History, Women and Gender in the Modern Middle East

This introductory text explores the gendered history of the modern Middle East, from the eighteenth century to the present, studying the various ways in which gender has defined the region and shaped relations in the modern era.

This book captures three aspects of change simultaneously: the events that mark the "modern" Middle East, women's encounters with the transition to modernity, and gendered responses to modernity. It contains both new fieldwork and a synthesis of secondary scholarship that highlight the role of gender in the modernization of Egypt, Turkey, Iran, the Levant, and the Persian Gulf states. Chapters are organized chronologically to chart the rapid developments of the modern era, but each chapter also stands on its own, with coverage of masculinity and femininity, sexuality, marriage and the family, labor, and women's contributions to Arab Spring uprisings. Through this comprehensive account, this book pushes back on stereotypes that the Middle East is an ahistorical region and that women have not been vital actors in the process of change.

Richly illustrated and accessible for a variety of readers, *History, Women and Gender in the Modern Middle East* is an ideal resource for undergraduate and postgraduate students in gender studies and Middle Eastern history.

Lisa Pollard is Professor Emerita of History at the University of North Carolina, Wilmington. She is co-editor of *Families of a New World* (2001) and author of *Nurturing the Nation: The Family Politics of Modernizing, Colonizing and Liberating Egypt* (2005). Additional publications include "From Husbands and Housewives to Suckers and Whores: Marital-Political Anxieties in the 'House of Egypt'" (2010) and "Teaching Muslim Women's History between Timeless-ness and Change: 18 Parts of Desire" (2014).

Mona L. Russell is an Associate Professor of History at East Carolina University. She is the author of *Creating the New Egyptian Woman: Consumerism, Education, and National Identity, 1863–1922* (2004) and *Egypt: Middle East in Focus* (2013). She has published widely on gender, education, and consumerism, most recently, "The New Woman, Her New Clothes, and Her Education: Missionary Encounters and Consuming the Exotic" (2021) and "Beauty Standards in Egypt: Popular Consumer Culture and the Representation of Women" (2021).

Gender History Around the Globe

Women, Gender and History in India
Nita Kumar

History, Women and Gender in the Modern Middle East
From Orientalism to the Arab Spring
Lisa Pollard and Mona L. Russell

History, Women and Gender in the Modern Middle East

From Orientalism to the Arab Spring

Lisa Pollard and Mona L. Russell

Routledge
Taylor & Francis Group
LONDON AND NEW YORK

Designed cover image: Girl in a vintage tram on the Taksim Istiklal street in Istanbul. Mikhail Sotnikov / Alamy Stock Photo

First published 2024
by Routledge
4 Park Square, Milton Park, Abingdon, Oxon OX14 4RN

and by Routledge
605 Third Avenue, New York, NY 10158

Routledge is an imprint of the Taylor & Francis Group, an informa business

© 2024 Lisa Pollard and Mona L. Russell

The right of Lisa Pollard and Mona L. Russell to be identified as authors of this work has been asserted in accordance with sections 77 and 78 of the Copyright, Designs and Patents Act 1988.

All rights reserved. No part of this book may be reprinted or reproduced or utilised in any form or by any electronic, mechanical, or other means, now known or hereafter invented, including photocopying and recording, or in any information storage or retrieval system, without permission in writing from the publishers.

Trademark notice: Product or corporate names may be trademarks or registered trademarks, and are used only for identification and explanation without intent to infringe.

British Library Cataloguing-in-Publication Data
A catalogue record for this book is available from the British Library

Library of Congress Cataloging-in-Publication Data
Names: Pollard, Lisa, author. | Russell, Mona L., author.
Title: History, women and gender in the modern Middle East : from Orientalism to the Arab Spring / Lisa Pollard ad Mona L. Russell.
Description: 1 Edition. | New York, NY : Routledge, 2024. |
Series: Gender history around the globe | Includes bibliographical references and index.
Identifiers: LCCN 2023037748 (print) | LCCN 2023037749 (ebook) | ISBN 9781138800366 (hardback) | ISBN 9781138800601 (paperback) | ISBN 9781032658063 (ebook)
Subjects: LCSH: Women—Middle East—History. | Sex role—Middle East—History. | MIddle East—History.
Classification: LCC HQ1726.5 .P65 2024 (print) | LCC HQ1726.5 (ebook) | DDC 305.40956—dc23/eng/20231012
LC record available at https://lccn.loc.gov/2023037748
LC ebook record available at https://lccn.loc.gov/2023037749

ISBN: 978-1-138-80036-6 (hbk)
ISBN: 978-1-138-80060-1 (pbk)
ISBN: 978-1-032-65806-3 (ebk)

DOI: 10.4324/9781032658063

Typeset in Times New Roman
by codeMantra

Contents

1 Introduction   1

2 Close to Home: Middle Eastern Women's Lives from the
   Eighteenth and into the Nineteenth Centuries   7

3 Middle Eastern Women in the European Imagination   29

4 New Fathers, New Brides, and New Daughters:
   Reform and Its New Men and Women   47

5 The New Woman through the New Man's Gaze   71

6 Beyond the "Woman Question": Women Define
   Themselves as Writers, Activists, and Revolutionaries   90

7 New States and Their New Women   108

8 Ethnic States and "Their" New Women   130

9 (Un)finished Business, but Not as Usual: Feminisms from
   the 1950s   155

10 Women and Work   179

11 Sexuality   200

12 Fashion, Clothing, and the Body   219

13 Houses in Motion: Women in War and Revolution   240

14 Arab Spring   264

Further Reading   *283*
Index   *289*

1 Introduction

The goal of this book is to present the history of the modern Middle East and of its women from the eighteenth century through to the present to students and readers with no previous knowledge of these subjects. Our intention is also to introduce our readers to the various ways in which gender—constituted and ever-changing categories of what it means to demonstrate masculinity and femininity—has defined the region and shaped relations between its subjects and citizens in the modern era. We define the Middle East here as Egypt, Turkey, Iran, the Levant, Lebanon, Syria, Iraq, Israel/Palestine, and Jordan and the Persian Gulf States. The North African states of Tunisia and Libya make a brief appearance in our chapter on Arab Spring.

This book is written as an anthem to one of our boldest and most clever undergraduates. At the end of a semester during which she had encountered all that our readers will find in these pages, this student exclaimed: "Who knew that there was so much history surrounding women in the Middle East?!" When encouraged to say more about her observation, she confessed to having anticipated a semester dedicated to women's absence, to the history of women's distance from the realms in which history is made. She had expected to learn about subjugation, illiteracy, and other forms of deprivation. She imagined herself encountering a history in which women are not actors in their own stories. She had really wanted to know how women negotiate what she had thought to be the isolations of seclusion, ignorance, and cover.

Undergirding this student's expectations about women was her sense that the Middle East is an ahistorical place, governed in the modern era as it has been from time immemorial. Her surprise at the rich history she had encountered was not, therefore, limited to Middle Eastern women: she had not expected to find any change over time, the classic definition of history, in region to which she attributed no change. How could women, she wondered, or for that matter, men, be historical actors in a region devoid of history?

While our student was bold in her assertions, she was not unique in her anticipations. Decades of classroom teaching and public speaking have provided us with countless opportunities, most of them pleasant, to present the Middle East and its male and female inhabitants within the rapidly flowing stream of change that has characterized the modern world—contrary to the expectations of our audiences. Encounters with stereotypes and misperceptions, however, while sometimes

DOI: 10.4324/9781032658063-1

fatiguing, have yet to dull the excitement we feel when our listeners rightfully conclude that Middle Eastern women have had starring roles in a region that has witnessed great change over the past 200 years. Some of the forces behind that change are familiar to Western students: industrialization, global capitalism, colonialism, nationalism, war, and diplomacy. Some are not so familiar; while the motors driving change in the modern era have been similar across time and place, responses to modernity have not been. Local histories, of governance, culture, class, and religion, some of them seemingly swept away or forever altered by encounters with modernity, have, in fact, informed and shaped those encounters. To be modern in the Middle East has not meant the simple renunciation of the past or the easy adoption of the new. Rather, modernity has required a facilitation of both the past and the present in all of the arenas that define modern life. Like women from different times and places, historically, women in the modern Middle East have felt the sweeping impact of both global and local forces and have sometimes been swept away by them. But like their counterparts in different times and places, modern Middle Eastern women have responded to change by mobilizing in response to it, capitalizing on it, and acting upon it. In a word, women have often done the sweeping.

Our goal therefore was to write a history of the region from which women, both real women and symbolic constructs of what it means to be a woman, cannot be subtracted. If we have been true to that goal, our readers will conclude that while women have not always been physically present for the decision-making that has accompanied and defined modernity in the Middle East, they have nonetheless been evoked, relied upon, and empowered by the events of the modern era.

If our book is true to its title, it presents the story of the facilitation of modernity in the Middle East on three levels. First, what follows is a history of the modern Middle East, from the end of its imperial era through its postimperial present. As such, we follow many of the conventions and the signposts that have marked traditional accounts of Middle Eastern history, focusing on the waning days of empires, on the rise of new nations and nationalisms, and on challenges to postimperial regimes, both from within and without. The stories of politics, diplomacy, and nation-building included herein do not exclude men; rather, they feature them. Our presentation of the imperial functionaries and heads of modern states who have negotiated encounters with the West since the eighteenth century, however, is concerned as much with the crises of masculinity that accompanied such encounters as it is with resulting treaties and reforms. How heads of states came to see themselves as masculine figures in comparison to those who ruled in the West and to those who had ruled before them both required and resulted in new ways of viewing women and of empowering them. New ways of imagining women also served to shape conversations among heads of state about the nature of the past and the path toward the future. Women's potential—past and present, harnessed or unfulfilled—has therefore undergirded the modern enterprise in the Middle East from its beginnings.

Second, while this book can be read as a straightforward narrative account of the events defining the modern Middle East, it is also intended to be read as an account of women's encounter with and facilitation of modernity, both as modernity manifested itself in changes to global economies and political systems and as a series of local responses. The local "factory girl," as she emerged in Istanbul, Beirut, Tehran, and Cairo ca. 1900, for example, was no more credited with the adoption of industry in the Middle East than was her counterpart in London ca. 1900. Nonetheless, like her Western counterparts, the Middle Eastern "factory girl" triggered fiery debates about modernity and its effects on women, shaping understandings of womanhood and of femininity at both the global and local levels. In cities across the Middle East, those debates—waged in registers reflecting affronts to local patriarchies, religious sensibilities, and family economies—were instrumental in shaping emerging sensibilities about place and history. Local stories about the "factory girl" similarly account for women's responses to men's fiery reactions to their participation in the public realm as laborers, students, and, increasingly, professionals. Local stories further illustrate women's choices regarding dress, education, and marriage—choices made in response to increased opportunities and to men's changing expectations of them. Just as industry facilitated the emergence of the female laborer (and of generations of female workers and labor activists), it also facilitated conversations about women that continue to shape place, identity, and gender relations.

Finally, this is a history of gendered responses to modernity. Reimagined masculinities and femininities by men and women in response to the challenges of the modern world make frequent appearances in this book. So, too, does the Middle East as a gendered region. Europeans ca. 1900 imagined the region as a fertile woman, ready to be penetrated by modern technologies and innovations, and as a defenseless woman, in need of protection from the wiles of Middle Eastern men. Those men, ca. 1900, some of them at the helm of reform programs designed to modernize their capital cities and territories, in turn, saw themselves as building "new women," by which they meant new cities, reconsolidated territories, and new ranks of educated female subjects. To protect new entities, ca. 1900 and ca. 2000, has therefore meant to protect women: gendered-feminine programs, cities, and territories. Such defense has been promoted by heads of state as a masculine affair. In each case, the gendering of modernization processes shaped relations among citizens and between them and the nations in which they reside, rendering women implicit to processes and projects that, on the surface, were entirely male affairs.

Reading a history of the Middle East through these three lenses makes it imperative to respond to our student with a resounding: "Yes, there is much history surrounding women in the modern Middle East!" Indeed, it is impossible to subtract women from that history.

History, Women and Gender in the Modern Middle East is organized chronologically, with several chapters dedicated to topics (clothing, sexuality, labor) designed to augment discussions began in previous chapters. While this book is intended to be read "in order," each chapter stands alone. Chapter 2 presents an overview of urban and rural women on the "eve of modernity" and illustrates the many ways women across classes contributed to sovereignty, the public good, business, education, manufacture, and agriculture, largely from their homes and in the local surroundings of their communities.¹ Chapter 3 presents an entirely different picture of homes as the source of women's power and production; in it, we discuss European portrayals of the region, which traded facts about women's contributions to their families and communities for fantasies about sex and power. Those fantasies would be easy to overlook in a history of the Middle East had they not been so instrumental in producing one of Europe's most overt justifications for intervention in the region: rescuing allegedly subjugated women.

Chapter 4 examines the masculine practice of creating "new women"—new cities, new entities, newly educated females—by Ottoman sultans and Qajar (Iranian) shahs as part of their efforts to reform and revitalize their governing institutions and territories. The chapter highlights the implication of women in the process of reform, the production of new kinds of women and men through modernization schemes, and the rise of new forms of masculinity and masculine sensibilities—including the birthing of new governing regimes.

Chapters 5 and 6 discuss the rise of "Woman Question" debates in Ottoman and Qajar territories ca. 1900. Those debates are considered by some to be the "big bang" events in women's history (globally and in the Middle East) because they ushered in a variety of new opportunities for women, particularly in education. "Woman Question" debates are also instrumental to women's history because they unleashed "woman" as a category through which all manner of things (some of them immediately relevant to women, others not) could be hashed out: history, identity, modernity, and tradition. Chapter 5 examines the body of literature produced by men in response to the "Woman Question," arguing that it presents women as symbols through which men worked out their place in the modern world. Chapter 6 by contrast examines women's contributions to the "Woman Question" debate as practical responses to a growing readership of women who were both anxious about change and emboldened by it. Chapter 6 also illustrates women responding to the "Woman Question" debate by organizing around civil initiatives dedicated to women's interests and to the needs of communities in transition.

Chapter 7 discusses WWI and its aftermath in the region. The war had devastating consequences for women in Ottoman territories, exposing them to starvation, dislocation, and physical and sexual violence. The war also brought women opportunities: to take up arms in the defense of territories; in various kinds of labor; and in the provision of charity and education. Those opportunities led to great disappointment when men, defeated by war and humiliated by the postwar presence of foreigners in the region, reasserted their privilege in the public realm by insisting that independence from Great Britain and France could not be had without women's sole attention to home and family.

Chapter 8 examines the application of "Woman Question" debates as state policy. New, secular regimes, beginning with that of Mustafa Kemal (also known as Atatürk), modern Turkey's first president (1923–1938), relied heavily on discourses produced from the beginning of the twentieth century about the relationship between reformed women and modern nations. Additionally, in a pattern that would be followed across the region, Atatürk placed Turkey's many women's associations under the supervision of his regime, harnessing the success of those associations while controlling their activities. The chapter ends with a discussion of the gender politics of the Islamic Republic of Iran (est. 1979) which, while reversing many of the policies of its secular predecessors, nonetheless continues to control and to define Iranian womanhood.

Chapter 9 examines feminisms independent of state control. We emphasize the ample civil initiatives that define Middle Eastern women's movements historically, as well as the increased inclusivity that defines them currently.

Chapter 10 discusses labor: white-, blue-, and pink-collar. In addition to examining the kinds of work women undertake in the region's formal and informal economies, we examine the various discourses and debates that have surrounded women's formal entry into the workforce since the turn of the twentieth century, beginning with that surrounding the emergence of the "factory girl."

Chapter 11 is dedicated to sexuality. We begin with a discussion of heteronormative marriage and its associated laws and customs, turning then to queer alternatives, both historical and contemporary, and their challenges to "masculine" and "feminine" categories.

Chapter 12 examines the multiple gendered meanings of various types of clothing associated with modernity. We illustrate that far from being a stand-in for religion (as it is often understood to be in the West), clothing in the modern Middle East has been a marker of tradition and of modernity, of subjects' and citizens' relationship to the nation-state and an expression of individuality.

Chapter 13 is dedicated to the women of Iran, Iraq, and Palestine, for whom the modern era has brought frequent displacement and upheaval. Accompanying such challenges has been a formidable presence of women's activism. Accompanying upheaval has also been a dizzying array of demands on women and expectations regarding their behavior.

Chapter 14 discusses the many contributions made by women to Arab Spring uprisings in 2011. Women appear in the chapter as heroines, villains, and scapegoats, illustrating the ambivalence of modern Arab states toward their female citizens. The chapter illustrates the rewards women have reaped by challenging the state and the high cost of women's alleged trespass into the public realm.

All of these chapters have been shaped by our students (in HIST 3680/6580, at ECU and HST 382/487 at UNCW) by their keen interest, their questions, suggestions, and objections. The many materials included in this text rest on the shoulders of our teachers, mentors, and colleagues, many of whose names make frequent appearance in our notes: Judith Tucker, Amira Sonbol, Mervat Hatem, Suad Joseph, Leslie Pierce, Leila Ahmed, miriam cooke, Asef Bayat, Marilyn Booth, Afsaneh Najmabadi, Beth Baron, Margot Badran, Nadje Al-Ali, Mary Ann Fay, Ellen Fleischmann, Eve Troutt-Powell, Libby Thompson, Cameron Amin, Sahar Amer, and Dror Ze'evi. We are grateful for the contributions of a new generation of historians of the Middle East, whose work on women, gender, and the body have pushed us to ask new and better questions: Elyse Semerdjian, Orit Bashkin, Reina Lewis, Hikmet Kocamaner, Melanie Tanielian, Noga Efrati, Liat Kozma, Mateo Muhammad Farzaneh, Arielle Gordon, Laura Bier, Shereen Abouelnaga, and Anne Marie F. Butler. Colleagues in Gender Studies (formerly Women's Studies at

ECU) and History at UNCW and ECU have provided consistent support. We are grateful for the assistance from the Thomas Harriott College of Arts and Sciences, which provided a variety of resources for the preparation of the text. Our friend and neighbor Patricia Conlon faithfully edited these pages, first by reading and, after she lost her sight, by listening to every word. Thank you.

Note

1 Abraham Marcus, *The Middle East on the Eve of Modernity: Aleppo in the Eighteenth Century* (New York: Columbia University Press, 1989).

2 Close to Home

Middle Eastern Women's Lives from the Eighteenth and into the Nineteenth Centuries

The story of Middle Eastern women on the eve of the modern era is one of continuity and change. Women's lives, both at home and in the world, were defined by customs accrued over the course of many centuries. At the same time, however, powerful contemporary forces, such as the rise of industrial Europe, concomitant changes in the global economy, and local, governmental efforts to centralize state power, brought powerful political, social, and economic changes to the Ottoman Empire, Egypt, and Qajar Iran. Women's domestic roles and routines, as well as their work patterns, were impacted by transformations in marketplaces and in consumption patterns, by challenges to local crafts and industries, and to agricultural production in rural areas. Those roles and routines were also changed by the introduction of new forms of education and, along with them, expectations for women. Throughout the region, such changes in expectations both expanded and diminished women's horizons.

This story about changes in women's lives across the eighteenth century and into the nineteenth century, particularly those changes that diminished the home as the seat of women's economic sufficiency, familial contributions, and, sometimes, political power, is by no means unique to Middle Eastern women. Indeed, in Europe, early industrialization brought women into cities and reduced their financial autonomy, as well as that of women who remained in rural areas, as factory work replaced cottage industry and agricultural subsistence. As local production and consumption patterns were altered by European industrialization and dominance in global trade, many women similarly faced migration to cities. Middle Eastern women lost opportunities in local production and trade and, with those losses, found themselves in increasingly difficult conditions.

This chapter focuses on the ways in which women of various classes lived and worked, first in the eighteenth century and then in the nineteenth century, as the Middle East began to absorb the changes brought about by transformations in the global economy and by the efforts of local rulers to adapt to global changes. This chapter argues that women's sovereignty, business acumen, and economic sufficiency were greatest when women were close to home and to the homes of other women.

Imperial Capitals—Royal Women

Just as it had been, historically, political sovereignty in the eighteenth-century Middle East was male. Across the Middle East, the maintenance of sovereignty, however, depended upon rulers' ability to control their governing classes. Marrying their daughters to local royalty and to high-ranking officials was one strategy that allowed sovereigns such control. Given the importance of ruling-class women to the negotiation of power, politics therefore depended upon what happened in royal harems (*andaruns* in Iran), which were the private, living quarters of the ruling and ruling-class families.

Harems were also the seat of reproduction for the Ottoman rulers, or sultans. As they consolidated their rule over the course of the fourteen and fifteenth centuries, the Ottomans married off their family members to royalty and to the governing elites of neighboring territories. Over the course of the sixteenth century, however, as their political and territorial control increased (and with it, the ever-present possibility of civil war), Ottoman sultans adopted a new strategy for consolidating and maintaining the power of their household: the purchase of white slaves from the Caucasus. Those women lived in the royal harem, located in the Topkapi Palace in Istanbul, and were educated to serve in the imperial harem in various capacities. They were also the sultans' concubines. Sultans manumitted concubines who produced male children for them, potential heirs to the Ottoman throne. Bearing now the title of *umm walad* or mother of a (sultan's) son, a royal, manumitted concubine and her adolescent son (the system operated under a one-concubine, one-son rule) were dispatched to live in a province within the empire. Upon the death of a sultan, his male heirs would return to Istanbul to vie for the throne by creating alliances with palace and military elites and by establishing favor with the public. Ottoman sultans rarely married their concubines due to the protections held by wives under Islamic law or *sharia*. Concubines were often known to reach the status of "favorite," but "wife" remained out of the reach of most.

The Ottoman harem grew in size and importance once the Ottoman sultans took up residence with all of their wives, concubines, and children in the residential quarters of the Topkapi Palace beginning in 1550 (and ending the practice of sending *umm walads* and their sons to the provinces). The Topkapi harem was made up of over 400 private apartments to house the many concubines (sultans could have as many concubines as they desired), their sons, and unmarried or widowed princesses who made up the royal family. The number one priority of the sultans' concubines was to produce a male heir who, with his potential ascension to the throne, might transform them into a *valide sultan.*

The importance of the Ottoman harem also increased after 1598, when the Ottomans established the cages or *kafes* system, in which Ottoman princes, including the crown prince, were confined to assigned quarters within the imperial harem in Istanbul. Such confinement curtailed the princes' movements and decreased potential threats to the power of the reigning sultan. The price of such a system was a decrease in Ottoman princes' skill at affairs of state; men who grew up in the *most* splendid of isolation were ill-equipped to govern a global empire. (Upon a sultan's death, aspiring princes no longer returned to Istanbul to vie for power. Rather, those who would not be sultan were strangled with a silk cord by their father or by a high-ranking public official). Never had concubines' skills at palace intrigue been so crucial: their number one job was now not only to produce a son, but to negotiate his ascension to power.

The Safavids, who ruled Iran through 1722, and the Qajar monarchs, who established their rule of Iran in 1797, used marriage to the daughters of powerful tribesmen, ruling officials, and religious elites to consolidate and keep their power. The Qajar monarchs engaged in a constant struggle to centralize their rule, and were often challenged by urban elites and religious clerics, and by the private armies of Iran's considerable number of tribes. Marriage of their sisters and daughters to such men was therefore a crucial ingredient in the Qajars' struggle to centralize their state.[1]

In Egypt, the Mamluks created fictive kinships through marriage and concubinage; both practices held Mamluk households together. The Mamluks were manumitted slaves, organized into household alliances. "Grandees" were the most powerful among them and those with the largest households. Mamluk grandees raised their male slaves and then married the favorites among them to their daughters, sisters, and concubines. This arrangement effectively produced fictive familial relationships. Those people "related" to the head of household, either through marriage, fictive kinship, slavery (see below), or service made up a Mamluk "*bayt*," or household. Political life was thereby tied to that of the family.[2]

Female members of ruling families in the Ottoman Empire, Iran, and Egypt influenced the patriarchal practices of sovereignty from the harem in a number of ways. Over the course of the sixteenth and seventeenth centuries, the Ottoman sultans' favorite concubines (*hasekis* or imperial concubines) came to have great power, as did the *valide sultans* (mother of the sultan). These women exerted their influence over their husbands and sons, attending to the shaping of their sons' character, and influencing their choices of wives and concubines. As the arbiter of marriages between the royal family and members of the families of the governing elite, the *valides* had the power to make or break the fortunes of the Ottoman ruling classes. Similarly, the *valides* sat at the center of networks connecting the ruling family to those who supplied the harem with goods and services, giving them influence over large and influential social and economic circles. The wives of Qajar monarchs enjoyed a similar influence over their sons and husbands. Rituals of state also fell into the hands of royal women. The Ottoman *valides* governed as regents for their sons and, sometimes, their grandsons. The wives of the Safavid shahs leant their calligraphy skills to the composing of diplomatic correspondence. The shahs' wives also served as their husbands' counselors and confidantes in matters of state. Safavid wives had a history of accompanying their husbands on official occasions, of ruling when their husbands were incapacitated, and of commanding the royal army in military campaigns against the Ottomans.[3] The wives of the Mamluk grandees frequently served as stand-ins for their husbands. For those men, the battlefield was where political power was won and lost and where Ottoman attempts to reassert their former control over Egypt were resisted. Consequently, Mamluk men were frequently absent from their households, sometimes for long stretches of time, and their wives were entrusted to supervise their husbands' wealth and property while those men waged wars. In the process, many Mamluk women became formidable business women and entrepreneurs.

In the imperial capitals, evidence of these royal women's presence was both frequent and elusive. While royal women spent little time outside of the harem, their contributions to the societies in which they lived were evident in the monumental architecture that such women had built in their names: mosques, schools, hospitals, and soup kitchens attested to royal women's sovereignty, piety, and concern for their subjects. For men and women, engaging in public works was both a means of pleasing God and of announcing one's status. For the many subjects whose lives were improved through access to education, medicine, and hygiene, the piety of royal women translated into accessible public services.

Residents of and visitors to eighteenth-century Istanbul were certain to take notice of the mosque complexes that had been built by the wives and mothers of a number of sultans. Hurrem Sultan, favorite concubine, and later wife, to Suleiman the Magnificent (r. 1520–1566), had bequeathed to the residents of Istanbul a building complex which included a mosque, a hospital, a soup kitchen, a religious college, and a primary school—all for public use (see Figure 2.1). In Edirne, the Ottomans' summer residence, Hurrem built a smaller complex, which included a mosque, soup kitchen, and an inn. Later Ottoman consorts and *valides* built similar complexes. The landscapes of Istanbul and Edirne reflected the glory of their devotion.

Figure 2.1 Hurrem Sultan Bathhouse, Istanbul. Sandor Szabo/Alamy Stock Photo.

A visitor to eighteenth-century Isfahan would have similarly taken notice of the contributions of the grandmothers, mothers, and sisters of the Safavid shahs. The buildings left behind by those women—bathhouses, educational complexes, hospices—are both testimonials to their piety and illustrations of the women's contributions to the life of the city.[4]

Royal women across the region drew the income necessary to fund, build, and maintain their charitable works from a number of sources. They brought substantial dowries to their marriages, to which they added royal stipends, using those funds as personal treasuries. Royal women also held substantial real estate holdings such as bazaars, bridges, and caravanserais, which were way stations for traveling merchants. Mamluk women developed substantial entrepreneurial skills as investors in rental houses, workshops, and tax farms. Salun Khatun, wife of a high-ranking Mamluk, received a small inheritance upon the death of her husband. By 1782, she had bought a share in a house, had purchased a workshop, two storehouses, three bakeries, two flour mills, and a tenement building. The next year, she added another house and four shops to her holdings. By 1790, Salun Khatun held more shops, equipment used for roasting coffee, and a mill for hulling lentils. By the end of her life, she had made a fortune.

While the power of royal women was thus visible to the eye, royal women themselves were secluded from public view, living in women's quarters within royal palaces or households. As such, they were both visible and hidden. But invisibility did not mean powerlessness. The sultans were always set apart from others, both at home and in public; their wives similarly did not leave the palace without an official retinue (see Figures 2.2 and 2.3).

Figure 2.2 Interior of Topkapi Harem, Istanbul. JL Photography/Alamy Stock Photo.

Over the course of the eighteenth and nineteenth centuries, Europeans would increasingly come to see the residents of such living spaces as inmates, imprisoned by their despotic husbands, and as hapless victims of their husband's taste for orgiastic sex (see Chapter 3). For royal women, the harem was a home, a place for raising children, visiting, learning, and in many cases, running businesses by proxy. For the female household staffs who worked in them, harems were training grounds and places of hard work.

As the seat of royal family life, harems were spaces in which comfort and privacy were paramount. Harems were indeed sanctuaries where women were safe from the "seedier side" of political life.[5] Harems were social and organizational spaces for the royal families (and for many elite families as well—see below) from which men who were not related to the family were excluded. In Mamluk Egypt, for example, grandee households had a *diwan* in which men met. Women had the run of the rest of the house and it was men whose movements were circumscribed.[6]

Within the segregated space of the harem, women observed a hierarchy of power. That hierarchy was based on status and authority and ran parallel to power structures among royal men. Within that structure, "matriarchal elders had power over other women and over young men." In the Ottoman imperial harem, the *valide sultan* was the "keystone of the harem institution." She received the highest stipend in the empire. Hers were a suite of apartments (only the sultan could boast of such magnificent living quarters), which linked her to the post of the black eunuch who guarded the harem, to the servants' courtyard, and the quarters of the sultan himself.

Figure 2.3 Exterior of Bayt al-Razzaz featuring mashrabiyya, Cairo. B. O'Kane/ Alamy Stock Photo.

Additionally, the Ottoman harem housed a large, paid staff to train the servants who attended to the royals. Members of the royal family called the harem "home," but for large, mostly female staffs, it was a place of employment and a training center. The *ketkhuda khatun* or harem stewardess, the senior administrative official in the harem, trained the women who were servants and concubines to the sultans. Household domestics took care of menial tasks such as food preparation, cleaning, laundry, tending fires, and working as bath attendants. By the eighteenth century, the highest salaries within the harem staff went to the *ustas* (mistresses) in charge of the palace, the laundry, and the pantry.

Harem hierarchies also reflected Iran's power dynamics. In the Imperial Household of Fath Ali Shah (r. 1769–1839) in Tehran, women of high rank and noble station were given the highest rank and therefore the greatest of the shah's favor. Fath Ali Shah had four permanent wives and many temporary wives, the favorite of whom was Tavus Khanum (Lady Peacock) "Taj el-Dowleh."[7] In deference to her rank, Tavus Khanum was given her own palace, replete with a series of private apartments (with men's and women's sections), a bath, and a mirrored reception hall that was similar to the one in the shah's imperial palace. Tavus Khanum had a private staff of more than 200 people at her command and a large kitchen budget, which fed the nobility who shared her quarters.[8]

In Mamluk Egypt, women were essential to family life. Mamluk women celebrated marriages and the birth of children and raised their children (boys left the harem at puberty and went to live in the men's quarters). Mamluk women enjoyed entertainments, visited with friends and family, and enjoyed the coffee, sweets, and plates of fruits that were brought to them by slaves. Women left the harem, wearing veils, on Fridays to visit the tombs of their family members. Mamluk women managed the staffs of their large households. Many managed properties and businesses and managed endowments from the harem, using *wakils*, or agents, to act as their intermediaries.

City and Town—The Upper Classes

The social practices of women from the upper classes of Muslims, Christians, and Jews across the region also included gender seclusion. The harem was essential to a social order in which knowing who one's father was held paramount importance, both for marriage and inheritance, and was therefore essential to a system in which virginity was women's greatest commodity.[9] Seclusion was also a practice through which elite families signaled to outsiders that their women did not work outside the home.

Elite women used the privacy of harems to facilitate business deals, engage with peers, and manage properties without navigating crowded urban streets.[10] From protected space, women organized and ran households, which could number up to 200 people. Harem and *andarun* women supervised servants, planned menus, and oversaw the raising of children. Some women taught other women the *hadith*, the collected sayings and traditions of the Prophet Muhammad and which—along with the Quran—form the basis of Islamic law (*sharia*).

Outside of their homes, harem women of all religions similarly used the modesty of their garments to negotiate public spaces without unwanted contact with men who were not their next of kin. As such, veils were portable harems in which women could conduct business, attend weddings and funerals, visit the harems of other women, go to bathhouses, and attend mosque or visit shrines.[11] In Qajar Iran, Tehran's streets were segregated from 4 p.m., allowing women a further layer of "veiled" protection from unknown men.[12] Non-Muslim women were prohibited from wearing clothing and shoes of particular colors and styles. Even in bathhouses, non-Muslim women differentiated themselves by their clothing.[13]

Elite women across the region were owners of urban property and of rural tax farms. In 1750, 4% of buyers and sellers of houses in Ottoman Aleppo were women who held titles to a third of the city's commercial buildings.[14] Across the region, women of lesser economic means put their money to work by purchasing a share of a house or a business or by renting rooms to boarders. Holding property in any of these fashions brought women social prestige.[15]

In Mamluk Egypt, the wives of religious scholars and merchants shared the elite status of their husbands. Like their husbands, many of these women possessed great wealth. One of the wives of the Sheikh of al-Azhar, Egypt's highest-ranking religious official, for example, was known to be a canny businesswoman. She invested, administered, and increased her husband's wealth buying houses, shops, and bathhouses.[16]

Elite women also loaned their money to men and women, both in and outside of their family networks, who sought similar investments. These women drew up their own contracts, which sometimes involved taking a client's home or other property as collateral. Such was the case of Aleppo's Amina bint Abd al-Qadir, who, ca. 1750, requested as collateral the home and the jewelry of one of her clients. Similarly, Aliha bint Ali Chalabi required that her client secure a substantial loan with his house.[17]

Affluent women were also active in various forms of urban improvement or urban renewal through their contributions to *waqf* endowments. Between 1746 and 1771, 38 of Aleppo's 97 *waqf* establishers were women.[18] In eighteenth-century Egypt, women made up almost 25% of all *waqf* holders. In Ottoman Anatolia, wives of lesser figures in the Ottoman bureaucracy used dowries from their marriages to establish *waqfs* with which to commission buildings.[19]

By cleverly utilizing *waqf* incomes and investments, women empowered themselves and others by skirting traditional inheritance laws, which favored men. If a female *waqf*-holder was to remarry, for example, she could use her property to provide wealth for her daughters (or favored children), provide for favored slaves, or redistribute wealth as she saw fit.[20] Women also earned income from their *waqf* properties through the transfer of *gedik*, the tools of production involved in an income-producing property, to themselves. Women who owned shops or commercial enterprises also transferred buildings or equipment to themselves or to their designated heirs. They also leased commercial or industrial space and invested the revenue from such real estate.[21]

City and Town—Female Slaves

Manumitted and child-bearing slave women also achieved rank and power in the Middle East on the eve of the modern era. African slaves, who served as domestic servants in middle- and upper-class households, originated from both the trans-Saharan slave trade as well as trade from the East Coast of Africa. Middle Easterners also purchased white slave women from the Caucasus, Circassia, and Georgia. Those women were most likely concubines, although many also worked as domestic servants. (Concubines were typically white, but there was no prohibition against black slaves being held in such a capacity.) Some slave women were prized for possessing specific talents as singers, dancers, or musicians. Owning slaves was a sign of status for well-to-do households; families bought slaves or received them as gifts from other families.

Slaves were the most disadvantaged class in Middle Eastern societies. Some, however, reached the status of respected protégées; when manumitted, they had business skills and held property. Others became part of the family that purchased them. Any slave who achieved the status of *umm walad* could not be sold. The offspring of such women were considered family members and they inherited wealth and property. Many slave women, some of whom married their owners, others of whom inherited their owner's property—or both—became quite wealthy in their own right. Manumission was also common upon the death of a master, particularly for favored slaves.

Slave ownership in the early modern era was not limited to Muslims. Christians and Jews owned slave concubines as well as domestic servants. Dealers trained slaves to work in Jewish households, teaching them the necessary skills such as attention to kosher dietary requirements and the performance of music that were necessary for work in Jewish homes. All slaves with such specialized talents fetched a higher price in market regardless of the religion of their potential owner.

City and Town: Working Classes

The vast majority of women living in cities and towns were urban poor struggling to eke out an existence. Urban women from the lower economic classes worked in the marketplace as laborers for local manufactures. In the textile industry, for example, women worked from home to prepare and spin thread. Women smoothed, dyed, and embroidered fabrics and worked as tailors. Urban women also worked in trade, selling commodities such as bread, wine, wheat, and thread. A majority of lower-income women, however, worked in service industries as dancers, singers, prostitutes, professional mourners, and above all domestic servants. Most affluent households had domestic servants (and slaves) who worked as cooks, attendants, and pages. Many less affluent homes could, at the very least, afford a maidservant.[22]

Among the most highly paid and well-fed of the domestic servants were wet-nurses, who supplied their own breast milk in cases where upper-class women could not or would not feed their own children. Healthy peasant women were often brought into harems as wet nurses. Once such a woman, known as a "*dada*," was installed in a harem, she became a permanent fixture and her husband and children became looked-after clients. A *dada's* children became like siblings to the children they nursed and were prohibited from marrying one another because of the close bond that they formed. The practice of wet-nursing lasted well into the twentieth century, even after the first expensive imported baby formulas began arriving in local markets.

During the eighteenth century, in both Ottoman and Qajar territories, changes in local economies and consumption patterns caused many women to begin flocking to urban centers, either alone or with their families. Across the century, Europeans began arriving in the region as representatives of European states (diplomats and consuls) and as missionaries, first for the Catholic Church and, later, representing Protestantism. Most of the Europeans who made their presence known throughout the region, however, were merchants, who introduced European commodities to Middle Eastern markets. Over the course of the century, imports slowly began replacing locally-produced products. Work patterns in the cities and in the countryside were therefore disrupted, both for men and women, as imported items became more available and more desirable to local consumers. The result was a host of region-wide migrations from the country to the city. Men and women alike left the countryside hoping to find work. In the Ottoman Empire, the flood of migrants to the cities led to an eighteenth-century imperial decree banning the migration of single or married men and women into Istanbul and Edirne except for medical treatment, business, or visiting relatives. In both cities, women in particular needed permission from authorities to conduct business.

Once migrant women had arrived in Ottoman urban areas, they became part of a surplus labor pool. In what is called the putting-out system, women worked from their homes to provide services as spinners and weavers throughout the eighteenth century and into the early nineteenth century in cities such as Bursa, Ankara, and Damascus. Women's labor remained separate from the male-dominated guild system, into which few women were welcomed. Only in the nineteenth century, when guilds lost their monopoly over production, did women's contribution to local economies begin to increase. It was this cheap pool of female labor however that buffeted the Ottomans against the initial flood of the European textile trade. In Ottoman urban centers and smaller villages, female laborers helped to produce printed textiles that mimicked highly popular imported calicoes from India.

Qajar women similarly formed a reserve army of labor. Urban women, who were the minority in a region that remained largely rural in the eighteenth and nineteenth centuries, participated in all kinds of production work: carpet weaving, embroidery, and the production of clothing, for example. Women worked in the production of tea, butter, and dried fruits. Women spun and manufactured silk and cotton, typically from home. Qajar women also worked in light industry, manufacturing guns, curing and preparing hides, and working in animal husbandry.[23]

Across the eighteenth century, service industries similarly provided employment for migrant women and for urban-born women. Bathhouses, for example, provided a number of different jobs in Ottoman and Qajar cities. Some bathhouses catered only to women. Others offered women-only days and times. In either case, the bathhouses needed female attendants, masseuses, water carriers, refreshment providers, and women to wash female clients (Figure 2.4).

Elite, secluded women met up with one another at bathhouses, often staying the whole day to chat and learn about local events and using "the bath water to make friends."[24] Indeed, region-wide, bathhouses provided women with the same kinds of social outlets that coffee houses, which were exclusively male spaces, gave to

Close to Home: Middle Eastern Women's Lives 17

Figure 2.4 Colored engraving, public baths for women, Ottoman Empire. Lanmas/Alamy Stock Photo.

men. Women brought food and drink to share with family members and friends. They sipped coffee, visited with one another, and shared news.

Women were also peddlers. In Cairo, a class of women called *dallalahs* brought commodities to secluded women. In Qajar Iran, Jewish women often performed the function of delivering goods to *andarun* women. As such, lower-class women reported news of other families' affairs, became harem women's confidantes, and kept harem women informed of events, serving as what one Iranian woman referred to as "walking and talking newspapers."[25] In both Qajar and Ottoman territories, female peddlers sold a wide variety of goods to their elite female clientele. Others were street vendors who provided food for day laborers or who offered seasonal snacks such as roasted corn in the summer and chestnuts in the winter. In Qajar Iran, Armenian women organized a wine trade for their community.[26] Other women went into urban areas from surrounding villages to sell their excess produce, eggs, milk products, and handicrafts on market days. Some women used their homes to launder or bake for clients; others provided those services in their clients' homes.

Female performers (*awalim*) formed another category of working urban women in the eighteenth century. They composed poetry and songs; they danced, entertained, and had prodigious improvisational skills. The most skilled and talented among these women could be selective about their audiences, and therefore performed exclusively for women (or when men were present, wore veils to protect their modesty). *Awalim* compromised their reputations when they performed unveiled in front of men.

Prostitution also provided women in urban areas with employment. The existence of slavery meant that the privileged class of men could purchase women and boys for pleasure. Slave dealers operated through a guild system, the laws of which prohibited slave dealers from selling women (or boys) into prostitution outside the market system. Guilds policed their own membership and had a vested interest in monitoring nonmembers who plied the trade. But there were creative ways to legally turn slavery into prostitution.

Women also used their voices to earn a living. Professional mourning, for example, was a way for the urban poor to boost their income. Upon the death of a family member, women were known to announce the death to their neighbors through high-pitched cries. But the wealthy in large cities (with the exception of Jewish families) often hired poor women to recite verses of from sacred texts, moan, gesticulate in funeral processions, and wail at burials.

Women were the more prominent of the sexes in death rituals. Widows wore plain black clothing, as did close family members of the dead, to express the mourning of the entire family. Women did most of the attending to and visiting of graves. Women also prepared and distributed food to families and neighbors. Secluded women had food delivered by their servants.

Weddings provided a variety of means for poor women to ply various trades. Some of their tasks were cosmetic: they removed hair from the bride's body, painted henna tattoos on a bride's hands, and arranged her hair. Other tasks performed by women helped the bride make the transition to married life: hired women helped explain the facts of life to the bride, for example. Hired women also witnessed the bloodying of the marital sheet and displayed the bloodied sheet to awaiting crowds.

Working-class women also parlayed sets of skills that ran the gamut from medical to magical. They served as midwives and doulas, helping mothers bring new life into the world, and tending to new mothers for 40 days after birth. Women of the working classes prepared the soups and teas that have traditionally been called for in various locales to reinvigorate the mother and to encourage lactation. Some midwives saw it as their duty to terminate unwanted pregnancies for unmarried women, women who had been raped, or women who had no means to support their children. Working-class women were also hired by elites to induce miscarriages by beating co-wives or concubines when such pregnancies threatened inheritance interests. While it was not unheard of for elite women to beat their pregnant competitors themselves, a safer route was to seek the assistance of a midwife.

Ordinary services also made up the repertoires of working-class women: some provided childcare services and health consultation on issues that had baffled mothers for centuries, such as colic and colds. Others provided consultations about marital problems, such as infertility or fear of the evil eye, and offered healing solutions and amulets. Some women were skilled in a range of services that we might call "sorcery." They read fortunes in coffee grounds to clients who were eager to know their futures.

Countryside

The peasant household required the labor of every member of the family, men, women, and children; and the pace of work differed according to the season. Throughout the region, families labored for subsistence, using the revenues they produced from agricultural production to pay their taxes. Families consumed what they produced and traded locally produced specialties like textiles, baskets, and bricks within and among other peasants.

Peasant women formed a sphere of agricultural production. They worked side by side with men in the fields as farmers and harvesters, picking crops such as cotton, olives, and citrus. Women collected water. They also collected firewood or cattle dung or the stalks of plants such as sugar cane with which to make fires. They tended and grazed animals. Women milked animals, processed milk, and made yogurt.

Peasant women also participated in cottage industry. In Nablus and the Galilee, for example, women and children not only picked olives, a staple of the Palestinian economy, but processed them as well, making olive oil and olive oil soap. Women also participated in the marketing of both products. [27] In Egypt, women raised and sold poultry and eggs. They raised livestock and made and sold cheese and ghee.[28] Because of their presence in the fields, peasant women occupied public space. At harvest time, they mingled with men and women from other families and other villages, unlike the secluded women from urban areas.

Within the family unit, in addition to laboring and selling homemade products, women were expected to give birth, nurture children, and tend to their households. The burden on women led one nineteenth-century British traveler to Anatolia to remark: "those [women] of the peasantry are active and laborious, performing much field and other heavy work in addition to their domestic duties, whilst the men may be loitering in idleness."[29]

In the countryside, the family had the greatest influence over women's lives. As it was in the cities, the family was the main unit of social organization in the countryside and the primary unit for production, reproduction, and consumption. The family was also the greatest generator of a woman's material means: families endowed their daughters with gifts and inheritances, their trousseau, and when necessary, divorce settlements and child support. In the absence of social security systems, families were the main agencies of social support.

Pastoralism

Many Westerners associate the pastoral lifestyle only with the arid Arabian Peninsula. Various forms of nomadism or semi-nomadism have existed throughout the Middle East since ancient times; however, and have carried both age- and gender-specific work roles with them. In groups that herd large animals, such as camels, young men typically grazed and watered the animals and protected the group from animal or human intruders. Older girls might also have had some responsibilities for the animals, including milking, some herding, attending to watering, and keeping watering areas clean. Small children and the elderly worked as close as possible to home—namely the tent. They collected wood or animal dung for fuel.

Other chores were more gender specific. Tasks that entailed handling the body of an animal, such as slaughter, shearing, and tanning, were generally assigned to men, while jobs that involved the processing of animal products, such as rendering animal fat, making yogurt, and making butter, were female tasks. Pastoral women historically were responsible for all medical care ranging from childbirth to concocting herbal remedies to managing severe injuries. The work of every individual was valued and required training. Thus, both parents participated in the upbringing of their children. Most scholars on the topic suggest that women were responsible for defending the camp. Furthermore, evidence suggests that while women were not leaders of groups, pastoralists valued their opinion. Evidence also points to women as having represented the interests of their families before various governmental entities during times when the Ottomans rounded up men for state projects.

Pastoral communities did not live in isolation from settled ones, but rather benefited from relationships of protection and trade with settled communities. Relationships with settled communities were not always perceived by either side as advantageous. The protection of the pilgrimage route was of utmost concern to Ottoman authorities, for example, and while one Bedouin group might have been entrusted to protect pilgrims, another could just as well have pillaged pilgrim caravans. Furthermore, as state centralization began (see below), the state's desire to settle nomadic populations encountered stiff resistance from those whose ancestors had long practiced this honored way of living.[30]

Fishing and Pearl Diving

Long before there was oil in the Persian Gulf, the traditional occupation of many coastal peoples from what is now Kuwait down to Oman involved fishing, pearl diving, shipbuilding, sailing, or trade. Pearl diving in particular was a risky business. Men would leave for over four months a year, enduring many grueling rounds of being submerged more than 20 meters with a basket of rocks. Back at home, women were responsible for all forms of production and the maintenance of family life (Figure 2.5).

The music of pearl diving communities reflected these gender-based hardships. Men performed *fjeri* song and dance, both on board ships and in coffeehouse celebrations. The *fjeri* performance at once praises Allah and demonstrates masculinity, celebrating the accomplishments, courage, and agony of the divers and sailors. Women, dressed in festive clothing, awaited the arrival of ships, singing joyfully of the return of loved ones. Conversely, women were wont to curse the ocean with stones or try to reverse stormy weather by dipping a cat in water. Women in

Figure 2.5 Drawing of fishing for pearls in the Persian Gulf, 1870. Chronicle/Alamy Stock Photo.

pearl-diving communities were known to decry the long voyages that separated them from their men folk and to mourn the loss of their men: women's words both cursed the ocean and praised the power of God.[31]

Little has been written about women in fishing communities. We do know that one notable feature that they share with sisters in urban settings is inheritance of property. In the same way that a woman who inherited property might be compelled to sell it to a male family member, so might a woman who inherited a lucrative fish trap. Even if a woman's hand was forced in the sale, she nonetheless was entitled to financial compensation for her possessions.[32]

Nineteenth-Century Change and Its Implications for Women

The French invasion of Egypt in 1798 and the Napoleonic wars helped to spur European economic activity in Ottoman territories. The invasion marked a new point in the intra-European competition for global trade routes and territories. The invasion also occurred in the early stages of the industrial revolution, which required increasing resources and markets. In response to the invasion, the Ottomans sent Muhammad (Mehmet) Ali (r. 1805–1848) to expel the French from Egypt's shores. Once he had accomplished the task of ousting the French, Muhammad Ali remained in Egypt and established himself as its de facto ruler. He created a new kind of state apparatus in Egypt, a model of independence for Egypt which included industrialization, military reform, economic restructuring, and educational reform. Muhammad Ali's reforms also included the transformation of the

Egyptian economy.³³ In both cases, transformations brought at the hands of the ambitious, upstart viceroy of Egypt brought changes that affected women's livelihoods, their control over their labor and products, and their home lives.

Between 1800 and 1820, Egypt had been a regional crafts and trade center of commodities like coffee, textiles, and spices. Between 1820 and 1850, however, Muhammad Ali's state emerged as the only exporter of crafts and textiles. At the same time, the state began to import manufactured goods from Europe, making local products less competitive and affecting the livelihoods of craftsmen and women. The state also used cash crops to bring quick revenue into its coffers. In this new system, the state dictated what would be grown throughout Egypt, assigned prices to crops, and held the monopoly on exports.

By the early 1840s, the state held the monopoly on cotton exports. While declaring their land to be "cotton-producing" gave owners a tax break, the result of state policy was less land for peasants to subsistence farm. Peasant families lost control over their relationship to the land. No longer could they balance crop production to meet consumption needs, pay taxes, or sell in local markets. As families increasingly labored for the state, they lost both their labor power and control over their land.

Military conscription into Muhammad Ali's army also affected the peasant family as male family members went missing for long periods of time. Women and men were drafted into the corvée labor that fueled agricultural and public works projects. By the 1830s, Egypt's agricultural production suffered as villages came to be populated only by women, children, the infirm, and the elderly. Families were left disassembled, hungry, and with little recourse to improve their lot, as agriculture and trade of agricultural production were replaced by large-scale agricultural production for the global market.

Urban women were also affected by Egypt's transformation to a cash crop economy. Women who had used their homes historically to clean and spin cotton and to produce cotton and silk thread, part of the putting-out system through which women sold their products independently and gained income for their families, continued to work as they had in the past. Beginning in the 1820s, however, they became state employees. State functionaries distributed materials such as flax and cotton to women's homes. Working within a quota system and receiving a set wage, women worked to spin those materials into the yarn that they were required to submit to the state at state-dictated prices. Women therefore lost control over both their labor and the sale of their products.

In the early years of the nineteenth century, Mohammad Ali endeavored to industrialize Egypt's textile production, and the number of textile factories and factory workers increased through the 1830s, to the alarm of European industrialists. As in agriculture, the state levied workers for its factories, most of which were shut down by the 1850s. Peasants were levied for factory work, in which they made a third of what they made in the fields. In Cairo, neighborhood leaders were ordered to round up workers, including women and children, whose cottage industry was replaced by wage labor (see Chapter 10).

In addition to engaging in reform and state centralization, Muhammad Ali had imperial aspirations. To stop the de facto Egyptian ruler's sweep through the region (his armies took territories in the Sudan in 1821 and stormed Lebanon and Syria in 1831), the Ottomans turned to the British for help. In exchange for British military aid, the Ottomans signed a trade agreement, the Treaty of Balta Liman (also known as the Anglo-Ottoman Treaty) of 1838. The treaty required that the Ottomans end their trade monopolies; allow British merchants and their partners full access to all Ottoman markets, and tax British merchants as well as their collaborators at the same rate as Ottoman merchants were taxed. The result was the arrival of European manufactured goods into Ottoman markets, the weakening of local manufacture, and the transformation of local labor practices. Male and female wage labor in workshops and on factory floors replaced family-based cottage industry.

In Anatolia and Iran, the production and export of carpets was also facilitated by new trade laws and undergirded by women's paid labor, both in cottage industry and factory work. Because of the unique nature of Anatolian and Iranian carpets, the local industry was not initially affected by European competition. The carpet industry changed only with the advent of increased foreign demand, greater foreign investment, and mechanization. By the mid-nineteenth century, as middle-class incomes in Europe and the US increased, consumers became enthralled with Oriental goods as a mark of social distinction. Exhibitions at the World's Fairs (beginning 1851), the rise of the field of interior design and the spread of women's magazines helped disseminate tastes for things Oriental among the upper and middle classes.[34]

The consuming desires of Europe and the US rapidly expanded demand for carpets from producers in places such as Uşak in Anatolia. Prior to the last quarter of the nineteenth century, this demand had been met by adding more workers from the same family unit to the production process, which was largely cottage-based.[35] As demand came to outstrip supply, local and European investors created new workshops that threatened traditional home-based production areas. Women who labored in workshops were not distracted by caring for children, tending livestock, and doing household chores. But mechanization and the transfer of labor out of homes and into factories nonetheless had negative consequences for women. The new companies utilized their own yarns, for example, which took away the jobs of spinners and dyers—work mostly done by women and children.[36] On the eve of the Young Turk Revolution (1908), women and children rioted over these changed conditions.

European influence in Iran arrived later than it had in the Ottoman Empire and Egypt. That influence, however, manifested itself in similar ways and had influences on women's lives. Russia sought territorial and commercial influence in Iran, and after defeating Qajar armies in Iran's north, imposed the Treaty of Turkmanchai in 1828. In a manner similar to the system Capitulations in the Ottoman Empire, the treaty gave Russia favorable trading status and low tariff rates. Nasir al-Din Shah (r. 1831–1896) granted the British similar advantages in a treaty signed with them in 1857. As the result of both treaties, Iran's economy became geared toward the export of raw materials and the import of manufactured goods. Carpet-making survived the arrival of European-produced goods because of the increased Western interest in "Persian carpets" that resulted from Iran's greater trade contact with Europe and, later, the US.

Prior to the nineteenth century, Persian carpet-making was a "tribal or village craft for domestic use and a form of personal savings against hard times." In agricultural villages and among nomadic pastoralists, carpet weaving had been the domain of women and children, who did their work in front of their huts.[37] Carpet production was a family affair, in which women provided labor and supervision.[38] Demand from the West, fueled by British, Italian, Swiss, American, and other Western investors, however, resulted in women and children becoming wage laborers in cottage industry. A late nineteenth-century visitor to Sultanabad, a center for carpet production, described Sultanabad as a typical village, except that each house had a loom in front of it, on which women worked to earn a wage.[39] As European imports weakened Iran's labor force (imported textiles, for example, put many Iranian textile producers out of work), women's labor assumed new importance. Cottage labor brought women cash and expertise. Carpet skills became selling points in marriage contracts: a father was not likely to give up a skilled daughter without adequate compensation.

Factory work emerged for women in Iran in the late nineteenth century in urban centers. Women worked long hours under the supervision of unknown males, threatening patriarchal sensitivities about women's roles and the proper conditions for women's work.[40] Women and children labored under the worst of conditions, including low wages, malnutrition, poor ventilation, and improper heating and cooling. As a result of these changes, Iranian carpet exports skyrocketed from £70,000 in the 1870s to £500,000 in 1910 and £1,000,000 by 1914[41] (see Chapter 10).

The Ottomans, both inspired and threatened by the example of Muhammad Ali, furthered their own series of reforms inaugurated decades earlier by their own Selim III (r. 1789–1807). Those reforms, known as *tanzimat* (1838–1876), resulted in a dramatic economic, social, political, and judicial reorganization of the empire. *Tanzimat* brought benefits to women's lives, especially in the form of the expansion of educational opportunities. But the reforms also brought challenges to women's livelihoods. The Ottoman land code of 1858, for example, introduced private property in Ottoman territories. The enforcement of the new Ottoman land code challenged traditional inheritance laws, which had historically protected women's interests. The *tanzimat*-era creation of new law courts restricted women's access to the courts—a staple of Ottoman life in previous centuries—and threatened women's ability to inherit and secure land and wealth. In places such as Egypt, the enforcement of new private property laws privileged various groups such as foreigners, bureaucrats, and the local nobility over non-elite members of Egyptian society. Through successive legislation, state-driven reforms created a system more in line with British property ownership, wherein the eldest male held the property title (but in which system inheritance continued to be divided according to *sharia* law). In Qina in Upper Egypt, for example, such legislation resulted in peasant women being disenfranchised from their property. Land disputes also led to the disappearance of peasant women as the result of an increase in honor crimes associated with landlessness.[42]

Reforms in the Ottoman Empire, Qajar Iran, and Egypt over the course of the nineteenth century encouraged greater state authority over citizens' lives. States taxed peasant and working-class women at higher rates. Their husbands were called to military conscription in larger numbers, which left women in evermore dire circumstances. Furthermore, changes in education, transportation, and communication transformed the nature of many traditional occupations along with social views of those occupations. For example, bathhouses, which had once provided a range of occupations for women, went out of style once indoor plumbing and bath fixtures arrived in the Ottoman Middle East.

The rise of an educated, urban middle and upper class of men and their increasing demands by men for the educated, "professional" housewives made many working-class women's occupations appear old-fashioned or superstitious. Practices such as the reading of coffee grounds, the hiring of professional mourners, and even the practice of folk medicine came to be considered outdated. Ca. 1900, when women's education began to breach the gulf attained by men, girls' textbooks lamented folk rituals as backwards, filthy, and disgusting, while at the same time touting the advances of modern housewifery.[43] In cities such as Istanbul, Cairo, Damascus, Beirut, and Tehran, "New Women" (see Chapters 4–6) sought education so that they could take more modern care of their own children. Urban, educated women began to rely on the professional care of doctors, gynecologists, and pediatricians, even as the midwife remained a staple of the countryside and of working-class women.

Female performers also endured changes as the result of nineteenth-century reforms, particularly in Egypt and Iran. After the occupation of Egypt, the French brought with them their own prostitutes, musicians, and theater troupes. At the same time, the French heavily regulated the taxation and organization of local prostitutes, dancers, and *awalim*. The French were also faced with an outbreak of the plague, the containment of which required high levels of surveillance and quarantine, including a ban on prostitution in Cairo. Between 1805 and 1834, Muhammad Ali was content to follow Ottoman guidelines regarding the regulation and taxation of prostitutes and entertainers. The dictates of public health and the safety of his army required that Muhammad Ali ban prostitution and public dancing in the capital in 1834.[44] Only after 1840, when the viceroy had finally consolidated his family's position, did Muhammad Ali focus on keeping brothels, coffeehouses, and taverns out of reputable neighborhoods. The enforcement of Muhammad Ali's rules tended to blur the lines that existed between prostitution, dancing, and refined entertainment. No longer would performance be a respectable career track. As gender segregation eroded ca. 1900, so too did women's opportunities in entertainment.

Conclusion

Early modern travelers to the Middle East often referred to women of the region as "timeless" or "unchanging." While women's lives in 1800 appeared quite similar to earlier eras, dramatic shifts were already underway, which were accelerated by the demand for resources and markets that came with the Industrial Revolution. Whereas families had been gravitating to urban areas, by the mid-nineteenth century, they now migrated in even larger numbers. The commercialization of agriculture, the creation of private property, and the rise of cash crops commodified both goods and labor in ways they had not been before. Subsistence labor, largely performed by women and children, became less valued in the monetized economy. The rise of stronger centralized states encouraged the settlement of nomadic populations. Gender roles, while differentiated in these communities, had placed greater value on female labor; and even in those communities that remained pastoral and nomadic, articulation with the merchant economy of the cities changed the nature of production and consumption, as in the case of carpets in Iran. Legal changes brought about by modernizing states circumscribed women's right to use the court and to own and inherit property. Modern education rendered many of women's traditional roles outdated or obsolete.

At the same time, women continued to rely on the sources of empowerment that had sustained them over the course of the centuries. Elite women, for example, continued to manage households, businesses, and properties. They continued to be educated and, in turn, to educate other women. While states increasingly placed *waqfs* under their care, women continued to use their endowments to fund public and charitable works. Like their counterparts in the working and peasant classes, women contributed to local cultures and economies and to their families. In each case, working close to home meant both proximity to family and distance from the tongues that wagged in response to women's increased participation in the labor force over the course of the nineteenth century. Working close to home also distanced women from the discourses that emerged over that century about the home and about modern women's proper place within it. It is to those discourses that we turn to in the next several chapters.

Notes

1. Camron Amin, *The Making of the Modern Iranian Woman: Gender, State Policy and Popular Culture, 1865–1946* (Gainesville: University of Florida Press, 2002), 18.
2. This section, aside from discussions of Safavid and Qajar Iran, is based on information from Mary Ann Fay, *Unveiling the Harem: Elite Women and the Paradox of Seclusion in Eighteenth Century Cairo*, Middle East Studies Beyond Dominant Paradigms (Syracuse: Syracuse University Press, 2012); Ülkü Ü. Bates, "Women as Patrons of Architecture in Turkey," in *Women in the Muslim World*, Lois Beck and Nikki Keddie, eds. (Cambridge, MA: Harvard University Press, 1978), 245–260; Afaf Lutfi al-Sayyid Marsot, *Women and Men in Late Eighteenth Century Egypt* (Austin, TX: The University of Texas Press, 1995); Leslie P. Pierce, *The Imperial Harem, Women and Sovereignty in the Ottoman Empire* (Oxford and New York: Oxford University Press, 1993).
3. Maria Szuppe, "The Jewels of Wonder: Learned Ladies and Princess Politicians in the Provinces of Early Safavid Iran," in *Women in the Medieval Islamic World*, Gavin Hambly, ed. (New York: St. Martin's Press, 1998), 325–348.
4. Stephen P. Blake, "Contributors to the Urban Landscape: Women Builders in Safavid Isfahan and Mughal Shahjanabad," in *Women in the Medieval Islamic World: Power, Patronage and Piety*, Gavin R.G. Hambly, ed. (New York: St. Martin's Press, 1998), 407–428.
5. Marsot, *Women and Men in Late 18th-Century Egypt*, 39.
6. This is one of Fay's main arguments in Unveiling the Harem.
7. Twelver Shia Muslims are free to practice *sigheh* or temporary marriage. In such marriages, the duration of the marital contract and the dowry are specified in advance.

8 Manoutcher M. Eskandari-Qajar, editor and translator, *Life at the Court of the Early Qajar Shahs* (Washington, DC: Mage Publishers, 2014), 4–14.
9 Fay, *Unveiling the Harem*, 38.
10 Fay, *Unveiling the Harem*, 184.
11 Susynne M. McElrone, "Nineteenth-Century Qajar Women in the Public Sphere: An Alternative Historical and Historiographical Reading of the Roots of Iranian Women's Activism," *Comparative Studies of South Asia, Africa and the Middle East* Vol. 25, No. 2 (2005), 304.
12 McElrone, "Nineteenth-Century Qajar Women," 303.
13 Abraham Marcus, *The Middle East on the Eve of Modernity: Aleppo in the Eighteenth Century* (New York: Columbia University Press, 1989), 41–42.
14 Marcus, *The Middle East on the Eve of Modernity*, 54.
15 Marcus, *The Middle East on the Eve of Modernity*, 192–193.
16 Marsot, *Women and Men in Late Eighteenth Century Egypt*, 77.
17 Marcus, *The Middle East on the Eve of Modernity*, 186–187.
18 Marcus, *The Middle East on the Eve of Modernity*, 210.
19 Bates, "Women as Patrons of Architecture," 248.
20 For a discussion of women's divided loyalties, see Iris Agmon, "Women, Class, and Gender: Muslim Jaffa and Haifa at the Turn of the 20th Century," *International Journal of Middle East Studies* Vol. 30, No. 4 (November 1998): 477–500.
21 James Reilly, "Women in the Economic Life of Late-Ottoman Damascus," *Arabica* 42, 1 (1995), 85–86.
22 For the Ottoman Middle East, this section is based upon Marcus, *The Middle East on the Eve of Modernity*; Reilly, "Women in the Economic Life of Late-Ottoman Damascus," 79–706, Marsot, *Women and Men in Late Eighteenth-Century Egypt*, Zarinebaf-Shahr, "The Role of Women in the Urban Economy of Istanbul, 1700–1850," 141–152; Karen van Nieukirk, "Changing Images and Shifting Identities: Female Performers in Egypt," in *Images of Enchantment: Visual and Performing Arts in the Middle East*, Sherifa Zuhur, ed. (Cairo: AUC Press, 1998), 21–36.
23 McElrone, "Nineteenth-Century Qajar Women," 303.
24 Badr al-Molok Bamdad, *From Darkness into Light: Women's Emancipation in Iran* (Costa Mesa, CA: Mazda Publishers, 2003), 15.
25 Bamdad, *From Darkness into Light*, 13.
26 McElrone, "Nineteenth-Century Qajar Women," 303.
27 Nahla Abdo, *Women in Israel: Race, Gender and Citizenship* (London: Zed Books, 2011), 70–72.
28 Marsot, *Women and Men in Late Eighteenth-Century Egypt*, 131.
29 Resat Kasaba, *The Ottoman Empire and the World Economy: The Nineteenth Century* (Albany: State University of New York Press, 1988), 84.
30 Dawn Chatty, *From Camel to Truck* (New York: Vantage Press, 1986); William Lancaster and Fidelity Lancaster, *Honour is in Contentment* (Berlin: de Gruter, 2011); Judith Tucker, *In the House of Law* (Berkeley: University of California Press, 1998), 29.
31 Nasser al-Taee, "Enough, Enough Oh Ocean: Pearl Divers in the Arabian Gulf," *MESA Bulletin* Vol. 39, No. 1 (June 2005): 19–31.
32 Richard B. Serjeant, "Fisher Folk and Fish Traps in Bahrain," *Bulletin of the School of Oriental and African Studies* Vol. 31, No. 3 (1968), 497, 502.
33 The section on Egypt's economic transformation under Muhammad Ali is taken from Judith E. Tucker, *Women in 19th-Century Egypt* (Cambridge: Cambridge University Press, 1984), Chapter 1 (unless otherwise specified).
34 Kristin Hoganson, *The Consumer's Imperium* (Chapel Hill: UNC Press, 2007), Chapter 1.
35 Donald Quataert, "Machine Breaking and the Changing Carpet Industry of Western Anatolia, 1860–1908," *Journal of Social History* Vol. 10, No. 3 (Spring 1986), 479–480.
36 Quataert, "Machine Breaking and the Changing Carpet Industry of Western Anatolia, 1860–1908," 481–482.

37 Leonard M. Helfgott, *Ties That Bind: A Social History of the Iranian Carpet* (Washington, DC and London: Smithsonian Institution Press, 1994), 159–160.
38 John Foran, "The Concept of Dependent Development as a Key to the Political Economy of Qajar Iran (1800–1925)," *Iranian Studies* Vol. 22, No. 2/3 (1989), 40.
39 Helfgott, *Ties That Bind*, 217.
40 Helfgott, *Ties That Bind*, 230.
41 Foran, "The Concept of Dependent Development," 40.
42 Zeinab Abdul-Maged, *Imagined Empires: A History of Revolt in Egypt* (Berkeley: University of California Press, 2013), 117.
43 See Mona Russell, *Creating the New Egyptian Woman* (New York: Palgrave, 2004), Chapter 8; Afsaneh Najmabadi, "Crafting an Educated Housewife in Iran," in *Remaking Women*, Lila Abu-Lughod, ed. (Princeton: Princeton University Press, 1998), 91–125; Reilly, "Women in the Economic Life of Late-Ottoman Damascus," 104.
44 Khaled Fahmy, *All the Pasha's Men: Mehmed Ali, His Army and the Making of Modern Egypt* (Cambridge: Cambridge University Press, 1997), 78–87.

3 Middle Eastern Women in the European Imagination

Introduction

Over the course of the nineteenth century, Western leisure travelers, entrepreneurs, and government officials began arriving in the Middle East in ever-growing numbers. Those men and women took a great interest in Middle Eastern women. In Western accounts of time spent in Ottoman and Qajar territories, it was not the executive and entrepreneurial acumen of elite Middle Eastern women that took pride of place. Nor was it the handiwork and labors of elite women's working-class contemporaries. Rather, Western travel writers in the colonial era dismissed any reflection on the similarities between Western and Middle Eastern women. Instead, Westerners favored an almost singular focus on the ways in which women's habits and customs marked differences between Western and Islamic societies. Western men and women created riveting and titillating but not wholly accurate accounts of their time in the Middle East. They did so through descriptions of veiling, accounts of polygamous marriages, and detailed depictions of harems. Through those accounts, the Middle East emerged in the imagination of Western readers not only as a region of bizarre and depraved customs but also as a place defined largely by women and their supposed habits and habitats.

The enduring legends of so-called Islamic depravity regarding women set in motion by travel literature captivated Western audiences to such an extent that the real habits and occupations of urban and rural women in Ottoman and Qajar territories largely eluded Westerners' notice. The allegedly depraved and imprisoned harem dweller, therefore, or her heavily-veiled figure in the public realm, were stand-ins for the real Middle Eastern women whose clothing, living arrangements, and domestic activities did not always match those of Europeans' descriptions. As Westerners' fixation with the harem intensified over the course of the nineteenth century, the harem's suggested practices became synonymous among Europeans with the region itself: travel writers of all kinds linked the harem's so-called "habits" to what they considered to be the region's backward political and economic institutions. What resulted from such Western imaginings was an increased determination on the part of Westerners to get inside the harem and to witness its depravities firsthand. A second result was an ever-intensifying rallying cry by leisure travelers, Christian missionaries, and government officials to reform the region and thereby rescue the so-called harem "inmate."

This call to reform Middle Eastern women was taken up in the late nineteenth and early twentieth centuries by European colonial officials, by local intellectuals, and by governing officials. As Chapters 5 and 6 illustrate, the Western race to reform and rescue harem women resulted in a similar focus on local women's habits and behaviors by Ottoman and Qajar elites. Male and female intellectuals across the region engaged in heated "Woman Question" (see Chapters 5 and 6) debates in the early twentieth century, both with Europeans and with one another. Those debates subsequently led to the emergence of nationalist movements in the WWI era whose language and symbolism similarly reflected a concern for women's reform (see Chapter 7).

Travel Literature and Women

European travelers to the Islamic world had long taken interest in Muslim women. It was during the seventeenth and eighteenth centuries, however, that European writers began focusing on harem women and writing about Muslim women as if they were markers of the essential differences between the Orient and the West.[1] As European empires expanded, Europeans' regard for the successes of Islamic civilizations—once conveyed in positive descriptions of Muslim women—shifted to attitudes of fear and threat. Depictions of Muslim women by Europeans subsequently represented the Islamic world as a vexing competitor and its allegedly hidden women as evidence of that world's inferiority relative to Europe. The early eighteenth-century transcription and translation from Arabic to French of *Alf Layla wa Layla*, known in the West as the *Arabian Nights*, popularized the image of an alleged captive harem inmate. The book's publication cemented the relationship in the European imagination between Scheherazade, who saved herself from death at the hands of a Muslim male (Shahrayar) by telling him nightly stories, and the Orient, where despotic males could kill their wives at whim.

With the ascent of the European middle class during the early colonial era, harems played an increasingly high-profile role in European travel literature. The growth of the middle class was accompanied by the changing notions about femininity, including the idea that a woman's domestic behaviors defined her as feminine. In the seventeenth and eighteenth centuries, European writers therefore began to focus on the domiciles and domestic practices of non-Europeans as a means of spotlighting European virtues. Harem literature was thus part of a process wherein Europeans used the ever-widening sphere of their colonial activities as an arena in which to understand and measure themselves relative to the behavior of others.

But where to find the Muslim women against whom to measure European women? Since most Europeans, particularly men, would not have been allowed inside a harem, travel writers had to rely upon literature. Consequently, Europeans who traveled to the Islamic world after the publication of the *Arabian Nights* relied on the texts as if they were ethnography and not fiction. Despite not having stepped inside a harem and using the *Arabian Nights* as their guide, eighteenth-century travelers nonetheless offered up salacious tales of lewd and violent men whose wives and concubines were victims of violence and promiscuity. As the eighteenth century progressed, the Muslim women who appeared in travel literature typically did so from behind the walls of the harem's so-called confinement.

There were some exceptions to eighteenth-century harem tales. Female visitors to the Ottoman Empire in the Enlightenment era, for example, were keen to depict the harem as a place where women knew liberty, albeit in a restricted space. Lady Mary Wortley Montagu (1689–1762) offers such an example. Her posthumously published *Embassy Letters* (1763), written during her brief sojourn in Istanbul and Edirne (1717–1718) as the wife of a European consular official and trade representative, were widely read among Europe's elite classes. In her *Letters*, Lady Mary suggested that Ottoman women's sartorial and domestic practices, in fact, allowed them great freedoms. Veils, she suggested, provided women perfect anonymity in the public sphere, allowing women to experience the curiosities of the world around them without the unwanted attentions of men. Harems and polygamy, she argued, gave Ottoman women the freedom not to be the singular focus of their husbands' attention and desire. In each case, the clothing and domestic arrangements that appeared to vex her contemporaries served as evidence for Lady Mary that Ottoman women were freer than they appeared.

Lady Elizabeth Craven, who spent 1785 and 1786 traveling between Crimea and Istanbul, similarly left ample record of her appreciation of Turkish women's "liberties." Writing at the end of the eighteenth century, Lady Craven did not have many positive things to say about the Ottomans. Claiming that the Sultan had spent too much time in the harem, she simply found him timid and ignorant. And the women? Craven claimed that they had spent too much time in the baths.[2] Her disregard for the Ottomans notwithstanding, Craven viewed the homosocial surroundings of the harem as far less likely to produce jealousy among women than European monogamous marital life. Similarly, she understood harem women to enjoy a great deal of sexual freedom:

> I think I never saw a country where women enjoy so much liberty, and free from all reproach, as in Turkey—A Turkish husband that sees a pair of slippers in the door of his harem must not enter; his respect for the sex prevents him from intruding when a stranger is there upon a visit.[3]

Harem tales had by 1850 become a calling card for nineteenth-century travel literature about the Middle East: one travel guide for visiting Ottoman territories, including Mesopotamia (roughly present-day Iraq), introduced the idea that travelers could not claim to know the region without having visited a harem. Like mosques, churches, and archeological ruins, harems appeared in nineteenth-century travel literature as places that had literally to be penetrated if one wanted to know the region intimately.[4] Nineteenth-century travelers were known to demonstrate frustration and sometimes hostility when they could not get inside homes to see women and their living quarters.

For male travelers to the region across the nineteenth century, the very promise of entering a harem, with all its alleged sexual licentiousness, offered a welcome antidote to the morals of the Victorian era.[5] Tales abounded about male travelers whose determination to get inside a harem led them to climb trellises and sequester themselves on the terrace of a house in order to peek at women nearby.[6] For men who were lured to the East by tales of its rampant sexuality, the Orient itself played the role of an imaginary harem.[7] In the accounts of such men, half-naked women lounged endlessly, waiting for a husband to arrive and fulfill their sexual longings. Samuel Graham Wilson, who visited Iran in the late nineteenth century, observed that an Iranian woman's role was "to maintain her husband's satisfaction. She aspires to the position of a slave to man's pleasure and comfort, and aspires to nothing more."[8]

Englishman Edward Lane, whose *Habits and Customs of the Modern Egyptians* served as an authoritative ethnography about Egypt for generations, urged readers to consider the harem's reproductive habits as evidence of depravity. He recounted that, for example, the harem women who wanted to get pregnant were known to step over the body of a decapitated man seven times. "And some, with the same desire, dip in the blood a piece of cotton wool, of which they afterwards make use in a manner I must decline mentioning."[9] Violence, sexuality, and peculiar customs combine in Lane's quote to create an image of the harem that was attractive as well as repulsive and as dangerous as it was delightful.

The idea that harem women might find themselves in the presence of a decapitated male was the result of another common figure in male-authored harem literature: the cruel and heartless master. If some writers found Muslim men to want nothing but sex from their wives, others found Muslim men to be indifferent to women's emotions:

> He is an uncivilized sacrificer [sic] who knows nothing about sweet feelings, the outpourings of the heart, the delicious abandon...There are no delicate moves, no different approaches, no gracious details; everything is rough and appears lifeless—merely a disgusting physical act.[10]

Other writers found the masters of harems to be physically cruel: Muslim men exhibited the same cruelty to their wives as they did to their male rivals. Evoking the *Arabian Nights*, travel writers noted that masters of the harem were wont to punish harem women for any and all manner of transgressions: writers alleged that, for example, the wives and concubines who were caught practicing lesbianism (said by travel writers to be the byproduct of their husbands' capricious attention to their needs) were said to be tied together and thrown into the sea.[11]

The sexuality of Middle Eastern men was also of enormous interest to European travel writers beginning in the eighteenth century. Circa 1750, Western travelers to the Ottoman Empire began criticizing same-sex practices between men. Those travelers claimed to find "unabashed homoerotic culture in coffeehouses and bathhouses and *Karagoz* plays" (shadow plays). Writers were now attuned to the sexual behaviors of both men and women.[12] In the military, writers claimed to find homosexuality in the Ottoman janissary corps. Some concluded that sodomy was worse than what was happening amongst women in the harem. Circa 1800 the Englishman Adolphus Slade, a naval officer who spoke Turkish and who was a frequent sojourner in Ottoman territories, condemned Ottoman society for what he called the widespread practice of sodomy. Slade based his conclusions on the slave market, where he observed that boys fetched a higher price than girls. Furthermore, he insisted that same-sex relations were rampant among the Ottoman male elites.[13] He described a party at which guests enjoyed wine, music, and dancing boys. As the boys began to dance, he wrote:

> some of the guests tore off their upper garments—fire in their eyes, froth on their beards—joined the dancers, their turbans half unrolled flying out as they reeled round the apartment, and but for the presence of the bey [master], scandalous displays would have ensued.[14]

Finally, Slade accused Sultan Mahmud II himself of sexual depravity with males, suggesting that the political and economic reforms the likes of which the Ottomans were undertaking in the nineteenth century (see Chapter 4) could not be accomplished by men who had sex with other men. Slade described sexual relations between men as a disease of state, in which the large percentage of government ministers were manumitted slaves, purchased by the sultan to pleasure himself, and lacking in all governing qualifications. "The political system prevalent in the empire is neither absolutist monarchy nor Oriental despotism. It is sodomy...Governed by sodomy and debauchery, their only law is social and political domination."[15]

European travelers to Iran were similarly fixated with same-sex relations between men. Frenchman Jean Chardin's claims to having written an authentic account of his sixteenth-century journey through Iran resulted in the book acquiring a kind of failproof stature: just as they had with *Arabian Nights*, readers trusted the text to be true. Chardin linked same-sex relations between men to the ubiquity of young male dancers who cross-dressed as females. Accounts such as Chardin's conditioned travelers to see the things they read about, even if they did not necessarily see them, resulting in the conclusion among Europeans that homosexual relations were prevalent in Iran. By the early nineteenth century, Iranian men themselves had come to understand that Europeans saw love between men to be a vice.[16]

Domestic Life

Female writers from the Victorian era were conditioned to believe that women needed to be exemplars of domestic practices. Travelers from that era therefore took great note of local women's household activities. In their writings, Middle Eastern women began therefore to take on the qualities of a mirror in which Western women could see their own domestic abilities and virtues reflected. To be sure, men as well as women took note of harem women's routines. The late nineteenth-century books and articles of French author Charles François Marie d'Harcourt (1835–1895), known to readers as le Duc d'Harcourt, included a fixation with women's domestic life. His work provoked a great deal of debate among Egyptian intellectuals at the turn of the twentieth century, in large measure because d'Harcourt's contempt for modern Egypt was expressed through his comments about domestic spaces. He wrote:

> When you go into the selamlik, the only part of the house accessible to a male visitor, you are struck in the houses of the richest pashas by the appearances of disorder, or rather unimaginable negligence. A thick layer of dust covers the gilded chairs, which seem to have never been dusted since they left the shop ... Everyone knows that ... disorder and negligence are signs of wasteful habits and extravagance.[17]

But female travel writers took especially careful measure of harem women's domestic habits and customs. Western women took note of harem women's table manners and their hygienic practices and used those customs as a means of accounting for what they saw as Muslim women's degradation. Household disarray was a most common trope. In numerous women's accounts of the Orient, harem women did little more than gossip, smoke, drink tea, tell stories, dance, and frolic. Wrote one visitor to an Egyptian harem:

> Pray, kind reader, just picture yourself surrounded by such a motley group of beings, gabbing, chattering to me in their unknown tongues ... and making grimaces like monkeys from four o'clock in the morning until ten at night incessantly; and then you may form some idea of life in the harem.[18]

In a similar vein, visitors to the Levantine harem wrote: "When you awake you will find music and dancing, the girls chasing one another, eating sweetmeats, cracking nuts and enjoying all sorts of fun."[19] Rarely was there any mention of harem women who excelled at running households and businesses.

The production of art accompanied that of travel literature in the late nineteenth century. Like literature, art produced for Western audiences a "glimpse" into Islam's so-called "hidden world." Jean-Léon Gérôme (1824–1904), perhaps the best-known Orientalist painter, placed on the canvas what travel writers captured in print: passive harem women and their cruel male counterparts. In Gérôme's "Moorish Bath" (1870), for example, the viewer is transported deep inside the harem to an elite woman's hidden bathing chamber (see Figure 3.1). A half-naked black slave bathes the semi-reclined, naked body of a harem woman. The bather's posture and placement suggest both pleasure and entrapment. Jean-August-Dominique Ingres (1780–1867) similarly evoked idle, supine, naked women trapped in the pursuit of pleasure in his 1862 "The Turkish Bath" (see Figure 3.2). In the painting, dozens of naked women inhabit an enclosed space. Some dance; others recline; yet others play musical instruments. The gaze and body language of most of the women suggest a combination of pleasure and boredom. Ingres' "Grande Odalisque," in which a harem woman reclines naked with her back to the painter, similarly evokes both

Figure 3.1 Jean-Léon Gérôme Moorish Bath, 1870. The Picture Art Collection/Alamy Stock Photo.

Figure 3.2 Jean-Auguste-Dominique Ingres, The Turkish Bath, 1862. Dennis Hallinan/Alamy Stock Photo.

the luxury and the depravity that were so commonly evoked by travel literature (see Figure 3.3). In none of these images do we see harem women managing their households or raising their children.

By the turn of the twentieth century, travelers could send evidence that they had seen, and therefore known, the Orient by sending a picture postcard home to their family and friends. Tawdry photographs of alleged harem women from French and British outposts in North Africa and the Middle East distorted the reality of harem women in much the same way as Orientalist paintings had, albeit for a more popular audience. European photographers stripped the orphans and prostitutes (who were asked to pose as harem women) of their veils, or of their clothing, or festooned them in jeweled turbans, beads, and baubles to offer viewers a peek into the alleged harem space.[20]

Orientalist painters also used their canvases to capture the so-called cruelty of Middle Eastern men. In his 1866 "The Slave Market," Gérôme utilized an open square to illustrate the cruel acts of Muslim men (see Figure 3.4). In "The Slave Market," men examine a white slave, brought most likely from the Caucuses, soon to become a harem girl. The naked female body emerges from Gérôme's painting both as a commodity and as the source of pleasures to come. Her Muslim male captor appears as a heartless trader in female flesh.

Perhaps the most evocative depiction of the brutality of the Muslim male is the product of one of Gérôme's students, Alexandre Georges-Henri Régnault (1843–1871). Régnault is best known for his "Execution Without Trial by the Moorish King" (1870), in which an Arab from fifteenth-century Spain serves as a stand-in for nineteenth-century Muslim rulers and in which unbridled tyranny appears to reign. The painting pictures an executioner, presumably a ruler, who looks on with

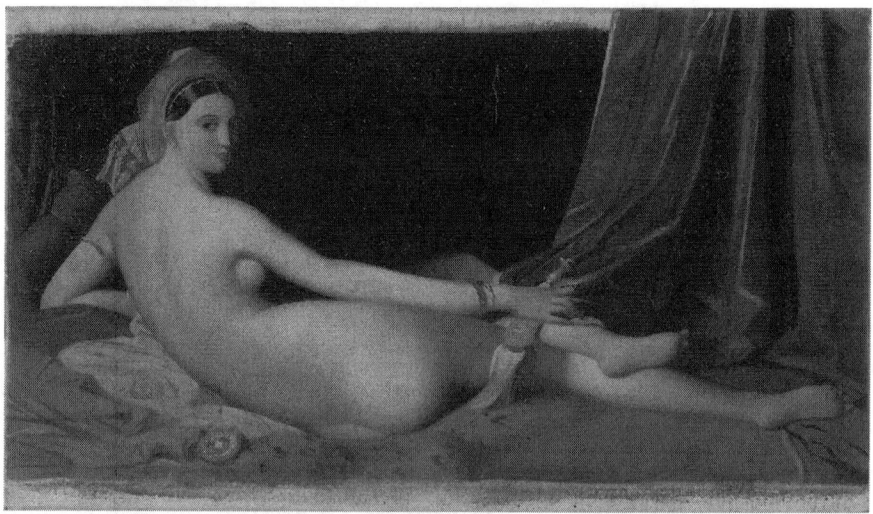

Figure 3.3 Jean-Auguste Dominque Ingres, Grande Odalisque, 1814. Art Collection 3/Alamy Stock Photo.

Figure 3.4 Jean-Léon Gérôme, The Slave Market, 1866. Artokoloro/Alamy Stock Photo.

detachment as blood from his recently decapitated victim drips between a body and its severed head.

Despotic men and harem women similarly represented the Middle East to late nineteenth-century American audiences in American travel literature about the region (e.g., Mark Twain and Herman Melville both wrote about their voyages there) and in American Orientalist art. The American painter Frederick Arthur Bridgman (1847–1928), a student of Gérôme's at the École des Beaux Arts in Paris, both diverged from and elaborated on his teacher's designs. Bridgman's 1878 "The Siesta," for example, depicts a clothed harem woman (see Figure 3.5). Her clothing leaves her slightly less titillating than her European-produced counterparts, but nonetheless attractive. Bridgman surrounded this woman, as his European contemporaries might well have, with the vehicles of both pleasure and subjugation. She is surrounded by rails, for

Figure 3.5 Frederick Arthur Bridgman, The Siesta, 1878. Artefact/Alamy Stock Photo.

example, which allude to her entrapment. Her tobacco pipe and her cup of tea remind us that her role is pleasure: her master's and therefore her own.

Europeans began combatting the trade in slaves from Africa and the Caucasus in Ottoman, Ottoman-Egyptian, and Qajar territories beginning in the 1840s, in part due to their conclusions regarding slavery and harem keeping. Beginning with the Qajars, Europeans acquired the right to search ships bringing slaves into Iranian ports. Those inspections succeeded in decreasing the number of slaves brought into Qajar territories and resulted in the signing of the 1882 Anglo-Iranian agreement to abolish the Persian Gulf slave trade.[21] The Anglo-Egyptian Convention of 1877 banned the import into Egypt of Sudanese and Ethiopian slaves and allowed the British to search ships suspected of carrying slaves in Egyptian waters. By the 1880s, as the British established hegemony in Egypt, they took on greater authority to suppress the trade, which was still being practiced despite the 1877 ban. It was not until 1904 that Britain's Consul General in Egypt announced that slavery had been eliminated in Egypt. In 1899, the Sultan banned slavery in the remaining Ottoman territories.[22]

The British government and the British and Foreign Anti-Slavery Society (BFASS) allegedly intervened in the regional slave trade in order to save women; they reserved their ire, however, for the masters (the patriarchs, as they were referred to by Europeans) who kept harems, even when those men married the women who had been their concubines. In the minds of British officials and BFASS members, the Muslim patriarch was unlike the English gentleman whose wife may have been confined to home but who was not enslaved by her husband—at least not in the minds of English gentlemen. By ending the slave trade, these men and women hoped to put an end to the harem altogether. But they also hoped to turn the Muslim patriarch into a reformed patriarch fashioned along European lines. Indeed, the British saw Muslim patriarchs to be an obstacle to any sort of Western reform in the region.[23]

Tawfiq Pasha (r. 1879–1892) of Egypt was an example of such a reformed patriarch. Tawfiq was placed in power in Egypt by the Ottoman sultan after Tawfiq's father, Ismail Pasha (r. 1863–1879) was forced to abdicate (see below). The British liked Tawfiq, in part, because he was monogamous and in part because he had openly expressed disgust for the slave trade. ("With one wife," he is known to have said, "there will not be any necessity for seclusion.")[24] While Tawfiq was wildly unpopular with his subjects (in large measure because of his cooperation with the British both prior to and after the 1882 occupation), the British held him up as a kind of "new man," monogamous and opposed to the harem—evidence that the Muslim patriarch could be reformed after all.[25]

Veiled Encounters

As Europeans became increasingly fixated by what they perceived to be women's habits and customs, veiling also caught the full force of their attention. Travel writers wrote about the street as an extension of the harem and increasingly described the veil as a public manifestation of women's imprisonment.[26] Earlier depictions of veiling, such as those of Lady Mary Wortley Montagu, as providing women with a level of liberty and dignity, gave way to descriptions of veils as evidence of the closed and secretive nature of Middle Eastern society. Over the course of the nineteenth century, writers increasingly compared veiled women to the dead. Similarly, writers referred to veiled women as mummies and witches. "In the crowd, too, are veiled women in black who would seem to be items detached from a funeral pageant…upon the addition of a conical hat … and a cat, [they] would turn into witches."[27]

Nineteenth-century European travelers, both male and female, also used the veil to discuss what they saw to be the sexual nature of Middle Eastern society. Travelers alleged, for example, that women could be found naked but for their veils, both inside and outside of their homes. One traveler suggested that:

> The veil seems to be the most important piece of their dress: their chief care is always to hide their face. There have been many instances of women who, upon being surprised naked, eagerly covered their faces, without shewing [sic] any concern about their other charms.[28]

This traveler even claimed that he had witnessed peasant girls running around naked with their faces veiled.[29]

Gendered Landscapes

In the nineteenth-century, travel writers attributed feminine characteristics to the Middle Eastern landscape. Writing from Syria, Englishman Robert Hitchens, author of popular accounts of Syria, Palestine, and Egypt, compared Damascus and Jenin to Eastern sirens who beckon to Western men. Hitchens also described the mountains of Moab as a tantalizing female, who lured travelers to her.[30] For one French traveler, Damascus was like "...the women I see passing in front of our camp, covering their embroidered dresses with a miserable cotton veil. They hide their treasures..."[31] In their account of their travels to Arabia, entitled *A Pilgrimage to Nejd*, Britons Wilfrid and Anne Blunt compared the Arabian Peninsula to the characteristics of a bride awaiting a bridegroom: fertile and luscious.[32]

The Middle East was also a feminine muse for Jews in the late nineteenth century, who longed for and wrote about the creation of a nation-state for the Jewish people in Palestine. Zionist writers from Europe and Russia, whose writings called for Jews to immigrate to Palestine and to work for the eventual establishment of a Jewish state there, imagined the land of Israel (Eretz Israel) to be female. Many of the men who imagined Eretz Israel to possess feminine characteristics had not actually seen the land they described. Nonetheless, they compared the land to a mother who would birth a new generation of Jewish men. Sometimes, they described the land as a lover for whom Jewish men would sacrifice anything, even themselves.[33] In his text on the creation of a nation-state for Jews in Palestine *Auto-Emancipation*, Leon Pinsker (1821–1891) described the land of Israel as the compassionate mother who would redeem the Jewish people—to whom he referred as children—who had been orphaned by the diaspora.[34] Writing from Palestine in the early twentieth century, the male Jewish settlers who took up the call of men like Pinsker and settled in Palestine described themselves as bridegrooms and the land as a woman's bosom.[35] In each case, descriptions of Middle Eastern landscapes were gendered: depictions of cities as veiled women and of landscapes as brides captured nothing of the activities that took place in sites like Damascus—agriculture, commerce, and education, for example—and rendered Ottoman and Qajar territories as feminine objects to be undressed and penetrated or by contrast protected.

European and, later, American geopolitical strategies in the Middle East over the nineteenth and twentieth centuries reflected Western understanding of the region in gendered-feminine terms: participation in the cutting of a canal in the Isthmus of Suez; taking of tantalizing, fertile, and luscious territories; penetrating institutions in order to know and reform them; protecting women from lascivious, despotic men; and reforming the women who were said to be synonymous with territory. Chapter 7 addresses the effects of European travel literature on governing policy at greater length, as does Chapter 13 on the 2003 American occupation of Iraq. Both chapters illustrate the enduring legacy of travel literature.

Reforming the Harem

During the final decades of the nineteenth century, missionary societies in Europe and the US sent increasing numbers of unmarried women into the field. Consequently, the number of Christian missionaries in the region increased substantially. Many of these women worked in schools and orphanages. A goodly number of the women who arrived in the Middle East to take up missionary posts in the later decades of the nineteenth century were also trained as nurses and doctors.

By law, the missionaries could not proselytize to or convert Muslim women. But in harems as well as in the dwellings of women of the lower economic orders, missionaries could introduce local women—Muslim and non-Muslim—to one of the hallmarks of nineteenth-century Christian civilization: the domestic sciences. In what they called *zenana* work, a term originally coined by Protestants who had worked in India, missionaries took up home visits to women of all classes to preach the virtues of Victorian domestic habits and mothering skills. Many missionaries found "visiting" to be the best form of preaching, especially to women in seclusion, even if no conversion resulted from their home encounters.[36]

From these visits, missionaries, like the ever-increasing number of travel writers who claimed to visit harems in the later decades of the nineteenth century, concluded that much was wrong with Middle Eastern women's domestic habits and child-rearing skills. Missionaries and travelers increasingly claimed that polygamy, sequestration, and indolence had produced women who were not fit to raise children. Writers and missionaries noted that harem women were inattentive to their children's hygiene, treating their children's illnesses with amulets and folk remedies rather than modern medicine, or blowing smoke up their children's noses rather than treating colds with tablets and other modern medicines.

The Western rallying cry to get inside the harem was therefore joined by a new call to educate and to reform harem women, both for their own sake and for that of their children. Some called for the Christian conversion of harem inmates: "Short of Christianity, no teaching can elevate the character and position of Mohammedan women in any land; for, as long as she accepts the Koran as a rule of faith, she will unhesitatingly acquiesce in the mutilated life to which she is condemned."[37] Others called for the conversion of the region's women to the domestic sciences of modern Europe and the US.

To accomplish this domestic conversion, European and American missionaries established a network of schools—from primary schools to colleges—across the region. The schools were designed to make women of all the social classes literate. They were also, however, designed to teach Western models of cleanliness, domesticity, and child-raising to Middle Eastern women. Missionaries hoped to make better mothers, homemakers, and wives out of harem women, hoping, in turn, to produce a generation of women who would insist upon monogamy and who would raise their children in suitably clean and orderly households.[38] Missionary schools ranged in quality and curriculum. In general, however, in addition to religious instruction, those schools provided basic literacy, arithmetic, and sometimes foreign language(s). Girls' schools usually provided instruction in some type of needlework, home economics, and some vocational training.

Males were also the target of such lessons, and missionary schools taught boys as well as girls. Missionary educators hoped that the young men who took courses in home economics, in addition to reading and math, would insist upon monogamy and upon raising their children in clean, well-ordered homes.[39]

Travel writers and their missionary counterparts concluded that men too needed to be reformed. Indeed, they claimed, the practice of polygamy and the daily interaction with allegedly childish harem women had ruined men and made them incapable of running their countries. Englishman Charles Perry attributed what he saw to be the ineffective nature of the Ottoman state to the fact that Ottoman rulers were educated in the harem. In isolation, and under negative "female influence," they were hardly raised for effective rule.[40] Writing later in the eighteenth century, a French traveler concluded that while the strength of Europe's nations lay in the positive role that women played in influencing homelife, the same could not be said of the Ottoman world.[41] By the mid-nineteenth century, travelers frequently pointed to the harem as evidence of Ottoman and Qajar misrule.

European writings and rumors about Khedive Ismail (r. 1863–1879) of Egypt illustrate Western apprehensions about the effects of the harem on elite men. Europeans held Ismail in an odd regard. On the one hand, they appreciated his many successes at modernization: the expansion and streamlining of government offices; the establishment of a nascent educational system for the elite classes; the opening of the Suez Canal; the building of libraries, theaters, and parks; the laying of miles of railroads; and the establishment of light industry—to give but a few examples. On the other hand, however, European accounts of Ismail reflected a tendency among Europeans to view the khedive as an oafish child, incapable of managing his affairs. Here, travel literature swayed the opinions of government officials: the Europeans who had been sent to Egypt beginning in the 1870s to supervise the Ottoman-Egyptian government's finances and to ensure that Ismail make good on repayment of loans to European banks, confessed that they drew on travel literature in their assessment of the khedive, his family, and his ministers. Sir Evelyn Baring (later Lord Cromer) who took up a post in Egypt as its controller general in 1879 and later served as Egypt's first Consul General (1882–1907), recorded in his memoirs that he had gleaned his knowledge of Ismail's private life from a traveler, William Nassau Senior, author of *Conversations and Journals in Egypt and Malta*. "The man's account of Ismail's private life is worth quoting. I do not doubt its accuracy."[42] Those accounts read much like the *Arabian Nights*, with a few modern twists: champagne now flowed in the harems that had ruined the Egyptian ruling elite. Europeans also attributed Ismail's alleged penchant for cruelty to his harem upbringing: the khedive was said to have acquired his habit for killing off the ministers who disagreed with him from his mother, Khosayr Hanem. That mother was allegedly so consumed by sexual desire that she sent for young men each evening, had her way with them in the confines of the harem, and disposed of their headless bodies in the Nile each subsequent morning.[43]

Such stories about the khedive's harem roots, and the fantastical images produced by them, seemed to override for Europeans any successes Ismail might have achieved in Egypt's modernization. When the British occupied Egypt in 1882, they pointed to the harem and its practices as legitimizations for an unpopular invasion. The argument of Cromer and his contemporaries was fairly simple: depraved habits and customs like the use of *harem* space had led Egypt to ruin. If Egyptian governing institutions were to be reformed, then the first step had to be saving women from their degraded state. One of Cromer's most often-cited musings claims that: "The position of women in Egypt, and in Mohammedan countries generally, is therefore a fatal obstacle to the attainment of that elevation of thought and character which should accompany the introduction of European civilization."[44] For Cromer and a generation of men and women who in both official and unofficial capacities made reforming the Middle East their rallying cry, the condition of women and the region's alleged shortcomings were one and the same.

Cromer also argued that Middle Eastern men would benefit from the reform of women. He and his contemporaries viewed the men who governed Egypt to be akin to small children, in need of constant care and supervision. Cromer frequently compared Egyptians to children in early stages of development: capable of little initiative and in need of constant adult supervision. His calls for the reform of women were joined with calls to improve Egyptian men. Reform, he wrote, would require Egypt to be "nursed and tended to slow maturity."[45] Like a mother, the officials of the veiled protectorate would raise Egypt to a new level of development.

Cromer's determination that Egyptian women be civilized was not, however, reflected in a generous allocation for women's education. Indeed, the percentage of the British government budget designated for the education of Egyptian boys and girls by Cromer and his successors ran in the single digits. Nonetheless, beginning in the 1880s, British officials in Egypt oversaw a slowly expanding educational system in which the reform of Egyptian households and the cleaning up of their alleged dirt and depravation was central to a curriculum aimed at both boys and girls.[46] By the early twentieth century, as Egyptians took a greater role in the state educational system, they, too, promoted a curriculum that emphasized lessons in hygiene, child-rearing, and household organization for girls.[47] Such curriculum joined with that of European missionaries who taught an increasing number of Muslim and Christian students that cleaning up their domestic practices was central to Egypt's progress. In each case, the lesson was clear: the problematic domestic practices that had led to the occupation had to be replaced with modern habits in order for Egypt to gain its independence. Modern mothers were at the heart of this educational-political enterprise: they were singled out as being the greatest influence on the future generations of Egyptians who would govern Egypt in Britain's stead.[48] Chapter 4 explores missionary and state education throughout the region more fully.

Cromer and others' use of domestic images to classify non-Western subjects and to shape colonial policy for ruling them was not a strategy that was limited to the Middle East. In India, for example, employees of the English East India Company and later British colonial officials claimed to be horrified by practices like *sati* (widow burning), laws prohibiting widows from remarrying, and laws allowing child marriage. It was seemingly easy for the British to justify colonial rule over people who engaged in such "backward" and "immoral" practices. It also seemed easy to use practices like *sati* to justify locking Indians out of positions in self-government. The British deemed Indian men effeminate when they could not protect their wives and daughters from the funeral pyre. How, the British asked, could such men be adequate to the task of running India?[49]

Conclusion

The harem women who nineteenth-century travel writers and missionaries claimed to discover were not women who planned menus, raised children, oversaw household staff, invested money, or managed businesses by proxy. Rather, European writers—male and female alike—depicted harem residents as inmates, imprisoned by men who had appetites for little more than sex and power. In the harem, all manner of bizarre, depraved, and perverse activities reduced women to being little more than slaves. As such accounts circulated and as they were reproduced in art and literature, Europeans began to equate the Middle East with the harem and with the subjugated women who inhabited it. On the eve of the modern era, literate Europeans had become accustomed to travel literature in which the harem had become a metaphor for the Orient.

Readers of travel literature thus did not see the extent to which modernizing reforms in both the Ottoman Empire and Qajar Iran had already produced a class of educated women whose habits largely resembled those of European women and a female laboring class whose difficulties were akin to their European counterparts. Rather, Western readers of travel accounts encountered an Orient that was alien to them, in which women—and men—lived depraved lives that had little in common with their own. Some readers of travel literature might have experienced an urge to journey to the Middle East and see such horrors up close. Others might have taken up the call of Christian missionaries who worked to civilize the region and to save harem women from their alleged degradations. Indeed, by the time of the arrival of officials like Cromer, travel writers had succeeded in creating harem inmates in need of rescue.

As the next several chapters will illustrate, European colonial regimes, members of local intelligentsias, and local state builders each used such "imagined" women to shape justifications for rule, to erect discursive strategies for nation building, and to build nations. In each case, a "new woman" emerged as the reformed antithesis to the allegedly depraved harem inmate who had emerged from the pages of travel literature.

Similarly, colonial regimes and local state builders put laws and educational systems into place so as to protect the "new woman" from the traditions of previous generations. New laws and systems often had little to do with the needs and demands of actual women. Instead, new institutions reflected obsessions with seclusion, veiling, and polygamy. Those obsessions, as well as cures for what supposedly ailed the harem woman, were taken up in the form of "Woman-Question" debates by the local intelligentsia. We will return to those debates in Chapters 5 and 6.

Notes

1 The theoretical underpinning of this chapter depends upon the work of Mohja Kahf, *Western Representations of the Muslim Woman from Termagant to Odalisque* (Austin, TX: The University of Texas Press, 1999), Introduction and Chapter 2, as well as Billie Melman *Women's Orients: English Women and the Middle East, 1718–1918: Sexuality, Religion and Work* (Ann Arbor, MI: The University of Michigan Press, 1995), Chapter 2.
2 Lady Elizabeth Craven, *A Journey Through Crimea to Constantinople* (London: G.J. and J. Robinson, Peter Norton Row, 1789), 5.
3 Craven, *Journey*, 205.
4 Lisa Pollard, *Nurturing the Nation: Colonizing, Modernizing and Liberating Egypt (1850–1923)* (Berkeley: UC Press, 2005), Chapter 2 "Inside Egypt."
5 One Englishman who had lived in Anatolia for a long while and who published an account of his time there admitted that what he knew about harem life he got from his wife. William J.J. Spry, *Life on the Bosphorous* (1895), cited in Judy Mabro, *Veiled Half Truths: Western Travelers' Perceptions of Middle Eastern Women* (London: I.B. Taurus, 1991), 53.
6 Mabro, *Veiled Half Truths*, 250.
7 Rana Kabbani, *Imperial Fictions: Europe's Myths of Orient* (London: Saqi Press, 2008), 113.
8 Cited in Guity Nashat, "Women in Pre-Revolutionary Iran: A Historical Overview," in *Women and Revolution in Iran*, Guity Nashat, ed. (Boulder, CO: Westview Press, 1983), 19.
9 Edward Lane, *Manners and Customs of the Modern Egyptians* (London, 1836), 75.
10 Sonnini de Manoncourt, *Travels to Upper and Lower Egypt (1799)*, 237–239, cited in Mabro, *Veiled Half Truths*, 142.
11 Elias Habesci, *The Present State of the Ottoman Empire, 1784*, 177, cited in Mabro, *Veiled Half Truths*, 139.
12 Dror Ze'evi, *Producing Desire: Changing Sexual Discourse on the Ottoman Middle East (1500–1900)* (Berkeley: UC Press, 2006), 167.
13 Ze'evi, *Producing Desire*, 154.
14 Adolphus Slade, *Records of Travels in Turkey and of a Cruise in the Black Sea with the Captain Pasha*, in the years 1829, 1830, and 1831, Vol. II (London: Saunders and Otley, 1832), 395, cited in Ze'evi, *Producing Desire*, 157.
15 Ze'evi, *Producing Desire*, 158.
16 Afsaneh Najmabadi, *Women with Mustaches and Men Without Beards: Sexual Anxiety in Iranian Modernity* (Berkeley: University of California Press, 2005), 34.
17 François Charles Marie le duc d'Harcourt, *Egypte et les Egyptiens* (Paris: Plon, Nourrit, 1893), 40–42, cited in Mabro, *Veiled Half Truths*, 187.
18 Emmeline Lott, *Harem Life in Egypt and Constantinople* (1865), Vol. I, 214–216, cited in Mabro, *Veiled Half Truths*, 66.
19 Isobel Burton, *The Inner Life of Syria, Palestine and the Holy Land*, 1875, Vol. I, 145–146, cited in Mabro, *Veiled Half Truths*, 85.
20 Malek Alloula, *The Colonial Harem* (Minneapolis: The University of Minnesota Press, 1987).
21 Vanessa Martin, *The Qajar Pact: Bargaining, Protest and the State in Nineteenth-Century Persia* (New York: I.B. Tauris, 2005), 163–164.
22 Paul E. Lovejoy, "Appendix: Chronology of Measures Against Slavery," in *Transformations in Slavery: A History of Slavery in Africa* (Cambridge: Cambridge University Press, 2012). https://www.cambridge.org/core/books/abs/transformations-in-slavery/chronology-of-measures-against-slavery/B759FB5758B1B5B963971E87A638ADAC.
23 Diane Robinson-Dunn, *The Harem, Slavery and British Imperial Culture: Anglo-Muslim Relations in the late Nineteenth Century* (Manchester: The University of Manchester Press, 2006), 41.

24 Robinson-Dunn, *The Harem, Slavery and British Imperial Culture*, 53.
25 Pollard, *Nurturing the Nation*; Robinson-Dunn, *The Harem, Slavery and British Imperial Culture*, 54.
26 Mabro, *Veiled Half Truths*.
27 Sir Frederick Treves, *The Land That Is Desolate: An Account of a Tour in Palestine* (London: John Murray, 1913), 52–53.
28 Carsten Neihbur, *Travels Through Arabia and Other Countries in the East* (Edinburgh, 1791) 118 cited in Mabro, *Veiled Half Truths*, 84.
29 Neihbur, *Travels Through Arabia*, 118, cited in Pollard, *Nurturing the Nation*, 63.
30 Mabro, *Veiled Half Truths*, 42–43.
31 S.A.R. le Comte de Paris, *Damas et le Liban*, 1861, 9, cited in Mabro, *Veiled Half Truths*, 44.
32 Melman, *Women's Orients*, 287–288.
33 Sheila H. Katz, *Women and Gender in Early Jewish and Palestinian Nationalism* (Gainesville: University Press of Florida, 2003), 82.
34 Leon Pinsker, *Auto-Emancipation*, cited in Katz, *Women and Gender in Early Jewish and Palestinian Nationalism*, 85–86.
35 Katz, *Women and Gender in Early Jewish and Palestinian Nationalism*, 86.
36 Heleen Muirre-Van den Berg, "Nineteenth-Century Protestant Missions and Middle Eastern Women: An Overview," in *Gender, Religion and Social Change in the Middle East: Two Hundred Years of History*, Inger Marie Okkenhaug and Ingrid Flaskerud, eds. (New York: Berg Publishing, 2005), 107.
37 Mabel Sharmon Crawford, *Through Algeria, 1863*, 55–56, cited in Mabro, *Veiled Half Truths*, 182.
38 Pollard, *Nurturing the Nation*, Chapter 5; Russell, *Creating the New Egyptian Woman*, 112; Heather Sharkey, *American Evangelicals in Egypt: Missionaries in an Age of Empire* (Princeton: Princeton University Press, 2015).
39 Russell, *Creating the New Egyptian Woman*, 112.
40 Charles Perry, *A View of the Levant* (London: T. Woodward, 1743), 54.
41 Claude Etienne Savary, *Lettres sur l'Egypte* (Paris: Onfroi, 1785), 158.
42 "Cromer's Situation in Egypt: Lord Cromer's Account," cited in Pollard, *Nurturing the Nation*, 88, fn 45.
43 Clara Asch Boyle, *Boyle of Cairo: A Diplomatist's Adventures in the Middle East* (London: Titus Wilson and Son, 1965), 36–38.
44 Cromer, *Modern Egypt* (London: Macmillan & Co., 1908), Vol. 2, 538–539.
45 Cromer, *Modern Egypt*, Vol. 1, 155, cited in Pollard, *Nurturing the Nation*, 98.
46 Pollard, *Nurturing the Nation*, Chapter 4; Russell, *Creating the New Egyptian Woman*, Chapters 6 and 7.
47 Pollard, *Nurturing the Nation*, 118–120.
48 Pollard, *Nurturing the Nation*, Chapter 4.
49 See Mrinalini Sinha, *Colonial Masculinity: The "Manly Englishman" and the "Effeminate Bengali" in the Late Nineteenth Century* (Manchester and New York: Manchester University Press, 1990).

4 New Fathers, New Brides, and New Daughters

Reform and Its New Men and Women

Over the course of the nineteenth century, rulers in Istanbul, Cairo, and Tehran worked diligently to gain admission to the league of modern rulers. Mastering Western technologies, displaying military force, and reforming and refashioning militaries, bureaucracies, and cityscapes were demonstrations of both prowess and power. In Egypt and Iran, Muhammad Ali and Fath Ali Shah levied the efficiency of reformed institutions in the service of control over their territories and their populations. Rulers who engaged in reforms—sultans, khedives, shahs—additionally portrayed themselves as the sole father of their subjects and as the sole sovereign of their domains.

Such mastery was frequently displayed as masculine force: new technologies—trains and telegraphs, for example—allowed rulers literally to penetrate their territories, to reach, control, and command the loyalty of their subjects as never before. As they dressed the old cities of Cairo, Tehran, and Istanbul in new garb, nineteenth-century rulers further demonstrated their manliness: they bulldozed old neighborhoods and discontinued the architectural styles of their predecessors. As they made "new women" out of old cities, nineteenth-century rulers similarly displayed their tastes for things modern, Western, and innovative. And in the streets and royal palaces of these new cities, reformers demonstrated their potency yet again in new portraits and statues of themselves. In each case, the consolidation of their rule, the command of Western technologies, and the representation of their masculinity were the antithesis of the images that had circulated about Middle Eastern rulers through travel literature.

And yet, gendered-masculine behavior also had a feminine side: in addition to bulldozing, these men also played the role of mothers of a new generation of men and women whose tastes, behavior, and expectations were "birthed" as the result of state-sponsored reform projects. These new sons and daughters would, in turn, shape the gender expectations of coming generations, their sartorial and marital choices, their publications, and their own active participation in reform programs. As the next several chapters will illustrate, the behavior of Egypt's newest generation was both a byproduct of the state and often a challenge to the state itself. Reform programs, once inaugurated, frequently escaped the state's control.

This chapter examines reform programs in Istanbul, Cairo, and Tehran to demonstrate the new forms of paternalism, patriarchy, and masculinity that issued from

DOI: 10.4324/9781032658063-4

state reform across the nineteenth century. Such new forms of power were visible in urban renewal programs, in which state power was reflected in novel settings and institutions in which "new" men and women encountered one another with increasing frequency and in which new expectations for men and women circulated. Some of those institutions were educational: new generations of increasingly literate women were evermore visible in the region's major cities. Those "new women" were championed by the state as being noticeable evidence of modernization and Westernization and heralded by the "sons" of new reformist fathers as sought-after wives and mothers.

Selim III: A Case Study for Middle Eastern Reformers

Selim III (r. 1789–1807), Sultan of the Ottoman Empire, who served as a model for reformist heads of state across the Middle East, both fit the harem literature mold and broke it. While his father Mustafa III (r. 1757–1774) was on the throne, Selim had witnessed firsthand the European-style military training that his father had initiated. Once Selim took power in 1789, after a stay in the cage system (see Chapter 2), he began creating the new infantry corps, the *nizam-i jedid* (New Force), for which Selim is well known and with which the modernization of the Ottoman Empire is said to have begun.

Selim's reforms were mainly limited to the military. He realized, however, that for the Ottomans to enter a new world order, he needed more efficient contact with Europe. That contact required more diplomatic missions and the construction of permanent embassies in major European cities. Selim possessed an overwhelming desire to be viewed in the same light as European monarchs, which he accomplished by having his portrait painted. Selim arranged for multiple copies of that portrait to be made so that he could present them to visiting European dignitaries, both as a token of his generosity and as a symbol of his ambitions.[1]

Selim's far-reaching plans for reform came at a difficult time and challenged the Ottoman status quo. His reign straddled the French Revolution and the beginning of the Napoleonic Wars in Europe; and it came after a series of costly wars between the Ottomans and Russia. Additionally, Selim had to deal with opposition to his new troops, which came mainly from his old fighting force, the Janissaries, and from the religious establishment, the *ulama*. Even those members of the *ulama* who supported the sultan's reforms listened to the Janissaries when they rebelled against him in 1807, claiming that Selim's reforms lay outside the parameters established by Islam. Selim consequently stepped down and was imprisoned within the palace. When the new Sultan Mustafa IV (r. 1807–1808) grew concerned about a plot to bring Selim back to the throne, he plotted to assassinate Selim. Mustafa also plotted to assassinate his own brother Mahmud II in order to secure the throne for himself.

While Mustafa was successful in assassinating Selim, it was his brother Mahmud II who actually took the throne in 1808 and who would rule through to 1839. Mahmud learned from Selim that reforming, removing opposition, and appearing civilized in the eyes of Europe would not be easily achieved. Mahmud would succeed where Selim failed in creating a New Force, but only after carefully laying the groundwork for his reforms, building consensus among the religious

Reform and Its New Men and Women 49

Figure 4.1 Sultan Mahmud II (r. 1808–1839). Heritage Image Partnership Ltd/Alamy Stock Photo.

establishment, and exterminating the Janissaries in 1826. He would not be satisfied with merely a new army: Mahmud's first modern schools, military academies, and military preparatory schools opened beginning in 1834.

Mahmud also learned from Selim that appearance mattered. Mahmud therefore adopted trousers and a frock coat, distinct from the robes and turbans worn by generations before him (see Figure 4.1). Mahmud's headgear, adopted by the military and the bureaucracy, would be the new sign of Ottoman modernity: the *fez*.[2] Mahmud had portraits painted of himself in this new attire; he presented portraits and cameos of himself to statesmen, foreign dignitaries, and notables from the Arab provinces. He also made himself visible: Mahmud was the first Sultan to regularly tour the empire to see how his people lived. Just before his death, Mahmud signed an edict designed to improve his subjects' quality of life. The massive reordering of society that resulted from that edict is better known as the *tanzimat*.[3]

Istanbul

Mahmud II did not live to see the Edict of Gülhane (1839), which was proclaimed to secure better quality of life for Ottoman subjects. The edict improved and equalized taxation and conscription practices (which meant minority rights) and improved the government through an overhaul of administrative practices. Mahmud's successor, Abdül Mejid (r. 1839–1861), only 16 when he came to the throne, sought more seasoned politicians, such as Mustafa Reşhid Pasha, to provide leadership in his stead. For all of these men, it was important that the empire appear as an equal to European powers. The Ottomans, therefore, participated in world events such as the Great Exhibition in London in 1851 and the World Fairs that followed, hosting the Ottoman Exposition in Istanbul in 1863.

Ottoman reformers also attended to education, albeit at a pace that was slow in comparison to other reforms. Through the mid-nineteenth century, only the military schools had been reformed by the Ottoman state. It was Christian missionary schools that provided Western education to the children of Ottoman elites, both in Anatolia and across the empire. Catholic missionaries, who had been operating in Ottoman lands since the sixteenth century, were joined by American and European Protestant groups. While the missionaries' implicit goal was to spread Christianity through the region, their explicit task was education. American and British Protestants worked actively in the region, spreading education to almost every city in Anatolia and establishing a variety of schools, including kindergartens, primary schools, and secondary schools, for boys and girls. Literacy rates among the communities served by these missionary groups soared. But so too did discontent: local church patriarchs were disturbed by the groups' proselytizing and by the allegedly radical ideas that converts to Western forms of Christianity were learning in schools.

By 1864, the Alliance Israélite Universelle, a French institution advancing a modern education for Jews in the Middle East, had founded its first school in Baghdad. Another soon followed in Ottoman Palestine. Within a decade, there were over four dozen more schools throughout the Ottoman Empire, including schools for girls.

The Ottoman state followed suit. In 1846, Mustafa Reşhid Pasha created an Education Council, which both sponsored the first nonmilitary modern schools and reduced the power of the religious establishment in providing education. By 1848, the first teachers' school had been opened in Istanbul. The Ottoman government overhauled its educational system in 1869, standardizing curriculum and instruction throughout a system that now served both the military and civilians. The overhauls of 1869 made elementary education compulsory for boys (7–11) and girls (6–10), proclaimed that each village would have an elementary school, and made distinctions between military and civil schools. Finally, the overhauls stipulated that higher-level schools would be distributed according to population, with preparatory schools planned in each provincial capital.[4]

The Ottoman state opened its first primary school for girls in 1858 in Istanbul. In 1863, Sultan Abdül Aziz opened a middle-level school for girls, with the goal of producing a new generation of well-educated wives and mothers to marry the new cadre of state functionaries who were also the product of his educational reforms.[5] In 1870, the state opened a teacher training college for girls which, by 1910, had produced 700 female instructors. By 1886, the state had opened several secondary schools for girls as well. Girls learned a mix of languages, handicrafts, and the basics of home economics. European governesses introduced Western habits and tastes into the harem, while imams tended to girls' religious education.[6]

Education for girls, both public and private, was appealing to a new generation of men, the Young Ottomans, who were the product of the *tanzimat*. Some Young Ottomans feared that their school-aged daughters might have contact with male teachers who they did not know and to whom they were not related.[7] Many of the daughters of such men received an education at home from private tutors. Such educational reforms, directed at both males and females, helped establish Ottoman rulers as modern, bourgeois (yet Muslim) monarchs and their "children" as modern, educated subjects.

This new generation of Ottomans was not of one mind regarding the role of the West in Ottoman reform ca. 1900. Nonetheless, they did seem to coalesce in their opinion that Ottoman women needed educating. For them, the moral emancipation of women was synonymous with their own liberation from the patriarchal customs that had curtailed their freedoms—and women's. But this generation's preference for the emancipation of women coincided not only with their desire for increased subjecthood; rather, their tastes had changed, tastes for new habits and conventions, such as marrying the spouse of their choice, smoking cigarettes (rather than water pipes), and wearing Western frock coats and trousers along with their fezzes. Such attire was typically donned by government employees as well as members of the elite classes.[8] A modern education undergirded these young men's tastes in women as well as fashion; women's education was designed to make women better wives to this generation of men.

Urban reform was also central to *tanzimat* reformers who worked to modernize the empire's capital city. As the *tanzimat* reforms were underway, Ottoman control of Istanbul had almost reached its 400th year. As the result of a trip to London in 1836, reformer Mustafa Reşhid Pasha had become determined to modernize the city. Ultimately, his goal was to bring order and to reduce any possibility of rebellion within Istanbul. At the same time, he hoped to reduce the threat of fires to the capital city. In any case, his attentions resulted in the arrival to Istanbul of new building materials and opportunities to design new neighborhoods.

At the forefront of change was the neighborhood of Galata, which had historically been an outpost for Genoese and Venetian merchants and, later, for Sephardic Jews. New citizenship and trading rights offered by state reforms brought new populations (Europeans, Russians, and Ottoman Muslims) to Galata. Many of these newcomers were either accustomed to or covetous of amenities such as street lighting, sidewalks, plumbing, and sewage. The result of their enthusiasm was a demand for more reform (see Figure 4.2).

Reform of Galata therefore became a pilot for new services, such as garbage collection and lighting, and for new styles of architecture in hospitals and

Figure 4.2 Galata and view of Pera circa 1900. Niday Picture Library/Alamy Stock Photo.

administrative buildings.[9] Later, a variety of schools, multistoried apartment buildings, and department stores would line the neighborhood's streets. In 1869, Galata became the site for the city's first public park, Taksim Garden, where promenades offered men and women places to stroll, cafes, beer gardens, music, and plays. The modernization of Galata attracted such attention that on more than one occasion, the police issued orders against Turkish women walking or riding in carriages in the park; the prohibition highlighted the distinction between modernized Galata and the rest of Istanbul where women did not yet engage in such activities.

Modernizing sultans could also boast of water taps similar to those found in Paris or Vienna. The city acquired modern quays, improved boat service, bridges, and later tramways. Railroad and tramway concessionaires began connecting neighborhoods within Istanbul and linking Istanbul to other parts of the empire. Train and tramway companies catered to local gender norms and—as in the case of ferry boats—provided separate compartments for women.

In the fast and furious days of the early *tanzimat* era, the young Sultan Abdül Mejid decided that the Topkapi palace was outdated and unsuited for a modern monarch. He therefore began construction on a new palace, the Dolambaçe, in 1843. The new palace incorporated state-of-the-art plumbing, gaslighting, and eclectic design elements ranging from European to Ottoman-Islamic, revealing the sultan's intent to present himself as both an Ottoman and a European ruler. After 1856, the tramway connected the palace to both the European and Asian sides of the city.

When Abdül Aziz (r. 1861–1876) took the throne, he walked in the tall shadow of his reformist brother and uncle. But he also had some lingering fears. In Egypt, Mohammed Ali's dynasty had been in place since the early nineteenth century. Egypt was subsequently part of the Ottoman Empire and yet its rival (see below). Shortly after Abdül Aziz took power, his maternal cousin Ismail became viceroy of Egypt. As a means of both raising his own stature as well as reining in his cousin, Abdül Aziz made a state visit to Egypt. Visiting Egypt only highlighted for him the need for further reforms at home. The visit also inaugurated a friendly competition between the cousins: Morse had received his patent for the telegraph some years earlier in Abdül Mejid's palace, but it was Egypt that boasted of telegraph lines. Similarly, it was in Egypt that the sultan took his first train ride.[10]

Abdül Aziz remained in competition with his cousin Ismail at home and abroad. Both monarchs visited France in 1867 for the Paris Universal Exposition, determined to be seen as equals among the crowned heads of Europe. At home, the rivalry manifest itself in forms both serious and superficial. To commemorate his successes, for example, Ismail had commissioned a number of pieces of statuary art (see below). News about those statues hit the Ottoman press several years before the first one was completed in 1872, giving Abdül Aziz time to commission a bronze bust of himself. The *valide sultan* did not approve of the project. Abdül Aziz continued to visit the commissioned English sculptor in secret. The sculptor, aware of the Sultan's tastes and proud of his own work, created a half life-size equestrian statue instead. Betraying all European stereotypes about harem women, the *valide* sultan had the statue thrown into the Bosphorus. Nonetheless, the Sultan had the statue retrieved from the water and displayed.[11]

Reformers hoped that Murad V (r. May 30, 1876–August 31, 1876), who took the throne after Abdül Aziz, would bring constitutional change to the Ottomans. If ever there was a sultan who could be seen as an equal in the eyes of Europeans it was Murad. All accounts of the sultan as a young man portray him as charming, musically inclined, and interested in the intellectual movements of the day. Queen Victoria was so enchanted by Murad during his visit to England that she even (unsuccessfully) tried to arrange a marriage for him.[12] Nevertheless, his mental and physical health only allowed him to rule for 93 days.

Murad's successor, Abdül Hamid II (r. 1876–1909), was aware of the track record of the reforming sultans who had preceded him. Security was therefore his passion, and he constantly sought to expand his networks: trains, telegraphs, *and* a network of men on the ground listened to potential voices of dissent. The new sultan used improved communication and transportation to extend his access to his empire. Over the course of his reign, the number of miles of Ottoman railroad lines tripled, distances covered by telegraph lines doubled, and telephone lines and electricity made their way to exclusive parts of the capital city.[13] In celebration of his 25th year on the throne in 1900, he broke ground on the Hejaz railway to facilitate pilgrimage travel (seen two years earlier with a visiting Kaiser Wilhelm II in Figure 4.3). Building this line would, he hoped, enhance his image as Caliph of the Muslim world.

Figure 4.3 Sultan Abdül Hamid II and Emperor Wilhelm II of Germany. PRISMA ARCHIVO/Alamy Stock Photo.

The extraordinary changes that had been brought to the Ottoman society were particularly visible in the capital and large provincial cities where both men and women had benefitted from those changes. New buildings demonstrated the power of the sultans (as well as their new tastes) and housed the ministries and bureaucracies through which new citizens' lives were managed. New forms of transportation brought Ottomans in contact with one another with greater frequency, transported them to new institutions, and exposed them to the new Ottoman order. The new school system had created students who looked toward their empire as a family and its leader as a patriarch. New ways of portraying the sultans demonstrated their efforts to be both fathers to their people and brothers to European heads of state.

Cairo

Where Mohammad Ali lived, how he built his palaces, and the type of architecture that he supported demonstrated his desire to consolidate power and to remove Mamluk influence. He created a Cairo that looked increasingly like a European capital and reinforced his image as a masculine sovereign among equal heads of state. He destroyed the homes and architectural styles of his vanquished rivals.[14] He banned the use of traditional wooden latticework in new structures, preventing fires while at the same time eradicating a style associated with his enemies. Among Muhammad Ali and his retinue, traditional Cairo was referred to as feminine, old-fashioned, and outdated: "she" could easily be refashioned.

Education was a means to an end in Muhammad Ali's quest for military and economic expansion. In order to create a powerful army and a bureaucratic elite to run his state, Muhammad Ali needed a new educational system. Some have referred to that system as "modernized" or "Westernized." While the viceroy implemented the latest Western technologies, however, he also insisted upon retaining Arabic as the language of instruction in his new schools. He also imposed a regime of strict discipline in order to distinguish his educational system from counterparts in the West. Muhammad Ali needed specialized schools for military science, engineering, and medicine. Collectively, the graduates of those new schools were the "New Men" of Egypt.

Muhammad Ali's keen interest in education was also corporal. After an outbreak of venereal disease in the army, during which Egyptian women were unwilling to be treated by male doctors (and whose recalcitrance blocked progress in stemming the disease's spread), the viceroy focused on training women as midwives. A French medical adviser to the viceroy suggested training Egyptian women. The result was the opening of the School of Midwifery in 1832. The first students at the school were female slaves and orphans. To increase the ranks of its medical personnel, the state employed a clever strategy: upon graduating, students were urged to marry a male graduate from the medical school in exchange for a promotion in rank, a home, a monetary award, and manumission (if they were enslaved). Such couples could be dispatched to the countryside to work as a pair.

A Committee of Public instruction followed the establishment of the School of Midwifery. The viceroy and his retinue were of one mind: the advancement of society depended upon the contributions of both women and men. Muhammad Ali first outsourced education to Christian missionaries, to whom he granted land, buildings, and numerous other bonuses. Accordingly, British and French missionaries opened schools in Egypt between the 1820s and the 1860s. These rapidly-expanding schools offered opportunities for girls through varied curriculums. Middle- and lower-class girls learned income-producing skills like needlework and embroidery. Girls from the upper middle class preferred schools that offered foreign languages, art, and music. For women who could not afford tutors to come to their homes, these schools offered skills that led to social mobility.[15] As Chapter 5 illustrates, men with modern education increasingly desired companionate, educated brides.

Muhammad Ali's own desire to place himself among European heads of state is evidenced in a portrait in which the viceroy's seating, dress, and sword are remarkably similar to a portrait done of Ottoman Sultan Abdül Mejid. In both paintings, the

Scotsman Davie Wilkie (1785–1841) employed methods common to European military portraiture of the era.[16] The viceroy also demonstrated his relationship to European heads of state by displaying the gifts that were given to him by Louis-Philippe of France, part of the two men's long-standing friendship and practice of exchanging gifts. Perhaps the greatest boost to Muhammad Ali's claim to membership in the ranks of heads of state came, however, with his receipt of Egypt as a hereditary *pashalik* through the Treaty of London in 1840. His heirs subsequently emulated European royalty by working, successfully, to establish the practice of primogeniture in Egypt.

Muhammad Ali's grandson Ismail (r. 1863–1879) wanted Egypt to "be a part of Europe." Ismail had been schooled in Vienna and Paris, and he was fluent in French, making him popular with many among the consular circuit; however, his home life, full as it was with 14 official wives and consorts, reinforced his ineligibility to be "like the rest" among European royalty. Adding to his ineligibility was the Ottoman sultan's refusal to grant him primogeniture, or to change his title from viceroy to khedive, until Ismail officially married the mother of his heir apparent, Tawfiq. Ismail then decided the future for his children: their marriages would be bourgeois, monogamous, companionate pairings of equals.[17] Seizing the moment, between January and February 1873, four of Ismail's children were wed in spectacular ceremonies that marked "new marriages." This appearance of monogamy, or serial monogamy, became a hallmark feature of the dynasty.[18] Tawfiq (r. 1879–1892) and Amina became the prototypical image of a royal couple for European and Egyptian consumption.

Ismail wanted to attract development and investment from European visitors at the grand opening of the Suez Canal in 1869. He and other elites in his circle had visited Europe for the 1867 World Exposition in Paris. Having seen the recently reorganized capital of France, the Khedive developed his own grandiose ideas about how to develop Cairo. Those ideas were facilitated by the presence of a multitalented state minister, Ali Mubarak, among Ismail's entourage in France. Mubarak would help Ismail modernize Cairo, advised by yet another member of the khedive's touring entourage: none other than Baron Georges-Eugène Haussman, who had recreated Paris with wide boulevards, better sanitation, and green parks.[19]

Energized by this tour, Mubarak set to work redesigning Cairo. He began with the so-called "Frankish" quarter around Azbakiyya, home to European accommodations, consulates, stores, and entertainment. Mubarak designed Azbakiyya as the central hub from which wide new roads radiated, creating new squares for appropriately modern European-style buildings (see Figure 4.4). Opera Square was home to the newly styled rococo Opera House and Khazindar Square was the "speculative" home for Egypt's first stock exchange.[20] In 1872, Opera Square would also be home to an equestrian statue of Ismail's father, hand ready by his weapons.[21] (See Figure 4.4). The government trampled over existing residents, forcing innovations on certain neighborhoods, including gaslighting. Neighborhoods that were not ready in time for the opening of the canal were whitewashed, cleaned, and covered to project a veneer of Europeanization to the khedive's guests.[22] Furthermore, Ismail had many historic sites, including some 400 Mamluk monuments, demolished in order to complete the construction of Muhammad Ali Street, which linked old and new Cairo.[23]

Recreating Cairo as a Paris of the East also meant developing parks in the city. The new park in Azbakiyya provided entertainment designed to please its European

Reform and Its New Men and Women 57

Figure 4.4 Statue of Ibrahim Pasha, Cairo. Artokoloro/Alamy Stock Photo.

and Euro-Egyptian clientele: there were a variety of restaurants, kiosks, games, a shooting gallery, a Chinese pavilion, an aquarium, a photographer, a theater, booths for the purchase of tobacco and toys, and paddleboats for use on a pond. A military band with European and "Eastern" members played rousing music in the evenings (see Figure 4.5). Other entertainment in the park included traditional forms of street entertainment. The park served as a model, not only for Cairo but for other cities, where parks were understood to bring order, harmony, and hygiene, and to provide a green haven for a growing Egyptian elite, newly arrived from the countryside.

The crowning glory in Ismail's urbanization project, however, was one that would surely make him the equal of all European sovereigns: a neighborhood named after himself, Ismailiyya. Ismailiyya Square sat at the heart of Cairo—we know it today as Tahrir square. To encourage the right kind of development in

Figure 4.5 Azbakiyya Gardens, Cairo. Artokoloro/Alamy Stock Photo.

his namesake neighborhood, Ismail granted free land only to those who would commit to building suitable mansions before the arrival of European guests for the Canal's opening (see Figure 4.6). While only a portion of Ismail's renovations were completed by 1869, he was nonetheless able to put on a spectacular demonstration of modernization for his European guests.

Those who attended the Suez festivities must certainly have taken notice of the changes that Ismail was bringing to Egyptian education. Some of Ismail's educational reforms consisted simply of reestablishing the schools that had been shut down under his predecessors, Abbas and Said (r. 1848–1863). Others were entirely new, such as Ismail's use of regularized testing, curriculum, and instruction. Furthermore, whereas all government schooling had previously been offered free of charge, Ismail introduced fees for those with the means to pay them. Girls' education was next. In 1867, he charged a commission with the task of studying the feasibility of a primary school for girls, hoping to show off the new school at the festivities surrounding the opening of the Suez Canal. His hopes were not met. Nonetheless, the Siyufia School opened in 1873, under the patronage of Ismail's third wife, Jashm Afet Hanum. She donated the palace in which the school was located, which could accommodate 200 boarding students and 100 day students under its roof.

From all accounts, the Siyufia School was luxuriously appointed and well staffed, offering a wide-ranging curriculum that appealed to women from both

Figure 4.6 Khedive Ismail and Ferdinand des Lesseps at the opening of the Suez Canal, 1869. Chronicle/Alamy Stock Photo.

upper and lower classes. Foreign languages, music, and art classes promised to make white slave women educated and amiable companions, suitable for "new men" with a modern education. The needlework and home economics provided girls of lesser means with income-producing skills. Once they had graduated, girls of lesser means could continue at the School of Midwifery, work in the factory that made clothing for government schools, or seek employment in the private sector. Demand for the school was so high that Ismail immediately set to work opening a second school and planning a third when he was deposed by the Ottoman sultan in 1879.

When the British occupied Egypt three years later, they claimed to champion girls' education. A number of British policies curtailed education for both boys and girls, however. The British not only limited access to schools, they also increased school fees (along with the number of families who had to pay them) and changed the schools' curriculum. The School of Midwifery, for example, became a training center for nurses instead of doctors. Additionally, the British introduced a two-track education system for males, aimed at providing basic literacy for the lower track and service to the state for the upper track. The curriculum in the girls' schools simply promoted home economics, which made them increasingly unpopular among families who wanted well-rounded educations for their daughters. It was only after the turn of the twentieth century that the British began promoting teacher training schools.

Like his grandfather's had, Ismail's reforms produced "new men" who, like their counterparts in Istanbul had, wanted a greater voice in public affairs. While united in their desire to reduce foreign interference in Egypt, this new generation did not speak with one voice. Many followed new trends like companionate marriage, wearing closely trimmed beards, smoking cigars and cigarettes, and insisting upon education for their daughters. Others more slowly adopted new patterns of consumption, still clinging to arranged marriages, water pipes, copious facial hair, and limited education for their daughters. Most were in agreement however that Ismail's debt and subsequent deposition pointed to the need for greater government accountability. A lively debate ensued in Cairo's multiethnic, multireligious Arabic press. That debate stressed the need for Egypt to retain an indigenous moral compass while seeking modern innovations.

The sons of the state brought these issues to the forefront in the Urabi Revolt of 1881. A group of army officers, led by a charismatic Egyptian officer, Ahmed Urabi, himself a "new man," began the movement, which was fueled by resentment: only a handful of native Egyptians had risen to the level of officer due to a system that favored the Ottoman (Turkish) elite. The officers were joined in revolt by large landowners, reforming intellectuals, and the urban bourgeoisie, all of whom demanded greater government accountability. Unlike the 1919 Revolution, which was a "family" affair involving men and women alike (see Chapter 7), the Urabi Revolt was a gendered-masculine affair in which the sons of the nation played starring roles—at least as the revolt is portrayed in popular memory and iconography. The revolt began with a stand-off between officers and the Khedive, continued with a massive bombardment by the British, and concluded with the "temporary" occupation that would last more than 70 years. While the daughters of the nation were not visible actors in the revolt, however, they were nonetheless participants. Their memory lives on in the recounting of the heroic actions undertaken by women and families who dedicated themselves to protecting the Urabists during the conflict.

In Cairo, as in Istanbul, the city that Muhammad Ali and his successors developed revealed signs of dynastic power and of change. The viceroy's wiping out of his opposition, widening of streets, elimination of old forms of architecture, and erection of new buildings were all visible signs of Muhammad Ali's power. His fascination with and use of new technologies, which would be imitated and continued by his sons and grandsons, allowed for the continued development of Egypt's infrastructure. Novel representations of Egypt's khedives, as well as new forms of pomp and ceremony, were instrumental in making the khedives' power visible, as were Egypt's many new buildings, bridges, train tracks, and canals. As in Istanbul, new forms of transportation, with compartments reserved for women, brought the khedives' subjects into increased contact with one another and delivered them to new houses of entertainment, new parks, and new schools. While Egypt did not have the compulsory education laws that the Ottomans developed, it did have a longer tradition of both "modern" education and various forms of girls' education. The female graduates of these new schools were the sought-after brides of the new generation of Egyptian men who, like women, were the byproducts of khedival reform. Those women, like their male counterparts, were increasingly politically-aware citizens. The longstanding presence of foreigners in khedival Egypt, first as investors and missionaries and later as occupiers, heightened Egyptians' national consciousness. As the next chapters illustrate, to understand, resist, adapt, and cope with modernity, the sons and daughters of the house of Muhammad Ali often focused on gender relations, using gendered terms to express their approval of or frustration with change.

Qajar Iran

The uniting of Iran under the Qajars in the late eighteenth century ended decades of regional fighting and control by warlords. The development of modern Tehran as a capital city was, like that of modern Cairo, the result of the consolidation of power. More than any other kind of reform, Qajar rulers used the transformation of their capital city to display their consolidated power to their subjects. The Qajars similarly used Tehran to demonstrate their eligibility for consideration as "modern" by European heads of state. Portraiture and rituals served to enforce the Qajar shahs' masculinity and sovereignty in a region known for opposition to central rule. Modernization schemes, similar to those of the Ottoman sultans and the Egyptian khedives, while not as extensive or comprehensive as they were elsewhere, helped the Qajar shahs not only to convince European rulers of the Qajars' civilized stature, but to demonstrate new forms of state building to their subjects.

Before they built Tehran's palaces and the created court rituals, the Qajars had not been much different from any other warlords. The Qajar state emerged with the ascension of warlord Agha Muhammad to power (r. 1794–1797). Prior to Tehran's elevation to capital city (under the reign of a man who had been castrated as a child to prevent him from becoming a political foe), the state's sovereignty had rested not in palaces, harems, or royal progeny, but rather in material, portable wealth: royal jewels sacred to the region and repeatedly plundered from one group by another.[24] Agha Muhammad's elaborate self-coronation in 1796, about two years after taking power, therefore involved following Safavid rituals and acquiring Safavid jewels. Agha Muhammad crowned himself on the Mughan Steppe in northwest Iran before he returned to his new capital city.[25] His assassination in 1797 cut short Agha Muhammad's rule.

Agha Muhammad's nephew and designated heir, Fath Ali Shah, was responsible for shaping the foundation of Tehran as well as for consolidating his family's power. He followed his uncle's ceremonial lead by providing an appropriate burial for his predecessor, punishing his uncle's assassins, and choosing a most auspicious coronation date, the Persian new year (Nawruz), March 21, 1798, which coincided with the Muslim holiday Eid al-Fitr, marking the end of Ramadan. The new shah crowned himself at Gulistan Palace, the existing base of a former dynasty's palace in Tehran, and from that time forward, the rebuilt palace would serve as a center for all court rituals.

As an expression of his power, Fath Ali Shah had commemorative paintings made of himself, some of them life-sized. He also had images of himself placed on the jewelry and the boxes that he would distribute to his opposition in order to intimidate them. In his first court portrait, a ruggedly handsome Fath Ali Shah is positioned on a carpet and wearing a *jiqqa* (a turban) instead of a crown in order to distinguish himself from his uncle, Agha Muhammad. The new shah's thick black beard, a sign of masculinity in Islamic culture, and his extravagant clothing were meant to set him apart from both his uncle and from his defeated enemies. In later portraits, Fath Ali Shah had himself depicted with images of the sun, which was a common image in political tracts from the period. The sun equated the king with a father who disciplines his children, further enhancing Fath Ali Shah's position as the ruler of a united region.[26]

Despite palace intrigue and various uprisings against him, Fath Ali Shah had consolidated his power by 1801. He celebrated this event by commissioning first the Sun Throne (later known as the Peacock Throne) in 1800, then the Marble Throne on the veranda of Gulistan in 1805, and finally by having a new crown made for himself. He wore this new crown in the many portraits painted of him over the course of his reign. To extend this authority visually to his enemies and to those in his own court who might defy him, Fath Ali Shah also had portraits of 11 of his sons painted wearing the crown surrounding their father. The Sun King was now physically and metaphorically the father of his people.

Fath Ali Shah drew on local standards of beauty and masculinity to portray himself to his people. In his 1809 portrait, for example, he has arched, close-set brows and almond-shaped eyes. He wears a long beard and is small-waisted. He is clothed in a luxurious jeweled gown, with heeled shoes, a scepter, and a sword (see Figure 4.7).[27] This portrait accompanied the shah's creation of a magnificent

Figure 4.7 Fath Ali Shah (r. 1797–1834). PRISMA ARCHIVO/Alamy Stock Photo.

reception hall, said to have been reminiscent of the large reception hall in the palace of Xerxes (r. 486–465 BCE). It was from this spectacular hall that Fath Ali Shah received visitors from England, France, and Russia (see Figure 4.8).

It was Fath Ali's son, Crown Prince Abbas Mirza, who began Qajar military and educational reforms along the lines of the Ottoman sultans and Muhammad Ali. In addition to making Iran more self-sufficient, Abbas Mirza wanted to strengthen its military. To accomplish both goals, Abbas Mirza brought in Europeans. Champions of reform applauded the French and British advisers who trained local officers. Opponents of reform focused on visible symbols of Europeanization—uniforms, flags, and shaved beards—as evidence of excessive imitation of the West. In 1811 and 1815, the Qajar state sent two small groups of students to England to study. Almost all of them enjoyed long and influential careers in government service. Crown Prince Abbas Mirza's unexpected death in 1883 brought an end to extensive military and educational reform in Iran for decades to come.[28]

Mirza's son, Muhammad Shah (r. 1834–1848), continued the tradition of portraiture instituted by Fath Ali. As Qajar contact with Europeans increased, particularly the Russians and the British, Qajar portraiture evolved. Muhammad Shah's portraiture shows continued accommodations to European convention: his beard is far shorter than his grandfather's and his waist is thicker. The shah's clothing in his seated portrait (1844) appears to be a melding of luxurious local fabric and a European military uniform. In 1836, Muhammad Shah set forth the symbols of his reign: the lion and sun. A lion, wielding a sword, standing with its paw holding a sword, emphasized the power of the state and a crown was a symbol for the nation.

Figure 4.8 Reception Hall, Gulestan Palace. B.O'Kane/Alamy Stock Photo.

64 *Reform and Its New Men and Women*

The lion and sun demonstrated the strength of the military and the monarchy. The crown positioned the king as father, while the sun evoked traditional standards of beauty. This emblem came in two forms, one for the military establishment and one which could be distributed to bureaucrats, men of religion, men of letters, and foreign dignitaries, as a reminder of the sovereign's power.[29] Thus, Iranian leaders could stand as equals to Europeans in bestowing such honors.

Muhammad Shah continued his father Abbas Mirza's military and educational reforms; however, he made these changes on a less ambitious scale. The British provided him with weapons and military training. Where his father had tried to find justification in Islam for the innovations, Muhammad Shah cast his justifications for reforms within the history of ancient Persia—a history he gestured to by using the lion and the sun in his court imagery. He allowed the first American and European missionary schools to operate in Iran, restricting the missionaries' sphere of influence to the small areas in the country's north, an area inhabited by Christians. By the mid-nineteenth century, these missionaries had opened Iran's first school for girls, which, at first, was attended by a very small number of students.

Muhammad Shah also reinitiated Fath Ali Shah's educational missions abroad. The shah sent a group of 40 or 50 students to France in 1845. Like the students who participated in Egyptian and Ottoman missions abroad, Qajar students were given strict instructions not to engage in extracurricular activities and—perhaps more importantly—not to lose their religion. Many of the returning students enjoyed long tenures of government service, as had their earlier counterparts.

Nasir al-Din Shah (r. 1848–1896), although a younger son of Muhammad, had already been designated as heir apparent. He owed his ascension to the machinations of his mother, Mahd Ulya, upon his father's death. Mahd Ulya was a political player who certainly defied Western stereotypes about harem women. In addition to military reform, Nasir al-Din Shah's reign was marked by the shah's utmost devotion to image. Indeed, it was during Nasir al-Din's tenure that the camera took on great significance in Iranian history. While he was a prince, British and Russian diplomats, all of whom competed for influence in the court, presented cameras as gifts to Nasir al-Din Shah. The shah took an immediate interest and became one of Qajar Iran's first photographers. He was so taken with photography that when one of his retinue traveled to Europe in 1858, he requested that they bring him back a European photographer for his court; that man taught the shah how to take and to develop his own photographs. Whether he used local or European photographers, Nasir al-Din Shah archived events large and small in the court and around the country. He had photographs taken of himself looking fierce and cruel and used those photographs to intimidate both his subjects and his political opponents. He worked to produce loyalty to the empire among his subjects by photographing historic sites and by circulating those images as widely as possible.[30]

Unlike Fath Ali or Muhummad Shah, Nasir al-Din Shah was clean-shaven, except for his large, elegantly crafted mustache, and he was keenly concerned about his image—one that he continuously reproduced (see Figure 4.9). Impressive mustaches were a way for Iranian men to maintain the masculinity of facial hair while at the same time adopting other European norms of modernity. And so

Reform and Its New Men and Women 65

Figure 4.9 Portrait Nasir al-Din Shah (r. 1848–1896). North Wind Picture Archives/Alamy Stock Photo.

it appears for Nasir al-Din Shah, who kept meticulous notes on the state of facial hair of various men whom he met during his first visit to Europe in 1873.[31] Unlike his great grandfather, who wore large amounts of jewelry, Nasir al-Din Shah wore jewelry discretely and kept his hair cut even shorter than his father had.[32]

Nasir al-Din Shah enhanced his image at home and abroad in three interrelated ways: the opening of a military college, Dar al-Fanun, in 1851; the expansion of his palace; and the renovation of Tehran, the capital city. Dar al-Fanun was the brainchild of Nasir al-Din Shah's chief minister, Amir al-Kabir, who wielded enormous influence over the shah in matters of state, the military, and finance. The Western-style school created and sustained an independent Iranian military, in addition to producing a cadre of bureaucrats who would be loyal to the shah (and who would decrease his dependence on costly European advisors). Amir al-Kabir also anticipated that the education of this new elite would act as a balance against the political and religious movements that were emerging against the Shah. The school was located on the northeast corner of the citadel and palace complex where military exercises had previously been conducted. A state press on the palace grounds produced textbooks for the school's use.

Amir al-Kabir was a victim of his own successes: in order to mitigate his minister's power, the shah had him executed less than two weeks before Dar al-Fanun opened its doors in 1851. The school nevertheless remained a barometer for change (or lack thereof) in the regime and in the city. Nasir al-Din Shah was a frequent visitor to the school in its early years, where he performed informal checks on this pet project and paid more formal visits to give out medals and present honors after exams. A further benefit of visiting the school was bringing European visitors as guests, to whom the shah could promote his modern image.

Changes to his capital city also occupied a great deal of Nasr al-Din Shah's time and attention. Over the course of 26 years, the shah made changes to the palace grounds, which comprised an enormous part of Tehran. These changes took place in three phases and were influenced both by the shah's concerns about security and by his travels to Europe. In the first phase of Tehran's renovation (1866–1873), the shah had a permanent theater constructed, in which he could have passion plays for which the Imam Husayn performed. But the new theater also served to promote Nasir al-Din Shah: there, new-fangled state rituals were staged, as were celebrations of the shah's birthday. Traditional celebrations and pyrotechnics were combined in modern celebrations in support of the father-ruler. As these celebrations grew in size and number, he cleaned up Tehran. In 1867, for example, he demolished one of the oldest, most congested parts of the city and began constructing new squares and boulevards. He created suburbs to the north of Tehran, and built decorative new walls, and gates. He surrounded the capital with a moat. The renovated city quadrupled the size of his great grandfather's capital.

Nasir al-Din Shah's first travels to Europe were reflected in the second stage (1873–1878) of his capital city renovations. His 1873 travels through Europe allowed him to visit many cities, collect European art, and visit the World's Fair in Vienna. The journey also allowed the shah to present himself to crowds who had gathered to see him along his way. He was said to have tired of the convention of greeting crowds but was nonetheless pleased with the stature that his visit gave him among the brethren of world leaders. While in England, Nasir al-Din Shah received the Order of the Garter from Queen Victoria. Her son, Prince Albert, found Nasir al-Din Shah to be "charming and civilized"—good news for a ruler courting European heads of state.[33]

After having been received by many such figures, Nasir al-Din Shah realized that in the game of nations, he needed a better place for receiving his own visitors and a better place to house his own possessions. In the asymmetric game of diplomacy, appearance, ceremony, and ritual were the shah's requisite tools. Accordingly, he created a new audience hall with specialized reception rooms. The hall's decorations represented the shah's self-image: there, he blended traditional Persian and Arab designs with those of modern Europe.

A final set of renovations continued up through 1892. The shah fortified his image as a rival to the Ottomans by housing gifts from Ottoman Sultan Abdül Hamid II at the White Palace. There, his audience hall displayed tiles depicting Nasir al-Din Shah reviewing his troops.[34] His ambitions were met with further recognition and praise: Englishman George Curzon, who visited Iran as a correspondent for *The*

Times, commented on the remarkable changes he had witnessed in Tehran over the years. Curzon noted that the old city was hardly recognizable among the new collection of courts, gardens, and buildings.

The shah feared that educational reform would introduce instability to his realm. The state consequently did little to reform education under Nasir al-Din Shah. One small change, however, was the creation of another polytechnic institute, a branch of Dar al-Fanun, in the city of Tabriz. Tehran's Dar al-Fanun had fallen into a state of benign neglect and by 1891 had become a high school. The school was replaced with a variety of specialized schools and secondary schools, including a military school (1875) and eventually a medical school (1906).

Christian missionary and community education took up where the state did not. American and British missionaries continued to operate schools in Iran's north, mainly focusing their efforts on Christians (whom the missionaries tried to convert). Both Muhammad Shah and Nasir al-Din Shah viewed these missions as minority concerns and intervened only when the Armenian community complained about the missionaries. The proselytizing operations of the missionary schools spurred the Armenians to create their own community schools later in the century.

After Nasir al-Din Shah's death, the continued state promotion of education was influenced by two phenomena: first, the Tobacco Concession crisis (see Chapter 6) had resulted in a more politically active citizenry, one which increasingly equated education with proper citizenship and governance; second, a new shah, Mozaffer al-Din (r. 1896–1907), was more receptive to educational reform. It was during his reign that the state's new schools, aimed at the promotion of basic literacy, began to compete with traditional religious schools. In 1898, a reformist prime minister pushed for the shah to establish a Society for Education, which helped to further the cause of the state's educational endeavors. Because the state schools competed for the same students that traditional schools drew on, Iran witnessed its first, large-scale opposition to state education. The Society for Education lasted only three years before being incorporated into other government entities, but its role in starting a dialogue within Iran about education was long-lasting.

The Constitutional Revolt (1906–1911) (see Chapter 6) helped spark the debate in Iran about the necessity of female education. It was in the midst of that crisis that the first government school for girls opened in 1910. No longer would the state allow foreign entities a free hand; the following year, it began licensing private schools, and by 1922, it had established curriculum guidelines for boys' and girls' schools.[35]

While the development of Cairo and Istanbul in the nineteenth century were also extensions of the patriarchal impulses of rulers, Tehran represented the quintessential whim of its ruler. Whereas some aspects of modernity spread throughout Egypt and the Ottoman Empire, in Iran, modern institutions largely remained limited to the capital. Due to overwhelming European imperial influence, Iran did not receive a North-South artery train until 1927, despite the efforts of many eager foreign investors. (Britain and Russia both feared the consequences of an Iran fully linked by railroads.) Consequently, the only train tracks built by the time of Nasir al-Din Shah's death was a five-mile stretch between Tehran and the pilgrimage city of Shah Abd al-Azim.[36] Tehran was, nonetheless, very much a symbol of the Qajar shahs' consolidation of power. New palaces and court rituals, new soldiers and students, and a cleaned-up capital city were testaments to Qajar presence on the throne. New forms of portraiture, photography, and court rituals captured the shahs as they worked to demonstrate the extent of their consolidated power. As in Istanbul and Cairo, military and educational reforms, like the buildings that housed them and the soldiers and students they produced, marked a new generation of subjects.

Conclusion

To consolidate their sovereignty and to proclaim themselves sole fathers of their subjects, eighteenth-century and nineteenth-century rulers in the Middle East engaged in reform programs. Their new militaries, the trains that cut through their territories, and the schools that turned out state servants demonstrated new kinds of masculinity, power, and paternalism. New forms of self-representation in portraiture, statuary, and cityscapes demonstrated the modernity of these reformist rulers, both to European heads of state and to local subjects.

Women were included in these reforms, in both symbolic and practical ways. The modernized cities of Istanbul, Cairo, and Tehran were the beloved projects of reformist rulers. Those cities and their new institutions, in turn, produced new generations of sons and daughters, men and women who were "birthed," at least symbolically, by the fathers of new states. As such, urban reform across the nineteenth century can be seen as a both masculine and feminine affair. At the same time, emerging state attention to women's education produced a new generation of women who, as Chapters 6 and 7 illustrate, both benefited from state education and used it to challenge state agendas. The state's new daughters (who were also intended to be brides to the state's new sons) were therefore not the docile and subservient subjects that state builders might have preferred.

In both symbolic and practical ways, the technology through which nineteenth-century reformers harnessed power and control over their subjects created changes both for women and in local gender relations long after reform programs were completed. In Egypt, for example, Ismail's successors continued to build suburbs around Cairo and tramways to connect the capital city to its new surroundings. The construction and extension of tramway lines provoked a variety of criticisms that were usually related in some way or another to gender. The foreign-owned enterprises that built the tramways, for example, threatened Egyptian men and their ability to provide for their families. The tramway employed very few people, whereas many men earned a livelihood in a system of horse-drawn omnibuses or cabbies. Egyptians felt that foreign investment groups were raping the land and reaping the benefits.[37]

Furthermore, despite the fact that there were separate ticket classes and gender segregation on the trams, Egyptians complained that the trams encouraged a dangerous mingling of the sexes. Even tramway stops were fodder for tension. The stop at the Sania School, for example, had to be moved due to the harassment of the girls who rode it: that harassment apparently came not only from boys, but also from women who searched the tramway stop for potential brides for their sons. But tramcars also provided women with spaces in which to engage in all kinds of conversations. Women from that era recollect, for example, having discussed feminist issues with foreign women in the ladies' car. Thus, the trams were also a source for "dangerous" ideas.[38]

Those "dangerous" ideas, and men's notions about the women who had them, will be the topic of the next two chapters.

Notes

1 Caroline Finkel, *Osman's Dream: The History of the Ottoman Empire* (New York: Perseus, 2005), 389–397.
2 Donald Quataert, "Clothing Laws, State, and Society in the Ottoman Empire," *International Journal of Middle East Studies* Vol. 29 (1997), 403.
3 Finkel, *Osman's Dream*, 440.
4 Michael Provence, "Late Ottoman State Education," in *Religion, Ethnicity, and Nationhood in the Former Ottoman Space*, Jørgen Nielsen, ed. (Leiden: Brill, 2001), 120.
5 Reina Lewis, *Women, Travel and the Ottoman Harem: Rethinking Orientalism* (New Brunswick, NJ: Rutgers University Press, 2004), 56.
6 Lewis, *Re-thinking Orientalism*, 19 and 80.
7 Deniz Kandiyoti, "End of Empire: Islam, Nationalism and Women in Turkey," in *Women, Islam and the State*, Deniz Kandiyoti, ed. (Philadelphia: Temple University Press, 1991), 24–25.
8 Ahmet Ersoy, "A Sartorial Tribute to Late Tanzimat Ottomanism: the Elibise-i Osmaniyye Album," *Muqarnas* Vol. 20 (2003), 196–197.
9 The section on urban renewal in Istanbul is based on Zeynep Çelik, *The Remaking of Ottoman Istanbul* (Berkeley: University of California Press, 1993).
10 On Barak, *On Time: Technology and Temporality in Modern Egypt* (Berkeley: University of California Press, 2013), 35.
11 Finkel, *Osman's Dream*, 473–474; "Sultan Abdül Aziz and his Statues," *Today's Zaman* (November 17, 2011), http://www.todayszaman.com/features_sultan-abdulaziz-and-his-statues_263096.html.
12 Çelik Gülersoy, *The Çırağan Palaces* (Istanbul: Istanbul Library, 1992), 129.
13 Douglas Howard, *The History of Turkey* (Westport: Greenwood, 2001), 69; on Hejaz railway, see Eugene Rogan, *Frontiers of the State in the Late Ottoman Empire* (Cambridge: Cambridge University Press, 1999), 65.
14 Nihal Tamraz, *Nineteenth-Century Cairene Houses and Palaces* (Cairo: AUC Press, 1998), 5, 17–24.
15 Mona Russell, *Creating the New Egyptian Woman: Consumerism, Education, and National Identity, 1863–1922* (New York: Palgrave, 2004), 102, 107–109.
16 See Khaled Fahmy, *Mehmed Ali: From Ottoman Governor to Ruler of Egypt* (London: Oneworld Publications, 2012), Chapter 4. Sir David Wilkie and John Woodward, *Paintings and Drawings by Sir David Wilkie, RA 1785–1841* (sl, sn), 20–21, University of California Libraries, https://archive.org/stream/paintingsdrawing00wilk#page/n3/mode/2up; Emilie Weeks, "About Face: Sir David Wilkie's Portrait of Mehemet Ali," in *Orientalism Transposed*, Julie Codell and Dianne Macleod, eds. (Aldershot: Ashgate, 1998), 46–62.
17 While it was common for royal women to marry for strategic and political alliances, the idea of men marrying equals was completely unnecessary according to Ottoman, Mamluk, and Abbasid precedent.
18 Ken Cuno, "Ambiguous Modernization: The Transition to Monogamy in the Khedivial House in Egypt," *Family History in the Middle East*, Beshara Doumani, ed. (Albany: SUNY Press, 2003), 247–270.

19 Ismail and Mubarak had been to Paris before and could therefore see the remarkable changes.
20 Andrea Humphreys, *Grand Hotels of Egypt* (Cairo: AUC Press, 2011), 61.
21 Lesley Lababidi, *Cairo's Street Stories* (Cairo: AUC Press, 2008), 56.
22 Unless otherwise specified, the section on Ismail's reforms and British occupation have been taken from Russell, *Creating the New Egyptian Woman*, Chapters 2, 3, and 6.
23 Lababidi, *Cairo's Street Stories*, 60. These changes literally produced two Cairos.
24 Abbas Amanat, "The Kayanid Crown and Qajar Reclaiming of Royal Authority," *Iranian Studies* Vol. 34, No. 1/4 (2001), 20.
25 Changes in the urban landscape of Tehran are covered in Jennifer M. Scarce, "The Architecture and Decoration of the Gulestan Palace: The Aims and Achievements of Fath Ali Shah (1797–1834) and Nasser al-Din Shah (1834–1896)," *Iranian Studies* Vol. 34, No. 1/4 (2001), 103–116; Kaveh Bakhtiar, "The Towers of Nasir al-Din," *Muqarnas* Vol. 21 (2004), 33–43.
26 Amanat, "Royal Authority," 17–20; Scarce, "The Architecture and Decoration of the Gulestan Palace" 107; Najmabadi, *Women with Mustaches*, 72.
27 Najmabadi, *Women with Mustaches*, Figure 2, 14.
28 Section on education in Iran is based on Monica Ringer, *Education, Religion, and the Discourse of Cultural Reform in Iran* (Costa Mesa: Mazda, 2001); Shiva Balaghi, "Nationalism and Cultural Production in Iran" (PhD Diss., University of Michigan, 2008); Maryam Ekhtiar, "Nasir al-Din Shah and the Evolution of Dar al-Fanun," *Iranian Studies* Vol. 1/4 (2001), 153–163.
29 Najmabadi, *Women with Mustaches*, 63–86. Over time, the sun would lose more and more of its female characteristics, and by the mid-1930s, it would lose its facial features altogether. On transformations of beauty, see Najmabadi, "Gendered Transformations: Beauty, Love, and Sexuality in Qajar Iran," *Iranian Studies* Vol. 34, No. 1/4 (2001), 89–102.
30 Ali Behdad, "The Powerful Art of Qajar Photography: Orientalism and (Self)-Orientalizing in Nineteenth-Century Iran," *Iranian Studies* Vol. 34, No. 1/4 (2001), 141–151.
31 Najmabadi, *Women with Mustaches*, 52, 151.
32 Scarce, "The Architecture and Decoration of the Gulestan Palace," 113.
33 David Motadel, "Qajar Monarchs in Imperial Germany," *Past and Present* No. 213 (November 2011), 191–235, quotation from 235.
34 Scarce, "The Architecture and Decoration of the Gulestan Palace," 116.
35 Camron Amin, *The Making of the Modern Iranian Woman* (Gainesville: University of Florida, 2002), 145.
36 Abbas Amanat, *Pivot of the Universe* (Berkeley: University of California Press, 1997), 429.
37 Egyptian industrialist Talaat Harb wrote a series of articles for *al-Ahram* that appeared over the course of the month of September in 1919 critiquing the foreign company.
38 Barak, *On Time*, 192.

5 The New Woman through the New Man's Gaze

Introduction

By the mid-nineteenth century, intellectuals throughout the Ottoman Empire and Iran had begun displaying an intense focus on women and their behavior. On the one hand, such attention was a response to Orientalist discourse: Middle Eastern men and women "spoke back" to European authors of harem literature. At the same time, however, "Woman Question" debates emerged in response to the region-wide reform and state-building projects which had promised to change women's position in society through educational and legal reforms. By the early twentieth century, discussions about "the Woman Question" had become powerful vehicles through which budding nationalists defined their past, critiqued their present, and offered suggestions about the future. By the turn of the twentieth century, women had come to embody the aspirations and platforms of reform programs and of emerging nationalist agendas.

Discussions and debates about the "Woman Question" also allowed local intellectuals to engage in global conversations about slavery and citizenship in the era following the abolition of the Atlantic slave trade. Because slavery was linked to the family in the Islamic world, participants in discussions about the practice also engaged in discussions about familial life and therefore about women. Discussions and debates about slavery and women in the nineteenth-century Middle East were consequently not merely approvals or refutations of European social models and political systems, but also platforms through which men and women discussed their domestic practices and their familial traditions. This chapter therefore opens with a brief discussion of "the Woman Question" within the context of the global conversations about slavery.

This chapter then examines three periods during which men spilled much ink about women. (Women's participation in the "Woman Question" debate will be taken up in the next chapter.) We begin with "early thinkers," who wrote before the first constitutional crisis in the Ottoman Empire and Iran ca. 1850. We then turn to the diffusion of the "Woman Question" after the Ottoman constitutional revolt of 1876, during which time heated debates about women accompanied discussions about new ways of defining "Ottoman" and about men's new demands on the Ottoman state. We end with a third generation of male intellectuals, which emerged

DOI: 10.4324/9781032658063-5

with the constitutional crises in Iran (1906–1911) and the Ottoman Empire (1908), in which the Qajar and Ottoman orders were challenged by subjects who were determined to become citizens and who used discussions about women to illustrate their demands for increased participation in their own self-rule.

Slavery, the Family, and the Colonial Order

The "Woman Question" emerged worldwide as part of larger debates about human and civil rights in the wake of the Atlantic Revolutions in America, France, and Haiti in the late eighteenth century. As male subjects became citizens, thorny questions surfaced about what role women and slaves would play in emerging nation-states. In the West, early nineteenth-century advocates for women's suffrage and for abolition were often members of the same organizations. American suffragists Elizabeth Cady Stanton and Lucretia Mott, for example, first met at the World Anti-Slavery Convention in 1840 and later organized the Seneca Falls Convention in New York (1848), where abolitionist Frederick Douglas played a key role in advocating for feminism. In the Ottoman Empire and Iran, while the "Woman Question" was similarly connected to human rights, discussions about women arose as a response to imperialism and cultural confrontation with the West. Men wrote in refutation of the Europeans who were actively writing about homes and families across Qajar and Ottoman territories. Local men wrote about women and slavery in reaction to European discourse about them and as a means of defining home and family in their own terms. In the Islamic World, the "Woman Question" was connected to slavery because slaves were frequently part of elite homes and families.

Both the landscape of the "Woman Question" in the Middle East and the nature of human bondage in the region differed vastly from the West. According to Islam, women have legal personhood, the right to conduct business, and to have their interests represented in court. Because of this recognition of women, Christian and Jewish subjects, male and female, historically used Ottoman courts to represent their interests as legal subjects. In other words, many of the issues for which Western women fought in the nineteenth and early twentieth centuries were simply not relevant for Middle Eastern women.

Similarly, abolitionist arguments about slavery did not apply to Islamic societies. Atlantic World slavery, for example, was a race-based slavery in which black African slaves were commodities who could produce further commodities for their owners. Slavery in the Ottoman Empire and Qajar Iran, by contrast, was multiethnic, multiracial, and multipurposed (see Chapter 2). It would be simplistic and incorrect to state that Middle Eastern slavery was kinder, gentler, or better. Nonetheless, to be a slave in the Middle East was not necessarily to be a slave for life. The Quran enjoins believers to free their slaves (2:77) (9:60) and even to marry them (24:32). Authoritative versions of the Prophet Muhammad's life similarly enjoin believers to see their "servants and slaves [are] like brothers."[1]

As debates over the abolition of slavery intensified, men in Ottoman and Qajar territories wrote about women and slaves in much the same way that Europeans did: as a means of working out who was eligible for citizenship and who was not and as a means of defining their household orders. Ottoman and Qajar men who wrote about "their women" and "their households"—households which sometimes included slaves and multiple wives—were sensitive to the claims made about their family life by Europeans, whose harem literature was often used as a justification for European intervention in Middle Eastern affairs. At the same time, Middle Eastern men, like bourgeois Europeans, also wanted political rights, as evidenced by a number of movements that emerged after the *tanzimat* reforms in the Ottoman Empire and in the lead-up to the constitutional crisis in Iran (see Chapter 6).

Debates about women and slavery, like calls for their own increased participation in politics, were therefore part of men's quest to order (and reorder) their political and social worlds. Europeans had used harem literature to deem the Muslim household order unsuitable to the modern world. Europeans also pointed to slavery in the Islamic world as a means of suggesting that Muslims had not yet entered the modern era. Just as European claims about their harems had been controversial, slavery was a contentious issue for Muslims. At a time when men were calling for their own political rights and for women's rights to an education, they also had to reckon with calls for an end to slavery. Middle Eastern reformers could call for the abolition of the slave trade. But how could they call for putting an end to an institution that existed in the Quran despite its encouragement of manumission? Regardless of Ottoman and Qajar attempts to ban the trade, thousands of women from the Caucasus continued to be brought into the region, where they served as highly valued slaves in upper-class households. The flow of black slaves from Sudan continued as well. Elite memoirs and other forms of anecdotal evidence suggest that slaves were beloved members of households, but there is also evidence to suggest that even into the early twentieth century people were bought, sold, and separated from their loved ones.[2] It was against this backdrop that men began writing about the "Woman Question."

Men Writing about Women

Men who wrote about the "Woman Question" in the Ottoman Empire, Egypt, and Qajar Iran did not speak with one voice. There were, however, some common features of "Woman Question" discourse from the late nineteenth and early twentieth centuries. Most of the elite men in the Ottoman and Qajar territories who wrote about women had either studied in Europe, in missionary schools, or in Westernized local schools. Most were profoundly influenced by French Enlightenment thinkers, but at the same time had not abandoned their own intellectual traditions. Indeed, expressing their ideas required that nineteenth-century Middle Eastern authors adopt new forms of writing and language expression. In the late nineteenth century, for example, the popular press competed with official newspapers across the region. In governmental presses, events of the day had for some time been listed in fixed and formulaic forms of Ottoman Turkish, Arabic, and Farsi—forms of each language that people did not use in everyday speech and which were accessible to only the most educated. The expansion of private presses not only allowed for the emergence of new literary genres but also for the circulation of more popular forms of local languages. Henceforth, newspapers, novels, plays, and treatises—written in more popular forms of local languages—were "conduit[s] for the diffusion of new ideas about the relationship between men and women ..."[3] Utilizing new means of printed expression helped break the molds of traditional languages and updated those languages with new terms.

While authors differed in emphasis, format, and content, one common element links their works: companionate marriage. "Woman Question" authors first addressed European condemnation of the polygamous home, which in reality was not the norm. Local writers then stressed the importance of marriage between intellectual equals, which was increasingly becoming the norm. While such intellectual equality carried some caveats, the basic formula was the same: harmonious marriages would create proper homes and families, which, in turn, would create proper nations. For Young Ottomans (and reformers elsewhere), the domestic body and the body politic were intricately connected.

Early "Woman Question" Authors

The Egyptian intellectual and civil servant Rifaat Rafai al-Tahtawi (1801–1873) was among the first Ottoman intellectuals to address the "Woman Question." Tahtawi was originally from the trading entrepôt of Tahta in Upper Egypt and had been trained by a renowned scholar at al-Azhar, Egypt's renowned Islamic university. Tahtawi later served as the imam who accompanied the first Egyptian educational mission to France in 1826. As a consequence of his tenure in France, Tahtawi became a scholar of French language and history and served for the remainder of his life in a variety of government posts in education and translation. One of his first publications was a description of his experience in Paris, *An Extraction of Gold in a Summary of Paris* (1834). The text contains Tahtawi's first thoughts about the connections between the domestic and the political realms.[4] In a series of essays, he describes in elaborate detail his voyage, the habits and customs of the French life (penned for the students on the educational mission), and even his thoughts on the July Revolution of 1830 in France.

While these subjects may seem random and disparate, they, in fact, illustrate Tahtawi's fascination with orderly homes and the connection of those homes to constitutional rule. He illustrates that the home in which a well-educated wife, rather than a servant, greeted visitors at the door was a building block for nations in which rulers consult their advisors. His translations to Arabic of European texts also made this connection between the home and the world outside of it. Tahtawi translated the Frenchman Georges-Bernard Depping's *Historical Background on the Manners and Customs of Nations*, in which the author divided the world into civilized and uncivilized, clean and dirty, well-governed and despotic peoples.[5] Depping claimed that well-governed people lived in clean and orderly homes, and only in clean and orderly homes. In his later work, *The Paths of Egyptian Hearts in the Splendors of Contemporary Morals* (1869), Tahtawi wrote further about nationalism, which he referred to literally as a love of the homeland (*hubb al-watan* in Arabic), and suggested that a people's behavior, both at home and in public, helped to shape national sentiment.⁶ In each case, he suggested that domestic behavior influenced the nation's progress.

During his tenure in Khedive Ismail's Ministry of Education, Tahtawi continued to develop these ideas about the relationship between the home and the family when a special committee requested that he write a textbook for girls and boys. Tahtawi began the tract called *A Trustworthy Guide to the Education of Girls and Boys* with a justification for girls' education based upon Islamic precepts, pointing out that educating women did not violate scripture and highlighting important exemplars of educated Muslim women. He also discussed evidence in favor of women's education from the collections of narratives about the Prophet Muhammad's life (*hadith*). Tahtawi argued that any disadvantages that might come from girls' education were far outweighed by the benefits, especially insofar as companionate marriage was concerned. He claimed that improved family life would result from a harmonious marriage and therefore that girls and boys should receive the same primary education.⁷ Tahtawi stood by his ideas: he put stipulations into his own marriage contract by giving his wife a document stating that he would not divorce her or take additional wives or concubines as long as she devoted herself to their home and remained "in affection, looking after his children, servants, and slaves."⁸

While modern in his views about women, Tahtawi was in the end a man of his time, and in Egypt, the times dictated that an elite bureaucrat was likely to have been a slaveholder. He apparently felt obliged to care for, but not manumit, his household slaves. Thus, for all of Tahtawi's precocious arguments in favor of reforming the family and the nation, he stopped short of calling for slavery's abolition. Tahtawi's views on Sudan, where he had been exiled for many years by Khedive Abbas I, were imperial and racist in comparison to his views about Egypt. Tahtawi called for a continuation of Egypt's colonial presence in the Sudan, a presence that he hoped would civilize the Sudanese.⁹

Elsewhere in the Ottoman Empire, other thinkers similarly supported the notion of companionate marriage over arranged marriages. Like Tahtawi, the Ottoman intellectual and reformer Ibrahim Şinasi (1826–1871) studied in France. He did so under the patronage of Mustafa Reşhid Pasha (1800–1858), one of the leading architects of the Ottomans' *tanzimat* reforms. Şinasi penned *The Poet's Wedding*, which broke molds in its ideas about marriage, its format, its use of a less formalized Ottoman Turkish language, and in its stylistic conventions. *The Poet's Wedding* was published in 1869, the same year that the first school for girls opened in Istanbul. The premise of the play was to satirize the system in which the bride and groom did not meet until their wedding day and in which others made decisions regarding marriage for young men and women. In short, Şinasi wrote *The Poet's Wedding* to promote companionate marriage. Indeed, the play ends with the protagonist, Müştak, married to his chosen companion.¹⁰

Among the most influential early Turkish-language newspapers were Şinasi's own *Picture of Ideas* (1862) and Ebüziyya Tevfik and Recaizade Ekram's *Progress* (1868). The men who established these newspapers were all products of Ottoman reform and at the same time its protagonists: Namik Kemal, Ahmet Midhat Efendi, and Şamseddin Sami, whose works were experimental grounds for new ideas and for creating a Turkish that was accessible to the masses. Historians mark Namik Kemal's 1867 article "A Memorandum on the Education of Women" as the first of many to link the progress of the nation to women's education.[11]

Şamseddin Sami (1850–1904) joined the Ottoman intellectuals' conversations about women in the 1870s. Using his own newspaper, *The Garden*, Sami published "The Tale of Talat and Fitnat," the first Ottoman Turkish serialized novel. Like Şinasi's *The Poet's Wedding*, Sami's story about the characters Talat and Fitnat focuses on the ideal of companionate marriage, using a combination of stock characters recognizable to local audiences from *Karagoz* shadow theater along with new notions such as romantic love, choice in marriage, and educated womanhood. In addition to the love that blooms between the tale's protagonists, Sami also used Talat's parents, Rifat and Saliha, as models of the changing ideals about marriage among his generation. Saliha was herself an educated bride, who like her husband had a say in the choice of her spouse from whom she demanded respect and good communication.[12]

The basic plot of the Talat and Fitnat's story takes place after Saliha was widowed and while Talat was still a school boy. While Talat attended school, Fitnat, the stepdaughter of a tobacco merchant, spent her days sewing and embroidering in an apartment located upstairs from Talat's family. One day, Talat happened to catch a glimpse of Fitnat and fall in love with her. Using the well-known device of disguise, Talat cross-dressed and posed as Ragibe, a woman who had happened upon Fitnat's apartment. Ragibe, or Talat in disguise, offers to pay Fitnat for sewing lessons by teaching her to read. Fitnat agrees, relishing the opportunity to advance her education. Meanwhile, Fitnat's stepfather, eager to marry off his ward, has found a man whom he believes to be the perfect groom: a wealthy older man, who unbeknownst to Fitnat is actually her biological father. Her distaste for this potential husband does not arise from the taboo of incest alone, but rather from Fitnat's own lack of say in choosing a husband and from the unsuitability of her stepfather's choice for her. Unlike *The Poet's Wedding*, however, Sami's story did not end well: Fitnat committed suicide rather than giving in to a marriage to the groom of her stepfather's choosing. Talat followed in her path by killing himself, determined not to marry anyone other than his chosen bride.[13]

A number of different currents fed into Sami's forward thinking about companionate marriage. He was from a family with Bektaşi roots, a Sufi order that promoted equality and encouraged the participation of men and women in its rites. Although Sami did not actually spend time in France as Tahtawi and Şinasi had done, he did study at a Greek school where he gained an appreciation for French knowledge.[14] Both his family's roots and his intellectual training made him an apt spokesman for choice in marriage.

Sami was not the only author whose background shaped his views on both the "Woman Question" and on reform within the empire. Namik Kemal came from a long line of Ottoman civil servants and reformers. His marriage, while characterized by devotion and respect, had been an arranged one. His grandmother had brokered his marriage to a 14-year-old girl, whose most common attribute to her husband was the loss of their mothers at a young age. Kemal's daughter was born in 1865, the same year of the birth of the Young Ottoman movement, which aimed to establish a constitutional government in the Ottoman Empire, and shortly before the opening of the Ottomans' first school for girls.[15] Like a number of the men in the Young Ottoman movement, Kemal had associations with the Bureau of Translation, which had exposed him to a wide variety of intellectual trends. Like others, Kemal used his newspaper as a platform to link domestic and political reform.

While the Young Ottomans viewed the domestic and political realms as two sides of the same coin, the first writings on the "Woman Question" in Iran were critiques of the political realm presented through discussions of domestic practices. For writers such as Mirza Fathi Ali Akhunzadeh, the "Woman Question" was a symptom of the larger problems in the country, particularly tyrannical government. Akhunzadeh, a self-proclaimed atheist, was influenced by Persian, Turkish, and Russian cultures. He wrote a series of treatises and plays that openly criticized current Iranian marital practices, corruption within the Qajar dynasty, and even the family of the Prophet Muhammad.[16] Akhunzadeh discussed the lack of choice given to the Prophet Muhammad's brides, arguing that modeling such limited choices had led men and women to various forms of subterfuge and extramarital liaisons. Akhunzadeh then suggested that those liaisons, in turn, had prompted rigorous Quranic injunctions that bound women to specific forms of clothing and to seclusion within their homes.

Although Akhunzadeh supported women's right not to veil, he argued that married women needed both the physical and metaphorical protection of the *hijab*, which, in addition to referring to a veil, also connotes a curtain separating women from men.[17] Akhunzadeh also supported the intermingling of the sexes and suggested that the lack of socialization between the sexes in Iran had contributed to what he referred to as social ills, such as homosexuality.[18]

Also writing from Qajar Iran, Mirza Abd al-Hossayn Khan Kermani (1854–1897) is best known for his famous treatise entitled *One Hundred Sermons*, four of which dealt with the "Woman Question." Kermani asserted that neither Islam nor the Muslim Qajar elite were of themselves capable of reforming the nation, let alone half of its population. He criticized veiling, seclusion, and polygamy, arguing that such practices hindered a woman's ability to attain an education. He also argued that such customs did not necessarily guarantee a woman's chastity. In concert with intellectuals elsewhere, Kermani claimed that monogamous marriage would remedy social problems and benefit both husbands and wives.

Kermani claimed that lack of interaction between the sexes and unsuitable marriages had led to various forms of social vice, including prostitution, homosexuality, and pedophilia—a host of relationships that in his opinion would not produce suitable children for the nation. Like many authors of his generation, he argued that the mother's womb was the first of several schools that each child would attend, continuing with their family, religion, government, and their physical environment. Guaranteeing the well-being of women therefore guaranteed the well-being of the nation, the social order, and the natural world.[19]

Writings after 1876

Without overly simplifying the platform of the Young Ottomans, they believed that the *tanzimat* reforms had not gone far enough in bringing about a modern unified society. What they wanted in addition was a constitution to limit the authority of the Sultan, representative government, and better education for both sexes. Without abandoning Islam, the moral compass of the empire, the Young Ottomans also called for the adoption of modern science and technology. Ottoman losses in continuing wars with Russia provided the Young Ottomans with the opportunity to wage a coup in 1876, bringing Sultan Abdül Hamid II to power. The new sultan, in turn, promised the Young Ottomans constitutional rule.

That constitution was in effect for just over a year (November 1876 to February 1878). Nevertheless, for a brief period, the Ottoman capital witnessed an atmosphere of free expression before Abdül Hamid II began imposing heavy censorship. (Thereafter, the movement for free expression lived on more robustly in the Ottoman provinces and among Young Ottomans in exile.) As censorship increased, fiction became an increasingly popular means through which intellectuals could address the reforms they longed for in both the domestic and political realms.

While Abdül Hamid II slowed the Ottoman Empire's movement toward constitutionalism and while he worked against free expression, he did continue with some of his predecessors' reforms. Abdül Hamid II, for example, has been described as a "patriarchal feminist" who opened new schools for girls and expanded teacher training for women.[20]

In this atmosphere of reform and repression, Şamseddin Sami once again took up his pen and wrote a progressive tract entitled *Women* (1879), published on the tenth anniversary of the Ottoman adoption of compulsory education for boys and girls. Sami argued that women, while not being the "same" as men intellectually, possess an equal capacity for intellectual development. Sami argued that the progress of civilization therefore depended upon educating women and upon allowing women to reach their full potential so as to contribute fully to the world around them. *Women* included a discussion of Sami's views about monogamy, which he viewed as the desired form of marriage in most circumstances.[21]

Sami's colleague Ebüziyya Tevfik published some 700 articles on various subjects between 1865 and 1913 in the five newspapers with which he was affiliated. As Abdül Hamid II clamped down on free speech in the 1880s and as other forms of publication such as books became more common, Tevfik began producing almanacs. In 1899, he published a women's almanac, in which he included biographies of notable Muslim women. Tevfik also included information that he deemed important for women, including tips on hairdressing, articles on feminism, and advice for dealing with domestic servants.

The prologue to Tevfik's almanac stressed the importance of women's advancement, both to women themselves and to the nation. The section on feminism argued that Islam had historically guaranteed women the rights that Western feminists were struggling to acquire at that time. Tevfik concluded, therefore, that feminism was not an appropriate movement for Muslim women. As for domestic servants,

Tevfik bemoaned Ottoman changes in laws regarding slavery in a fashion that was reminiscent of Tahtawi. Formerly, slaves had been part of households. With the demise of the slave trade, the real possibility of hiring non-Muslims to work as household servants led Tevfik to worry about the kinds of women who would replace slaves.[22] Tevfik was indeed progressive in his views about women; his views about slavery, like Tahtawi's, nonetheless reflect an adherence to tradition.

In the late nineteenth century, the novels of Ahmed Midhat (1844–1912) reinforced the idea that the reformed Ottoman household would henceforth be the foundation of a properly functioning society. Midhat believed that "freely contracted companionate marriage, with the sexes defined in a complementary fashion, produced enterprising and altruistic citizens and resulted in a prosperous economy and moral society."[23] But Midhat's first novel, *Felatun and Rakim*, demonstrated that reformed households were not necessarily Westernized households. In *Felatun and Rakim*, Midhat juxtaposes the hardworking Rakim who marries for love, and Felatun, a wealthy philanderer. Rakim's love story is not a Western love story, however, as his "true love" is a white slave woman named Canan. Rakim purchased and educated Canan and had her tended to by his *dada* Kalfa, the black slave woman who had raised him. Because she developed a true affection for her owner, Canan gave up the "opportunity" of being emancipated from him and moving on to a better household. Instead, she, Rakim, and the *dada* Kalfa lived a comfortable life together.

Several things are noteworthy about this novel, first published in 1875, and about the household it describes. Despite the 1854 prohibition against the trade in white slaves, slavery in the Ottoman Empire still existed. While Rakim chose not to have intercourse with Canan until such point as she returned his affections (which, coincidentally, happened only after she got an education), Rakim nonetheless had the power to both buy and sell her. The underpinning of their marriage was, therefore, slavery and not equality. Similarly, Rakim's household was maintained by Kalfa, his black *dada*: it was she who was responsible for Rakim's upbringing and for the steady maintenance of his household. Throughout the story, *dada* Kalfa is a loving figure, who, in fact, enables Canan to get an education and to tend house according to her husband's wishes. Thus, promoting companionate marriage, which was based on education and on a supposed equality between the sexes, required men like Ahmed Midhat to reckon with the relations both between men and women and between masters and slaves. When a foreign family comes to visit their household, to literally take the harem tour described in chapter three, Rakim explains the enforcement of gender segregation: "You won't be able to see any women, just a black [woman's] arm thrusting a platter through the door."

Midhat's use of a "thrusting" image of the black woman is meant to threaten the foreigners, despite the loving role Kalfa plays throughout the story. *Dada* Kalfa is indeed a loving figure, who, in fact, enables Canan to leave the house, according to her husband's dictates. Not everyone would have had the luxury of sending their concubine or daughter to a governess under the protection of a *dada*. Eventually, the establishment of girls' schools and the need for trained female teachers to work in them created even more porous gender boundaries in the empire.

As for slavery, in his *Just Seventeen*, Midhat used the story of a Christian prostitute to level a blow against Europeans for trying to stop the Ottoman slave trade. He wrote:

> Hey you Europeans! Here you are tossing around a few words about the promotion of civilization and love of freedom and trying to block slavery in Turkey. Among us, no slave would be sold in whorehouses like these to service the dirtiest of scoundrels.

Midhat blamed Europeans for encouraging local Christians to take up the European practice of requiring the woman's family to provide a dowry, causing the downfall of women whose families could not afford it. Midhat maintained that the traditional practices of slavery and concubinage, in fact, protected Muslim women from rapacious capitalists, out for women's dowries.

As censorship conditions in the Ottoman capital worsened under Abdül Hamid II, Egypt became a center for publication and journalism (although the first years after the British occupation in 1882 did witness some censorship). Cairo and Alexandria were generally freer for writers and journalists than Istanbul was at the time, and those who wanted to publish therefore flocked to Egypt from all parts of the empire where they joined local intellectuals in conversation. The "Woman Question" filled the pages of the Egyptian press where it was debated by both secular nationalists and Islamic reformers who hailed from Egypt and from other parts of the Ottoman Empire.

Writing from Cairo, Muhammad Abduh (1849–1905) was an influential theologian who took up the issues of women's education and of the reform of Islamic law to help answer the "Woman Question." Abduh was an advocate for women's education, and after the British cut funding for Egyptian schools, he worked with the royal family in Egypt to solicit funds to open schools for boys and girls.[24] While Abduh recognized that polygamy was supported by the Quran, he argued that the practice of polygamy among the early Islamic community had been determined by historical circumstances. He pointed out Quranic verses in which the contemporary practice of polygamy might not hold, such as a husband's ability to treat all of his wives equally. In short, Abduh sought answers to the "Woman Question" within an updated Islam rather than through the rejection of indigenous values.

Abduh contributed regularly to several newspapers and belonged to a number of intellectual circles and salons through which he influenced other intellectuals, including Qasim Amin (1863–1908), who has been credited with placing the "Woman Question" at the forefront of intellectual debate in turn-of-the-twentieth-century Egypt. Amin, who was educated both in Egypt and in France, called for advancing women's education, for reforming divorce laws, and for rethinking the use of the *hijab* in Islamic societies. Amin was both praised and criticized for his views. Those who responded to his work shared the idea that women and their activities, both at home and outside the home, reflected Egypt's political progress.

Indeed, Amin's agenda in his two best-known works, *The Liberation of Women* (1899) and *The New Woman* (1901), had less to do with liberating women than with responding to European critiques of Egyptian society by exposing Egyptian domestic practices. By lifting the *hijab* or veil off Egyptian domestic life, Amin aimed to show Europeans that Egypt was modern.[25] Amin took up the pen largely in response to the publication of *Egypt and the Egyptians*, an offensive piece of travel literature by French author Charles-François-Marie Le Duc d'Harcourt[26] (see Chapter 3). His work supported British imperialism by contrasting Egyptians to Europeans and by suggesting that Egyptians were similar to children who were not ready for self-government. D'Harcourt was critical of Egyptian marital and domestic practices and suggested that men who engaged in the practices of polygamy and seclusion were not fit to run their nations.

Amin's books called for an educational system that would allow women to be "a sister to man, a companion to her husband, [and] a tutor to her children—a refined individual." He hoped that "this transformation" would take place in Egypt, arguing that it would be the "the most significant development in Egypt's history."[27] But Amin also called for the reform of Egyptian men. Amin likened Egypt's governing institutions to its domestic practices, and argued that a despot was no different than a tyrannical, patriarchal husband and father. He therefore suggested that only a constitutional order, governing a nation of homes in which women were educated and in which men were partners, rather than tyrants, would suit Egypt in the modern era.[28]

Amin's work created a firestorm in the press precisely because it challenged the entire structure of gender roles in society and questioned what it meant to be a modern Egyptian man as well as a modern Egyptian woman.[29] Before publishing his famous texts, Amin had used a local newspaper to publish a series of articles called "Reasons and Results." He used those articles to respond to d'Harcourt's insinuations that Egyptian men lacked the physical strength and the intellectual vigor to build a modern nation.[30] Amin argued against seclusion, for example, and for the education of women precisely because he saw uneducated mothers as prone to weakening the physical and moral fitness of their sons and daughters. Modern motherhood by contrast produced men and women who were physically and morally equipped for the task of ushering Egypt into the modern world.[31]

Amin's most notable opponent (Muhammad) Talaat Harb (1867–1941) is best remembered in Egyptian history for his role in starting a national bank and other national industries several decades after he tussled with Amin. While establishing Egyptian national institutions was still among Harb's pipe dreams, he wrote *The Woman and the Veil* (1899) to reclaim the Egyptian domestic realm, which he felt Amin had allowed the West to colonize. Like Amin, Harb was an advocate for women's education. Unlike Amin, however, Harb used religious justifications for educating women. Harb thought that Muslim, Christian, and Jewish girls alike should receive a religious education aimed at making them better wives and mothers. More importantly, Harb argued that women should wear the *hijab* and that women should reside within the home, which is to say within the demarcated realm of the *hijab*.[32] Ultimately, however, he agreed with Qasim Amin that education was a means of ending the subjugation of Egyptian women.

Ibrahim Ramzi also joined the Egyptian "Woman Question" debate. Ramzi idealized companionate marriage and the bourgeois nuclear family. He acknowledged the important role that well-raised children, and, therefore, women, played in the national project. And he praised the modern Egyptian homes in which Western habits had taken root. For Ramzi, however, the ultimate arbiter of the household was the father, whose task was to physically, emotionally, and metaphorically demarcate the *hijab* over his wife and family. Ramzi insisted that women could not be freed from their obligation to the *hijab* until men allowed them greater access to education (or until God intervened on behalf of the Egyptians to provide them with the economic privileges of Europeans.)[33] For Ramzi, the woman was at the mercy of her husband, the British, and God. As a result, the *hijab* had to stay.

Like other Egyptian intellectuals of his day, Ramzi had his own problematic views on race. While he did not write about the slave trade, he did blame black Africans, particularly the Sudanese, for perpetuating Egyptian women's bad habits (or what he claimed were their bad habits). Specifically, he pointed at women's custom of visiting saints' tombs and participating in *zar* or ritualized possession by spirits. Ramzi called the Sudanese "the nearest thing to black *afarit*," or spirits, and argued that dark foreigners who came from outside the Egyptian nation taught women unwholesome practices.[34] Who better than Egyptian nationalists to teach women to eschew such customs and be modern—at least according to Ramzi.

In Iran, Qasim Amin's *The Liberation of Women* was translated just one year after its publication in Egypt. The book's translator Yusuf Ashtiani (1847–1938), however, took some rather interesting license with Amin's work. Ashtiani chose to drop Amin's chapter on the veil. And where the veil was mentioned, Ashtiani creatively paraphrased Amin's words, either to suit his audience or to air his own views. The below example shows, first, Amin's original and then Ashtiani's translation:

> [Amin] Were women's socialization effected in accordance with religious and moral principles, and were the use of the veil terminated at limits familiar in most Islamic schools of belief, then these criticisms would be dropped and our country would benefit from the active participation of all its citizens, men and women alike.
>
> [Ashtiani] Provided the education of women is carried out according to fundamentals of our solid religion and rules of morals and manners, and with due regard to conditions of *hijab*, we will reach our goal, bitter conditions will be behind us, and sweet days will emerge.[35]

Ashtiani clearly advocated women's education, but suggested that advances in education, like changes regarding veiling, had to remain in line with Iran's "fundamentals" and "manners." In Iran, as in Egypt, men ca. 1875 still debated women's education, just as they continued to link women's progress with that of the nation. Iranian reformers maintained their arguments over the veil: was it an impediment to progress or a symbol of indigenous values? Like Ashtiani, many Iranians viewed the veil as central to Iranian identity.

The spread of writing about the "Woman Question" in the Ottoman Empire after 1876 and in Qajar Iran reflects the rise of print capitalism and the inclusion of an increased number of participants in the debates. While there was general agreement that bourgeois, companionate marriage would lead to national harmony and good citizenship, questions lingered about the extent to which Islamic societies could incorporate change all the while remaining authentic. As fervent as male writers were about the "Woman Question," at greater concern was their own role in changing societies and their own political future.

The Third Generation

The Tobacco Concession crisis (1890–1892) (see Chapter 6) that led to the constitutional uprising in Iran from 1905 to 1911 and a second constitutional crisis at the tail end of the reign of Abdül Hamid II inaugurated a third generation of writers on the "Woman Question." The Young Ottoman movement and its corresponding movement in favor of reform in Iran both raised questions about the role of men and women in a reformed political and social order. Thus, the "Woman Question" received new attention within the political debates that erupted in Iran as the result of the Tobacco Crisis of the 1890s.

The crisis itself brought debates about women to the fore, witnessed women's participation in demonstrations against Qajar concessions to Europeans, and created new bonds between various exiled Iranian intellectuals. Kermani, who wrote from exile in Istanbul, met Iranian expatriate pan-Islamist Jamal al-Din al-Afghani (1838–1897), who had also been exiled from Qajar territories because of his calls for political reform. From Istanbul, Kermani also corresponded with another Iranian expatriate Mirza Malkam Khan (1833–1908), who edited the London-based, Farsi-language newspaper *Qanun*. While only five of *Qanun*'s 40 issues dealt with the "Woman Question," Malkam Khan used the journal to suggest that Qajar society had to be reformed and brought under the rule of law.[36] He used *Qanun* to recruit women to his cause. That cause was a kind of humanist creed: when Iranians were fully aware of their humanity, he argued, they would attend to the improvement of women as well as men's condition. Malkam Khan attributed the need for reform in Iran to the despotic Qajar regime, its taxation practices as well as the continued practices of slavery and concubinage. Malkam Khan claimed that women had informed him of their readiness to reform the Qajar state and its customs, printing a letter in *Qanun* from an alleged noblewoman: "Yes, it is up to us to destroy this bazaar of dishonor…The torch of humanity is now in our hands."[37] In *Qanun*'s 19th issue, published ca. 1892, Malkam Khan issued a call for readying those women to reform Iranian society by providing them with education. He argued that his "humanism" was consistent with Islam in calling women to be educated mothers and partners to their husbands.[38]

In the same period, Kermani joined forces with a Babist shaykh, Ahmed Ruhi, and with him coauthored a book called *Eight Heavens* (1892). In this forward-thinking work, the two men called for women to be the equals of men "in all affairs and rights… including learning, education, government, inheritance, industries and commerce."[39] In their calls for women's equality, the two men "were actually more progressive than the leaders of the emerging Bahai movement." Kermani and

Ruhi nonetheless encouraged male superiority over women in legal, fiscal, and governmental matters as had Şamseddin Sami in Istanbul two decades earlier.[40]

During the Constitutional Revolt that began in Iran in 1906, the Bahai intellectual strain mirrored both the Western liberal tendencies and Russian social democracy that lay behind the revolt.[41] Like the Young Ottoman movement and the Urabists in Egypt, Iranian constitutionalists called for limits to the shah's powers. Unlike their contemporaries in Istanbul and Cairo, however, Iranian constitutionalists worked with the clergy (mullahs) to implement change. While the mullahs and the secular constitutionalists had different frameworks through which to argue for limitations to the shah's powers, both sides agreed that the Qajars had misgoverned Iran. Increasing hostility to the Qajar shahs and to their representatives in Iran ca. 1900 is a story that has been told in gendered terms: quite literally of the Qajars raping the countryside of its women and consequently stirring up the movement that is known as the Constitutional Revolt.[42] Iranian women did not gain political rights as the result of the Constitutional Revolt (see Chapter 6). Representatives to the new parliament *(majlis)*, which was established as the result of the revolt, did, however, discuss women's right to join associations and to participate in the press.[43]

In the waning days of Abdül Hamid II's reign, Arab intellectuals such as Jurji Zaydan (1861–1914) and Farah Antun (1874–1922) used historical fiction to argue that the oppression of women was intricately connected to the oppression of society as a whole. Zaydan, a Syrian Christian and a graduate of the Syrian Protestant College (later to become the American University of Beirut), made Egypt his home, where he established Dar al-Hilal press. Zaydan wrote nearly two dozen novels, mostly historical fiction, which he serialized in his journal *al-Hilal*. A typical Zaydan novel had three or four settings, spanned several historical events, and added a blend of "romance, sexuality, and adventure." Using this genre allowed Zaydan to put forward "radical political suggestions about the rights of women by situating his plots in distant locations or in the medieval past."[44]

In his fiction, Zaydan used the allegory of the harem as a stand-in for authoritarian rule. Zaydan critiqued the physical and metaphorical *hijab* demarcating public and private space. And he critiqued the *hijab* as a personal cloak. In Zaydan's fictional harem, the master of the household represented despotic and arbitrary rule. Zaydan presented the homosocial world of the *harem* as a space in which women were supported and in which they had networks of family and friends. But Zaydan presented women who were educated and who could choose their own grooms as having a position in society that was more enviable than that of *harem* women. In each of his novels, Zaydan demonstrated the importance of companionate marriage. As such, he used fiction to "respond to, appropriate, and comment upon themes discussed by prominent intellectuals."[45] Like Iranian authors such as Akhunzadeh, Kermani, and Malkam Khan, Zaydan equated the downfall of the patriarchal system that supported segregation with the downfall of tyrannical government.

While there was no room for gender segregation, tyranny, or the *hijab* in Zaydan's work, his feelings about race and slavery were more complex. Zaydan did not condemn slavery. And he described black slaves as animals. Concubinage was the only form of slavery that Zaydan criticized.[46]

Egypt was not unique among Arabic-speaking regions in the Middle East in producing writers, nor were novels and treatises the only means for the participation in "Woman Question" debates. In 1904, the Iraqi poet Jamil S. al-Zahawi (1863–1936) wrote about women's condition in Arab society. Both in poetry and in prose, Zahawi strongly supported the role of women in building society and the woman as "barometer of the nation's progress and civilization." Zahawi typically used his poems to discuss the legal aspects of women's inequality in divorce and inheritance laws. In the company of most "Woman Question" debaters, Zahawi believed that harmonious marriage, in which couples had a say in their future, was the strongest foundation for society. For Zahawi, seclusion had to end in order for marriage to be harmonious. Zahawi also found the veil to be a social impediment and argued that women needed it only for prayer. He went so far as to say that veiling caused psychological and hygienic problems, not the least of which were homosexuality and women's reduced ability to reproduce.[47]

The Nation as a Woman

A crucial byproduct of these reforms and debates, in the regions discussed above and in other parts of the Ottoman Empire, was the appearance over the first decades of the twentieth century of the idea that emerging nations embodied the qualities of reformed women. Male cartoonists in the Ottoman, Egyptian, and Iranian press used satirical depictions of "old" and "new" women to depict the dilemmas of social change and to illustrate the many forms that new nations might take. In the period immediately after the Young Turk Revolution, for example, the female image of "Türkiye" embodied an emerging Turkishness that was neither ultra-Westernized nor, by contrast, hesitant to modernize along Western lines. While "Türkiye" took many forms, her beauty and grace confronted the aggression of other nations, and she embodied honor and virtue.[48] "Lady Egypt," similarly represented ongoing debates about Egypt's nature. She was often arrayed in clothing representing Egypt's Pharaonic past; on other occasions, cartoonists portrayed her in traditional attire. Sometimes she wore a mixture of European and traditional fashion. Like the "Türkiye," she embodied the nation's assets and protected the nascent nation from European aggressions.[49] Nations in feminine guise were rallying symbols for the aspirations of a growing number of nationalists who linked allegedly feminine virtues with emerging national projects.

Often, these female representations of the nation glorified the contributions of Ottoman, Egyptian, and Iranian women as wives and mothers to the national cause. In 1907, during the Constitutional Revolution, an image of "mother Iran" was shown protecting the infant *majlis* (parliament) from its enemies.[50] In Istanbul, the *nesli çedid* or "new generation" was announced by a young mother contributing to the nation by rocking a cradle. In it, a baby soldier sports a fez and carries a rifle.[51] During the years following the 1919 Egyptian Revolution, "lady Egypt" was depicted breastfeeding the nascent Bank of Egypt, a project which—according to the cartoonist—was certain to succeed because it was nurtured by mother Egypt.[52] In each case, the success of the nation rested on women's maternal roles.

Like the harem dweller of the nineteenth-century European imagination, these women were not real. Rather, they represented the fears and ambitions of male intellectuals and politicians who sought to transform the nature of local rule and to respond to European imperialism. While women certainly benefitted from the educational projects that accompanied state reform, women's aspirations for themselves were not necessarily depicted in "Woman Question" debates or in symbolic, gendered-feminine representations of the nation. Nonetheless, as debates about women became incorporated into state-building projects, women whose objectives were different from those of male nationalists frequently found themselves in conflict not only with men but with the symbolic "ladies" who male reformers had constructed to represent them.

Conclusion

Across Ottoman and Qajar territories, intellectuals and government officials devoted half of the nineteenth century to writing about the "Woman Question." In their writings, women, their domestic lives, marriages, education, and clothing served as stand-ins for topics that were just as often about men as they were about women. This is not to suggest that the men who took up their pens to debate the position of women in their societies did not care about the conditions under which their mothers, wives, and daughters lived. Many of the men who took part in "Woman Question" debates over the course of the nineteenth century (and again into the twentieth century) worked devotedly—and successfully—for the improvement of women's lives, including advocating for educational and legal reforms. For such men, the interests of real, flesh-and-blood females were both real and pressing.

At the same time, however, the "woman" represented in questions about "her" was an abstraction, a concept, a vehicle through which men discussed questions that were relevant to them. As the beginning of this chapter suggests, the "Woman Question" first emerged in the wake of late eighteenth-century and early nineteenth-century revolutions, at the heart of which were questions about citizenship and rights. In the revolutions that swept through the Atlantic World, the question of "who shall rule" was no less important than the question of how former subjects would be turned into citizens. What sorts of rights would these citizens hold and how would those rights be demonstrated and protected? In the West, newly minted citizens debated about those who still did not hold rights—women and slaves. In the Ottoman and Qajar territories, subjects who did not yet have the rights that we associate with democratic revolutions, used debates about slavery and women to discuss as-of-yet unanswered questions regarding their own place in society. Debates about the home, in which women were central, served as useful tropes for discussing hierarchies (both racial and governmental), the limits of patriarchal rule, and the benefits and liabilities of tradition and change, as well as the rights and responsibilities of citizens toward one another. Debates about the home and family and, along with them, women served as arenas in which intellectuals and government officials rehearsed such questions, tying public and private together in ways that were quite distinct from their eighteenth-century antecedents.

Men also used the "Woman Question" to debate and discuss what kind of men they would be in an era of rapid transformation. As Europeans attributed childlike characteristics to Ottoman and Qajar men, those men "wrote back," indicating that—unlike children—they made choices for themselves, including about the women they would marry and the way in which their children would be raised. Such men suggested that as husbands and fathers, they were demonstrating adult behavior, assuring not only the future of the nation but also a comfortable position for their wives and children in that nation. As they participated in "Woman Question" debates, men discussed and debated the limitations of untrammeled political power and of the limitations of their own power within their households, including the power that they held over their slaves. Similarly, they debated the potential and the liabilities of tradition and of religion for answering questions about political and social reform, indicating that to be Ottoman and Qajar meant to incorporate institutions and ideologies from worlds outside their own.

As we will see in the next chapter, women who participated in "Woman Question" debates had similar but competing agendas. While women were certainly engaged in questions about political and economic reform and in debates about the contributions of women to the societies in which they lived, female contributors to "Woman Question" debates tended toward the practical rather than the abstract or the symbolic. For them, education was an end to a better life of the mind, not a means for advancing society to its next step. Choosing a spouse was not a demonstration of women's modernity as much as it was a determination to live with a partner and companion. For women, writing about women from the Islamic and European pasts was not an exercise in using women to symbolize the merits and limitations of those societies. Rather, women became biographers of other women in order to glean examples about how to live in the world.

It is to the practical application of the "Woman Question," as women discussed and debated to it and to the mobilization of women that was the byproduct of reform that we turn to next.

Notes

1 While men often married concubines who bore them children, the idea of marrying slaves was not one that carried through the early Islamic period for women. The ideals of both the Quran and the traditions of the Prophet did not hold true in late nineteenth-century Egypt. According to the historian Gabriel Baer, judges would not perform marriages for manumitted female slaves. See his "Slavery in Nineteenth Century Egypt," *Journal of African History* Vol. 8, No. 3 (1967), 436 (n. 130); 438 (n. 140).
2 Eve Troutt Powell, *Tell This in My Memory* (Stanford: Stanford University Press, 2012), 144–147.
3 Irwin Schick, "Print Capitalism and Women's Agency in the Late Ottoman Empire," *Comparative Studies of South Asia, Africa, and the Middle East* Vol. 31, No. 1 (2011), 202.
4 Rifaat Rafai al-Tahtawi, *Takhlīṣ al-Ibrīz fī talkhīṣ Bārīz*, in '*Usul al-Fikr al-'Arabi al-Hadith*, M. Hejazi, ed. (Cairo: al-Hay'a al-Misriyya al-'Amma lil-Kitab, 1974).
5 George Bernard Depping, *Aperçu historique sur les moeurs et coutumes de nations* (Paris: L'Encyclopédie Portative, 1826).
6 Rifaat Rafai al-Tahtawi, *Manahij al-al-bab al-Misriya* (Cairo: Ragha'ib Company, 1912).

7 Rifaat Rafai al-Tahtawi, *al-Murshid al-Amīn lil-bināt wal-banīn* (Cairo: Royal Schools Publishers, 1289 [AH]). esp. 6, 32, 48–49, 66–68, 91, 101–106, 120–121, 134, 195–207, 215–256, 273–277, 372–373.
8 Leila Ahmed, *Women and Gender in Islam* (New Haven: Yale University Press, 1992), 137.
9 Eve Troutt Powell, *A Different Shade of Colonialism* (Berkeley: University of California Press, 2003), 48–55.
10 Ibrahim Şinasi, *The Wedding of a Poet: A One Act Comedy*, trans. Edward Allworth (Whitestone: Griffon House Publications, 1981).
11 Nermin Menemencioğlu, "Namik Kemal Abroad: A Centenary," *Middle East Journal* Vol. 4, No. 1 (October 1967), 32. George Gawrych, "Şamseddin Sami, Women and Social Consciousness in the Late Ottoman Empire," *Middle Eastern Studies* Vol. 46, No. 1 (2010), 98–99.
12 Gawrych, "Şamseddin Sami," 98–100.
13 Gawrych, "Şamseddin Sami," 100.
14 Gawrych, "Şamseddin Sami," 98.
15 Menemencioğlu, "Namik Kemal Abroad," 29–30, 33.
16 Camron Amin, *The Making of the Modern Iranian Woman* (Gainesville: University of Florida Press, 2002), 26–27.
17 Afsaneh Najmabadi, *Women with Mustaches, Men Without Beards: Gender and Sexual Anxieties of Iranian Modernity* (Berkeley: University of California Press, 2005), 134.
18 Najmabadi, *Women with Mustaches*, 148.
19 Amin, *The Making of the Modern Iranian Woman*, 30–33; Afsaneh Najmabadi, "Crafting an Educated Housewife in Iran," ("Crafting") in *Remaking Women*, Lila Abu-Lughod, ed. (Princeton: Princeton University Press, 1998), 91–93.
20 Elizabeth Frierson, "Unimagined Communities: State, Press and Gender in the Hamidian Era" (PhD Dissertation, Princeton University, 1996), 90, cited in Özgür Türesay, "An Almanac for Turkish Women: Notes on Ebüziyya Tevfik's *Takvimü'n Nisa*," in *Social History of Late Ottoman Women: New Perspectives*, Doygu Köksal and Anastasia Falierou, eds. (Leiden: Brill, 2013), 229.
21 Gawrych, "Şamseddin Sami," 101–104.
22 The entire discussion of the almanac comes from Türesay, "An Almanac for Turkish Women," 234–243.
23 The discussion of Midhat and his writings comes from Holly Shissler, "The Harem as the Seat of Middle-Class Industry and Morality: The Works of Ahmet Midhat Efendi," in *Harem Histories*, Marilyn Booth, ed. (Durham: Duke, 2010), 319–341.
24 Mona Russell, *Creating the New Egyptian Woman* (New York: Palgrave, 2004), 216 (n. 112).
25 Pollard, *Nurturing the Nation*, 154.
26 Charles-François-Marie Le Duc d'Harcourt, *L'Égypte et Les Égyptiens* (Paris: Librairie Plon, 1893).
27 Amin as cited in Russell, *Creating the New Egyptian Woman*, 1.
28 Pollard, *Nurturing the Nation*, 156–157.
29 Marilyn Booth, "Woman in Islam: Men and the 'Women's Press' in Turn-of-The-20th-Century Egypt," *International Journal of Middle East Studies* Vol. 33, No. 2 (2001), 178.
30 Ahmed, *Women and Gender in Islam*, 162; Pollard, *Nurturing the Nation*, 155–162; Wilson Jacobs, *Working Out Egypt* (Durham: Duke University Press, 2010), 59–62; Marilyn Booth, "Women in Islam: Men and Women's Press in Turn-of-the 20th-Century Egypt," *International Journal of Middle East Studies* Vol. 33 (2001), 171–174.
31 Pollard, *Nurturing the Nation*, 159.
32 M. Talaat Harb, *Tarbiyat al-mar'a wal-hijab*, 2nd ed (Cairo: Matba'at al-Manar, 1905 [1899]). He followed this work by another book, *The Definitive Message on the Woman and the Veil* (*Fasl al-Khitab fi al-mar'a wal-hijab*) in 1901.
33 Booth, "Woman in Islam," 179, 184, 193.

34 Booth, "Woman in Islam," 182.
35 Quoted in Najmabadi, "Crafting," 101.
36 Amin, *The Making of the Modern Iranian Woman*, 32.
37 Cited in Amin, *The Making of the Modern Iranian Woman*, 32.
38 Amin, *The Making of the Modern Iranian Woman*, 33.
39 As quoted in Amin, *The Making of the Modern Iranian Woman*, 31.
40 Amin, *The Making of the Modern Iranian Woman*, 31.
41 Janet Afary, "Steering between Scylla and Charybdis: Shifting Gender Roles in Twentieth Century Iran," *National Women's Studies Association* Vol. 8, No. 1 (Spring 1996), 30.
42 This is the argument of Afsaneh Najmabadi, *Daughters of Quchan* (Syracuse: Syracuse University Press, 1998).
43 Amin, *The Making of the Modern Iranian Woman*, 38.
44 Orit Bashkin, "Harems, Women, and Political Tyranny in the Works of Jurji Zaydan," in *Harem Histories*, Marilyn Booth, ed. (Durham: Duke, 2010), 292.
45 Bashkin, "Harems, Women, and Political Tyranny," 312.
46 Bashkin, "Harems, Women, and Political Tyranny," 313.
47 Sadok Masliyah, "Zahawi: A Muslim Pioneer of Women's Liberation," *Middle Eastern Studies* Vol. 32, No. 3 (July 1996), 161–171.
48 Palmira Brummet, "New Woman and Old Hag: Images of Women in the Ottoman Cartoon Space," in *Political Cartoons in the Middle East*, Fatma Müge Göçek, ed. (Princeton: Markus Weiner, 1998), 13–58.
49 Baron, *Egypt as a Woman*; Pollard, *Nurturing the Nation*.
50 *Mulla Naser al-Din*. March 31, 1907, no. 13, cited in Afary, *The Iranian Constitutional Revolution*, illustrations insert.
51 *Kalem* 85: 5, May 5, 1910, cited Palmira Brummet, "New Woman and Old Hag: Images of Women in the Ottoman Cartoon Space," in *Political Cartoons in the Middle East*, Fatma Müge Göçek, ed. (Princeton: Markus Weiner, 1998), 36–37.
52 *Al-Lata'if al-Musawwara*, August 2, 1920, cited in Pollard, *Nurturing the Nation*, 191.

6 Beyond the "Woman Question"

Women Define Themselves as Writers, Activists, and Revolutionaries

The harem continued to exist and to function as a practice into the early decades of the twentieth century, but it looked little like the harems of the Western imagination. Far from being silent prisoners, elite women continued to be mothers to their children, supervisors of their households, managers of their *waqfs* and businesses, and students and teachers of their religions.

The lives of secluded elite women were witnessing changes, however. Political and social reformers continued to promote girls' education over the course of the nineteenth century. An increasing number of men sent their daughters to school or brought tutors into their homes to educate their wives and daughters. The local press burgeoned in urban centers like Istanbul, Tehran, Beirut, and Cairo, and provided literate women and men with access to increasing varieties of information. The spread of the printed press throughout the region also provided women and men with platforms for publishing their ideas. Elite women might still have had limited access to the public realm; nonetheless, they were increasingly well educated and engaged with both local and global events.

From the mid-nineteenth century, elite women in Anatolia, Iran, and the Arabic-speaking world contributed to the flurry of discussions, publications, and debates about reform, European imperialism, and the "Woman Question." Women wrote prose and fiction and had their works published by the privately owned presses that grew in number across the region. Women throughout the region funded and published their own journals beginning in the 1860s and targeted those journals to a largely female audience. Women's writings addressed topics that were of interest to women specifically; those topics also resonated within larger discussions about the historical and contemporary roles of men and women within a rapidly changing society.

The matters women discussed in their journals looked similar to those taken up by men: critiques of Orientalist literature about their homes and families; new readings of Islam and Islamic history; and the call for increased education for women. Like male writers, women wrote about religion, taking up their pens to critique conservative interpretations and to illustrate their religion's inherent approval of women's education.

And yet women's discussions of "Woman Question"-related topics tended toward the practical rather than the symbolic. Women used their journals, for

DOI: 10.4324/9781032658063-6

example, to publish women's histories and biographies and to provide their female readers with realistic examples of women's struggles and successes. Female contributors to women's (and men's) journals asked and answered questions such as how Muslim and European women participated in and responded to the world around them; how they lived, raised children, and worked; how they practiced their religion; and how they negotiated the world of politics.[1] For such writers and their reading audiences, these reflections on female historical figures were intended to provide models to emulate or critique. Similarly, women treated the home as a real place requiring knowledge and skills and not as a symbol of their region's backwardness or advancement. Finally, by the turn of the twentieth century, women used their journals to decry the lip service being given to women's education, both by local reformers and Europeans, and to make concrete demands for women's increased access to schools and universities.

The women who wrote for and read both the male- and female-authored press did not wait for men to answer the "Woman Question," especially with regard to women's education. Rather, numbers of elite women established philanthropic societies dedicated to opening primary and secondary schools for girls. Women's organizations provided literacy and vocational training to women of the lower classes whose economic situation had worsened as local economies became harnessed to European industrialization. Harem women's organizational and business skills enabled them to become successful social activists, and to work, first from their homes and later from their meeting spaces to effectively address the educational and health needs of women and children across classes. Such contributions to the public realm contradicted European assumptions about harem women and tested European and local men's ideas about women being best suited for domestic and family life alone.

Non-elite women were also participants in challenging the words and practices of local and foreign men. From the late nineteenth century, the increased presence of Europeans in the region brought locals of all classes into conflict with their own governments and with the European powers which were increasingly present in the region. During the 1905 Constitutional Revolution in Iran, elite women drew on their organizational skills and financial resources to contribute to local struggles, defying social conventions by organizing and participating in public demonstrations. Women of the lower classes drew on protest models from earlier conflicts with local governments and made their presence (and their discontent) known to both local and foreign officials. The public presence of women often drew the ire of local governments and of conservative religious figures. Women of all classes nonetheless risked their own physical safety in order to bring about political, economic, and social change.

In each of these cases, women called for their right to participate in the new constitutional orders that men were fighting for. Women's forays into writing, organization, and activism, and their increasing claims to the public realms, were therefore sources of much gender anxiety for men, who felt their domain to be encroached upon by women. That anxiety, as Chapters 7 and 8 illustrate, led men to insist that the domestic realm was the best place for women. Gender anxiety also led men to shape legal and educational platforms through which to control women's activities. Nonetheless, the actions and activities of these pioneer writers, organizers, and demonstrators shaped the outlooks and agendas of women and women's movements over the course of the twentieth century.

This chapter examines writers and activists across the region, illustrating women's efforts and activities in print and philanthropism, and concludes with a discussion of women's participation in Iran's 1905 Constitutional Revolution during which women wrote, organized, and took to the streets, translating their thoughts and skills into direct action.

Writing

In Ottoman Turkish, Arabic, and Farsi, books and essays written by women began appearing prior to the full eruption of "Woman Question" debates in the last decades of the nineteenth century. Women certainly lent their voices to that debate ca. 1900. But an earlier generation of women had already begun to respond: as the Young Ottomans began to offer new interpretations of Islam and of Islamic history, female authors, like men, questioned and debated the sanctioned roles of women within the context of religion. As new forms of education swept the region and as men and women acquired European habits and tastes, women questioned local customs like arranged marriages, polygamy, and concubinage. As local sartorial, educational, marital, and domestic customs slowly changed for the elite and emerging middle classes, women searched for role models after which to pattern their behavior and shape their morals. While women thus wrote about a disparate number of topics, what linked their discussions was the suggestion that education, both of males and females, would lead to more equitable interpretations of Islam and therefore to the improvement of women's conditions in society.

In Anatolia, Fatma Aliye (1862–1936), the daughter of an Ottoman civil servant and *tanzimat* reformer, began a prolific writing career by challenging both European and conservative Islamic views of Ottoman society. Aliye's writings challenged Orientalist depictions of the Ottomans and offered new readings of Islam and Islamic history. Aliye argued that the oppression of women in Ottoman society stemmed from social customs and traditions and not from Islam. Aliye's *Women in Islam*, published in 1891, offered a correction to what the author saw to be the ignorance of her fellow Ottomans regarding their own customs and about the origins of those customs. Aliye worked to tease out that which was required of women by their religion from the practices that the Ottoman society had inherited (and acquired) from the world around them.

Aliye also wrote *Women in Islam* to challenge Western misconceptions about the harem.[2] Mid-nineteenth-century Ottoman women, she claimed, were contemptuous of Western visits to their living quarters; they were equally disapproving about the commentary published about them after foreign women claimed to have visited a harem. In the words of one offended Ottoman woman:

> What did these women imagine they would find and see?…Women in gauzy trousers sitting on the floor? In their abysmal ignorance these foreigners did

not realize that many of the veiled ladies of the harem were better born [and] better raised…than some of their [Western] most famous society women.[3]

Female authors such as Aliye therefore busied themselves publishing more realistic accounts of harem life.[4] Aliye's work took readers inside the harem to illustrate that the lives of secluded women were hardly titillating.[5] She illustrated elite Ottoman women's devotion to organizing and supervising their households. She wrote about the delight that harem women took in the company and in the intellectual engagement of their extended families and of many (male and female) visitors.[6]

Like many of her male counterparts, Aliye was a champion of companionate marriage. In *Women in Islam* and in her many published novels, Aliye critiqued customary arranged marriage, promoting love and companionship between men and women in its stead. While Aliye was a proponent of monogamy, she nonetheless had reservations about the nuclear family living arrangements that were becoming fashionable among upper-class Ottomans. In her 1892 novel *Stories*, for example, Aliye contrasted harem life, which she happily spent among her extended family and many friends, to what she saw as the lonely confinement of women in arranged marriages and single-family dwellings. Aliye viewed women in such domestic arrangements as isolated, subject to the whims of their husbands alone, and without recourse to their extended families. She went so far as to compare arranged marriages and single-family dwellings to slavery. Aliye likely wrote from her own experiences: her husband, Farik Pasha (b. 1853), to whom she had been betrothed by arrangement and with whom she lived alone in an Istanbul apartment, forbade her from reading, writing, and translating for the first ten years of their marriage.[7]

With a logic that was similar to that of men involved in the Young Ottoman movement, Aliye took up the call for women's education. Aliye argued that as participants of everyday life, women themselves were part of—and indeed indispensable to—Ottoman public life. Aliye's argument stood in contrast to many male authors who limited educated women's role to that of motherhood by suggesting that the sons of educated women offered the greatest contributions to the Ottoman public realm.[8]

Aliye also contributed to debates about Islamic traditions regarding women. In 1899, she participated in a published debate with Mahmud Emin Seyidşehri, a legal advisor to the Ottoman Minister of Finance and a prolific author. Seyidşehri published two texts about women. In his first book, *A Defense of Polygamy*, Seyidşehri defended polygamous marriage by illustrating the role of polygamy in the Quran and throughout Islamic history. In his second book, *A Defense of Polygamy: Addendum*, Seyidşehri invited Aliye to respond. She took up his challenge, using the opportunity not to critique Islam, but rather to attack the logic of Muslim men who she viewed as using religion to justify their own sexual gratification and pleasure.[9] In each case, Aliye intimates that it was not the world of women that needed reforming, but rather the habits of men.

In Iran, Bibi Khanom Astarabadi similarly used the pages of her 1894 *The Vices of Men* to challenge male authors of "Woman Question" texts. Astarabadi did not challenge conventions such as veiling. Rather, in a fashion similar to Aliye's,

Astarabadi challenged men's prerogative to interpret Islam in ways that supported and perpetuated customs that were to their liking, such as sex with young boys, infidelity, gambling, and drinking. Astarabadi argued that male authority over women needed to be conditioned not on the Quran per se, but on the moral uprightness of male authorities. She praised men like Nasir al-Din Shah, for example, who demonstrated that they could treat each of their wives equally and argued against polygamy when practiced by men who had neither the financial nor the emotional resources to do the same. Astarabadi championed companionate marriage and argued that vice among men would decrease only in proportion to their marital and domestic happiness.[10]

In Egypt, thanks to a father who was determined to have his first-born daughter educated, Aisha Taymur (1840–1902) became learned in Arabic, Farsi, and Ottoman Turkish. She additionally studied the Quran, grammar, and Islamic jurisprudence.[11] Her education facilitated her work as a translator for the khedival court, employment which required her to leave her home to go to work. After she married, Taymur left her position in the court in order to raise and educate her children. When her children were grown, she turned to writing, publishing books of poetry and prose.[12]

While the "Woman Question" debate is typically—if falsely—understood to have been started with the publication of Qasim Amin's *The Liberation of Women* in 1899, Taymur had already published a social critique of relations between the sexes in Egypt in late 1887. In *The Consequences and Circumstances of Words and Deeds*, Taymur argued that in order for nations to advance, rulers needed to improve the education of young men. In a logic that was similar to that of Aliye and Astarabadi, Taymur suggested that it was uneducated fathers and husbands who weakened the social order through their subjugation of women. Taymur was also a proponent of educating women: through a series of essays, including a treatise on the importance of women's education entitled "Families Will not be Rectified But by the Education of Women," Taymur took up the importance of women's education to the improvement of the status of women in her society. Like others, she suggested that educating women would lead to an improvement in relations between men and women and therefore to the advancement of society as a whole.[13]

Taymur was an advocate of maintaining the strong presence of religion in Ottoman-Egyptian society, just as Aliye had been. In her long essay "The Mirror of Contemplation," Taymur provided an interpretation of the Quran that was far less patriarchal than most contemporary interpretations. Indeed, Taymur's reading of the Quran situated the roots of companionate marriage and women's education within the context of religion and argued that there was no contradiction between contemporary education and religious tradition.[14]

Many women's publications were innovative in style as well as content and displaying new ways of crafting poetry and prose. Combining traditional Arabic forms of biographical writing with the European tradition of writing biographies of famous women, Zeinab Fawwaz (1860–1914) from Lebanon published a biographical dictionary of famous Muslim women called *Scattered Pearls in the Lives of Harem Dwellers* (1895). The book chronicled the lives of famous women, from both European and Islamic societies, including figures from Greek mythology, Biblical characters, the Prophet Muhammad's first wife, Khadija, his youngest wife, Aisha, and Isabella II of Spain.[15] In each entry, Fawwaz highlighted women's social and political contributions to the societies in which they lived.

Fawwaz was not the first to publish such a dictionary: in 1879, her fellow Lebanese immigrant to Egypt Maryam Nasr Allah al-Nahhas (1859–1888) published *The Fine Woman's Exhibition of Biographies of Famous Women*. The book, which like Fawwaz's later text was an exposé of the lives of both European and Muslim women, was funded and sponsored by the Egyptian Khedive Ismail Pasha's third wife, Princess Jeshm Afet Hanem. Similarly, after immigrating with her family to Egypt in 1908, the Palestinian author Mayy Ziyada (1886–1941) wrote biographies of prominent women writers, including the Egyptian author Aisha Taymur, from which a later generation of women writers across the region drew inspiration.

Writing biographies, published as books and as short sketches in the growing periodical press, gave women a voice in a "Woman Question" discourse that had frequently reduced women to types and ideals.[16] By contrast, female-authored biographies gave women access to a wide variety of examples after which to pattern themselves. In Egypt alone, 571 biographies of women (written by both women and men) appeared in the press between 1892 and 1939.[17]

Drawing on Arabic literary traditions and combining them with new, European forms of storytelling, Arab women began publishing novels. Often, those novels were situated in the context of the region's political and social struggles: Zaynab Fawwaz's *Fine Consequences*, published in 1899, told a story about relations between families during Lebanon's mid-nineteenth-century feudal struggles for power. Labiba Hashim's *A Man's Heart* (1904) narrated the journey of Christian exiles from Mount Lebanon who had struggled to rebuild their lives in places like Beirut and Egypt after Lebanon's sectarian strife had displaced them in the 1860s. Afifa Karam (1883–1924) used her *Badia and Fuad* to criticize the blind imitation of Western habits and customs by her fellow Lebanese.[18] In each case, women used their education and adopted new literary forms to recount history and to engage in social critiques.

The establishment of salons and literary societies accompanied women's forays into writing. In Ottoman Syria, Labiba Hashim encouraged women to establish literary societies so that they could exchange ideas and form friendships with one another.[19] Consequently, prominent women in Damascus society began hosting discussion groups. Similarly, women across the region opened their homes to educated women (and, sometimes, men) who, in addition to entertaining themselves by playing games and listening to music, engaged topics in science and literature.[20] Princess Nazli, the niece of Khedive Ismail, held a literary salon in her home in Cairo, as did Alexandra Khuri Avierino, publisher of a women's journal, in Alexandria. The Associates of the American Girls' School in Cairo met twice-monthly to discuss literature at their salon beginning in 1899.[21] To meet and to discuss the world around them became a defining feature of the elite, late Ottoman era women's culture.

Press

From the late nineteenth century, a nascent women's periodical press provided an increased number of women with platforms through which to address polemics; discuss topics such as the domestic sciences, history, and literature; and advance the cause of women's education. Women wrote because they "understood that their own liberation was dependent upon liberating the collective consciousness from traditional values."[22] Women encouraged each other to take up their pens. Wrote Alexandra Khuri Avierino, founder of one of the first women's journals in Egypt: "I solicit female champions of knowledge."[23] As the women's press continued to evolve and to publish sophisticated writings by women, an increasing number of women wrote and submitted their essays and stories.

Women's journals were often funded by women of means. Some female publishers received subsidies from wealthy patrons. Others received funding by associating their journals with a philanthropic or literary society. Others raised capital through private business or through advertising. In each case, women's periodicals reached increasingly higher numbers of literate female readers.

In Anatolia, women established their first journal in 1869, followed quickly by a host of others. Ottoman women used their press to discuss women's rights and the compatibility of those rights with Islam. Topics also included the inequality of women in Muslim families and about the importance of women's education. Fatma Aliye, author of *Muslim Women*, contributed to Anatolia's longest-running women's periodical *The Ladies' Own Gazette* (1895–1909), the goal of which was the encouragement of Ottoman women to be good wives, mothers, and Muslims. Such themes appeared in the men's press as well: Halide Edib used the Young Turk daily paper *Tanim* to discuss relationships between men and women and the effects of those relationships on Ottoman society.[24]

Between 1892 and 1939, 24 women's journals emerged in the Arabic-speaking world, in Cairo, Alexandria, Damascus, Beirut, and Baghdad, among other cities.[25] The publishers of these journals were Jewish, Christian, and Muslim women. In Egypt, Hind Nawfal first published *The Young Woman* in Alexandria in 1879. Aleppo would see the publication of a journal dedicated specifically to women in 1893 when Nadima al-Sabuni published *Woman*. Alexandria saw a spate of publications with the 1896 appearance of Louisa Habbalin's *Paradise*; the emergence in 1897 of *The Intimate Companion* by Alexandra Khuri Avierino; and of Esther Moyal's *The Family* in 1898.[26] In Lebanon, 1906, Labiba Hashim published *The Eastern Girl*. From Damascus, Mary Ajami dedicated *The Bride* (1910) to "those who believe that in the spirit of women is the strength to kill the germs of corruption…"[27] `Ajami was editor in chief of the journal and worked with a staff of Syrian women who wrote under pseudonyms for fear of reprisals.[28] In Palestine, both men and women contributed to a women's journal, established in 1919, called *Mirror of the East*.

In Iran, the women's press emerged in 1910 with the appearance of an eight-page weekly magazine called *Danesh* or *Knowledge*. The journal's first issue offered the disclaimer that it would refrain from discussing politics and events facing the nation in favor of discussing domestic issues. That disclaimer appeared in response to (male) members of Iran's first parliament or *majlis* (see below) who enjoined women to stay out of politics. *Danesh*'s editors responded to men's critiques by limiting their discussions to family matters, hygiene, and child care. Occasionally, the paper addressed the unhappiness that Iranian women of all classes experienced in marriage.[29] The journal frequently advocated for women's education.[30]

On Saturdays, in Isfahan, readers could buy a copy of *Women's Language*, published in 1919 by Sadiqah Dawlatabadi. In Tehran, readers enjoyed *Women's Universe*, published by the Association of Graduates of the American Girls' School, who used the profits from their journal to open medical clinics for women and to support literacy projects for women.[31] Contributors wrote about a variety of topics, such as the growing presence of foreigners in the region and their influence on local societies; veiling and women's rights (including, as the century progressed, the right to vote); and child marriage and its societal liabilities. Dawlatabadi, who had been forced to marry at 16, was an outspoken critic of child marriage. She used the pages of her journal as a platform for campaigning against the practice.[32]

Across the region, the topics of scientific housekeeping and proper child-raising techniques also took pride of place in women's journals. The family was a topic of great interest, and a goodly number of articles discussed the roles of men, women, and children within the nuclear and extended family units. Biographies of women and men illustrated both sexes' contributions to their societies and to their families. Journals offered women advice on how to arrange their homes and how to use the new household gadgets that were appearing in local marketplaces. The women's press also contained articles on labor and on men and women's work conditions, which many authors decried as a threat not only to workers, but to the social order around them. Finally, women's journals carried literature: short stories, novels in serial form, and poetry.

Journals provided women with an arena in which to add their voices to the debates that preoccupied men of the era, and to offer their own interpretations of the roots of traditions like veiling and polygamy. While women also used the press to champion nationalism and to suggest—as had men—that reformed households would form the bedrock of new nations, women's discussions of home life combined ideals about the future of the nation with concrete knowledge about how to be educated subjects and individual consumers. Women's journals also promoted women's roles in nationalist causes, suggesting that—as contributing members of the social order—women had much to contribute to the struggle against European imperialism.[33]

Organization and Activism

Beginning ca. 1900, women of the elite class established service societies, dedicated to helping the needy, particularly women and children. Some well-funded women's philanthropic organizations also taught fellow Ottoman and Iranian subjects to read, provided them with vocational training, and cared for them when they were ill. Some societies opened maternity clinics. Others widened their communities' educational network by establishing primary schools. Philanthropy was an arena in which women's public presence was considered legitimate, respectable, and honorable.[34]

From philanthropy, women later turned their attention to women's causes such as education and suffrage, and used their organizations—many of which became feminist organizations in the 1920s—to lobby local governments for women's rights. Finally, women used their organizational skills to challenge both local and colonial states as women participated in demonstrations, boycotts, and strikes. Women's activism thus extended from philanthropy to clashes with local and colonial regimes.

In each case, women's activities were political: women's philanthropic efforts created state-like institutions at a time when local governments were challenged by foreign intervention and fluctuating economies.[35] At the same time, women made demands of regimes that claimed to support women but failed to provide them with education or medical care. Networks of organized women also challenged both foreign and local governments, participating in movements in favor of local economic autonomy and political inclusion. In the post-WWI era, women would draw on their earlier experiences to organize anti-colonial resistance movements and women's movements.

Philanthropy

The late nineteenth century saw the rise of new forms of philanthropy across the Middle East. Charity and philanthropy were not new to the region. Judaism, Christianity, and Islam each enjoin believers to care for the needy. Late nineteenth-century organizational forms of philanthropy were new, however. As state reform and the rise of new European-geared economies swept the region, old forms of community organization broke down. The new state institutions that replaced traditional organizations attempted to fund projects for the poor and the needy, but their efforts fell short of providing for the steadily increasing number of people who relied on their services. As new economies weakened traditional forms of agricultural and commercial practices, as communities of migrant farmers moved to cities to find work, and as immigrant communities arrived in places like Istanbul, Cairo, and Alexandria to find work, they were not necessarily provided for by the state. New philanthropic associations arose to provide them with aid.

Beginning ca. 1850 and gathering momentum from the 1880s, the region increasingly witnessed the appearance of a growing civil society of beneficent organizations. Locals formed and joined those organizations, donating their time, efforts, and financial resources to help community members. By the end of the nineteenth century, the landscapes of Anatolia, the Arab provinces, Iran, and Egypt began to witness the appearance of schools, libraries, meeting spaces, and hospitals built by such service societies.

In 1847, the Ottoman Syrian provinces saw the establishment of the Sisters of Love association, whose members organized their efforts to build a hospital, a tuberculosis sanitarium, and a hostel for girls. In 1880, Beirut witnessed the emergence of Syrian Dawn, a women's society whose devotion to charity and to women's education was evidenced in the opening of a convent and a school. In the 1880s and 1890s elite women founded local "national" schools to compete with missionary education in cities like Beirut, Damascus, Tripoli, and Homs. By 1900, Lebanese women were extensively involved in charitable organizations, whose focus was on expanding women's educational opportunities and on providing vocational training.[36] Anbara Salam Khalidi attended the school of a charitable organization in Beirut ca. 1900 called "The Fruits of Benefaction." The school's motto that the future of the nation had its roots in girls' education reflected the goals of many philanthropist-educators across the region.[37] On the eve of WWI, almost a generation after she had attended this school, Khalidi herself joined Beirut's "The Awakening of the Young Arab Woman Society." In their activities, members found a common cause in funding girls' schools and in providing female students with housing and clothing. In addition to philanthropy, what Khalidi describes as the women's "feverish" efforts to promote girls' education, provided "a means to vent our... emotions" as war appeared increasingly imminent.[38]

Iran's religious minorities were the first to have access to foreign and missionary education and to open schools of their own. Educated Armenian women subsequently opened several schools in Iran across the nineteenth century; girls in Isfahan, Tehran, and Tabriz began attending such schools between 1858 and 1879.[39] Christian women in Iran's then largest city, Tabriz, opened the Armenian Women's Beneficent Society in 1890. The group opened girls' schools, providing scholarships to needy students. Isfahan saw the opening of a similar society (*anjuman*) in 1892, and by 1895, Tabriz had a second Armenian women's society dedicated to girls' education.[40] The curriculum in the Armenian girls' schools was similar to that of foreign missionary education and included courses in child-rearing, housekeeping, and cooking, in addition to Armenian- and Persian-language instruction and other academic subjects.[41]

Muslim Iranian women began establishing *anjumans* in the early twentieth century, beginning with the Women's Freedom Society in 1907. The association, which took the form of an elite coed salon, had the goal of encouraging women to speak in public; indeed, the task of lecturing and speaking at the salon's meetings was left fully to women.[42] The society was short-lived: the groups' practice of mixing of men and women ran contrary to local culture, and the group's meeting place was soon attacked by mobs. Members nonetheless retained a long-lasting interest in women's education.[43] The organization's rosters included two of Nasir al-Din Shah's daughters and two emerging champions of women's education, Sadiqah Dawlatabadi and Shams al-Muluk Javanhi Kalam.[44]

Women's education in Iran was also taken up by the 1907 Women's Society, which petitioned Iran's *majlis* to support women's education. The group was reconstituted in 1910 as the Society of Ladies of the Homeland, whose membership advocated for and organized boycotts of foreign goods and foreign loans (see below). The group engaged in charity and social work, including the establishment of schools for girls, adult educational programs, and an orphanage.[45]

Several members of Iranian women's *anjumans* became pioneers of girls' education. Durrat al-Muali, for example, a member for the Society of Ladies of the Homeland, later opened the doors of the Pearl of Schools in 1909.[46] Al-Muali's home was a regular center for women's meetings and for a literary salon. Safiyah Yazdi, the member of the Association for the Freedom of Women, founded a girls' school in 1910. By 1911, women's efforts had led to the enrollment of approximately 2,000 girls in elementary schools in Tehran alone.[47]

Because many of Iran's clerics were opposed to the education of women, a schism quickly developed between them and the members of the women's associations. Clerics and women's associations later found common cause during Iran's Constitutional Revolution of 1905–1911 (see below). Nonetheless, as they worked tirelessly to see young women educated, women resented the clerics' depictions of them as "load-carrying animals."[48]

In Istanbul in 1897, Fatma Aliye founded the Ottoman Women's Association for Aid, one of Anatolia's first women's associations. Aliye later helped to establish the Society for the Defense of Women's rights (1908). That group, which would later agitate for women's suffrage, opened a number of women's philanthropic organizations in the Ottoman capital. Aliye received a medal from Sultan Abdül Hamid II for her efforts on behalf of the poor.

In Egypt, in response to a wave of infant mortality, the royal family's Princess Ayn al-Hayat joined with a group of elite women to open the Mohammad Ali Dispensary in 1909.[49] In her memoirs, organizer and activist Hoda Shaarawi accounted for the Dispensary's early days, writing about the elite women who met with the princess and who pledged hefty sums of money to her project. Shaarawi recounted the furnishing of a rented building with donated beds and desks; the European and Egyptian doctors who gave their time and services; and the women who later helped to expand the project to include a school. She described charity fêtes, held in royal palaces, where people paid to see the belongings of the royal family. Shaarawi noted that male guests were secluded from women and could only peep at the festivities despite having paid a handsome price for admission.[50]

In Damascus, provision of medical relief to the poor inspired Nazik al-Abid Bayhum (1887–1959) to establish the Red Star Association (later to be called the Red Crescent) in 1909. Nazik al-Abid, who later fought against the French as they occupied Syria in 1920, also established the Light of Damascus Society, which spearheaded a literacy campaign. Al-Abid was also active in several societies dedicated to advancing the interests of women.[51]

Organization and the Promotion of Women's Rights

Like Nazik al-Abid, members of charitable societies across the region began turning their attention and organizational skills toward the promotion of women's interests. In 1908 Cairo, Fatima Rashid established the Society for the Advancement of Women, which advocated the recognition of women's rights. The society sponsored lectures for its membership given by prominent women of the day, some of whom were members of the organization themselves. Nabawiyya

Musa (1866–1951), who was the first woman in Egypt to take and pass the state secondary school exam and who dedicated her life to expanding educational opportunities for Egyptian women, addressed the group. Similarly, the author and orator known as Bahithat al-Badiyya (Searcher in the Desert), also known as Malak Hifni Nasif (1886–1918), spoke to a gathering. In 1911, Nasif presented the Egyptian Nationalist Congress with a list of demands regarding women. Those demands included the right to a full education, the right to work at a meaningful vocation, and the right to participate in congregational prayer. As the result of these women's efforts, special lectures were opened to women at the Egyptian University in Cairo, beginning in 1908.[52]

In 1908, in Anatolia, Halide Edib opened a woman's association called the Society for the Elevation of Women. The group had ties to British suffragettes and to a local men's association called the Society for the Defense of Women's Rights. Members of the group discussed the compatibility of women's rights with Islam. The group also supported further education for women. Members of the society petitioned the Ottoman government for universal suffrage.

In Iran, by 1910, members of women's organizations began discussing topics that had been taboo up to that point: divorce, polygamy, and veiling. In her memoirs, one of Nasir al-Din Shah's daughters, Taj al-Sultanah, discussed her own woes: her forced marriage, her husband's philandering, and her recourse to abortion. She argued that many of Iran's ills stemmed from the practices of veiling, arranged marriages, and men's habit of cheating on the women whom they had married for wealth or social position. She and others argued that men's treatment of women had to be altered in order for Iran to advance.[53]

Organization and Political Demonstrations

The remainder of this chapter focuses on Iranian women, whose forays into demonstrations against the actions of local and foreign governments ca. 1900 presaged a century of Middle Eastern women's activism. The exclusion of Iranian women from the constitutional regime they fought to establish similarly presages mounting anxieties about gender roles throughout the region. While men seemed to welcome women's assistance in securing new forms of self-governance, they did not welcome what women's participation in organized politics appeared to herald: departure from tradition.

Men's objections belied a century of Iranian women's active participation in protesting state policies, however. Throughout the nineteenth century, urban, lower-class women, whose veils allowed them to protest without being recognized, had formed a substantial presence in bread riots. Those riots occurred in response not only to escalating bread prices but also to slumps in the Iranian economy, increases in the cost of living, and the famines and diseases that had disrupted local economies and left the price of bread outside of their reach. Protests started by women were then joined by networks of bazaar merchants, the ulama, and members of guilds. Tehran witnessed such bread riots in 1834, 1861, and 1871. The women of Shiraz protested against the price of bread in 1865 and again in 1873. A protest in

Isfahan in 1840 was so serious that the Shah himself marched to the city, where he was greeted and addressed by a crowd of female protesters.[54]

Across the 1880s, Iranians protested against tax increases, government corruption, the rising cost of living, and the state's increased export of Iranian produce. In the countryside, it was common for entire villages to rise up against the Qajar state. In cities, the poor used protests to demonstrate their anger at the increase in prices of basic commodities such as bread and tea.[55] Food shortages "frequently brought crowds of lower-class women into the streets, damaging shops and punishing" those who hoarded their goods.[56]

In the 1890s, Iranian men and women began protesting Nasir al-Din Shah's practice of granting concessions to Europe. One particularly onerous concession had been granted by Nasir al-Din Shah to a British businessman for control of Iran's tobacco production. Tobacco had been a crop from which farmers and the merchant classes had made a profit in Iran for several centuries. Granting a concession for the crop's cultivation and distribution therefore worked against the interests of a large percentage of the local population. An alliance quickly grew between the clergy, who thought that Nasir al-Din Shah was giving too much power to Europeans and the merchants who had a stake in overturning the concessions. By issuing a *fatwa*, or a legal injunction, against tobacco use, a prominent cleric hoped to get people to stop using tobacco and therefore to limit British profits.[57] A boycott of tobacco use then began, uniting Iranians of all classes. Smoking was popular among Iranian women and they, like men, observed the boycott. Even the shah's wives and concubines were said to have smashed their waterpipes.[58]

Women also participated in demonstrations against the concessions, attacking shops whose owners had not participated in the boycott, shouting insults at the shah (they questioned his masculinity by calling him a "female with a moustache") and physically attacking one of his sons.[59] While Nasir al-Din Shah subsequently canceled the tobacco concession, a shortage of food led riots and protests to continue. In Tabriz, a woman named Zainab Pasha led riots against the governor and merchants who had been hoarding food.[60]

After Nasir al-Din Shah's 1896 assassination, his son and successor, Muzzafir al-Din, continued to grant concessions to Europeans. The new shah's policies were offensive to the same class of people who had been offended by Nasir al-Din Shah: the urban class of merchants, the *bazaaris*, were hard hit by the shah's policies. To both the *bazaaris* and the *ulama*, the shah's practice of granting concessions to Christians was also an offense. To Western-educated reformers, the shah's policies were corrupt and autocratic. The three groups united in a common opposition to Muzzafir al-Din and called for a constitution to limit his power. By 1905, most Iranian cities had become home to secret political societies of constitutionalists. Between 1905 and 1911, supporters of a constitutional regime—men and women—would use their secret societies to organize and hold protests in favor of constitutionalism.

The first phase of revolutionary uprisings began in the summer of 1905 when men and women gathered in Tehran to demand the resignation of a Belgian customs administrator.[61] In December of 1905, protestors occupied a popular shrine just a few miles south of Tehran in order to force the shah to stop concessions. Women lent their support to male demonstrators by climbing on the roof of the shrine and throwing stones at the shah's soldiers. They also participated by forming human barriers between the soldiers and the clerics, chanting: "Oh, King of the Moslems [sic], command that these leaders of the Moslems be respected!"[62] Other women marched to the shah's palace. A Women's Revolutionary Committee sent a letter to the shah and threatened his life if he did not comply with the people's demands.[63]

In Isfahan, during the summer of 1906, as prices went up and hunger was rampant, merchants encouraged their wives, unrecognizable under their veils, to attack the British Consulate. Mass demonstrations had begun in July 1906 when the shah's army shot a prominent cleric. Both men and women used their *anjumans* to spread information about meeting places and to continue discussions about the importance of a constitution. When 12,000 male demonstrators occupied the British Legation in Isfahan, both to protest concessions and in support of a constitution, elite women pooled their financial resources to support them. Rich and poor women alike sold their jewelry and their household items or gave cash donations to support male protesters.[64] Women's societies, like the Society for Women's Freedom, organized strikes and boycotts and lent their financial support to the male constitutionalists.[65]

Over the remainder of the summer of 1906, men and women continued to facilitate strikes and to organize boycotts of foreign goods. In Tabriz, for example, women's societies encouraged locals to wear their old clothes instead of buying new garments produced in Europe. In response, Muzzafir al-Din agreed to the promulgation of a constitution and to the establishment of an elected assembly or *majlis*.

Women, however, did not hold seats in Iran's first *majlis*, which met from October 1906 to Muzzafir's death in 1907. The *majlis* drafted a constitution that effectively limited the shah's power, placing final authority over the country's finances in the legislature's hands. The national bank project, which women had helped to fund during the uprisings by selling their jewelry and by purchasing shares, was made official by the *majlis* soon after its opening.[66] Their efforts notwithstanding, the *majlis* failed to promiote women's interests. Wrote one woman to the local press: "Why is it that the Constitution has prevented women from gaining their rights?" Another petitioned the *majlis* to let women run the country for a trial period, so as to uproot the autocracy that the new constitution had seemingly not done away with. The women who protested in front of the *majlis* remained committed to that body's anti-foreign agenda. But they were angered by their exclusion from the institution they had so recently helped to establish.[67]

Muzzafir al-Din died in 1907 and was replaced by his son Muhammad Ali. As inflation began to hit Iran and as Russia and Great Britain exerted increased pressure on the shah in order to protect their economic interests, another wave of rebellions erupted. During those rebellions, two prominent members of women's societies, Sadiqah Dawlatabadi and Durrat al-Muali, visited tea houses to encourage men not to use imported sugar in their tea. The two women similarly visited fabric stores to encourage patrons to use only locally produced materials. Women also protested in print by writing to local papers about their dissatisfaction with the *majlis*' actions. And despite their dissatisfaction with the *majlis*, women continued to sell their personal belongings in order to support the new institution against anti-constitutionalist forces.[68]

A civil war broke out in Iran when the shah had his troops close the *majlis* in June 1909. As the shah reestablished his control over Tehran, the center of constitutionalism moved to Tabriz. The shah's troops held Tabriz under siege for 11 months. During the siege, women fought and died alongside men to defend the city. The press applauded women for their "exceptional courage and devotion to duty," as they had organized to capture food from hoarders. Women washed and nursed wounded protesters. Women also wrote to state officials to report that they would rather starve than give up the fight.[69]

In Tehran, women flouted anti-protest laws and demonstrated in the streets. Numerous stories of women's bravery emerged from the streets of Tehran, which were occupied by the shah's soldiers. One woman hid a pistol under her chador and shot and killed an anti-constitutional orator as he addressed a crowd in the city's center. A female protester by the name of Laila Gilani joined the constitutionalists after having been raped by a landlord. A Kurdish woman joined the protestors after her husband had been executed by the shah's forces. Asfik, the 13-year-old daughter of nationalist leader Yephrem Khan, joined the ranks of constitutionalists who fought to secure Tehran.[70] By the summer of 1909, the city was retaken by constitutionalists and a second *majlis* was established. In recognition for women's contributions, the *majlis* took up more serious discussions about women's education.

Majlis members failed to reach consensus about education or suffrage for women. The first *majlis* had made universal education the law, but it would be another decade before that law was applied to women. A second *majlis* excluded women from enfranchisement, along with illiterate men, minors, lunatics, criminals, and murderers.[71] In the words of one member: "God has not endowed them [women] with the ability to be electors…"[72]

Nonetheless, after the constitutional uprisings were over, women continued to fund and to teach in girls' schools. Sadiqah Dawlatabadi, for example, continued to agitate for women's education in lectures and newspaper articles delivered and written in and outside of Iran. She took a degree from the Sorbonne in 1922 and lectured widely about the importance of women's education to the nation. She was Iran's delegate at an international women's conference in Paris in 1926 and used that forum to advocate for women. When she returned to Iran in 1927, she was one of the first women there to remove her veil. In her will, she wrote, "I will never forgive women who visit my grave veiled."[73]

Conclusion

As the result of state reform and educational projects across the nineteenth century, an increasing number of women in Ottoman and Qajar territories received traditional and European educations. Women used their increased access to knowledge to write. In their collective writings, women offered their own answers to the "Woman Question," contested harem literature, and advocated for women's education.

At the same time, educated elite women began associating with one another to help the poor and the needy and to promote women's rights. In Iran, in the late nineteenth and early twentieth centuries, women's associations expanded their agendas to include challenges to Qajar territorial and economic sovereignty. As participants in the Tobacco Rebellions of the 1890s and the Constitutional Revolution of 1905–1911, women worked to guard against European encroachments into Qajar domains. They demonstrated on behalf of the economic well-being of their communities. At the same time, women asserted their right to participate in the spoils of their contributions: a constitutional regime. While Iranian men were grateful to the women who risked their physical safety to secure an independent *majlis*, they were anxious about women in the public, specifically political realms. They wondered if women's morality could be safeguarded in the presence of men who were not their relatives. They wondered about their own ability to protect their women, both from fellow Iranian men and from the guiles of Westernization. As the result, women were excluded from the political realm for which some had risked their lives.

As we will see in the following chapter, the patterns and results of women's participation in the Iranian Constitutional Revolution would repeat themselves throughout the region in the early decades of the twentieth century, as women continued to draw on their increased educational and organizational experience and to participate in nationalist movements. Male members of those movements, conflicted about what would happen to women if the public realm were opened to them, made arguments in favor of women's place at home.

Notes

1 This is the thesis of Marilyn Booth's *May Her Likes Be Multiplied: Biography and Gender Politics in Egypt* (Berkeley: University of California Press, 2001).
2 Irvin Cemil Shick, "Print Capitalism and Women's Sexual Agency in the late Ottoman Empire," *Comparative Studies of South Asia, Africa and the Middle East* Vol. 31, No. 1 (2001), 206.
3 Musbah Haidar, *Arabesque* (London: Hutchison, 1944), 172–174, cited in Reina Lewis, *Women, Travel and the Ottoman Harem Rethinking Orientalism* (New Brunswick, NJ: Rutgers University Press, 2004), 16.
4 Lewis, *Rethinking Orientalism*, 110.
5 Lewis, *Rethinking Orientalism*. Lewis argues that Ottoman women reacted to harem literature by writing their own "insiders' accounts" about their experiences in the harem.
6 Elif Ekin Akşit, "Fatma Aliye's Stories: Ottoman Marriages Beyond the Harem," *Journal of Family History* Vol. 25, No. 3 (2010), 210–211.
7 Elif Ekin Akşit, "Fatma Aliye's Stories," 211.
8 Elif Ekin Akşit, "Fatma Aliye's Stories," 210.
9 Shick, "Print Capitalism and Women's Sexual Agency," 204.
10 Camron Michael Amin, *The Making of the Modern Iranian Woman, Gender, State Policy and Popular Culture, 1865–1946* (Gainesville, FL: The University of Florida Press, 2002), 35–36.
11 Mervat Hatem, "A'isha Taymur's Tears," in *Remaking Women: Feminism and Modernity in the Middle East*, Lila Abu Lughod, ed. (Princeton: Princeton University Press, 1998), 76.

12 Hoda Elsadda, "Egypt," in *Arab Women Writers: A Critical Reference Guide, 1873–1999*, Radwa Ashour, Ferial J. Ghazoul, and Hasna Reda-Mekdashi, eds. (Cairo: The American University in Cairo Press, 2008), 103.
13 Mervat Hatem, *Literature, Gender and Nation-Building in Nineteenth-Century Egypt* (New York: Palgrave MacMillan, 2011).
14 Elsadda, "Egypt," 103–135.
15 Nabila Ramdani, "Women in the 1919 Egyptian Revolution: From Feminist Awakening to Nationalist Political Activism," *International Journal of Women's Studies* Vol. 14, No. 2 (2013), 43.
16 Booth, *May Her Likes Be Multiplied*.
17 Radwa Ashour, Mohammed Berrada, Ferial J. Ghazoul and Amina Rachid, "Introduction," *Arab Women Writers*, 4.
18 Yumna Al-'Id, "Lebanon," Ashour et al., *Arab Women Writers*, 17–19.
19 Elsadda, "Egypt," 106.
20 Heghnar Zeitlian Watenpaugh, "The Harem as a Biography," in *Harem Histories: Envisioning Places and Living Spaces*, Marilyn Booth, ed. (Durham: Duke, 2010), 225.
21 Beth Baron, *The Women's Awakening in Egypt: Culture, Society and the Press* (New Haven, CT: Yale University Press, 1994), 176.
22 Al-'Id, "Lebanon," 14.
23 Elsadda, "Egypt," 106.
24 Lewis, *Rethinking Orientalism*, 38.
25 Ashour et al., "Introduction," 4.
26 Elsadda, "Egypt," 99.
27 Baron, *The Women's Awakening*.
28 http://al-hakawati.net/english/Arabpers/Mary_Ajami.asp.
29 Janet Afary, *The Iranian Constitutional Revolution, 1906–1911* (New York: Columbia University Press, 2004), 200.
30 Firoozeh Kashani-Sabet, "Patriotic Womanhood: The Culture of Feminism in Modern Iran, 1900–1941," *British Journal of Middle Eastern Studies* Vol.32, No. 1 (2005), 31.
31 Parvin Paidar, *Women and the Political Process in Twentieth-Century Iran* (Cambridge: Cambridge University Press, 1997), 50.
32 Paidar, *Women and the Political Process*, 50.
33 Mona Russell, *Creating the New Egyptian Woman* (New York: Palgrave, 2004).
34 Margot Badran, *Feminists, Islam and Nation: Gender and the Making of Modern Egypt* (Princeton: Princeton University Press, 1995), 47.
35 Baron, *The Women's Awakening*, 175.
36 Rita Stephen, "Women's Rights' Activism in Lebanon," in *Mapping Women's Movements: A Century of Transformation from Within*, Pernille Arenfeldt and Nawar al-Hassan Golley, eds. (Cairo: The American University of Cairo Press, 2008), 115.
37 Anbara Salam Khalidi, *Memoirs of an Early Arab Feminist: The Life and Activity of Anbara Salam Khalidi*, Tarif Khalidi, trans (London: Pluto Press, 2013), 13.
38 Khalidi, *Memoirs of an Early Arab Feminist*, 57–58.
39 Jasamin Rostami-Kolayi, "Origins of Iran's Modern Girls' Schools: From Private/National to Public/State," *Journal of Middle East Women's Studies* Vol. 4, No. 3 (Fall 2008), 62.
40 Susynne M. McElrone, "Nineteenth-Century Qajar Women in the Public Sphere: An Alternate Historical and Historiographical Reading of the Roots of Iranian Women's Activism," *Comparative Studies of South Asia, Africa and the Middle East* Vol. 25, No. 2 (2005), 309–310.
41 Rostam-Kolayi, "Origins of Iran's Modern Girls' Schools," 65.
42 Badr al-Molok Bamdad, *From Darkness into Light: Women's Emancipation in Iran* (Costa Mesa, CA: Mazda Publications, 2013), 29; Afary, *Iran's Constitutional Revolution*, 185.

43 Paidar, *Women and the Political Process*, 67–69.
44 Bamdad, *From Darkness into Light*, 29.
45 Paidar, *Women and the Political Process*, 69.
46 Rostam-Kolayi, "Origins of Iran's Modern Girls' Schools," 70.
47 Rostam-Kolayi, "Origins of Iran's Modern Girls' Schools," 70.
48 Afary, *The Iranian Constitutional Revolution*, 190.
49 Baron, *The Women's Awakening*, 172.
50 Huda Shaarawi, *Harem Years: The Memoirs of an Egyptian Feminist*. Margot Badran, editor and translator (New York: The Feminist Press of CUNY, 1986), 94–98.
51 Pauline Vinson and Nawar al-Hassan Golley, "Challenges and Opportunities: The Women's Movement in Syria," in *Mapping Arab Women's Movements: A Century of Transformation from Within* (Cairo: American University in Cairo Press, 2012), 66.
52 Baron, *The Women's Awakening*, 176–177.
53 Afary, *Iran's Constitutional Revolution*, 197–198.
54 Vanessa Martin, *The Qajar Pact* (London: I.B. Tauris Press, 2005), 100–102.
55 McElrone, "Qajar Women in the Public Sphere," 312.
56 Paidar, *Women and the Political Process*, 41.
57 Paidar, *Women and the Political Process*, 50.
58 Paidar, *Women and the Political Process*, 50; Bamdad, *From Darkness into Light*, 9.
59 McElrone, "Qajar Women in the Public Sphere," 313.
60 Paidar, *Women and the Political Process*, 50.
61 Paidar, *Women and the Political Process*, 53.
62 Bamdad, *From Darkness into Light*, 10.
63 Paidar, *Women and the Political Process*, 53.
64 Afary, *The Iranian Constitutional Revolution*, 179.
65 Afary, *The Iranian Constitutional Revolution*, 185.
66 Afary, *The Iranian Constitutional Revolution*, 64.
67 Paidar, *Women and the Political Process*, 55–56.
68 Afary, *The Iranian Constitutional Revolution*, 188–192.
69 Paidar, *Women and the Political Process*, 58; Afary, *The Iranian Constitutional Revolution*, 194.
70 Afary, *The Iranian Constitutional Revolution*, 195.
71 Paidar, *Women and the Political Process*, 63.
72 Ellen Fleischmann, "The Other 'Awakening: The Emergence of Women's Movements in the Modern Middle East, 1900–1940," *Globalizing Feminisms, 1789-1945*, Karen Offen, ed. (London and New York: Routledge Press, 2010), 109.
73 Afary, *The Iranian Constitutional Revolution*, 187.

7 New States and Their New Women

Introduction

WWI (1914–1918) tested the conclusions reached by men who had advocated for women's exclusion from the public realm ca. 1900. The local impacts of war required elite women's beneficent associations to double their efforts, women to fill jobs vacated by men, and the Ottoman government to mobilize women for agricultural and public works projects. Battle called women with nursing skills to tend to wounded soldiers. The exigencies of war meant that women could not (or would not) simply stay at home.

Similarly, the postwar era required women's contributions. As former Ottomans and Egyptians rose up against the Europeans who now (or still) occupied their territories, women risked their lives by joining in demonstrations and participating in armed struggles. Through their philanthropic organizations, women served their aspirant nations by opening schools, orphanages, soup kitchens, and hospitals. To further serve, women also began to demand suffrage and full inclusion in the nation-states to whose future they had already contributed.

Women's efforts to become enfranchised citizens were met by resistance on two fronts. As a means of assuring their own position in the public arena, local men, who themselves were not yet free to shape the public realm to their own liking, once again made recourse to debates about women's "rightful place." At the same time, European administrators, reliant upon the cooperation of local men, supported and often facilitated those men's efforts. The arena in which women waged a lengthy struggle for suffrage was therefore shaped by competing patriarchies, none of them fully willing to translate women's war efforts into political inclusion.

This chapter chronicles women's contributions to the public realm during the WWI years, during the struggle for independence in Anatolia and Egypt, and against the rise of mandate states in Syria, Lebanon, Iraq, and Israel/Palestine. We examine the ways in which women saw themselves as nationalist agitators and illustrate the resistance that women met from men who worked to keep women in their place. We end with a discussion of symbolic "nations as women." As men fought to protect these symbols in the WWI era, they cemented a relationship between women and nation in which home would long remain women's rightful place.

DOI: 10.4324/9781032658063-7

WWI

In August 1914, members of the Committee of Union and Progress (CUP), the Young Turks who had deposed the Ottoman Sultan Abdül Hamid II in 1908, took the Ottoman Empire to war against France, Great Britain, and Russia. The defeat of the Ottomans led to France and Great Britain's occupation of the Arab provinces and to the occupation of Anatolia by Allied forces. The immediate postwar struggle, for men as well as women, therefore involved armed struggles against occupying armies. The postwar era also witnessed local demonstrations in favor of implementing the ideals of self-determination that were the byproduct of the postwar peace process.

The impact of WWI was total in a region that, for the most part, lacked the infrastructure for industrial war.[1] That impact was made heavier still by the combatants' full utilization of local food supplies, fodder, animals, and manpower. Balances between feeding local populations and providing military needs were precarious at best. As early as October 1914, grain shortages were legion in Lebanon. By 1916, in one Lebanese village, 47 people starved to death in a 12-day period. In another, it took just three days for 19 to die.[2]

Across Ottoman Syria, households suffered intense dislocation as three quarters of all men between the ages of 17 and 55 were conscripted to the war effort. One in five men never returned. Women became heads of household and worked in fields and factories to provide for their children. The Ottoman Military governor of Syria, CUP member Jamal Pasha, organized work brigades, dispatching women to harvest wheat and other crops. In cities, women filled in for absent artisans, worked in textile mills and weaving shops, and sold supplies in markets.[3]

Deprivations were legion. Plagues of locusts hit Ottoman Syria in 1914. Famine struck in 1915 and 1916. Those same years, heavy snows cut Mount Lebanon off from food supplies and killed 50,000–80,000. Hot winds in June 1916 badly affected Syria's grain-producing region; half a million residents died from hunger.[4] The Entente blocked Syria's seaports. Trade routes were disrupted or shut down by the movement of troops. Neither men nor women could feed their families.

Palestine witnessed equal devastation: "famine, locust plagues, deforestation, currency devaluation, and a complete disruption of the economy." Disease and poverty were rampant in Palestinian cities.[5] When British forces arrived in Jerusalem in 1917, they encountered a population that, in addition to suffering from malnutrition, had also fallen prey to typhus, malaria, and cholera (See Figure 7.1).[6]

In Egypt, the buildup of troops from Britain and from British India overwhelmed existing resources. Demands for supplies required that the British tighten their rule in Egypt, which they had largely governed through collaboration with the Egyptian government (See Figure 7.2). As Egyptian men were drafted into labor corps, peasant women replaced their husbands in the fields. The cost of living soared for Egyptians of all classes.

Gender anxieties resulted in each locale. The horrors of war were accompanied by the trauma of men's inability to protect their wives and families. Men were haunted by the specter of the hungry women who begged in the streets. Halide

110 *New States and Their New Women*

Figure 7.1 Capture of Jerusalem, WWI, c.1917–1918. The Print Collector/Heritage Images/ Alamy Stock Photo.

Figure 7.2 Giza, Egypt, WWI. The Protected Art Archive/Alamy Stock Photo.

Edib, present in Beirut in 1916, became inured to hearing women and children cry out in hunger.[7] Women risked imprisonment for black-market purchases.[8] Men funneled their anger at the war toward women, whom they accused of breaking gender norms by working in public, by begging in public, and by taking on roles traditionally reserved for men.[9]

Despite men's anxieties, women marshaled their organizational skills in order to relieve the misery around them. Edib's Society for the Elevation of Women established a 30-bed hospital in Istanbul, where club members worked as nurses and their husbands often worked as surgeons and pharmacists.[10] The group also provided courses in nursing, domestic sciences, and child-rearing for the urban poor. As women attended to injured and dying men, they broke taboos regarding the mixing of the sexes. In Palestine, women participated in poor relief; 1918 witnessed the establishment of the Palestine Women's Council and the Social Service Association, which provided aid to the hungry and the ill and refuge for orphaned girls.[11] In Beirut, Nazik al-Abid Bayhum's Red Star provided medical relief to the poor and opened mothers' societies and dispensaries throughout Greater Syria. Bayhum and her colleagues also established a local network of orphanages, schools, clinics, and training programs for nurses.[12] In Cairo, the Mubbarat Muhammad Ali opened its first dispensary in Cairo on the eve of WWI. During the war, the group continued to provide aid to mothers and infants. The organization carried on its mission for decades after the war had ended.[13]

Women's associations were of great use to local governments. Beirut's governor, Azmi Bey, commissioned sewing work from a workshop sponsored by the Syrian Ladies Association (SLA).[14] By 1917, the SLA's efforts had caught the eye of Jemal Pasha, governor of Greater Syria. The governor pledged both a continuation and an expansion of state funds to the organization. He also announced a plan to make the women's refugee and training centers permanent to Beirut. Jemal Pasha's commitments allowed the organizations to expand their activities: women subsequently opened four refugee centers and two workshops. One of those workshops reportedly employed 1,800 women.[15]

Women also demonstrated during the war. Lebanese women protested against Jemal Pasha's practice of executing men accused of participating in the Arab nationalist movement and against the war's increasingly dire circumstances.[16] Palestinian women participated in demonstrations against Zionism: indeed, the most important feature of the women's movement in Palestine prior to WWI had been its participation in the national struggle against Zionist immigration and settlement in Palestine.[17] European and Russian Jewish immigrants had been purchasing land and building settlements in Palestine since the early 1880s, motivated and organized by Zionism, the goal of which was building a nation-state for Jews. As the number of Jewish settlements in Palestine increased, so too did Palestinian landlessness and poverty. Palestinian women, particularly peasants, had been rebelling against the Palestinians' decreasing economic well-being since 1884, when women participated in a demonstration against Jewish settlers in the village of Afula. The number of demonstrations against Zionism and the British would increase after WWI, as would women's participation in them.[18]

The Postwar Era

Agreements stemming from the postwar Conference of San Remo placed Anatolia under the jurisdiction of an international community and awarded spheres of influence in Anatolia to the Allies. The Arab provinces were detached from the remaining Ottoman territories and made into the French and British mandate states of Syria, Lebanon, Iraq, Transjordan, and Palestine. Egypt remained occupied by the British after the war.

Women across the region protested against the presence of Europeans on their soil and against the establishment of an unwanted postwar order. Participation in rebellions brought women new challenges and increased opportunities to participate in the region's future while remaining active in social activism and philanthropy. Women viewed their struggles as nationalist ones and their roles as similar to men's: rescuing the nation from the imposition of outside rule.

Once the Ottoman Empire had been defeated and Anatolia occupied, a wave of popular uprisings erupted. Across Anatolia, elite and middle-class women formed patriotic societies, such as the Anatolian Women's Association for Patriotic Defense (est. 1918). Women broke with gender conventions by taking up roles as orators, stirring their listeners by giving impassioned speeches in favor of Turkish independence. Halide Edib made such a speech in Istanbul in May 1919.[19] Other

Figure 7.3 Mustafa Kemal and Halide Edib (Adivar) at Gebze Station, Turkey. Archive PL/ Alamy Stock Photo.

women, including Edib herself, joined the armed resistance against the occupying forces. Peasant women smuggled weapons, food, and medicine to their male compatriots, later receiving the commendation of the future president of independent Turkey, Mustafa Kemal, later to be known as Atatürk (r. 1923–1938) (See Figure 7.3).[20]

Beginning in March 1919, Egyptian women of all classes joined in the organized boycotts and demonstrations against the continued British presence. Those protests and demonstrations continued until the Egyptians had succeeded in gaining a limited independence from the British in 1922. Peasant women protested the continued British interference in Egyptian politics by burning fields and by engaging in other acts of sabotage. Peasant women also joined urban women in boycotting British goods and in taking to the streets in protest of Great Britain. Some "women of the people" lost their lives to British bullets: on March 14, 1919, Hamidah Khalil became the first female martyr to the revolution. She was killed by a British soldier in Cairo's old city.

Elite women assisted the Wafd, a delegation of politicians who determined to represent Egypt in the postwar peace conferences in France. The British refusal of their request and the Wafd's subsequent exile from Egypt led to the outbreak of the 1919 Revolution. During the revolution, the wives of Wafd members, such as the noted philanthropist and social activist Hoda Shaarawi formed the Wafdist Women's Central Committee (WWCC). WWCC members raised money, participated in demonstrations, and acted as stand-ins for male Wafd members during their exile (and, later, as they were in Paris to negotiate Egypt's independence). Women marched carrying flags reading "Down with the Protectorate" and "Freedom and Total Independence." Shaarawi later wrote that "The revolution manifest itself the same way everywhere because there was only one way to act and that was to revolt."[21]

In Syria, women took up arms in favor of Amir Faysal's Arab nationalist movement. Faysal was the son of Hussein bin Ali, Grand Sharif of Mecca, to whom an Arab kingdom had been promised by the British. Faysal was also the field commander in the Arab Revolt against the Ottomans. He was made King of Syria by local notables in 1918. After failing to expel the French, he was made king of Iraq by the British. The Syrians engaged in armed resistance against the French between 1919 and 1926, first in favor of Faysal and then in support of independence from the French (which would not come until 1946). In 1920, rural women engaged the French in direct combat during the battle of Khan Maysalun outside of Damascus. Elite women were also participants at Khan Maysalun: the noted social activist and organizer Nazik Abid Bayhum fought there. Abid had earlier established the Red Star Society which she and Faysal, who was the society's patron, modeled after the Red Cross. For her efforts, Faysal awarded Abid an honorary military rank in the Syrian army. On July 24, 1920, Abid led a battalion of nurses onto the battlefield to tend to the sick and the injured. The Syrian Nationalist minister of defense, Yusuf al-Azma, allegedly died in her arms.[22] After the battle, Abid was dubbed the "Joan of Arc of the Arabs."[23]

The largest armed uprising against the French was the Syrian Revolt of 1925, during which women in both Syria's cities and countryside participated in street

Figure 7.4 Bazaar of Hama destroyed during aerial bombing of Damascus. The Picture Art Collection/Alamy Stock Photo.

demonstrations and smuggled food, weapons, and medicine to troops. Women often hid food and supplies under their cloaks at French checkpoints. Dozens of women died in combat; hundreds of others died in French aerial bombardments of Syrian cities as the French asserted their control over Syria (See Figure 7.4).[24] After the uprising, Syrian women continued to use the streets to challenge the French in matters ranging from public health to limitations on women's right to work.[25]

In Iraq in 1920 local revolts against the British Mandate were led by all spectrums of the Iraqi population: urban nationalists, Shia religious leaders, and tribal leaders in Iraq's south. The uprising lasted for several months, spread over one-third of Iraq's countryside and was difficult for Great Britain to contain. Women's support of the nationalist movement was headed by Naima Sultan Hamuda or Umm Salman, wife of the patriarch of a powerful urban family who established a women's committee in Baghdad. Naima and other elite women also contributed by donating their money and jewelry and by encouraging other women to support the uprising.[26] Veiled and dressed in black, women in Baghdad participated in funeral processions, which frequently turned into nationalist demonstrations, chanting nationalist slogans against the British.[27] In Iraq's countryside, women

Figure 7.5 Female refugees sewing army clothing in Baghdad, WWI. Chronicle/Alamy Stock Photo.

carried weapons and accompanied male combatants. Peasant women rallied men to fight by chanting poems and other kinds of encouragement.[28]

In Palestine, British Mandate officials attempted to balance the needs and interests of both Jews and Arabs: the 1917 Balfour Declaration had placed Great Britain in the position of supporting the rights of both Jewish and Arab residents there. High Commissioner Herbert Samuel suggested several unitary forms of government, all of which were rejected by the Palestinian community (as to accept them would have been to legitimate Balfour). As the result, the 1920s witnessed a mandate government under which Jews and Arabs came increasingly to resent one another while at the same time developing their own, independent political institutions.[29]

In January 1920, Palestinians mounted their largest demonstration against the British Mandate and against Jewish settlement. About 40,000 Palestinians, among them women, came together in Jerusalem to protest. Afterward, women formed part of a delegation that went to meet with the British High Commissioner to demand the abrogation of the Balfour Declaration.[30] In 1921, women worked to raise money to send a delegation of men to London to protest the Balfour Declaration. Committees in all of Palestine's major cities worked to collect funds for the effort.[31]

Organizing, Redux

In Egypt elite women who had been involved in the establishment of the Mubarrat Muhammad Ali joined ranks with a group of middle-class women and established The New Woman Society in 1919. Members of the group understood charity to be a national responsibility, shouldered by Egyptians with means, and partaken of by those who had suffered during the war years.[32] The New Woman Society opened a crafts workshop to help girls to earn a living. The group also taught the girls to read and write and provided them with instructions in hygiene, morality, and comportment.

In the mandate states, members of women's organizations had a dual challenge. On the one hand, their efforts to promote women's education and health care filled gaps that were left by the frequent inattention of the mandate governments to women's issues. Women's efforts in the public realm clashed with British and French governing strategies, however, which often favored the cultivation of local men's loyalties at the expense of women's aspirations. British and French colonial officials brought their own notions about the "proper" position of women in the mandate states over which they governed. As European ideas about women's education, marital rights, and inclusion in the political realm mingled with local customs and traditions and became law, women had to contend both with local patriarchies and with new state laws designed and implemented by their foreign occupiers. Those laws placed women where European men thought they should be: under men's jurisdiction.

In Syria and Lebanon, the gender anxieties that had been the byproduct of WWI were heightened upon the imposition of French Mandate rule. Henri Gouraud (1867–1946), French High Commissioner in Syria and Lebanon, governed through alliances with local patriarchs: heads of religious sects, heads of tribes, rural landowners, and urban notables. Those men served as intermediaries between the French and the locals over whom they held jurisdiction.[33] Under such a patronage system, the French worked to fulfill their League of Nations mandate to heal the region through the implementation of public health and education programs. French advisors oversaw the efforts of thousands of Syrian and Lebanese civil servants, whose job was to lay the foundations of new sates. The men who honored their new French "fathers" received the benefits of land and privilege.

As the French delegated state programs for women to women's philanthropic organizations, women found ample opportunity to serve. The mandate governments saw women's health as secondary to the state's mission and provided few resources for women. Consequently, the French subsidized and relied upon women's philanthropic societies to take care of women's needs and those of their children. The Red Crescent Society had served needy women and children in Beirut and opened mothers' societies for women with infants in Damascus, Aleppo, Alexandretta, and Latakia beginning in 1919. The Red Crescent subsequently built a network of orphanages, schools, clinics, and nurses' training programs in both Lebanon and Syria. In Damascus, women established the Drop of Milk Campaign in 1922 to provide sterilized milk to impoverished children and medical advice and care to impoverished women.³⁴ After the Syrian uprising, women mobilized once again, this time to offer training programs to women. Adila Bayhum al-Jazairi organized crafts workshops during the revolt in order to ensure that women had the vocational training necessary to earn a living. In 1927, she joined ranks with Nazik Abid to establish the Syrian Women's Awakening Society, which provided education and medical attention to displaced women and children.³⁵

Lebanon was an active center of women's associational activity in the years following the war: between 1920 and 1939, 36 groups registered their organizations with the state. These groups emphasized the dual goals of providing education and health care to Lebanese women. In Beirut, Linda Sursuq led the Orthodox Society of Compassion for Ladies which supported education for poor girls. Muslim members of the Arab Girls' Awakening Society opened the Islamic Orphanage in 1922.³⁶

In Iraq, women's participation in uprisings against the British led to a great flurry of women's organizational activities. Elite women founded the first women's association, the Women's Awakening Club (WAC) in Baghdad in 1923.³⁷ The club's 60 members included the wives of prominent Iraqi politicians, who, in addition to organizing meetings and symposiums for their membership, dedicated themselves also to educating poor and orphaned women.³⁸ The club had as its goal the preparation of women to help themselves, to assist their families, and to serve the Iraqi nation.

Under the British Mandate, Iraqi women had to negotiate between the traditional values of their society and Mandate government's translation of those values into a code of law.³⁹ By the early 1930s, the British would rule Iraq through practices that embodied both direct and indirect rule. But prior to the 1930s, the British had ruled Iraq directly. To do so, they used methods gleaned during the WWI era, during which time they gained the loyalty of Iraq's many tribal chiefs through the implementation of the Tribal Criminal and Civil Disputes Regulation (TCCDR), laws that would remain in place in Iraq through 1958. Through the TCCDR, conservative tribal customs—including those pertaining to women—were sanctioned and legalized by the state. Such customs included tribes handing over women to other tribes to settle blood disputes, excluding women from inheritance, and honor killings. While the British described tribal customs pertaining to women to be "harsh" and "uncompromising," they nonetheless implemented those customs as national law for fear of losing the loyalty of Iraq's tribes.

Similarly, in order to gain the allegiance of Iraq's religious elites, the British left personal status laws in the hands of religious leaders. The Iraqi Constitution of 1925 stated that only religious courts, in accordance with each sect, could settle matters such as marriage, divorce, and child custody. Through the end of the monarchy in 1958, Iraqis tried unsuccessfully to amend British policy. Consequently, challenges to limits on education, to polygamy, unfavorable custody laws for women, equal access to divorce, and the raising of Iraq's minimum marriage laws were not reformed.

As Iraq's constitution enshrined tribal and religious views women who advocated for women's education, for example, were met with a tremendous amount of hostility. In the 1930s, families who sent their children to school in Baghdad, for example, received death threats. Girls were sometimes pelted with stones as they walked to and from school.

In 1921, Palestinian women organized their first women's group. The Palestinian Women's Association (PWA) was a philanthropic association focused on literacy movements, hygiene campaigns, and employment of the poor. The British government in Palestine was notoriously parsimonious when it came to education and social services for women, even while claiming that Palestinians needed the British Civilizing Mission. Women therefore stepped in to fill those voids.[40]

The PWA was also nationalist in orientation and attended to the mobilization of women to increase Palestinian national consciousness. As such, the association was designed not only to help Palestinian women, but also to help Palestinian men secure an independent nation. In 1921, women also established the Society of the Arab Women's Union of Nablus, both to attend to charity and to benefit all of Palestine. Palestinian women's organizations proliferated in the 1920s, as women opened welfare centers, Girl Scout troops, student groups, and women's labor unions.

In the 1920s, Jewish immigrants to Palestine similarly engaged in beneficence. European Jewish women saw non-European Jews in Palestine (which is to say native-born Jewish women or Jewish immigrant women from the Middle East) as less civilized than they were and therefore suitable targets for civilizing philanthropic activities. Some groups of Jewish women also extended their philanthropy to Palestinian women, teaching them hygiene and prenatal care. In providing such services, female Zionists hoped—as did male Zionists—to make Jewish settlement more bearable to Palestinians. The Women's International Zionist Organization, which was funded by Jewish women in Europe, sponsored the Domestic Science School in Nachlat Yitzchak, which taught Jewish and Arab women modern hygiene, nutrition, and housekeeping. An American woman, Dr. Olga Pickman Fainberg, left her home in Chicago to live in Jericho among Palestinians. She tended to the sick, ran a sanitarium, and organized a nursing school.[41]

Across the region, teaching was an important arena in which women demonstrated their nationalist aspirations. In the mandate states, European officials and Christian missionaries argued that local women needed to be civilized. Many of those men carried stereotypes about harem with them to the Middle East and therefore attested that education was crucial to transforming local women into "useful citizens." Mandate governments devoted very little of their budgets to women's education, however. What they did allocate to girls' schools was limited in courses in domestic sciences and child-rearing, with the goal of civilizing Arab women by transforming them into European women. Women's organizations across the region stepped in to provide women with a more ample education.

State Building and Feminist Campaigns

Women who participated in emerging nationalist movements expected inclusion in the political realm when the struggle was over. Disappointment over their exclusion from that realm did not lessen their commitment to nationalism, however. Rather, when women throughout the region were not enfranchised postindependence, they channeled their energies once again into serving their nations through social activism. As the result of their exclusion from the political order, members of feminist or women's movements continued to serve their nations through increasingly large and sophisticated philanthropic networks. Those networks allowed women to confront their states—the very states they hoped to build—for suffrage and full inclusion in the public realm.

In Egypt, in March 1923, women formally separated themselves from the Wafd and organized an independent feminist organization called the Egyptian Feminist Union (EFU). Saad Zaghloul was made semi-independent Egypt's first Prime Minister in 1923. When Egypt's first constitution was written, women were not given the right to vote or to participate in politics. After their long struggles in demonstrations and in organizing for the Wafd, the members of the WFCC were rightfully dismayed. Hoda Shaarawi wrote: "The Egyptian woman, from the moment of the first spark of the Revolution of 1919, entered public life from the most honorable door, the door of the national struggle for freedom and independence." Shaarawi, Nabawiyya Musa, and their counterpart Ceza Nabarawi (1897–1985) therefore organized and mobilized other elite women to promote and provide women's education and healthcare to campaign for suffrage and to fight for women's legal equality.

In 1924, the EFU opened a center in a working-class neighborhood and called it the House of Cooperative Reform. From the center, the EFU ran a dispensary for poor mothers and children and a domestic arts and crafts workshop. A second center, built in 1932 and called the House of the Woman, had space for a larger school and a meeting room in which the EFU held conferences. Through fundraising, the EFU opened hospitals, day care facilities for working women and vocational educational centers. The EFU used its own periodicals to discuss the importance of women to the family structure and of the family to the health and strength of the nation.[42] The EFU also used its periodicals to address British regulation of prostitution, which had been in place since the 1882 occupation. EFU members wondered how the British, whose occupation of Egypt claimed to champion women, could also institutionalize prostitution.[43]

The EFU also rallied for a reform of personal status codes, especially laws regarding polygamy, divorce, and child custody rights. Over the course of the 1920s, the EFU waged successful campaigns to get the minimum age of marriage age raised for both females and males (16 for women and 18 for men) and to change custody laws to favor mothers. They began campaigns that would occupy them for decades: to limit polygamy and to regulate divorce.

Finally, the EFU began a suffrage campaign. Feminists both in and outside of the EFU continued to press the Egyptian state for suffrage through 1956 when their demands were finally met (see Chapter 9). EFU members maintained their ties with the International Alliance of Women and attended most of the organization's international congresses in favor of suffrage.[44]

By the late 1920s, Syrian and Lebanese women emphatically emphasized their roles as female citizens and addressed their right to participate in the public order.

The Women's Union in Syria and Lebanon became the vanguard of a self-conscious women's politics.[45] The group supported Arab nationalism and cross-sectarianism, coordinated the activities of its member groups, and organized a public conference on women in Beirut in 1928. The group promoted women's issues through petitions to government offices and through continued demonstrations. The group additionally helped to sponsor the first of several Eastern Women's conferences in order to help women forge transnational ties.

Women in Lebanon and Syria had begun demanding suffrage beginning in the immediate postwar era. In April 1920, just prior to the French occupation, the Syrian Congress had discussed a proposal for women's suffrage. Some local men were sympathetic to the demands of the Syrian women who had been campaigning for suffrage and for full inclusion in politics: Ibrahim al-Khatib, a delegate to Congress, suggested that women of a certain age who held a secondary school certificate should be allowed to vote. Faysal and his supporters agreed. Detractors—typically Faysal's opponents—saw suffrage as a threat to Syria's gender hierarchy. They suggested that enfranchised women would mix with men; they also suggested that because women's suffrage was a Western practice, implementing it in Syria and Lebanon was tantamount to another round of European rape of Arab women. Many Syrian legislators were eager for the West to know that women's rights had been on their agenda, but women were subsequently denied the right to vote.

When the suffrage debate was taken up by the Lebanese Representative Council in 1923, some men complained that women were taking men's work and threatening to take men's place in the public realm. Others suggested that as men's companions, women should share in all aspects of life. Members of the Council agreed to work for an increase in women's education and to support women's associations and publications and to take up the suffrage question again in 1924. When it came for the Council to vote, however, women were once again denied the right.

The Lebanese and Syrian men who resisted women's appeals suffered from the humiliation of having foreigners on their soil. Indeed, the arrival of Gouraud to the region in 1920 had aggravated an already simmering crisis of paternity: the local men who had suffered on the battlefield and who could not protect their wives and daughters while they were away at war were now further insulted by the imposition of mandate rule. Additionally, locals had chosen Faysal to be the father of the Syria. Through the imposition of the mandate system however, France was to be the "mother" to the nascent states of Syria and Lebanon, and Gouraud was the father who would rule over his new Lebanese and Syrian "children" with a stern hand. Control of women's behavior was often the result of men's struggle to reassert themselves over this new French "father."

Debates about suffrage were often waged in religious language in the French mandates. As the British had done in Iraq, the French left the definition of personal status laws to the patriarchs of both the Muslim and Christian communities in Syria and Lebanon. Debates about suffrage, therefore, often reflected religious rather than political concerns. Men frequently depicted women who wanted to vote as betraying their religion and as betraying their religiously defined positions as mothers and wives. As in Iraq, some local nationalists viewed the relegation of personal status to the religious elite to be an obstacle to state building.

Syrian women protested against their exclusion from politics and against men's debates about their behavior by showing their faces. Syrian women had used unveiling as protest beginning in 1919: elite women lifted their veils in Damascus in front of the American King-Crane Commission, who were in the region to gauge local responses to the postwar settlements. After fighting in the battle of Khan Maysalun in 1920, Nazik Abid had herself photographed unveiled in her military uniform in protest of the Mandate. In 1922 in demonstrations against the French arrest of Arab nationalists and in a 1925 demonstration against a visit of Lord Balfour to the region, women also lifted their veils. While women in Syria and Lebanon did not link their political rights with their right to unveil, they did use the uncovering of their faces as a means of protest.

As the result of men's resistance to women's campaigns for unveiling and suffrage, Lebanese and Syrian women shifted tactics. Instead of continuing to fight for suffrage, women in Syria and Lebanon adopted motherhood as a nationalist political strategy in the late 1920s. In 1928, 27 women's groups from Lebanon and Syria participated in a women's conference in Beirut. Participants in the conference advocated for women's right to participate in civic life and for the future of independent Arab nations. They would start by raising a generation of sons who could liberate their countries from the French.

On the one hand, the adoption of patriotic motherhood by Syrian and Lebanese women was a retreat from earlier demands for suffrage and the right to unveil. At the same time, advocating for motherhood was a self-conscious strategy to sidestep men's resistance to women's participation in public. Members of the Women's Union hoped that by sidestepping politics they could enter politics once again. The women who organized the Eastern Women's Conferences in Damascus (1930) and Tehran (1932) therefore highlighted the need for social reforms for women who, they argued, would best support the nationalist cause if they were better educated, if they knew their rights and responsibilities in marriage, and if their important economic contributions through home industry were protected by the state.

What appeared to be a rejection of women's earlier political agendas in actuality grew the base of the women's movement. Motherhood united women and gave the women's movement a mass base, moving the movement away from polarizing issues like suffrage and veiling and therefore increasing the number of participants. The result was a kind of agreement with men in the nationalist movement that independence would precede women's rights. Both women and men kept their side of the bargain: ca. 1930, 1,000 women held membership in over 40 women's groups, the focus of which was not political, and men waited until the 1940s to take up seriously the subject of women's full inclusion in politics.

Palestinian women's political activism increased from the late 1920s in response to escalating tensions between Jews and Palestinians.[46] The 1929 riots over access to the Western Wall (Wailing Wall) of the Haram al-Sharif (the compound that encloses the Dome of the Rock and al-Aqsa Mosque) led to the deaths of 116 Arabs and 113 Jews and to the arrest of over 1,000 Palestinians and to the execution by the British of several of those who had been arrested. The Palestinian community responded strongly to the executions. A desire to "help the men" led to the establishment of the Arab Women's Association (AWA) in 1929. One of the AWA's founders Matiel Mughannam wrote: "There are times when you can't do anything except to go out and do something. We had to do something to help the men."[47]

And yet, helping the men was only part of the mission of the women who joined the AWA. Advancing Palestinian women's quest for increased access to education and to inclusion in the civic order certainly motivated women to join. Women were also motivated by the paucity of state services being provided for the Palestinians by the mandate government. As in the early 1920s, women stepped in as service providers to fill in the gaps in state assistance.

The first accomplishment of the AWA was the organization and launching of the First Arab Women's Congress in 1929. As the result of the "substantial organizational acumen" of a core of women (many of whom were married to prominent members of the nationalist movement) from notable Jerusalem families, the Congress brought together approximately 200 middle-class and elite women from throughout Palestine. "It was a bold step to take in view of the traditional restrictions which, until then, prevented the Arab woman in Palestine from taking part in any movement which might expose her to the public eye."[48] The meeting had several agendas. One was the consolidation and focus of women's efforts and activities. The other was political: attendees elected an Arab Women's Executive (AWE) to deliver its objections to mandate policies to High Commissioner John Chancellor, head of the mandate government.

The women of diverse classes and religions who joined the AWA did so for a number of reasons. Some were motivated by the same spirit of beneficence that defined women's participation in charitable associations in the early 1920s. For those women, serving the poor took the greatest priority. For others, the AWA was a respectable organization through which to exert pressure on Great Britain and through which to mobilize demonstrations against the mandate and against Jewish immigration.

But women in the AWA understood that women's agendas were secondary to establishing an independent Palestine. When the struggle for Palestinian nationhood intensified over the course of the 1930s, women committed their efforts to the national struggle and thereby left women's issues for a later day. Because Palestinian women understood their goals within the context of a sought-after nation-state, they accepted—as did women in Syria and Lebanon—that securing the nation took priority over feminist agendas. In the words of a former president of a women's association in the Palestinian city of Tulkarem: "How could women demand rights when the men did not have any?"[49]

States and Gendered Anxieties

As Palestinian men struggled against the British, they also struggled with one another over women's correct comportment and behavior during a time of war. The Palestinian press was united in its praising women's contributions to the national cause. But rebels were not so unified, and as factions grew between men over strategies for securing and then governing Palestine, women quickly became symbolic of those factions. For some men, Western clothing of any sort was linked to imperialism and women who donned it were deemed guilty by association. For others, veiling was an "Arab" garb and Christian women, like Muslim women, demonstrated their commitment to the struggle for Palestine by wearing it. In either case, controlling or attempting to control women's behavior and morality marked men's visions of the nation's future.

In pointing to women's behavior as reflecting that of the nation, however, Palestinian men were influenced by more than factionalism. Indeed, as Chapter 5 illustrates, the "Woman Question" around which men rallied in the pre-WWI era defined women's contribution to sought-after nation-states as wives and mothers. While national struggles seemed to require the contributions of male and females alike, women's roles in those struggles—as demonstrators, weapons' smugglers, and insurgents—seemed to threaten women's real domain in national life: the home.

In Egypt, during the 1919 revolution, the Egyptian press had been full of men's praise for women's contributions, sacrifices, and heroism. The press had also been full of photographs of women participating in demonstrations, carrying flags, and occupying public space. In this now iconic photograph of the uprisings, from April 1919, a group of women (see Figure 7.6) in an open carriage appear in a crowd of men. One woman raises the Egyptian flag as the crowd cheers her on. The caption to the photograph reads: "An Egyptian lady in her carriage raises her hand to greet the people, and to acclaim the nation and Egypt."[50] A second photo (see Figure 7.7) reveals women parading in celebration of Saad Zaghlul's return from abroad. In that photo "Egyptian ladies and girls parade[ing] for the leader and cheer[ing] him."[51] In each case, women wear cloaks and thin face veils *(yashmaks)*, and in each case, men applaud their contribution to public pageantry.

Figure 7.6 Women protesting in Cairo, 1919. *al-Lata'if al-musawwara* (April 21, 1919) as cited in Baron, *Egypt as a Woman.*

Figure 7.7 Women amidst protesters during Zaghloul return. *al-Lata'if al-musawwara* (April 12, 1921) as cited in Baron, *Egypt as a Woman.*

Such images were accompanied by reminders of the "Woman Question," however. In the following ad (see Figure 7.8), which markets a brand of artificial breast milk called Lactogol, women are dressed up as demonstrators. They wear the same garb as female protestors did and like their real counterparts, these women carry placards. On those posters, however, is not the standard 1919 call for "freedom and total independence" from the British or for an "end [to the] occupation." Rather, this sign reads: "Nationalist mothers: Your most sacred duty is to raise healthy sons for the Nation. So feed them Lactogol."[52]

The essential role of motherhood to the Egyptian nationalist movement was a common theme in revolutionary era advertisements and political cartoons. Mother Egypt (see Figure 7.9), for example, nurtured the aspirant nation's institutions: here, mother Egypt breastfeeds the Egyptian national bank project (Bank Misr) and ensures its success.[53] Nationalists encouraged women to be like mother Egypt, to raise good children, and to instill a love of nationalism in them. Nationalism in the 1919 era was, indeed, presented as a family affair, one in which reformed, educated "new women" served the nation from the home. For Egypt to succeed, it had to have strong mothers at home.[54]

The 1919 Revolution had its "first couple," Saad and Saffia Zaghloul who were lauded as the mother and father of the nation that was partially won from the British as the result of the uprisings. The Zaghlouls' home, which was known as "the house of the nation," was the meeting place for demonstrators, both in 1919 and in subsequent uprisings. Saffia Zaghloul, who was a reformed, educated "new woman" by the standards of the era, was known to keep house in all of the ways that were

New States and Their New Women 125

Figure 7.8 Lactogol advertisement. *al-Lata'if al-musawwara* (August 27, 1919) as cited in Pollard, *Nurturing the Nation* and Russell, *Creating the New Egyptian Woman*, respectively.

Figure 7.9 Mother Egypt Breastfeeding National Bank. *al-Lata'if al-musawwara* (August 20, 1919) as cited in Pollard, *Nurturing the Nation*.

described as "proper" in the Egyptian nationalist press. While the Zaghlouls were childless, the nation's home was nonetheless suitable for raising Egypt's children and it was from that home that Mrs. Zaghloul presided.[55]

Two images of womanhood and its role in public culture therefore sat in seeming contradiction to one another. On the one hand, women helped to secure the nation, and on the other, once the nation had been secured, women's departure from the home threatened the foundation of the semi-independent nation whose existence was attributed to women's contribution.

Anxieties about women in the public realm were evident in Greater Syria as well, both before and after the establishment of the French Mandate. The specter of hungry women marked the Arabs' wartime experience under the Ottomans, during which time households were disrupted as fathers and husbands were sent off to war. The image of women, whose absent husbands and fathers could neither protect them from hunger nor from the dishonor of begging in the streets, shaped a generation of Syrian men who experienced the powerlessness of conscription and famine.

The French ruled Syria and Lebanon through a system in which the French were both mother and father figures. As governing officials in a mandate system designed to infantilize the locals until they could demonstrate readiness for self-rule, the French positioned themselves as father figures, frequently stern and disciplinarian. At the same time, the French ruled through a maternalist, civilizing mission in which the job of the Mandate state was to nurture, reform, and teach the Syrians and Lebanese so that they might ultimately emancipate themselves.

Reasserting the Arab woman's role as mother and as denizen of the household seemed to shore up Arab men's sense of themselves as fathers and heads of household, despite the presence of the French and despite the difficulties Arab men faced in protecting their women during the war years. Many men felt a second assault to their masculinity as women demonstrated their ability to protest and to fight like men, and then claimed rights in a public realm that even men could not claim control over. As the following cartoon suggests, men were not certain where they stood in Mandate era gender hierarchies (see Figure 7.10). In a cartoon called "His Wife is Busy," a meek gentleman pushes two infants in a baby carriage and explains to a more robust man who is clearly chastising him that he is tending to his children because his wife is otherwise preoccupied.[56]

Within such a context, it is not surprising that men sought to reassert a paternal order in which they were heads of the national and the familial households. Defining women's behavior in public, debating the proper way for women to dress and, perhaps most importantly, assigning women the role as housewives and mothers rather than fellow soldiers and parliamentarians allowed men to reassert their authority in a world turned upside down.

As the next chapter demonstrates, men who struggled to reassert their masculinity in the postwar order either kept women out of the public arena or circumscribed women's places within that arena until the business of building independent nations had been completed.

New States and Their New Women 127

Figure 7.10 His wife is busy *al-Dabbur* (June 18, 1928) as cited in Thompson, *Colonial Citizens*.

Notes

1. Kristian Coates Ulrichsen, *The First World War in the Middle East* (London: Hurst and Company, 2014), 2–3.
2. Melanie S. Tanielian, *The Charity of War: Famine, Humanitarian Aid and WWI in the Middle East* (Palo Alto: Stanford University Press, 2018), 4.
3. Elizabeth Thompson, *Colonial Citizens: Republican Rights, Paternal Privilege, and Gender in French Syria and Lebanon* (New York: Columbia University Press, 2000), 26.
4. Thompson, *Colonial Citizens*, 20. Deprivations of the war chronicled in autobiographies and family stories, for example, Almaz Abinader's *Children of the Regime* (Madison: University of WI Press, 1997).
5. Ellen L. Fleischmann, *The Nation and Its 'New' Women: The Palestinian Women's Movement, 1920–1948* (Berkeley: University of California Press, 2003), 107.
6. Ulrichsen, *The First World War in the Middle East*, 114.
7. Thompson, *Colonial Citizens*, 20.
8. Thompson, *Colonial Citizens*, 27.
9. Thompson, *Colonial Citizens*, 35.
10. Reina Lewis, *Rethinking Orientalism: Women, Travel and the Ottoman Harem* (Rutgers, NJ: Rutgers University Press, 2004), 113–114.
11. Fleischmann, *The Nation and Its 'New' Women*, 107

12 Yumna Al-'Id, "Lebanon," in *Arab Women Writers: A Critical Reference Guide, 1873–1999*, Radwa Ashour, Ferial J. Ghazoul, and Hasna Reda-Mekdashi, eds. (Cairo: The American University in Cairo Press, 2008),15; Tanielian, *The Charity of War*, 191.
13 Margot Badran, *Feminists, Islam and Nation: Gender and the Making of Modern Egypt* (Princeton: Princeton University Press, 1994), Chapter 5.
14 Tanielian, *The Charity of War*, 194.
15 Tanielian, *The Charity of War*, 196.
16 Thompson, *Colonial Citizens*, 95.
17 Soraya Antonius, "Fighting on Two Fronts: Conversations with Palestinian Women," *Journal of Palestine Studies* Vol. 8, No. 3 (Spring, 1979), 26.
18 Julie M. Peteet, *Gender in Crisis: Women and the Palestinian Resistance Movement* (New York: Columbia University Press, 1991), 43.
19 Lewis, *Rethinking Orientalism*, 70.
20 Deniz Kandiyoti, "The End of Empire: Islam, Nationalism and Women in Turkey," in *Women, Islam and the State*, Deniz Kandiyoti, ed. (Philadelphia: Temple University Press, 1991), 36–38. Lewis, *Rethinking Orientalism*, 116.
21 Shaarawi cited in Badran, *Feminists, Islam and Nation*, 75.
22 Subhi Hadidi and Iman al-Qadi, "Syria," in *Arab Women Writers: A Critical Reference Guide, 1872–1999*, Radwa Ashour and Hasna Reda-Mekdashi, eds. (Cairo: The American University of Cairo Press, 2008), 61.
23 Thompson, *Colonial Citizens*, 120.
24 Thompson, *Colonial Citizens*, 48.
25 Thompson, *Colonial Citizens*, 98.
26 Noga Efrati, *Women in Iraq: Past Meets Present* (New York: Columbia University Press, 2012), 119.
27 Noga Efrati, "The Other 'Awakening' in Iraq: The Women's Movement in the First Half of the Twentieth Century," *British Journal of Middle Eastern Studies* Vol. 31, No. 2 (November 2004), 164.
28 Efrati, "The Other 'Awakening' in Iraq," 164.
29 Cleveland, *A History of the Modern Middle East*, 6th ed. (Boulder: Westview Press, 2016), 233–234.
30 Peteet, *Gender in Crisis*, 43.
31 Fleischmann, *The Nation and Its 'New' Women*, 108.
32 Badran, *Feminists, Islam and Nation*, 51.
33 The below materials come from Thompson, *Colonial Citizens*.
34 Pauline Vinson and Nawar al-Hassan Golley, "Challenges and Opportunities: The Women's Movement in Syria," *Mapping Arab Women's Movements: A Century of Transformations from Within*, Pernille Arenfelt and Nawar al-Hassan Golley, eds. (Cairo: The American University of Cairo Press, 2012), 66.
35 Thompson, *Colonial Citizens*, 97.
36 Thompson, *Colonial Citizens*, 96.
37 Efrati, "The Other 'Awakening' in Iraq," 159.
38 Efrati, "The Other 'Awakening' in Iraq," 159; Efrati, *Women in Iraq*, 121.
39 The below materials come from Efrati, *Women in Iraq*.
40 The below materials, unless otherwise specified, come from Fleischmann, *The Nation and Its 'New' Women*.
41 Sheila Katz, *Women and Gender in Early Jewish and Palestinian Nationalism* (Gainesville: University of Florida Press, 2009), 117–118.
42 Badran, *Feminists, Islam and Nation*, Chapter 11.
43 Liat Kozma, *Global Women, Colonial Ports: Prostitution in the Interwar Middle East* (New York: SUNY Press, 2017).
44 Badran, *Feminists, Islam and Nation*, Chapter 11.
45 The below materials are taken from Thompson, *Colonial Citizens*.

46 The below materials, unless otherwise noted, are taken from Fleischmann, *The Nation and its 'New' Women*.
47 Matiel Mughannam cited in Fleischmann, *The Nation and Its 'New' Women*, 145.
48 Matiel E. Mogannam, *The Arab Women and the Palestine Problem* (London: Herbert Joseph, 1937), 70 cited in Antonius, "Fighting on Two Fronts," 26.
49 Mogannam, *The Arab Women and the Palestine Problem* 70 cited in Antonius, "Fighting on Two Fronts," 26.
50 *Al-Lata'if al-Musawwara*, 21 April 1919, 4 cited in Beth Baron, *Egypt as a Woman: Nationalism, Gender and Politis* (Berkeley: University of California Press, 2005), 125.
51 *Al-Lata'if al-Musawwara*, 12 April 1921, cited in Baron, *Egypt as a Woman*, 130.
52 *Al-Lata'if al-Musawwara*, 27 August, 1919, cited in Pollard, *Nurturing the Nation*, 192.
53 Al-Lata`if al-Musawwara, 20 August, 1919, cited in Russell, *Creating the New Egyptian Woman*, 96.
54 Pollard, *Nurturing the Nation*, Chapter 6, "Reform on Display."
55 Baron, *Egypt as a Woman*, Chapter 6, "Mother of the Egyptians."
56 "Al-Dabbur," 18 June 1928, p. 6 cited in Thompson, *Colonial Citizens*, Figure 15.

8 Ethnic States and "Their" New Women

Politicians translated debates about the relationship between women and the successes of the nation into state-building platforms in the decades following WWI. Beginning in the 1920s, as new regimes worked to assert power, governing elites transformed the reforms and debates from earlier decades about women's role in society, past and present, into strategies for ordering and governing. At the same time, those politicians used reforms directed at women to define and to cultivate ethnic nationalisms. In some Middle Eastern countries and over the course of many decades, state-sponsored feminisms have remained instrumental to the building of new states and of new ethnicities. In others, women-focused platforms have been used to transform secular states into Islamic ones, as was the case in the Islamic Republic of Iran (see Chapter 13).

This chapter examines the use of women by governing officials to advance state- and ethnicity-building agendas across the region. It evaluates the state feminism practiced by the first president of Turkey, the shahs of Iran, and the heads of Iraq, Syria, and Egypt. It also looks at the foundational years in Israel's history to examine the extent to which women's prescribed behavior served as the basis for the new Jewish state. This chapter illustrates that in the era of state-building that came after WWI, defining and controlling women's role in society have served as useful tools, both for managing populations and for building national identity. This chapter also illustrates the extent to which debates regarding women's proper contributions to the nation have continued through the present, as heads of state define and redefine the agendas of their regimes.

Chapter 9 will look at women's movements as they developed alongside state feminisms. It will illustrate how state feminisms often worked at cross-purposes with women's movements, circumscribing and co-opting their activities and agendas, even as state feminisms empowered the very women whose lives they sought to order and control. In the immediate WWI era, "New Woman" debates became the pillars of the secularization and modernization platforms of Mustafa Kemal (r. 1923–1938; known as Atatürk after 1923) and Reza Shah Pahlavi (r. 1926–1941) as both men steered their newly-created nations away from the traditions and institutions of the dynasties that preceded them. Both men came to power through the military; both men successfully reestablished order on the heels of the chaos and the foreign occupation that accompanied the postwar years. Both men

DOI: 10.4324/9781032658063-8

Ethnic States and "Their" New Women 131

Figure 8.1 Reza Shah Pahlavi and Atatürk. UtCon Collection/Alamy Stock Photo.

harnessed their military successes to wrestle their societies away from the customs and institutions of the Ottoman and Qajar dynasties to build new, secular, ethnic states. In their physical appearance, as well as their state-building activities, both men represented the shift from the old order to a new one (see Figure 8.1).

Mustafa Kemal came to power when, at the conclusion of WWI, the Allies reduced the Ottoman Empire to a rump state: Committee for Union and Progress members fled the country and the Allies controlled Istanbul. A grassroots campaign to regain not the entirety of the empire but simply Anatolia or "Turkey" grew among former army officers and civilians who were successful in creating the new Turkish Republic. Mustafa Kemal gained notoriety during the immediate postwar era not only for his role as a field officer in the resistance movement but also for his growing leadership in the nationalist movement. He was elected as independent Turkey's first president in 1923. As such, Atatürk implemented reforms through a republican form of government in which he held almost total authority.

In Iran, Reza Khan, a colonel in the Cossack Brigade, used the atmosphere of anti-foreign sentiment that permeated Iran after WWI to end Qajar rule, to take increased powers into his hands and by 1926 to establish himself as a new royal. In 1921, Reza Khan led a battalion into the capital and forced the last Qajar Shah to accept his choice of prime minister. Two years later, Reza Khan became prime minister himself. In 1925, he encouraged the Qajar Shah to take a vacation from which he never returned. The Qajar dynasty was deposed and the *majlis* endorsed a new dynasty, named the Pahlavi dynasty. Reza Khan was now Reza Shah Pahlavi, "king of kings."

For both Atatürk and Reza Shah, women and their position in society were symbolic both of the old order and of the new. In Turkey, Kemalism, or the platforms established and promoted by Atatürk and his retinue of reformers, shifted national culture away from Islam toward "the original culture of the Turks before they accepted Islam."[1] Atatürk saw feminism in Turkey as a function of state reform, in which Kemalist reformers worked to promote equality between women and men, an equality that they believed characterized pre-Islamic Turkish society. Atatürk and men such as Ziya Gölkalp (1876–1924), who is considered by many to have been one of the greatest intellectual figures of the early Turkish republic and a visionary figure in the creation of modern Turkish identity, supported what is known as the "Turkish history thesis." This thesis suggests that Turks contributed to civilization long before the establishment of the Ottoman Empire and argues that women were central to pre-Islamic Turkish civilization. Indeed, Gölkalp saw women as the guarantors and protectors of the Turkish past. Atatürk's state feminism was the product of Gölkalp's thesis, and it sat at the heart of Kemalist state-building.[2]

Reza Shah similarly adopted state feminist platforms in order to work against the past and to negotiate the present. Like Atatürk, Reza Shah viewed the Qajar-era women's customs as emblematic of a failed order. He worked to replace those customs with new ones, in which "virtue, civilization, progress, Islam and ancient Iranian custom" were made visible.[3] Reza Shah's platforms for women were designed to be evidence of modern Iran's progress.

On the one hand, such state platforms for women were pragmatic. In both Turkey and Iran, the state inaugurated increased educational opportunities for women, continuing and expanding Ottoman and Qajar modernization platforms. By increasing Turkey's number of primary and secondary schools, for example, Atatürk made education fully compulsory for both sexes by 1924. Over the course of the 1930s, Turkish women gained increased access to higher education, taking degrees in medicine, engineering, and law. The result was the proliferation of female professionals in Turkey by the end of the 1940s. In Iran, similarly, girls were encouraged to attend new state-run primary and secondary schools by 1928. In 1934, a number of teacher training colleges opened and the state encouraged women's enrollment in them. After a 1934 visit to Turkey, where he was impressed by Atatürk's reforms, the shah began further implementation of primary and secondary schools for girls nationwide. In 1935, Reza Shah established Iran's Women's Center (also known as the Women's Society). The Center was established to promote the "physical and spiritual training of women." It promoted unveiling (see below), women's physical fitness, and women's education.[4] Consequently, the University of Tehran opened its doors to women and men in 1935. By the late 1930s, women were visible among the ranks of Iran's burgeoning civil service in which they worked as typists and clerks.[5] They also held an increasing number of jobs as teachers by the end of Reza Shah's reign.[6]

On the other hand, Turkey and Iran's state platforms were symbolic. As both Atatürk and Reza Shah worked to cultivate Turkish and Iranian nationalisms and to marginalize or to lessen the role of Islam in their countries, they waged powerful campaigns against those things that they deemed reminiscent of the Islamic past. Fashion became a means through which both men manufactured secular Turkish and Iranian identity. For Turkish and Iranian men, this focus on clothing meant campaigns and laws against the wearing of the fez, turbans, and other forms of traditional headgear. For women, the state's focus on fashion signaled either the mandated abandonment of various forms of veiling, as was the case in Iran, or by contrast, a lack of allegiance to a new, secular, Turkish order. The content of most of Atatürk's speeches about women was focused on the veil. He emphasized the need for Turkish women to adapt to the necessities of modern life and pointed to his wife Latife Uşakligil (1898–1975) as a model of Turkish modernization; she was unveiled in public appearances and in photographs (posing both alone and with her husband, who favored top hats and fedoras). In emphasizing unveiling, Atatürk claimed that he was reviving ancient Turkish culture.[7] Uşakligil was put on show for the nation and foreign dignitaries. All the wives of high-ranking officials were expected to know ballroom dancing and other Western social graces in order to socialize at state functions. Atatürk's views of women and progress did not necessarily align with contemporary feminists: competing in beauty pageants, beginning in 1929, was for the Turkish leader a sign of the new nation's progress. In any case, women were at the forefront of progress, from what they wore on their heads to their bathing-suit-clad bodies.

Atatürk applied these sartorial reforms to himself as well: he shed the image of military leader in uniforms and donned the Western-style suit and fedora. Even his grooming habits demonstrated a tilt toward the West. Historically, facial hair has been a sign of masculinity in Islamic culture, but Atatürk did not need facial hair to prove his manliness. The size of his mustache declined considerably from before the Young Turk Revolution when it was large, bold, and waxed to a smile-length mustache on the cover of *Time* magazine in 1923 to a later clean-shaven look. As president of the Republic, Atatürk worked to distinguish himself from what he considered to be the effeminate, secluded sultans of the past, clad as they were in "Eastern" clothing.

Unlike Atatürk, Reza Khan eagerly emulated the Qajar shahs because he desired to inherit the Persian monarchy. He continued to wear the military uniform because the Qajars had done so. Military uniforms easily delineate class and rank, and because Reza Khan would fight his entire career to transform himself into Reza Shah and to earn the title King of Kings, he never abandoned his uniform.

Reza Shah issued legal injunctions against veiling in 1936. Unveiling was a key feature of Reza Shah's Women's Awakening project. The state targeted men's clothing as well: in 1928, the shah required men to abandon traditional forms of headgear, to don the Pahlavi cap, and to dress in European attire.[8] By 1935, wearing a hat was compulsory. Just as it had been at the turn of the twentieth century, clothing was now a stand-in for the nature and potential of the nation and of dramatic rupture from the past: neither men nor women were consulted about their preferences.

Other reforms mixed pragmatism with symbolism. As a means of lessening the power and prestige of the religious establishment and to give Turkey a further layer of Westernization, Atatürk replaced the *sharia* with Western civil codes. His 1926 adoption of the Swiss Legal Code for matters pertaining to the family gave women greater access to divorce and to custody of their children, while at the same time cementing the husband as head of household and reducing women's rights with regards to inheritance. Reza Shah similarly introduced the Marriage Law of 1931, requiring marriages to be registered with the state, outlining specific conditions for divorce, and raising the minimum age of marriage to 15 for females and 18 for males.

In both countries, the state encouraged women to be informed wives and mothers and to make domestic activities their primary concern. In Kemalist Turkey, professional women acquired a greater esteem in society than housewives and mothers did. Nonetheless, Kemalism stressed women's biological role as mothers and insisted that women devote themselves to bearing children. Kemalism also insisted that women nurture the new nation. Ideal women, at least in Turkey and Iran's urban areas, were therefore professionals, mothers and—hearkening back to the early twentieth century—members of philanthropic organizations. Women in Kemalist Turkey therefore faced pressure to perform their modern Turkish identity at home, in the workplace, and in civil society.[9] Iranian women faced a similar pressure to bear the various burdens of modern Iranian womanhood: companionate marriage, motherhood, and devotion to professionalism. Women did, in fact, benefit from state reforms in both the early Turkish republic and Reza Shah's Iran. Both nations' top-down reforms, however, were not aimed at representing women's interests. Rather, state reforms were designed to transform the nation along the lines of Atatürk and Reza Shah's visions and at emancipating women without concern for their private lives.[10]

Immediately after the establishment of the State of Israel in 1948, members of the secular Labor Party, whose ideologies largely defined Israel through the 1970s, enshrined women as part of the public sphere. To do so, Israel's first Prime Minister David Ben-Gurion and other state builders drew on the ideals of their generation, on the left-leaning, socialist outlook of the second and third *aliyahs* (1904–1923), or waves of immigration to Palestine. Those men and women, whose presence in the new Yishuv (as Jewish settlements in Palestine were known through 1948) was largely concentrated in agricultural collectives (*moshavim* and *kibbutzim*), cultivated and promoted equality between the sexes. The early Zionist pioneers from central and eastern Europe worked to create the new Yishuv and—in it—a New Jew, one who was physically fit, capable of self-defense, and economically self-sufficient as the result of the hard physical labor of farming. The result was a hypermasculine culture in which women existed "less as individuals than as part of the group which the men dominated."[11]

When Israel was established, women were nonetheless asked to participate in masculine, *sabra* culture (or the culture of the early settlers and their descendants) by serving in the new state's military. The lore of the *sabra* generation, of the men and women who were educated in a culture of pioneer settlers and defenders, presented Israel as an example of a new and model society, in which men and women had participated equally.[12] This equality was canonized in the Israeli

Declaration of Independence (1948), which asserts the "equality of all citizens without discrimination of religion, race or sex."[13] The Defense Service Law of 1949 appears to be the first Israeli government's commitment to equal rights for women and to a vision of the new Yishuv's history. At the same time, the law appears to acknowledge women as individual contributors to the building of a new society and not simply as indistinct members of a crowd.

But the Defense Service Law exempted married women, pregnant women, and women with children from service in Israel's defense, assuming that wife and soldier are contradictory positions and elevating motherhood to women's duty to the nation.[14] In initial debates over women's place in the military, Ben-Gurion argued that the state "should not obstruct a woman from becoming a mother" and that "motherhood is the unique destiny of women." One Labor Party member asserted that if the Jewish state were to remain Jewish, Jewish women had to make babies: "He who worries about Jewish demography should worry about the family. We cannot afford to draft married women because it will decrease the birth rate."[15] Some women from the Revisionist Zionist opposition to Ben-Gurion felt it was their duty *as mothers* to fight for the nation. Tzila Amidror Heller, for example, whose autobiography covers the years surrounding Israel's emergence as an independent state, pushed aside her domestic duties to organize and fundraise for the Yishuv's underground militia, the Irgun (see Figure 8.2).[16]

In pointing to the Jewish family and to demographics, male members of the Labor Party drew on a second facet of new Yishuv history: that of the promotion and elevation of motherhood by emerging Jewish proto-state institutions such as the Histadrut, the Yishuv's national federation of labor. From the 1920s through to the time at which the Defense Service Law was passed, Histadrut participated in the circulation of manuals through which elite, educated Jewish women, largely of European origins, learned their duty as "mothers of the nation."[17] *Sabra* culture promoted the myth of gender equality; in fact, however, women of the new Yishuv were "subjected to an unremitting program of education" and indoctrination about their obligation to produce and nurture children.[18] The strong bodies of the new Jewish males were attributed to the breast milk of the Ashkenazi (European) Jewish women who followed these manuals correctly. Manuals distinguished Jewish women of European background—who allegedly took child-rearing literature most seriously—from Palestinian Arab women and Jews from Arab countries and Iran who were said, in these same manuals, to abandon their children or leave them at home tied to their beds while they labored. Ashkenazi women were encouraged to be teachers and to instruct immigrants from the Arab world and Iran in how to be proper mothers.[19] Israel's military could not then promote the potential sacrifice of women who sacrificed themselves at home to the production and nurturing of the next generation of Israelis.

By including non-married women in the Defense Service Law, the new Israeli state perpetuated a beloved myth about women's equality while at the same time enshrining motherhood as women's national duty. The state's simultaneous promotion of European, scientific motherhood, based on cleanliness and order, worked to distinguish "Jewish Israeli" as an ethnicity apart from the new state's Arab neighbors.

136 *Ethnic States and "Their" New Women*

Figure 8.2 Girls training for the Irgun, 1948. Everett Collection Inc/Alamy Stock Photo.

Women were similarly useful vehicles for advancing the cause of secular Arabism and pan-Arabism in places like Syria, Egypt, and Iraq. In the late 1940s, the coauthors of Baathist ideology Michel Aflaq (1910–1989) and Salah al-Din al-Bitar (1912–1980) dedicated the Baath to eradicating backward thinking about women, suggesting that to do so would liberate Arabs from the feudalism and tribalism from which the party sought to distance its followers. Baathists focused on the reform of women in Arab societies, both to promote Arabism as a progressive platform and to criticize old regimes such as the Hashemite dynasty in Iraq. Baathists argued that the efforts of the previous governments at educational and legal reforms for women had produced little in the way of progress in the years following independence from the British and French mandate states.[20] Aflaq and al-Bitar embodied Baathism to such an extent that even after their control over the party had been usurped by others, their physical presence was both threatening to and a defining force for men like Saddam Hussein and Hafez al-Assad who both used Baathist ideology to rule Iraq and Syria.

Baathist platforms included the development of practical programs designed to allow women to participate in public life, work toward their own liberation and, along with it, the liberation of Arab society.[21] The Baath Party constitution of 1951 declared that the family was at the center of the Arab social order and that women were at the heart of the family. Furthermore, the constitution asserted that Arab nationalism considered women and men to be equals. Finally, the document suggested that the Arab nationalist movement championed the elevation of the cultural and social status of women.[22]

In 1950s Egypt, pan-Arabist Gamal Abdul Nasser (r. 1956–1970) articulated his own vision of "the New Woman." Like the Baathists, Nasser used women-focused platforms to distance his socialist agendas from the governing strategies of an earlier generation of elite politicians. He also used the "Woman Question" as a means of wrestling "Arab" from those Egyptians who had begun in the 1930s to attach Arab identity to the Islamic past rather than to secular agendas. Nasser's vision of society required a double duty of women: they were to serve the nation through their roles as wives and mothers while at the same time remaining highly visible as workers and symbols of the state's industrial progress.[23] His family planning program was designed as much to tackle Egypt's burgeoning population as it was to promote small families as symbols of modernity and industrialization. As Chapter 9 illustrates, Nasser's reforms wrestled much control from women's charitable organizations and from the women's movement. When pan-Arabist ideology was transformed into governing platforms in places like Iraq, Syria, and Egypt, the result was state-mandated agendas for women. Arab socialist forms of feminism became national causes. The Egyptian Constitution of 1956 and the National Charter of 1962 formally recognized women as citizens, and Nasser used reforms directed at women as evidence of his commitment to achieving freedom, unity, and socialism in Egypt (and during the Egypt-Syrian Union of 1958–1961). The Nasser regime gave women the right to vote and to run for political office in 1956, and extended education and health care services to an increasingly large number of Egyptians. Egypt had its first female parliamentarian, Rawya Attiya (1926–1997), in 1957. Similarly, the regime granted women the right and the duty to work and passed laws protecting female workers by guaranteeing them maternity leave. Nasser's 1964 laws regarding secured employment for university graduates also increased the number of women in the workforce.

Suffrage and secured employment did not necessarily translate into women's freedom to define themselves outside of Nasser's vision of Arab socialism. The same year that Nasser granted women the right to vote, for example, he forced Egypt's very active women's movement to limit itself strictly to social issues, effectively placing the state in the position of shaping women's movements. At the same time, Nasser resisted the reform of Egypt's personal status laws, furthering women's inequality within the conjugal family unit (see Chapters 10 and 11).[24]

Nasser's concern for women was born of the Suez Crisis. The invasion by Britain, France, and Israel catapulted Nasser to fame not for winning the war but rather for standing up to imperialist aggression. In the period that followed the crisis, Nasser expelled a goodly number of foreign communities from Egypt and nationalized a large number of Egyptian industries. He therefore needed skilled and unskilled workers to contribute to Egypt's labor force. Thus, he turned to women as a solution to his labor shortage.

The Suez Crisis transformed Nasser into a hero in the decolonizing world. To promote that image, Nasser wanted to distance himself from the elite politicians of the past, the tarboosh-wearing (fez-wearing), French-speaking lawyers with deep pockets who were deemed effeminate in comparison to the masculine, uniformed, English-speaking officers of the new generation. Nasser combined his charisma, good looks, and charm with his stance against corruption to produce an image of an ideal, new Arab leader. His photograph hung in the homes of all Egyptians through to his death in 1970, and it covered the walls of Arab cities.[25] In the photographs that flooded the Arab world, Nasser was portrayed as a leader in uniform, sometimes as a brother to fellow Arab leaders, sometimes as their father. Nasser posed with farmers and students as well as workers and children to show his paternal relationship to his fellow Arabs (see Figure 8.3). His image also appeared in paintings and statues that can still be seen throughout the Arab world. When Nasser became the president of the United Arab Republic (1958–1961), he became not only Syria's ruler, but established a model for the Arab cult of personality that would define the region for years to come.[26]

In Iraq, the brief rule of Abd al-Karim Qasim (r. 1958–1963), who, along with a group of Free Officers, brought the military to power and who worked to overturn the platforms of the monarchy, witnessed a view of secular Arabism that was similar to Nasser's (despite the fact that Qasim worked diligently to distance himself from and distinguish himself from Nasser). Qasim promoted women's education. One of Iraq's most famous female artists, Suad al-Attar, for example, remembers state education in the Qasim era as encouraging and supporting. "My high school gave me two rooms to show my work at an exhibition. What school would do that nowadays?"[27] Qasim took women's demands for increased legal equality seriously, implementing a progressive personal status code in 1959. The new code granted women equal inheritance rights, restricted polygamy and unilateral divorce, and emphasized women's rights to set their *mahr* or bride price. The new code also made women's consent to marriage mandatory.[28]

As much as Qasim worked to distinguish himself from Nasser, he emulated the Egyptian president by having his photograph taken in uniform. This photograph, like Nasser's, was hung ubiquitously throughout Iraq.[29]

As the Baath consolidated its control of Iraq after 1963, first under `Abd al-Salam `Arif and then from 1968 under Ahmed Hassan al-Bakr, the state increasingly granted women full citizenship rights and promised them full political participation as members of the party. Iraqi Baathist officials considered marriage to be a national duty, and the new state therefore encouraged and facilitated marriage through continued education and health care reforms for women. In the economic realm, the state pursued attitudes and strategies comparable to Nasser's, promoting women's work outside the home and equipping women to work effectively. A 1970 labor code made men and women equal at work. As the government was the single largest employer in the country, it was in a position to apply the code and to ensure equality in pay, training, pensions, and benefits.[30] As in Nasser's Egypt,

Figure 8.3 Gamal Abdul Nasser. mosamem/Alamy Stock Photo.

the unveiled woman working outside the home became symbolic of the state's progress and of its modernity.

The Baath's commitment to women's education quickly bore fruit. By 1976, women made up roughly 39% of the educational field and 31% of the medical field. Twenty five percent of laboratory technicians were female as were 15% of accountants, 11% of factory workers, 4% of engineers, and 3% of holders of high government posts.[31] The 1973 oil boom prompted the state to continue pumping resources into women's education and vocational training and to elevating the female worker to the same symbolic status she enjoyed in Nasser's Egypt.[32] For many women, the first decade of the Baath Party rule was a golden age—economic reform and expansion, women-friendly laws, and a flourishing middle class.[33] Iraqis of that era pointed to women and their accomplishments as symbolic of the ideologies that shaped Iraq after its independence from the British: Iraqi nationalism, pan-Arabism, and democratic political pluralism. Men encouraged women to participate in an open political arena as philanthropists, political activists, and demonstrators.

While Iraq's Baathist state continued to advance women's education and their participation in the labor force, it also co-opted many women's associations, including a massive organization called the Iraqi Women's League into a Baath Party apparatus for women, called the General Federation of Iraqi Women. Through the General Federation, party officials supervised women's activities and behavior.[34] Iraqi women in the General Federation took on illiteracy campaigns, volunteer activities, and vocational and industrial training, each designed to advance women's skills and opportunities. The state's issuance of Law 39 in 1972, signaled however that the most important function of the General Federation of Women was to mobilize Iraqi women for Iraq's various proclaimed struggles (e.g., against American imperialism, the state of Israel, and the perceived backwardness of Iraqi society), effectively subordinating women's individual interests in favor of national agendas.[35]

While Iraqi women resented an increasing state role in their private and public lives, their dissent tended to be buffered over the 1970s by a flourishing, oil-driven economy from which many benefited—including women.[36] After taking power, Saddam Hussein (r. 1979–2003), who had been the vice chairman of the Baath Party and vice president of Iraq from 1968, claimed that women were half of society. Accordingly, he encouraged women's education, implementing programs to work against women's illiteracy. He also encouraged women's participation in an economy that was increasingly buoyed by oil. As part of Saddam Hussein's "New Iraqi Woman" discourse, women's salaries went up and state assistance for working mothers increased. In 1971, Saddam Hussein gave a speech, in which he said: "An enlightened mother, who is educated and liberated, can give the country a generation of conscious and committed fighters."[37] Iraqi men were fined if they failed to allow women to participate in education and labor. Iraq in the 1970s was thus a decade of contradictions between a state that both repressed women and supported their advancements.[38] One woman recalled: "I was not a Baathist, and I hated the regime. But at that time there was something constructive happening in the country. The education system improved tremendously. We got excellent health care …. You can't have a perfect situation."[39]

In image, Saddam was a man of many seasons. He began his career as a hit man for the Baath Party (see Figure 8.4). Essentially, he was a thug. Iraq had witnessed many military coups; hence, in 1976, Saddam gave himself the position of military general in order to create the image of a military strongman. After Nasser's death, other leaders in the region, such as Libya's Muammar al-Qadhafy and Anwar Sadat of Egypt, had all competed to be the great, pan-Arab leader in uniform. Saddam Hussein participated in that competition for Nasser's mantle. While he also feared being overthrown, his struggle to assert himself as the region's most powerful military figure mediated against his anxiety about being ousted. Saddam Hussein repeated what nineteenth-century rulers had previously done, which is to erect statues of himself across Iraq, sometimes as a military figure.

Like Nasser and Qasim, or perhaps surpassing them, Saddam Hussein had numerous photographs of himself made and hung throughout Iraq. In those images, he was variously portrayed as a father to the nation (an armed father; his gun was always present, even when he was holding and kissing a child). State-supported media, Friday sermons, and textbooks supported the image of Saddam the father. While Saddam frequently sported military attire, he was also a consumer of Western clothing, shoes, and hats.[40] For his 65th birthday, for example, he commissioned the

Ethnic States and "Their" New Women 141

Figure 8.4 A young Saddam Hussein. Album/Alamy Stock Photo.

statue that would later capture the world's attention as American soldiers invaded Iraq and topped Saddam's statue in Firdos Square. (Currently, a statue of a family has replaced the old statue; see Figure 8.5.) That statue represented Saddam Hussein in a business suit rather than a military uniform.

To build the Baathist state in Syria, Hafez al-Assad (1971–2000) implemented policies that were not dissimilar to those of neighboring Egypt and Iraq. From previous regimes, Syrian women had received the right to vote (1953). When the Baath took over Syria in 1963, the party began making substantial investments in education, emphasizing equal access to both elementary and higher education for women, a policy that al-Assad continued to support throughout his 40-year presidency. By 1975, when literacy rates for men in the region averaged 51%, half of Syrian women were literate.[41] The compulsory education act of 1981 made education a requirement for boys and girls between six and 12.[42] As women gained greater access to university education, their presence in the workforce increased; by the mid-1990s, more than half of all university students were women and the percentage of women working outside the home had increased from 5.5% in 1970 to 26.1% in 1995.[43] As in Nasser's Egypt, the Syria state has needed and mobilized women for the workforce.

As in Iraq and Egypt, the Baath Party used women as symbols of Arab modernization. Syria's 1973 constitution guaranteed women the state's commitment

Figure 8.5 Firdos Square, Baghdad. Johnny Saunderson/Alamy Stock Photo.

to women's equality. Article 45 of the 1973 Constitution stated, for example, that "the state guarantees women all opportunities and removes all restrictions."[44] As in Iraq and Iran, the Baathist state placed the women's movement under state supervision by creating an umbrella organization called the General Union of Syrian Women in 1967. The state encouraged women to participate in the public sector and guaranteed women employment. What the state did not allow, however, was women's participation as independent political actors, and it therefore corralled women's movements and women's civil society organizations and put them under state control.[45]

Syria has greater religious heterogeneity than Iran, Iraq, and Egypt, and therefore the hand of the state has been less heavy regarding women's affairs as it has been in neighboring countries. While the Syrian Baath improved women's lives in education and labor, it left the personal status laws that govern women's rights in marriage and divorce in the hands of the religious elite. Because those laws vary greatly among religious communities, changes in such customs as age of marriage, *mahr* price, divorce, and custody have not been systematically applied nationwide as they have been in countries like Iraq and Egypt. As will be discussed in the following chapter, Syrian women's movements have encountered sectarian rather than state resistance as they have worked for women's legal equality.[46]

Like Nasser, Hafez al-Assad rose to leadership from humble origins and from a military background. Unlike Nasser, however, he lacked charisma. The ubiquitous projection of his image through the Baath Party mechanisms helped al-Assad to make up for that lack. He portrayed himself variously as a farmer, a worker, and a father. The most common image was that of al-Assad in a military uniform, however, sporting sunglasses to hide his eyes and his emotions[47] (see Figure 8.6). As

Ethnic States and "Their" New Women 143

Figure 8.6 Hafez al-Assad. Japhotos/Alamy Stock Photo.

the Syrian nation's father, al-Assad worked to promote expansion of education to include women and to implement laws that protected women in the workplace. It would be under Bashar al-Assad who assumed rule in 2000 (see below) that Syria would see the implementation of state feminist programs.

In Iran, Mohammed Reza Shah (r. 1941–1979) accelerated his father's pattern of linking women's emancipation with modernizing agendas. Muhammad Reza Shah liked to wear a uniform despite the fact that he was not a military figure like his father had been. Also, unlike his father, Muhammad Reza Shah was clean shaven.

In the early years of Reza Shah's reign, Iran's diverse array of political parties each had branches for women. As will be discussed in Chapter 13, Iranian women's organizations proliferated; they worked with political parties and with the state to advance women's education and integration into the workforce. Women's associational life witnessed a reflourishing in this period.[48] In 1951 and 1952, under the brief administration of Prime Minister Mohammed Mossadegh (1882–1967), women participated in municipal elections. When after a US-sponsored coup and the shah retook power from Mossadegh, he outlawed many political parties and women were subsequently excluded from Iran's political life. When the shah commenced his White Revolution in 1963, however, he extended women's right to political participation, giving Iranian women the right to vote and to run for office. Six women were elected to Iran's *majles* that year; the shah appointed a female minister in 1965. The years between 1963 and 1979 witnessed rapid modernization, funded—as in Iraq—by oil revenue. State revenues were channeled into state-sponsored education at all levels and the number of female workers and professionals increased dramatically. Labor laws, passed in 1974, made the workplace safer for women and allowed breaks for nursing mothers. Abortion was made legal in 1977.

Seemingly-progressive laws were coupled with increased state supervision of women, however. After 1953, the shah began placing women's activities under state control. Between 1956 and 1966, he worked to bring women's activities under the state's supervision through the establishment of the High Council of Women, an umbrella organization to oversee the charitable organizations that would, henceforth, be women's sole domain, and to strengthen the state's control over the legal and educational domains. In 1966, the High Council was replaced by the Women's Organization of Iran (WOI) which, while continuing to contribute to women's education, was also a bureaucratic apparatus (by 1977, it had 400 branches and 70,000 members) through which the state oversaw women's activities.[49] The WOI continued to promote many of the policies that had been central to Iran's earlier state feminism, suggesting that while professional women were crucial to promoting both shahs' vision of modernity, their primary responsibility was to home and family.

As had been the case under his father's tenure, Mohammed Reza Shah's reforms helped mainly the middle and upper classes. As the shah cracked down increasingly on Iranians' political freedoms, even the women whose lives were ostensibly improved by state-driven reforms became hostile opponents of the state. By the end of the 1970s, Iranian women found themselves in a situation similar to Iraq's, in which state advancements for women were coupled with harsh state repressions.

In Egypt in the 1970s and 1980s, Anwar Sadat (r. 1970–1981) made women's issues high profile, championing platforms pertaining to women, both as a means of sustaining the projects undertaken by Nasser and as a means of differentiating his regime from that of his predecessor. The president's wife, Jehan Sadat (1933–), was also an advocate of women's issues, including literacy and economic self-sufficiency (see Figure 8.7). President Sadat promulgated a constitution guaranteeing a balance between women's private and public roles and duties. He set up a quota system whereby women would be guaranteed seats in Egypt's legislature. On June 20, 1979, he issued a presidential decree which added 30 seats for women to parliament and which allocated 10%–20% of seats on government councils nationwide to women. That year, nine out of 390 elected members of parliament were female.[50] It was this version of the constitution that his successor Muhammad Husni Mubarak (1981–2011) inherited in 1980.

Sadat continued Nasser's commitment to education. He departed from Nasser's economic agenda by privatizing national industries and by opening Egypt up to increased foreign trade. (While Sadat plied his image as a boy from a poor peasant village, his new economic policies made it possible for him to import designer suits, both military and otherwise). Sadat also opened Egypt up to development by the West and by the oil-rich nations of the Persian Gulf. The result was a rise in employment opportunities for women, including the new service industries that accompanied increased tourism in Egypt. According to government estimates, the number of working women doubled between 1978 and 1980.[51]

Figure 8.7 Anwar al-Sadat and his wife, Jehan. Dennis Brack/Alamy Stock Photo.

Sadat's administration also produced a host of conditions that would bring women back into the spotlight as objects of heated debate. The flooding of the public realm with professional women increased crowding in urban areas, the country's increasingly high cost of living, and an emerging cultural conservatism combined to bring traditional forms of dress back in vogue. As the *hijab* became increasingly popular, debates about idealized womanhood intensified, both among women and men (see Chapter 12). Sadat's self-promotion as a pious person and his subsequent re-inclusion of Islamists into acceptable public discourse and his increased attempts to appease their determination to include Islam in politics elevated the "Woman Question" to a position reminiscent of the early twentieth century, and seemingly divided Egyptians over the relationship between women's behavior, women's access to the public sphere, and the state of the body politic.

This division continued through Mubarak's regime. His policies both resembled and departed from Sadat's. Mubarak's educational and health policies perpetuated the turn-of-the-twentieth-century idea that women best contributed to society as wives and mothers. The government could not keep the contract that it had made with the people in the 1960s, and by the Mubarak era, it was easier to send women home than it was to provide them with jobs. Mubarak therefore promoted the family ideal that had its roots in the early twentieth century: in 1985, for example, he attempted to repeal Sadat's reforms of the personal status laws as a gesture toward those who saw those reforms as departing from Islamic tradition. It would not be until 2000 that Egyptian women could divorce without their husband's permission.⁵² Mubarak made the protection of the female body high profile after Egypt hosted the 1994 International Conference on Population and Development. When international attention was subsequently drawn to women's issues in Egypt, including the practice of female genital mutilation, Mubarak made gestures toward abolishing the practice and toward improving women's access to education and health care. His continuation of Sadat's neoliberal economic policies intensified the gap between the rich and the poor, increasing illiteracy and unemployment, rendering such gestures insufficient and ineffective. At the same time, however, the Mubarak regime witnessed the reemergence of organized women's movements, ending Nasser and Sadat's practices of limiting and supervising them.⁵³

Mubarak's devotion to Sadat's economic policies allowed him to wear imported clothing and to promote an image of himself as an elite, cosmopolitan businessman. Like Nasser's, this image proliferated: Mubarak's picture was ubiquitous in Egypt's public sphere.

Over the course of the 1970s, in Iran, Mohammed Reza Shah's increased crackdowns on human and political rights created fertile soil for the cultivation of a "Woman Question" debate that was far from the secularizing discourse of the Pahlavi dynasty. Followers of the exiled Ayatollah Ruhallah Khomeini (1902–1989), a powerful voice of opposition to the shah, rekindled debates that were also reminiscent of discussions and debates from the earlier in the century, equating the secular Iranian state's failures, in part, with women's departure from their proper domestic roles. As the revolution progressed, women—secular and otherwise—used the chador as a symbol of protest against the regime. For many men, veiled women were symbolic of the new order that they worked to usher in. For these men, veiled women were once again symbolic of Iran's break from its past: this time, from a secular past. The Islamic Republic that emerged from the Iranian Revolution of 1979 saw resurgence of traditional forms of dress and the ideological linking of women's dress to the potential of the new republic. The new regime reversed several of the Pahlavis' policies toward women, particularly the Family Protection Law of 1967. The new government also closed family planning centers and while continuing to support women's education, applied quotas for female university applicants in a wide range of scientific and professional fields. (In each case, the state later revised its actions in response to women's reactions against state restrictions of their rights.) Women retained the right to vote and to be elected to public office, but the new constitution of 1981 reinstated Islamic law, defined the family as central to the state, and the state to defining the family. Motherhood reemerged as Iranian women's primary responsibility; new dress codes, including required veiling, would protect mothers. The legal age for marriage was set at 13 for girls and 15 for boys. For some, such state-mandated reforms were a dramatic betrayal after a revolution in which women often took active roles. Said one Iranian woman: "Of the Revolutionary triad 'Independence, Freedom, Islamic Republic,' all we got was the Islamic Republic."⁵⁴

The state's use of women to define its agendas in the years following the revolution represented not only a continuation of earlier debates, but also presaged a pattern of defining state agendas through the circumscription of some women's activities and the promotion of others. A lengthy war with Iraq (1980–1988) required women to work in realms the regime had previously defined as "masculine," leading to the relaxation, if not the transformation, of labor and educational policies. By 1989, a population crisis required the state to rethink its stance against family planning. That same year, Iran's parliament passed a limited divorce reform bill, which required court permission for divorce.[55]

After Ayatollah Khomeini's death in 1989, "Woman Question" debates rose to the surface once again. A fairly free press allowed for the circulation of debates and discussions about reform in the Islamic Republic. The state in the post-Khomeini era also encouraged women to reenter the labor force and the educational arena. During the presidency of Mohammed Khatami (r. 1997–2005), for example, 60% of the student body in Iran's universities was female. The 2000 return to power of politicians who preferred Khomeini-era laws and norms once again witnessed crackdowns on women's dress, behavior, and circulation in public spaces. Mahmoud Ahmedinejad (r. 2005–2013) used his tenure as Iran's president to promote reforms reminiscent of the immediate postrevolutionary era. He urged the scrapping of birth control, promoted revision of Iran's already early legal marriage ages for both sexes, endorsed a family protection bill that removed men's need for their wives' consent to polygamy, and twice introduced quotas in Iran's universities, particularly in the medical and scientific fields. During Ahmedinejad's tenure, the moral police (*komitehs*) actively raided citizens' homes, beauty salons, gyms, and cafes to police interactions between unmarried males and females and to regulate women's dress.

The administration of Hassan Rouhani (r. 2013–2021) witnessed the most substantial economic hardships of the on-again, off-again sanctions campaign that Iran has withstood since the 1990s. Despite Rouhani's ties with moderate and reformist politicians, his tenure witnessed a resurgence of scrutiny of women's behavior in the public realm. A prominent human rights lawyer, Nasrin Sotoudeh, was recently given a lengthy prison sentence for defending women who practice "bad *hijab*" (see Chapter 12). The harshest sentence she received linked the defense women's clothing with corruption and prostitution.

Chapter 13 takes up Iran's current administration and the 2022–2023 uprisings that followed the murder of Mahsa Amini. Her death at the hands of state security for a *hijab* violation triggered waves of protests in which the *hijab* laws have rallied Iranians and symbolized their disfavor with an increasingly autocratic regime.

In Saddam Hussein's Iraq, years of wars and sanctions resulted in changes in gender ideology. Operation Desert Storm (1990–1991) and the subsequent UN sanctions accelerated for Iraqis the difficult living conditions that the Iran-Iraq War (1980–1988) had started. By 1997, women's employment levels—the highest in the Middle East at that time—had dropped from 23% to 10%. As sanctions made food and medicine less available, women spent increased amounts of time searching for scarce resources. As the state's infrastructure continued to deteriorate, the public realm became less safe for women. Women therefore attended school in decreasing numbers, and by the late 1990s, illiteracy among Iraqi women had reached 55% (up from 8% in 1985).[56]

Iraqi women also bore the burden of changes in gender ideology that were the byproduct of Saddam Hussein's reactions to war and sanctions: state discourse shifted away from one that favored women's participation in the workforce in favor of more conservative and traditional roles for women.[57] Saddam Hussein's state promoted a discourse in which women were expected to resign from their work, return home, and allow men to take over scarce jobs. The housewife replaced the working woman as Saddam Hussein's state-sponsored icon.[58] Saddam Hussein became more conservative, pointing to Islamic tradition rather than secular values a means of solving Iraq's crises. He became obsessed, for example, with the idea that Iraqi women had given up their morals in favor of prostitution and acted aggressively to repress women's sexuality. Dress codes consequently became stricter. Men in both urban and rural areas began demanding that women wear the *abaya*, equating women's dress with Iraq's many years of crisis.[59] One young woman explained:

> I know why my father is doing this and I am not angry with him … I think that it is not only my father who is doing this, but that it may be all fathers in Iraq. They are doing the same to protect their daughters from the risk of becoming the victims of bad rumors.[60]

In the aftermath of the American invasion and occupation of 2003, the sectarian- and ethnic-based groups who still struggle to gain control of the Iraqi body politic employ women and women's behavior as symbols of their agendas. Women and gender continue to be used by Islamists and others as a means of articulating anti-Baath, anti-Western, and anti-imperialist agendas[61] (see Figure 8.8). Islamist militias, both Sunni and Shia, have used dress codes, gender segregation, and *fatawa* or legal injunctions against women leaving their homes as a means of claiming control of the political arena and of defining Iraq to their liking.[62]

In Bashar al-Assad's Syria (2000–), it has been the president and his wife, Asma al-Akhras al-Assad, who have taken the helm of state feminism. Two years after her Western-educated husband inherited the presidency from his father, Asma al-Assad established the Fund for Integrated Rural Development (FIRDOS), in order to improve the lives of rural women through the granting of microloans. Her Modernizing and Activating Women's Role in Economic Development (MAWRED), established in 2003, has supported the entrepreneurial activities of women across classes. In addition to the efforts of his wife, al-Assad has continued many of the policies of his father: state-supported education, health care, and public sector employment for women. While Bashar al-Assad's continued attention to education has benefitted women in Syria a great deal, the pressures on women to be good housewives and mothers have carried over from the 1990s. Syrian women have had considerable success as government ministers and educators. Through 2011 (see Chapter 10), the Syrian state maintained supportive laws for women in the workplace, including paid maternity leave and access to on-site daycare.[63]

In the early years of his presidency, to make up for his lack of military credentials, Bashar al-Assad portrayed himself as an intellectual and as a concerned

Figure 8.8 Graffiti of George W. Bush and Saddam Hussein, kissing. Blake-Ezra Cole/ Alamy Stock Photo.

physician. Monikers such as the "Young President" and "The Doctor Leader" celebrated the youth of the new president.[64] In his early years, Bashar al-Assad was most frequently depicted in photographs with his father, whose policies he was eager to promote (see Figure 8.9). Bashar al-Assad married Asma ("Emma" to her friends), his girlfriend from his schooldays in London, almost immediately upon coming to power and produced a son, Hafez, named after his grandfather. Once his power was consolidated after 2005, Bashar al-Assad began portraying himself as half of a couple: he and his wife sported stylish clothing and appeared surrounded by children, wrapped in the Syrian flag (see Figure 8.10). Since 2011, the Syrian president has begun appearing in military uniform, as had his father.

In Turkey, Kemalist single-party rule gave way to political pluralism in the years following WWII. Nonetheless, Atatürk's vision of republican motherhood continued to define state agendas for women through to the end of the 1950s.[65] The preservation of Kemalism was, in fact, the goal of the 1960 military coup. From 1961 to 1983, as the multiparty, political life flourished in Turkey (albeit punctuated by two subsequent military interventions), parties of various orientations politicized women by recruiting them in order to expand their base of support. While those parties frequently had women's auxiliaries, they rarely promoted women's issues, addressing pressing problems such as Turkey's population increase, rapid urbanization, and outward migration while overlooking gender equality.[66] Constitutions penned in 1961 and 1982 expanded civil and social liberties but left Kemalist era family codes favoring men as head of household in place. In the area of education,

150 *Ethnic States and "Their" New Women*

Figure 8.9 Hafez and Bashar al-Assad. Goran Šafarek/Alamy Stock Photo.

Figure 8.10 Bashar al-Assad and his wife, Asma. SOPA Images Limited/Alamy Stock Photo.

however, devotion to Kemalist-style commitment to women appeared to have waned: by 1975, only 48% of Turkish women were literate compared to 75% of men.[67]

From the early 1980s, those in Turkey who continued to champion Kemalism have been joined increasingly by other political orientations, including those who support an increased role of Islam in the political realm. The electoral victory of the Motherland Party in the 1983 elections brought a coalition of Islamic revivalists and secularists to power. Since the election of the Justice and Development Party (AKP) in 2002 and under the leadership of Prime Minister (later President) Recep Tayyip Erdoğan (r. 2003–), moderate Islam has joined both secular voices and more radical religious orientations, each possessing agendas for women. In 2001, the Turkish Grand National Assembly (TGNA) amended the 1926 Turkish Civil Code, redressing inequalities in marriage and divorce, and raising the minimum age for marriage to 18 for both sexes. While the amendment resulted, in part, from activism from within Turkey, the TGNA's decision to address gender inequality, particularly the 1926 clause that made men the head of household, came as the result of Turkey's desire to join the EU. The dictates of the EU related to Turkey's ascension, specifically full promotion of liberal democracy and human rights ultimately helped women: TGNA issued the amendment despite the objections of Islamists who came to power the following year.[68]

Secularists and Islamists in Turkey regularly square off over the continued application of Atatürk era bans on wearing headscarves in the public sector, which have since been extended to include universities. Contemporary debates about veiling are reminiscent of those from an earlier era, and women and their dress have once again emerged as potent symbols in discussions about whether or not Turkey belongs in the West or in the Islamic world, about the role of secularism in Turkey, and about the place of Islam in Turkish society. Those debates are not about women's rights.

After a failed coup against them in 2016, President Erdoğan and the AKP have largely consolidated their hold over Turkish politics. Erdoğan has purged his political opponents—the military, the media, academia, and civil society—by arresting their personnel and shuttering some of their institutions. Women are among the tens of thousands who have been swept up and imprisoned—or who are still awaiting trial—for alleged anti-state activities. Voter-approved amendments to Turkey's constitution during the summer of 2018 changed the country's democratic structure by placing powers previously held by parliament in the hands of the president. Emboldened by his new powers, Erdoğan presents himself as Turkey's sole defense against internal and external enemies. As such, he has advanced what has been a trademark of the AKP since it took power in 2002: a family values agenda designed to "correct" what the AKP sees as damages done to the social fabric by Kemalism. Women who choose maternity over employment and who bear more than two children are not only heralded by Erdoğan's government, but financially rewarded by it: The state pays newlywed women to leave their job within a year after they marry.[69] The state's commitment to increasing government-sponsored religious education is designed to create a new generation of religious youth for whom the values of the secular state will no longer apply. Women who chose employment over motherhood are, according to Erdoğan's family politics, incomplete beings.[70]

In each of the above examples, women appear as symbols of backwardness or success, as objects of reform, as emblems of ethnicities and as tokens in state-building projects and revolutionary movements. While political reforms have brought women increasingly into the public realm as educated professionals and enfranchised citizens, women are at the mercy of state agendas that promote or revoke women's access to that realm at the expense of their interests and needs. Studying women in these capacities reveals the crucial role that women have played in the shaping of the modern Middle East—as justifications for European interventions, topics of powerful debates, symbols of nationalist agendas, and targets of state reform—but does not provide a full picture of women's histories or experiences. While examining women within the context of the "Woman Question" in all its forms is a type of women's history, it is a history that stands in partial isolation from that which focuses on women as subjects—both in step with national agendas and working against them. These women will be taken up in the next chapter.

Notes

1 Ayşe Durakbaşa, "Kemalism as Identity Politics in Turkey," in *Deconstructing Images of "The Turkish Woman,"* Zehra F. Arat, ed. (New York: Palgrave, 1999), 139.
2 K.E. Fleming, "Women as Preservers of the Past: Ziya Gökalp and Women's Reform," in *Deconstructing Images of "The Turkish Woman,"* Zehra F. Arat, ed. (New York: Palgrave Press, 1999), 128.
3 Camron Michael Amin, *The Making of the Modern Iranian Woman: Gender, State Policy and Popular Culture, 1865–1945* (Gainesville: The University Press of Florida, 2002), 80.
4 Firoozeh Kashani-Sabet, "Patriotic Womanhood: The Culture of Feminism in Modern Iran, 1900–1941," *British Journal of Middle East Studies* Vol. 32, No. 1 (2005), 41.
5 Amin, *The Making of the Modern Iranian Woman*, 170–171.
6 Amin, *The Making of the Modern Iranian Woman*, 185–186.
7 Durakbaşa, "Kemalism," 148.
8 Amin, *The Making of the Modern Iranian Woman*, 82.
9 Durakbaşa, "Kemalism," 146–147.
10 Jenny B. White, "State Feminism, Modernization and the Turkish Republican Woman," *National Women's Studies Association Journal* Vol. 13, No. 3 (2003), 147.
11 Haim Watzman, "Introduction" to Oz Almog, in *The Sabra: The Creation of the New Jew* (Berkeley: University of California Press, 2000), xv.
12 Almog, *The Sabra*, 2–3; and Nitza Berkowitz, "Motherhood as a National Mission: The Construction of Womanhood in the Legal Discourse in Israel," *Women's Studies International Forum* Vol. 20, No. 5/6 (1997), 609.
13 Cited in Berkowitz, "Motherhood as a National Mission," 608.
14 Berkowitz, "Motherhood as a National Mission," 609.
15 Cited in Berkowitz, "Motherhood as a National Mission," 610.
16 Tzila Amidror Heller, *Behind Prison Walls* (Hoboken: KTAV, 1999).
17 Sachlav Stoler-Liss, "'Mothers Birth the Nation': The Social Construction of Zionist Motherhood in Israeli Parents' Manuals," *Nashim: A Journal of Jewish Women's Studies and Gender Issues* Number 6 (Fall 5764/2003), 104.
18 Stoler-Liss, "Mothers Birth the Nation," 105.

19 Stoler-Liss, "Mothers Birth the Nation," 107.
20 Orit Bashkin, "Representations of Women in the Writings of the Intelligentsia in Hashemite Iraq, 1921–1958," *Journal of Middle East Women's Studies* Vol. 4, No. 1 (Winter 2008), 53–82.
21 Amal Rassam, "Revolution Within the Revolution? Women and the State in Iraq," in *Iraq: The Contemporary State*, Tim Niblock, ed. (London: St. Martin's Press, 1992), 91.
22 Cited in Bashkin, "Representations of Women," 68.
23 This is the thesis advanced in Laura Bier, *Revolutionary Womanhood: Feminisms, Modernity and the State in Nasser's Egypt* (Stanford, CA: Stanford University Press, 2011).
24 See Mervat Hatem, "Economic and Political Liberation in Egypt and the Demise of State Feminism," *International Journal of Middle East Studies* Vol. 24 (1992), 231–251.
25 Hazim Saghieh, "'That's How I am, World!' Saddam, Manhood and the Monolithic Image," *Imagined Masculinities: Male Identity and Culture in the Modern Middle East*, Mai Ghoussoub and Emma Sinclair-Webb, eds. (London: Saqi Press, 2004), 236.
26 Zaher Omareen, "The Symbol and Counter-Symbols in Syria," in *Syria Speaks: Art and Culture from the Frontline*, Malu Halasa, Zaher Omareen, and Nawara Majfoud, eds. (London: Saqi Press, 2014), 89.
27 Suad al-Attar, cited in *Iraqi Women: Untold Stories from 1948 to the Present* (London: Zed Books, 2012), 69.
28 Nadje Al-Ali, "The Iraqi Women's Movement: Past and Contemporary Perspectives," *Mapping Arab Women's Movements: A Century of Transformation*, Pernille Arenfeldt and Nawar al-Hassan-Golley, eds. (Cairo: The American University of Cairo Press, 2011), 95.
29 Saghieh, "That's How I am," 236.
30 Rassam, "Revolution Within the Revolution," 92.
31 Rassam, "Revolution Within the Revolution," 92.
32 Al-Ali, "The Iraqi Woman's Movement: Past and Contemporary Perspectives," 97.
33 Nadje Al-Ali, *Iraqi Women: Untold Stories from 1948 to the Present* (London: Zed Books, 2012), 112, 113.
34 Al-Ali, *Iraqi Women*, 136–137.
35 Marion Farouk-Sluglett, "Liberation or Repression: Pan-Arab Nationalism and the Women's Movement in Iraq," in *Iraq: Power and Society*, Derek Hopwood, Habib Ishow, and Thomas Kosinowski, eds. (Oxford: Ithaca Press, 1993), 74.
36 Al-Ali, *Iraqi Women*, 131–137.
37 Saddam Hussein, cited in Al-Ali, *Iraqi Women*, 132.
38 Al-Ali, *Iraqi Women*, 131–137.
39 Fadwa K, cited in Al-Ali, *Iraqi Women*, 128.
40 Saghieh, "That's How I Am," 241.
41 Sally K. Gallagher, *Making Do in Damascus: Navigating a Generation of Change in Family and Work* (Syracuse, NY: Syracuse University Press, 2012), 51.
42 Gallagher, *Making Do in Damascus*, 66.
43 Sara Lei Sparre, "Educated Women in Syria: Servants of the State or Nurturers of the Family?," *Critique: Critical Middle Eastern Studies* Vol. 17, No. 1 (Spring 2008), 7.
44 Cited in Vinson and Al-Hassan Golley, "Challenges and Opportunities," 75.
45 Sparre, "Educated Women in Syria," 8.
46 Vinson and Al-Hassan Golley, "Challenges and Opportunities," 71, 73.
47 Zaher Omareen, "The Symbol and Counter-Symbols in Syria," in *Syria Speaks: Art and Culture from the Frontline*, Malu Halasa, Zaher Omareen, and Nawara Majfoud, eds. (London: Saqi Press, 2014), 91.
48 Nikki Keddie, *Women in the Middle East: Past and Present* (Princeton: Princeton University Press, 2006), 190.
49 Parvin Paidar, *Women and the Political Process in Twentieth-Century Iran* (Cambridge: Cambridge University Press, 1995), 150.

50 Earl L. Sullivan, *Women in Egyptian Public Life* (Syracuse, NY: Syracuse University Press, 1986), 43.
51 Sullivan, *Women in Egyptian Public Life*, 179.
52 Kenneth Cuno, "Divorce and the Fate of the Family in Modern Egypt," *Family in the Middle East: Ideational Change in Egypt, Iran and Tunisia*, Kathryn M. Yount and Hoda Rashad, eds. (New York: Routledge, 2008), 32.
53 Margot Badran, *Feminism in Islam: Secular and Religious Convergences* (Oxford: One World Press, 2009), 132.
54 Haleh Esfandiari, *Reconstructed Lives: Women and Iran's Islamic Revolution* (Baltimore: Johns Hopkins University Press, 1997), 54.
55 Keddie, *Past and Present*, 114.
56 Al-Ali, *Iraqi Women*, 198.
57 See Nuha al-Radi, *Baghdad Diaries: A Woman's Account of War and Exile* (New York: Vintage Press, 1998).
58 Al-Ali, *Iraqi Women*, 188–189.
59 Al-Ali, *Iraqi Women*, 201–203.
60 "Aliya," cited in Al-Ali, *Iraqi Women*, 203.
61 Nadje al-Ali and Nicola Pratt, *What Kind of Liberation: Women and the Occupation of Iraq* (Berkeley: University of California Press, 2009), 13.
62 Al-Ali, *Iraqi Women*, 240–242.
63 Vinson and Al-Hassan Golley, "Challenges and Opportunities," 76–78.
64 Omareen, "The Symbol and Counter-Symbols in Syria," 94.
65 Zehra F. Arat, "Introduction: Politics of Representation and Identity," in *Deconstructing Images of the Turkish Woman*, Zehra F. Arat, ed. (London: Palgrave Macmillan, 1998), 13.
66 Arat, "Introduction," 17–18.
67 William Cleveland and Martin Bunton, *A History of the Modern Middle East*, 6th ed. (Boulder: Westview Press, 2016), 268.
68 See Yesim Arat, "Women's Rights and Islam in Turkish Politics: The Civil Code," *Middle East Journal* Vol. 64, No. 2 (2010), 235–251.
69 Hikmet Kocamaner, "The Politics of Family Values in Erdogan's New Turkey," *Middle East Report*, no. 288 (Fall 2018).
70 Ayça Alemendaroğlu, "The AKP's Problem with Youth." *Middle East Report*, no. 288 (Fall 2018).

9 (Un)finished Business, but Not as Usual

Feminisms from the 1950s

Disenfranchisement in the 1920s led feminists to retreat temporarily from the struggle for women's rights and to define feminism as men had: service to the nation through philanthropy and patriotic motherhood (see Chapter 7). Heads of states subsequently defined feminism in measures both liberating (suffrage) and restricting (state-controlled women's organizations) (see Chapter 8). Neither definition met the mark of the women who sought to translate their civil and patriotic initiatives into agency: freedom to define (or decline) roles for themselves within emerging public realms. Feminism in the Middle East was not halted by disenfranchisement and state control, however. Rather, new generations of feminists have fulfilled goals advanced by the WWI generation, particularly the right to vote. New cohorts have also widened the scope of what it means to be a feminist. Agency is therefore the topic of this chapter.

A word about language. Middle Eastern women who call themselves feminist have placed themselves, historically, in the company of female activists around the world who define securing parity with men in the public realm as a feminist act. Nonetheless, women who have adopted "feminist" have relied on an imported and contested term; an affectation of elite women; a Western, imperialist import; and an unwieldy houseguest in a society in which parity between the sexes is not always understood as it is in the West. Some have preferred, therefore, to label their organizations "women's." Still others question the nature of a "women's movement": must associations support and address issues labeled "women's" in order to be considered part of a larger "women's movement?"

We define feminist movements as associations of women whose activities have addressed issues of concern especially to women and as movements whose civil initiative has seen much fruit in the form of charity and educational initiatives *and* whose civil initiative has included fighting for the establishment of a nation, or for regime change, or for changes to national identity. As such, we also include women's associations whose explicit goal over much of the twentieth century and into the twenty-first century has been suffrage and legal parity with men with regards to rights in marriage and divorce.

We also include as part of the feminist movement women whose goal is not to wrestle parity from men or from the state. Rather, as part of what has been labeled the "Islamic feminist movement" ("feminist" does not easily fit here either, for all

DOI: 10.4324/9781032658063-9

the reasons listed above), women have increasingly pointed to their right *not* to be considered a man's equal. So-called Islamic feminists seek parity within their own realm, the domestic, wherein fulfilment of their duties as wives and mothers puts them on what they see as the proper footing with men.

Finally, we include the many women whose movement through the public realm is now a given: movement through education, movement in the workforce, and movement through all of the halls that make up "the nation," including the ranks of government.[1] Women are simply an undeniable presence in the public realm. A clever sociologist has recently suggested that the overwhelming (if not routinely uncontested) presence of women in the public realm constitutes an unintended women's movement through which women have captured that which they fought for in the early decades of the twentieth century.[2] While the ultimate goal of full parity with men in the legal realm still eludes women (organized or otherwise), access to the public realm does not.

In each case, we advance what the late (and tremendous) scholar of Middle Eastern women's movements Rula Quawas captured so well prior to her untimely death: "…feminist thinking and practice emphasize a vision wherein everyone's needs are respected, everyone has rights, and no one needs to fear subordination or abuse."[3]

Recoupling

Struggles for national definition, liberation, and defense over the second half of the twentieth century have brought new generations of women into the public realm in ways that mirror earlier decades. Like their predecessors, women have leveraged contributions to political struggles into further opportunities—some of them within the political realm itself. Others have concluded that that the public realm has let them down. In each of the examples below, women's agency has been central.

Yemen (then South Yemen) experienced from the 1950s what many women across the region had in the early decades of the twentieth century. Women in Aden emerged into the public realm in the 1950s through journalism. The male-authored press in Yemen was ablaze with the "Woman Question" in the 1940s and 1950s. Mohammed Luqman, known as the Qasim Amin of Yemen, used his own newspaper to make the case for women's liberation. Women first joined these debates in the men's press, later establishing their own journals. Mahia Naguib, former editor of a column dedicated to women in the weekly *al-Nahda*, founded her own paper *Fatat Shamsan* in 1960. Hers was incidentally the first women's journal in the Arabian Peninsula.[4]

Readership of *Fatat Shamsan* included Aden's increasingly well-educated female elite and middle classes, many of whom had been joining women's groups since the 1950s. Women's participation in charitable organizations in Aden began in 1943 with the opening of the Aden Women's Club, which was linked to the British Council.[5] Purdah customs initially kept Muslim women away (and made their fathers or husbands uneasy). Nonetheless, over the course of the following decade, Muslim women slowly joined European and non-Yemini women in charitable activities. Once a Muslim woman, Madiha Hasan Ali, had been elected the group's president in 1954, most of the non-Yemeni women left the club.[6] Under Ali's guidance, the Aden Women's Club organized cultural activities more suited to the interests of women of Yemen's middle and upper classes.

Primary among those concerns was veiling.[7] In 1959, a handful of women from the Club, some of them *sans hijab*, marched through Aden to the offices of two prominent local newspapers. (Thirty other unveiled women followed in their cars.) There, they gave statements to the press about the *hijab* as a hindrance to their participation in social and public life.

But politics also occupied these women's attentions. A newly, reconstituted Aden Women's Club held lectures about the weight of colonial rule. Following foreign aggression against Egypt in 1956, club members raised funds and formed committees to encourage the local boycott of British and French goods. British persecution of Yemini trade union members brought members of the Club to protest in 1958, as did a proposal to place Aden in a Federation of South Arabia in 1962. The 1962 demonstrations ended with the arrests of male and female demonstrators and prompted a name change: the Club became the Arab Women's Society (AWS). Its slogan: One Nation, One Responsibility.

The following decade saw splits within the AWS along with the rise of new women's groups. The 1960s also saw a new wave of educated young women taking up issues related to women (e.g., the inadequacy of girls' education). A more left-leaning faction in the AWS joined Yemen's National Liberation Front (NLF), leading demonstrations, selling their jewelry, and collecting donations to support male fighters. In Aden, women smuggled arms (their counterparts in rural areas took up arms directly against the British). Women served as unit commanders. And they formed the ranks of the fallen. In a rival organization, the Front for the Liberation of Occupied South Yemen (FLOSY), women similarly worked delivering weapons and information and performing administrative tasks (see Figure 9.1). But sit-ins organized by women in late 1963 and 1964 were these women's finest hour: to force the British to return male detainees, women staged a 15-day sit-in at Aden's Asqalani Mosque. Hundreds of women took up station in the mosque's courtyard. It took a second sit-in on February 4, 1964, to convince the British to meet their demands.

The British left South Yemen in 1967 and the NLF-dominated People's Democratic Republic of Yemen (PDRY) rose to take their place. Women's contributions to the nationalist struggles were not without their cost: they speak of the 1960s as a struggle both against Great Britain and against their families and their traditions. Women warriors definitely broke purdah rules. In doing so, they were supported by male members of the NLF and FLOSY. But their families threatened to lock activist women out of the house if they did not come home from demonstrations at a respectable hour and men of religion spoke out against women who took up the national struggle in arms.

The rewards were nonetheless sweet. A new constitution gave women legal rights. In 1970, women gained the right to vote. A 1974 family law—considered revolutionary in the Arab world at that time—made women's consent to marriage a

158 (Un)finished Business, but Not as Usual: Feminisms from the 1950s

Figure 9.1 FLOSY members, Aden. James Davis Photography/Alamy Stock Photo.

legal requirement and forbade polygamy except under exceptional circumstances. The new law raised the legal age of marriage to 16 for females and 18 for males. The law prohibited unilateral divorce by males and limited bride price gifts (*mahr*).[8] Finally, the law required men and women to share household expenses, when able. In 1977, women stood for public office for the first time.

Such a quick turnaround from independence to women's suffrage has not been typical, however. Indeed, suffrage has taken pride of place in women's organizations in the period following independence in many countries, as women worked to fulfil the goals of the region's first wave of feminist activism. Beginning in the 1930s, pro-feminist leaders across the region granted suffrage by state fiat (see Chapter 8). Behind each fiat, however, were members of women's organizations who demonstrated and lobbied for the vote. Even Atatürk was not immune to the pressures of suffragettes.[9]

Some stories of women's successful campaigns for suffrage have high-profile heroines. In 1946, Doria Shafik used primetime strategies to tip the Egyptian state's hand. Shafik, a committed feminist and, at least initially, a comrade-in-arms to Hoda Shaarawi, founded a new women's journal, *Daughter of the Nile*. The journal's editorials targeted members of parliament hoping to sway their opinions regarding women's enfranchisement. Lobbying men of politics was only one of Shafiq's strategies: members of her women's union (also called Daughter of the Nile) organized and participated in public demonstrations in favor of suffrage in 1952. In 1954, Shafik called on the International Association of Women, hoping thereby to increase international pressure on Egypt's government. Her final strategy, however, was the most successful. In 1954, Shafik joined eight other women in a high-profile, pro-suffrage hunger strike. The hunger strike drew great attention to Nasser—who wanted the world to regard him as a modern leader. By 1956, Egyptian women had the right to vote.[10] The cost was high, however: Shafik spent the remainder of her days under house arrest and more than likely took her own life.

In other parts of the region, changes in social values have been the heroines. In Kuwait, which achieved independence from the British only in 1961, women did not participate in elections for the nation's first parliament in 1963. Women benefitted from the policies of Emir Abdullah Al-Salim Al-Sabah (r. 1965–1977), who provided state subsidies, health care, and education to families, health care, and free and compulsory education for both sexes, but were not included in the nation's election laws.[11] Divisions over women's rights within and between Shia and Sunni communities hampered efforts of women's groups to effectively lobby for the vote over the course of the 1970s and 1980s. It was the Gulf War, however, during which Kuwaiti women joined the underground resistance, sometimes sacrificing their lives in the struggle to rid Kuwait of Iraqi troops, which began to change the tide in society's acceptance of women's suffrage. In 1999, then Emir Jabar al-Ahmad Al-Sabah (r. 1977–2006) issued a decree granting suffrage. His decree was overturned by Kuwait's parliament. But the Emir's advocacy made it such that disenfranchisement—which many Kuwaiti men and women found to be "morally problematic and unjust"—was no longer a majority position, and the anti-suffrage stance of Islamists, both Sunni and Shia, lost some currency.[12]

Women's quest for political rights also gained greater acceptance among Kuwaitis after the September 11, 2001, attacks on New York's World Trade Center forced a collective reckoning among Kuwaitis regarding their country's identity. In the aftermath of the Emir's rejected 1999 decree, Kuwait's oldest women's organization, the Women's Cultural and Social Society (WCSS) had formed its Committee on The Political Rights of Women. After 9/11, moderate Sunni and Shia women's groups began aligning themselves with the WCSS in greater numbers. New suffragist groups also joined.[13] By 2000, these women's groups linked suffrage to the future of Kuwait and to its development as a modern nation. Kuwaitis opposed to women's suffrage were cast as extremist, anti-national, anti-progress, and closed-minded. As women increasingly framed women's rights as "everyone's issue," even conservative forces began to yield. In April 2005, in one of Kuwait City's largest ever demonstrations, a diverse crowd—men and women of all ages, veiled and unveiled women—gathered in front of Kuwait's parliament building in support of women's full inclusion in the political process. This time, parliament agreed.[14]

Today, women across the Middle East have the right to vote and to run for office. (Saudi Arabian women were the last to join the ranks of women voters in 2015.) Women across the region hold offices ranging from city councils to parliaments. Women holding high-ranking positions as cabinet ministers is no longer exceptional. Israel, Turkey, and Tunisia have had female prime ministers. Some nations have quotas for women in local and national legislative bodies. Decades of women's activism has yielded parity, at least in the casting of votes.

Conflicts have also set back women's struggle for political inclusion, as was the case in Lebanon during its civil war. Lebanon's 1958 political crisis, the subsequent invasion of American troops, and a civil war that engulfed the nation between 1975 and 1990 both provided Lebanese women with new opportunities for activism and fragmented what had once been a large and successful transconfessional women's movement. Enshrined within the independent Lebanon nation's Constitution (1943) was a system designed to represent all of the nation's confessional groups—but not equally. A National Pact based on a 1932 census (overseen by the French) gave undue political representation to Christians, who, after the influx of Palestinian refugees in 1948, no longer constituted the nation's majority by the late 1950s. While the Pact represented substantial compromise (Lebanon would be both a French-speaking, Western-leaning nation and an Arab Muslim nation), in fact, divisions within communities were heightened rather than diminished by Lebanon's political contract. The *zuama*, or bosses, who represented the political interests of their communities often placed Lebanon's national interests behind those of their communities. These political "fathers" to Lebanon's many communities further heightened patriarchal power in a nation historically structured along patriarchal lines. Within such a community or series of communities, women who organized in service of the nation had not only a national father to contend with, but also clerical fathers, their own fathers, and their husbands.

But organize they did. By 1947, two substantial groups dominated women's associational life: the Lebanese Women's Union (est. 1920) brought together Arab nationalists and political leftists. The Christian Women's Solidarity Association (est. 1947) represented the interests of some 20 Lebanese Christian associations. Both groups focused on aid for the poor and the needy. And both groups focused on improving women's living standards. By 1950, the groups formed a joint executive committee, which took on suffrage as its first project.[15] In 1952, members of this joint executive committee formed a permanent organization: the Lebanese Council for Women. The Council could claim a long string of successes from 1953: suffrage, elections of women to parliament, partial reform of inheritance laws for Christian women, and reformed citizenship laws.[16] In 1974, the Council helped secure the right of Lebanese women to travel abroad without their husband's permission.[17]

Women's organizations also maintained a presence in Lebanon's street politics in this era. In 1958, tensions escalated surrounding then president Camille Chamoun's (r. 1952–1958) decision to seek an unconstitutional second term in office. His actions provoked tensions between Lebanon's Muslim population, who rallied behind Gamal Abdul Nasser's pan-Arabism, manifest in the United Arab Republic with Syria (1958–1961), and the Lebanese Christians who supported Chamoun. The US, fearing Nasser more than communism, invaded in July 1958 at Chamoun's request, remaining in Lebanon through October and overseeing what would be the end of Chamoun's presidency (see Figure 9.2). Various influential women and women's organizations petitioned the US embassy in Beirut, urging the American government not to intervene in Lebanese affairs. Women's associations demonstrated, and the sight of women protesting in the streets inspired a new generation to do the same.[18]

Lebanon's identity crisis did not end in 1958, a year seen as a dress rehearsal for the civil war. New members of the Lebanese "family" made an already fractured body politic untenable: Palestinian refugees, approximately 100,000 of them in 1948, followed by another wave after 1967, occupied refugee camps, some of them located in places from which strategic incursions against Israel were possible. But it was the arrival of Palestine Liberation Organization (PLO) leadership to Lebanon in 1970, following their expulsion from Jordan, that upped the ante of identity politics. The PLO became a state within a state. (After the 1973 War, the situation became particularly tense as Lebanon became the nerve center for

Figure 9.2 American troops land in Lebanon. Kurt Schraudenbach/Süddeutsche Zeitung Photo/Alamy Stock Photo.

anti-Israel resistance.) Armed members of the PLO became a commonplace sight. Christian militias followed suit; the start of the civil war can be traced to the deaths of Palestinians, women and children included, when Phalangists attacked a PLO bus full of left-leaning Arab nationalists. Syria quickly sent forces to Lebanon. Israel invaded in 1982, hoping to turn Lebanon into a client state. In a word, armed fathers (and brothers) of competing communities fought against one another for Lebanon's future.

Within such an environment, women's choices were limited. Some joined the militias of various parties, working within party and paramilitary structures to fight (perhaps 15% of Lebanese women were armed combatants). Other women filled supporting roles in militias: logistics, communications, supply, and transport.[19] Conservative Shia militias, Amal and Hizbollah, were notable for encouraging both traditional roles as mothers of fighters and martyrs and public roles, most importantly the ideological training of other women.[20]

Jocelyn Kweiri, who lived across the street from the Phalangist (Maronite Christian party) headquarters and who served in a Phalangist militia, recollects the period between 1973 and 1975 as one of intensive training. Her weekly training consisted of martial arts and use of firearms. This training conflicted with her participation in the Legions of St. Mary, an international Catholic organization. But when the Mother Superior gave Kweiri the choice between "Jesus and Lebanon," she chose the latter. Youth who trained in such a manner gained the admiration of their parents. Only some outsiders "and a few party members" frowned upon their activity and found it to be unladylike.[21]

Other women chose to avoid participation in the armed struggle, a choice which also brought them danger. Many Lebanese left the country during the civil war or, at least, left Beirut if they had the chance. For those who stayed—combatants or not—survival was a daily undertaking. Women's memoirs attest to war's transformation of everyday occurrences into struggles: moving from zone to zone in Beirut, visiting family, gathering food, dealing with outages, losing loved ones, and supporting the fight in any way possible. Female authors like Zeina Abirached portray the transformation of Beirut into a warzone as various militias controlled different parts of the capital (and country), providing poignant descriptions of how women and their children moved from place to place to avoid sniper fire.[22]

Survival was also contingent upon self-medication: drugs, alcohol, and sexual encounters—some of them dangerous. Darina al-Joundi (b. 1968), who came of age during the war, recounts a childhood in which religious identity was fluid: when the war broke out, she was attending the School of the Holy Family and did not know that her parents were Muslims (although she did know that her father was a practiced atheist).[23] After the Israeli invasion of 1982, Darina and her sisters wanted to take up arms; however, her father refused to allow it (Darina was 14 at the time; she had already learned, at the age of eight, to assemble a Kalashnikov from a high-ranking PLO operative, a friend of her parents).[24] Instead, al-Joundi's father suggested that his daughters volunteer for the Red Cross, which frequently ran short of the supplies. But service did not bring al-Joundi relief. What she also recounts in *The Day Nina Simone Stopped Singing* was a substantial descent into self-medication. Her father saw teaching al-Joundi to drink as part of her "liberation." He also taught her that men were dogs.[25] Nonetheless, sex joined alcohol as al-Joundi's preferred medications.

Danger brought a halt to the activities of Lebanon's trans-confessional women's movement. The Council of Lebanese Woman was inactive during the civil war. But some of its members were not. Founding member Laure Moghaizel and her husband Joseph, both lawyers, established the Lebanese Association for Human Rights in 1985. With this council's help, a number of laws favorable to women were passed or amended. By 1999, in remembrance of the Moghaizel's work, the Lebanese government adopted partial reforms to laws related to honor killings, requiring judges to convict rather than simply acquit men found guilty of such acts.[26] Nevertheless, citizenship remains yoked to fatherhood and women still cannot be heads of households.[27]

Lebanon's civil war ended in 1989 with the signing of the Taif accords in Saudi Arabia. While the business of war ended, the business of fragmented confessional politics did not. Indeed, the papers signed in Taif set Lebanon back to where it had been in 1975.[28] Al-Joundi recollects being in Damascus at the time of the accords and rushing home, but finding that "nothing had changed. ... An army of assassins had vanished into thin air with a wave of a magic wand called amnesia."[29]

Unaddressed and unfinished business from Lebanon's pre-civil war era has led tensions to resurface, manifest in assassinations, political instability, protests, and outside interference. In 2005, former prime minister and real estate mogul Rafik al-Hariri was assassinated, sparking the "Cedar Revolution." Women actively participated in the 2005 uprisings, including "feminine" touches such as appeasing soldiers by handing them flowers.[30] Syria left Lebanon in April 2005.

In 2015, an infrastructural crisis involving garbage collection brought organized women's movements into the streets. "Sukleen," a company in the government's employ roughly since the end of the civil war, failed to get the government to renew its quite lucrative contract. Garbage soon replaced the barriers that had once filled Beirut's streets.[31] The simple demand, for the government to collect trash, was offered in voices free from confessional overtones. The role of feminists and of members of Lebanon's LGBTQ community in the demonstrations suggested, to some observers, a new model for Lebanese citizenship and perhaps a newly invigorated women's movement.[32]

In October 2019, the streets of Beirut once again filled with protestors, this time over an announcement about new taxes. The presence of large numbers of women in the demonstrations attracted the attention of regional and international media. Women's demands went beyond the simple rescinding of taxes: in addition to calling for the resignation of Lebanon's cabinet and prime minister, women called for an overall restructuring of the government to overturn the sectarian-based confessional system (see Figure 9.3). Targets of the protestors' agenda were the nationality laws and personal status laws.[33] One year later, Lebanese citizens continued to protest government corruption against the backdrop of the worldwide pandemic. A massive explosion of ammonium nitrate occurred at the port of Beirut. Overwhelming evidence indicates that both action and inaction by the government caused the explosion of the hazardous materials.³⁴

In neighboring Israel, the 1973 Yom Kippur War served as a wake-up call for women who might previously have taken their full inclusion in their nation's public realm for granted.³⁵ Indeed, Jewish women in prestate Palestine had won the right to vote in the Yishuv's governing bodies prior to the establishment of Israel—a right the state guaranteed them after 1948 and gained in large measure by women's organizations. The newly established Israeli Defense Force (IDF) required women, like men, to serve after 1949. In agriculture, women continued to work alongside men; indeed, photographs of bronzed men and women working the fields together in prestate Palestine and in Israel after 1948 were iconic demonstrations of Zionism's "thrilling level of gender equity relative to the times."³⁶

But the extent to which the Yom Kippur War brought civilian life to a standstill in the autumn of 1973 forced a reckoning among women regarding their real exclusion from aspects of Israeli public life. As men went off to war, they left behind no women trained to drive buses, on which Israel's public transportation depends. IDF women were relegated to the "legitimate" roles of nursing and caring for both combatant and civilian populations. Non-deployed women baked and knitted for men at the front while taking care of their families at home. Wartime and postwar

Figure 9.3 Graffiti, Lebanon 2019. JSK/Alamy Stock Photo.

decisions were made without female voices, civilian or military. When men finally came home from war, they replaced the women who had replaced them during the war, costing Jewish Israeli women wartime gains in the labor force. Where had the thrilling gender equity gone?

Perhaps Jewish Israeli women's quick successes in 1948 had blinded them to the realities of Israel's victory over the Arab states in 1967: war now defined Israel's way forward, and men dominated the Israeli military (and, along with it, the Israeli public realm). "Chicks with guns" had given early state Israel an air of the avant-garde.[37] After 1967, however, "dudes with guns" were king. The post-1967 era brought Israel great national pride, international acclaim, an economic boom, and a female prime minister, Golda Meir (r. 1960–1974). But that era also brought gender gaps in the Israeli workforce and an overrepresentation of women in lower-paying jobs. Some wondered if Jewish Israeli women amounted to little more than wombs for the production of the next generation (see Figure 9.4).

The absence of female bus drivers in the fall of 1973 therefore brought about a period of reckoning for Jewish Israeli women, just as it brought them opportunities for activism.[38] Women's organizations emerged in Haifa, Tel Aviv, and Jerusalem, each with a different focus. Haifa's group, Nilahem, focused its energies on the

Figure 9.4 Bronzed Israeli bodies defend a kibbutz. Gilad Flesch/Alamy Stock Photo.

degree to which a male-dominated, military-dominant society suppressed women, while women in Tel Aviv focused on women's liberation as a civil right. Women in Jerusalem linked feminism with poverty and with Israel's occupation of the West Bank. In each case, women linked women's rights to demands for the reform of Israel's social order.

Accompanying the rise of new feminist organizations was an increasing representation of Israeli Jewish women in the Knesset. Four women from the RATZ party (Citizens Rights Movement) were seated in the Knesset in 1973, including Shulamit Aloni, founder of the Citizens Rights movement and a driving force behind the reemergence of Israeli feminism. In 1975, the International Year of the Woman, then Prime Minister Yitzhak Rabin established a commission to look into the status of women in Israel. The report of that commission, which surprised many Israeli women and men for the scale of inequality it revealed, led to the creation of a new governmental position: Advisor to the Prime Minister on the Status of Women. Over the course of the following decade, dozens of the commission's recommendations were implemented, many of them dedicated to women's better integration into the workforce.

In 1992 a woman-friendly and woman-strong Knesset established a Committee on the Status of Women, a government body (part of Israel's ministry for Social Equality since 2009) designed to liaise between the government and nongovernmental organizations (NGOs) who take up women's issues. That cooperation led to the taking up in Knesset of a number of critical issues over the course of the 1990s, particularly education as it relates to gender equality, the status of the LGBTQ community in Israel, and the status of Arab women in Israel. As of 2000, Jewish Israeli women can serve in any position in the military.

Since 1973, the frequency of wars and military incursions involving Israel have led Jewish Israeli women to organize and demonstrate for peace. These women's organizations have linked women's activism to critiques of militarism and to the protection of its victims (on both sides). The Women in Black, established in 1988 in response to the beginnings of the Palestinian *intifada* in 1987 (see Chapter 13), holds vigils against Israel's continued occupation of the West Bank every Friday from 1 to 2 pm in Haifa, Jerusalem, and Tel Aviv (see Figure 9.5). Mothers of fallen Israeli soldiers in south Lebanon established Four Mothers in 1997. The group led a protest movement that sought to pull Israeli troops out of southern Lebanon (mission accomplished in 2000). Some have called Four Mothers the most successful anti-war movement in Israel's history.[39] Since 2001, the women who make up Machsom (Checkpoint) Watch observe and document interactions (and infractions) at military checkpoints in the West Bank and between the West Bank and Israel. Their goal is to monitor and document the conduct of Israeli soldiers (some of whom might be their partners or children) as they process Palestinians through IDF checkpoints. Women Wage Peace (WWP), founded in the aftermath of Israel's 50-day Operation Protective Edge in Gaza in 2014, has grown to be one of Israel's largest grassroots peace movements. WWP gathers women to protest war, to "unite [women] and take the future of this small place into our own hands." In 2022, WWP, which includes women of many ages and political persuasions,

Figure 9.5 Women in Black, Jerusalem. Nir Alon/Alamy Stock Photo.

Jewish, Arab, Druze, and Bedouin, began a collaboration with Women of the Sun, a Palestinian women's peace movement.⁴⁰

In Turkey, political divisions have provided feminists with opportunities to organize in ways not seen since the pre-Atatürk era. Organized feminism in Turkey has subsequently worked for women's rights as individuals and to define women's rights in ways that transcend state feminism definitions. Those rights include freedom to veil. Feminists in Kurdistan have worked to challenge exclusive definitions of "Turk" and to articulate a feminist agenda that corresponds less with Turkish feminist agendas.

Turkey experienced a military coup in 1980 in reaction to the ideological divides (and subsequent violence) that had overwhelmed the secular nation over the course of the 1970s. As the result of the coup, political parties (and the women's and youth branches associated with them) were largely closed down and a new constitution (1982) curtailed Turks' rights and freedoms. Despite these limitations, Turkish women who had over the course of the 1970s found their avenues limited by male-dominated political parties that took advantage of the dismantling of the party system to return to organized feminism 1920s style. Feminists organized and demonstrated in response to a judge's suggestion that women needed to be beaten in order to be controlled: 3,000 women took to Istanbul's streets in 1987. Other campaigns followed, such as the Purple Needle Campaign, which addressed aggressions against women on public transportation. The Purple Roof (est. 1990) provided a hotline for at-risk women. Feminists in the 1980s, located largely in Turkey's urban areas, also turned their attention to inequalities within marriage (such as automatic use of the husband's surname, the husband's right to make decisions regarding children's schooling), but it was the problem of escalating violence against women in Turkish streets and in Turkish homes that dominated their agenda.[41]

Over the 1980s and 1990s, secular Turkish feminists amassed a substantial number of accomplishments. Some of women's activities in this era harkened back to an earlier age: the opening of a Women's Library to collect and house literary and academic works by women and about women in Istanbul in 1990; the circulation of 63 women's journals; the establishment of women's studies programs at universities in Istanbul and Ankara; and the establishment of the Flying Broom Association to facilitate networking between women's organizations (which had increased in number from approximately ten ca. 1980 to over 350 by 2004).[42] Women from Istanbul and Ankara united in 1986 to petition the government to comply fully with the UN Convention about the Abolition of All Discrimination Against Women (CADAW) (see below). In 1990, the Turkish Prime Ministry established a department specifically designed to improve the rights and status of women. In 2001, the efforts of women's organizations joined with pressure from outside Turkey to influence the government to amend the 1926 legal code and to make men and women equal partners in marriage. Indeed, the slogan of many women's organizations in that campaign was: "Democracy in the Family means Democracy in Society."[43]

While these women criticized the legacies of the Kemalist state, it is also correct to say that women accepted those legacies. In other words, these were the women Atatürk hoped to create—secular, unveiled, married—asking the state for more rights and for more attention to their challenges (often evoking the 1960s Western feminist slogan "the personal is political).[44] As such, feminism had not created space for women who were not ethnically Turkish or who were not committed secularists. The Kurdish challenge to the Turkish state in the 1990s forcibly widened these women's definitions beyond the Kemalist paradigm to include women who were not veiled, not Turkish, and not, perhaps, interested in the heterosexual marriage contract.

The rise of the Kurdish nationalist movement forcibly changed these women's perspectives. The Kurdish question dates back to 1984, when the Turkish Workers' Party (PKK) attacked military installations in Turkey's southeast. By 1990, the conflict between the PKK and the Turkish military had spilled into the streets, where communities of Kurds and Turks protested the government's policies of emptying or destroying villages known (or imagined) to house PKK members. Kurdish women were not absent from these protests. Indeed, the conflict gave Kurdish women the opportunity to organize around issues related to gender, specifically the violence wrought by conflict. Additionally, the conflict brought Kurdish women increasingly into politics, where they joined parties, demonstrated in protests, and, occasionally, went to prison. The Saturday Mothers, for example, gathered collectively in a square in Istanbul to protest the imprisonment of their sons. KAMER, a widespread feminist organization in Turkish Kurdistan, in addition to addressing violence committed against men and women as the result of the Kurdish struggle, focused on the home as a place where violence against women is also committed. Women have also participated in Kurdish political parties, such as the Democratic Society Party (DSP), in which the ratio of women to men is higher than other parties in support of the Kurdish movement and from which Kurdish women have secured seats in parliament. Support for and participation in such projects brought Kurdish women to conclude that it was both the patriarchy of Kurdish society and the "imperialism" of the Kemalist project that had resulted in their marginalization within Turkish society, in general, and Kurdish identity politics in particular. Turkish feminists, they conclude, who have historically been urban, educated, and Westernized in the Kemalist fashion, had ignored the plight of women in Turkey who do not meet this definition. Consequently, the Kurdish question pushed Turkish feminists to "question how they relate to the state and to Kemalist ideology."[45]

Interaction and cooperation between Kurdish and Turkish women's organizations, particularly surrounding the issue of violence, have consequently increased since the mid-1990s, providing new avenues for activism as well as criticism of state agendas. Interactions between Kurdish and Turkish feminisms have resulted in some Turkish feminists distancing themselves from state policies, as is reflected in a number of Turkish feminist periodicals. Such distancing has prompted, if not forced, Turkish feminists to include women who are not heterosexual and who are not secular into the feminist fold, and to question some of Kemalism's limitations, such as unveiling, which will be discussed further in Chapter 12.

Decoupling, Redux

Conservativism has swept the Middle East since the 1970s, and with it, an embrace of Islam as a substitute for secular politics. The failure of the Arab states in 1967 dealt a blow to the certainty of Arab socialist nationalism, as did Nasser's death in 1970. Anwar Sadat gave pride of place to new forms of Islamic piety, both as an expression of his own religiosity and as a means of distinguishing his regime from that of his predecessor. Petrol economies in the Gulf depended on steady streams of guest workers from throughout the region, many of whom returned home with new religious sensibilities or heightened commitments to religious practices and identities. In Turkey, greater political pluralism led to increased demands for a place for Islam in public life. In Iran, the 1979 revolution gave way to the rise of an Islamic Republic (see Chapters 8, 12, and 13). In each case, resurgent religion was visible (and audible) in public—new forms of dressing, of self-fashioning, of greeting one another, and of defining the political realm.

Within such an environment, an increasing number of women cultivated alternatives to models of feminism from previous generations. Some refer to themselves as Islamic feminists. Many do not, however, shying away from or openly rejecting feminism as a Western import instead. Similarly, they reject the determination of Middle Eastern feminists from the 1920s to achieve political and legal parity for women. For many of these women, whom we refer to here as supporters of women's rights within Islam and as Islamic feminists, men and women are differently equal, one created for life in the public realm and the other for the private. Some, like Egypt's Safinaz Kazem (1937–) extol women to embrace a religious approach to women's rights while at the same time encouraging women to be involved in the workplace and in politics.[46] These women's way of looking at equality does not ipso facto place them in contention with women who define feminism as equal rights.[47] Rather, women who advocate for equal rights within Islam promote women's empowerment through the measured cultivation of modesty, sole devotion to marriage, homelife and family life, and subservience to a husband's roles as paterfamilias, breadwinner, and representative of his family's political interests in the public realm. Empowerment for these women means flourishing within a role dictated less by the nation and its prerogatives and more by religious imperative.

Such inclusion of Islam has led to new ways of organizing, although traditional forms, like charitable service to the community, have also remained robust among these women. Similarly, organized Islamic feminist groups work to irradicate the conditions that limit women's horizons, such as illiteracy and access to health care. For some, Islamic feminism is a wholly private affair, announced perhaps by clothing and manners but not by public declaration. For others, the movement among women seeking their rights within Islam is cultivated in gatherings, particularly in mosques. In what is described as the "women's mosque movement," women unite to study, to listen to women preachers, and to cultivate new ways of understanding and interpreting the Quran and the *hadith*. Some wish to cultivate more women-friendly interpretations of Islamic scripture. Others simply seek to know and understand their rights and duties within an Islam that is absent of men's voices. For some, attendance of such women's circles has no particular connection to politics. For others, the movement is political because it aims to restore piety to the public realm; these women suggest that without such piety the public realm cannot function. Dawa, or preaching, is a central practice for many of these women. Their goal, like that of many Islamic movements that have developed over the course of the twentieth and twenty-first centuries, is to circulate in public space, teaching and preaching what they see as correct Islam, and the gender segregation that accompanies their version of it.[48]

In Syria from the 1990s, challenges to the hegemony of state feminism have come in increasingly Islamic registers. As economic challenges led fewer Syrian women to be employed by the public realm, their allegiance to the Baathist emphasis on "women as workers" has shifted toward a discourse that promotes women as mothers and wives. The result has been women's increased participation in religion, both as a means of practicing piety and as a path toward leadership. An increase in veiling has been accompanied by the rise of women preachers, including the *sheikha* or female spiritual guide.[49] Within Sufi tradition, *sheikhas* are understood to possess that which God grants only to select individuals: *baraka*, a blessing that brings with it religious enlightenment. Within women's circles, *sheikhas* bring the teachings of right Islam and the conveyance of grace. Some circles are named after their *sheikha*, as is the case of the Qubaysiat, one of Syria's most popular women's groups, named after its founder Sheikha Munira al-Qubaysi.[50] Sunni women have also claimed a greater space in Syria's mosques, where they "lead lessons, prayer and *dhikr* [the devotional act of remembrance through repetition of the names of God or religious phrases] for other women."[51]

In Kuwait, the *Baydar al-Salam* (Threshing Fields of Peace, est. 1981—Kuwait's oldest religious association for women) has Sufism as its structural apparatus. The group forms part of Kuwait's Federation of Women's Associations. As such, it is allied with the government to serve the community. The goal of the Federation is also to "raise women's awareness of their religion, their identity and their role in the family."[52] Baydar al-Salam has a *sheikha* to whom members show respect and devotion; she, in exchange, shares her "chains of grace" with members of the group. To join *Baydar al-Salam* is, therefore, to embark on a spiritual journey and to involve oneself in educational and charitable activities through which the greater community is served.[53]

Internationalism, Re-dux

Since the late 1970s, the attentions of women's movements have turned to the international, as they were in the early twentieth century. The UN General Assembly (UNGA) declared the years 1975–1985 the "Decade of Women." With that declaration came a series of conferences, at which participants, including representatives from the Middle East, discussed topics such as pay equity, violence against women, and basic human rights. A final conference took place in Beijing in 1995, resulting in the promulgation of the Beijing Declaration and Platform for Action, which encouraged governments and NGOs to "mainstream gender through the implementation, monitoring and evaluation of legislation, politics, and programs." To encourage a closer relationship between states and women's organizations, the Platform also called for the establishment of various "machineries" of implementation (women's agencies, commissions, ministries, committees, advisors) in which women are well represented and for the continued holding of conferences in which women's voices serve to influence discourses and agendas.[54] The Platform yielded two instruments of measure for gauging women's empowerment: the UNDP's Gender and Development Index (GDI) and the Gender Empowerment Measure (GEM). Such rubrics have given women across the world a means of measuring inequality and a framework within which inequalities can be addressed.[55]

Against the backdrop of these conferences (which also included the Cairo Conference in 1994 regarding women's reproductive rights), the UNGA instituted the international treaty known as the Convention for the Elimination of all forms of Discrimination Against Women (CEDAW) in September 1981 (see Chapters 10 and 11). Like the Beijing Platform, CEDAW provides a means of measuring women's equality.

The UN's turn toward the mainstreaming of gender and its placing of women's rights within the category of human rights was the result of international feminist networking over the course of the 1970s. Women from around the world arrived at UN conferences with extensive research and information, much of it generated by their own networks.[56] As such, the UN provided a framework for advancing the agendas of transnational advocacy networks and global discourses about human rights.[57] Indeed, the decade and its conferences helped establish the legitimacy of women's issues and drew attention to inequalities faced by women worldwide.

Preparations for the Beijing Conference were sites of forced interactions between representatives of states (many of which had passed laws limiting the scope and activities of civil society) and representatives of women's associations and NGOs. While forced, those interactions led to a substantial interaction between states and women's associations in the lead-up to Beijing. In 1992, the government of Lebanon established the National Commission for Lebanese Women to prepare Lebanon's representatives to the Beijing conference.[58] In Yemen, a coalition of women in academic and NGOs established the *Mahdhuma* (The Collective of NGO Groups Concerned with Women) to prepare a delegation for Beijing.[59] Royal women represented both the state and its female citizens: Jordan's Princess Basma Bint Talal (b. 1961) led preparatory meetings for Beijing and was part of Jordan's official delegation.[60]

Since Beijing, women have sustained a presence in the "machineries" of implementation, the "instruments of government tasked with work relating to women's rights and needs."[61] Some governments have established Ministries for Women. Others added "women" to already-existing ministries. Others still have created a National Women's Council in lieu of a ministry. In Lebanon, for example, the government established a National Committee for the Follow up of Women's Issues, made up of representatives of both the state and civil society. The Follow Up Committee, itself an NGO, is tasked with the coordination of the membership and activities of various other NGOs dealing with women's affairs.[62]

The post-Beijing era also brought with it substantial international funding for women-focused NGOs. Consequently, those NGOs proliferated in the region ca. 2000 (Turkey additionally was awash in internationally sponsored NGOS as the result of its 1990s drive to join the EU). While NGOs brought opportunities, they also became targets for criticism. Conservative elements saw them as agents for foreign ideas about women. Some criticisms came from the very women who worked within or allied their interests to these NGOs: were the agendas of foreign donors being met at the expense of local interests?

In addition to forcing contact between states and women's associations, the Beijing Conference put momentum behind women's movements and renewed their legitimacy. The Beijing Platform, unevenly and imperfectly applied across the region, lacked adequate targets for measuring the impacts of its programs.[63]

Since 1995, however, the Middle East's measures of equality have inched up, not down.[64] As such, the women who made the Beijing Conference possible can claim to have more than the attending of international conferences in common with their early twentieth-century predecessors. Some called Beijing a "reset moment."[65]

And yet, when looked at from the perspective of the early days of women's activism, women's movements in the Middle East continue to face many of the challenges with which they started. The rehabilitation of the reputation of *harem* women is no longer an issue. But veiling (and unveiling) by choice is still not always a woman's prerogative. (While Western nations are no longer poised to intervene to save *harem* women, they do continue, as did American President George W. Bush in 2001, on the eve of the American invasion of Afghanistan, to see rescuing "women of cover" as their prerogative.[66]) Women's organizations still fight for women's access to education and health care. Civil society organizations, including women, still provide assistance to citizens who fall outside the state's reach (despite laws limiting and controlling civil society organizations). Women work and vote (and are elected to office) in the public realm, and yet violence against women in that realm is high. Similarly, the realities of domestic violence remain real as women continue to fight for equal rights in marriage and divorce.

Indeed, reforms to personal status codes remain as integral to women's agendas as they were among the first generation of feminists. Issues that appeared to be "feminist" ca. 1920 are no longer considered radical. Women's demands to hold citizenship and to pass it on to their children, and for equality in marriage and divorce, however, are still seen by men and by states as radical demands.[67] The efforts of women's organizations have succeeded in winning nationality rights, with few exceptions (see above). Equal access to divorce and child custody have remained elusive, however. Fathers are still dominant, both in the public and private realms; marriage and divorce laws remain largely in the hands of religious authorities. Women's organizations are therefore accused by conservative clerics as "acting against God" when they work for women's right to a unilateral divorce.[68]

The suggestion that women have come "full circle," however, overlooks the extraordinary debt that regimes across the region hold to the efforts of women's organizations, steadfast in their respect for the needs of their compatriots, committed to advancing the rights of everyone, and determined to end subjugation and abuse. What the state has refused to yield says nothing about the strength of the feminist vision (or its many accomplishments).

When women wielded this vision against states in the Arab Spring of 2011 (and across the decade preceded it), the results were mighty. Women's organizations shaped Egypt's Kefaya Movement in 2004 and Lebanon's Cedar Revolution (which led to regime change) in 2005[69] (see Figure 9.6). During the Arab Spring, organized women, champions of many causes (labor rights, nonviolence, education, politics, children's advocacy, cyberactivism, and LGBTQ rights) helped to mobilize millions against autocracy, applying new technologies to long-dependable networks, strategies, and methods. Perhaps most importantly, they kept pressure—and continue to do so—on states to pass legal reforms protecting women

174 *(Un)finished Business, but Not as Usual: Feminisms from the 1950s*

Figure 9.6 Cedar Revolution, Lebanon. char abumansoor/Alamy Stock Photo.

and their rights. Since 2013, Saudi Arabia, Bahrain, Tunisia, Morocco, Egypt, Algeria, Lebanon, and Iraq have all passed laws granting women greater rights and protections in the workplace and in the courtroom. In 2014, Tunisia passed the first constitution in the Arab world to speak of equality between men and women. In 2016, Egypt passed legislation imposing criminal penalties for sexual harassment in the workplace. In 2017, women in Saudi Arabia gained, among other rights, the freedom to drive.[70]

Conclusion

Even women who do not hold membership in a woman's association or women who do not openly avow feminist agendas (while perhaps harboring them in secret) contribute to the women's movement—or so says Asef Bayat, our clever sociologist. The public realm is now awash in women, feminist and otherwise. These women's presence in the public realm is not what it was in the 1920s when feminists took to the streets to make women's presence in public acceptable. A century on, women's movement into or through the public realm is all but unavoidable.

According to Bayat, the now mundane circulation of women in the public realm despite ideologies that urge them not to (or laws that prohibit their circulation in certain arenas) constitutes a movement in and of itself. Bayat calls it a non-movement, however. As the result of laws limiting women's participation in civil society, he suggests, the days of autonomous organizing, successful lobbying, and unfettered civil initiatives are no longer. In their stead, women—often unwittingly—keep pressure on men and on governments by simply taking up space in public. Women impose themselves as public players, says Bayat, by taking care of everyday business in public: they shop; they go to school (and accompany children to and from school); and they run errands. As they stand in line at the bank or in the market, they might complain, perhaps loudly, about the service or about increased prices. As such, they make their voices heard and their presence known.[71]

In Chapter 10, we look at women who work outside of their homes, for whom encounters with and movement through the public realm are daily affairs. Unwitting feminists or not, they walk in the tall shadows of women who began marching over a century ago.

Notes

1 See Asef Bayat, "The Feminism of Everyday Life," in *Life as Politics: How Ordinary People Change the Middle East*, Asef Bayat, ed. (Stanford, CA: Stanford University Press, 2013), 86–105.
2 Bayat, "The Feminism of Everyday Life."
3 Rula Quawas, "Barefoot Feminist Classes: A Revelation of Being, Doing, and Becoming," in *Women Rising in and Beyond Arab Spring*, Rita Stephan and Mounira M. Charrad, eds. (New York: New York University Press, 2020), 15–16.
4 Amel Nejib al-Ashtal, "A Long, Quite and Steady Struggle: The Women's Movement in Yemen," in *Mapping Arab Women's Movements: A Century of Transformation from Within*, Pernille Arenfeldt and Nawal Al-Hassan Golley, eds. (Cairo: American University in Cairo Press, 2012), 207.
5 Asma' Reimi, "Al-Mar'a al-adaniya fi-l-haya al-ijtima`iyya wa-l-thaqafiya wa-l-iqtisadiya wa-l-siyasiya fi-l-fatra min `am 1937–1967," *Majallat Saba'*, 1999, 114 cited in al-Ashtal, "A Long, Quite and Steady Struggle," Arenfeldt and Al-Hassan Golley, *Mapping*, 200.
6 Nadira Abdel Qoodos, *Mahia Naguib: al-rayada* (San'a: Markaz 'Ubadi al-l-Dirasat wa-l-Nashr, 2005), 43, cited in al-Ashtal, "A Long, Quiet and Steady Struggle," 202.
7 The below information is from Asmahan Al-`Alis, *Awda' al-mar'a al-yamaniya fi zil al-idara al-baritaniya li 'Adan 1937–1968* (Aden: Dar Jami'at 'Adan li-l-Tiba'a wa-l-Nashr, 2005), cited in al-Ashtal, "A Long, Quiet and Steady Struggle."
8 Maryann Howe, "South Yemen Cautiously Easing Restrictions on Women," *The New York Times*, May 28, 1979.
9 Cagla Diner and Şule Toktaş, "Waves of Feminism in Turkey: Kemalist, Islamist and Kurdish Women's Movements in an Age of Globilization," *Journal of Balkan and Near East Studies* Vol. 12, No. 1 (March 2010), 44.
10 Cynthia Nelson, *Doria Shafik, Egyptian Feminist: A Woman Apart* (Gainesville: University of Florida Press, 1996).
11 Mary Ann Tétreault, Hellen Rizzo and Doron Schultziner, "Fashioning the Future: The Women's Movement In Kuwait," Arenfeldt and Al-Hassan Golley, *Mapping*, 254.
12 Tétreault, Rizzon and Schultziner, "Fashioning the Future," 267–269.
13 Haya Al-Mughni, "From Gender Equity to Female Subjugation: The Changing Agenda of Women's Groups in Kuwait," in *Organizing Women: Formal and Informal Women's*

Groups in the Middle East, Dawn Chatty and Annika Rabo, eds. (New York: Berg Publications, 2001), 181, cited in Arenfeldt and Al-Hassan Golley, *Mapping*, 269.
14 Tétreault, Rizzo and Schultziner, "Fashioning the Future," 270.
15 Iman C. Chkeir, *Nis'a fi l imra'a: al-sirat Laure Moghaizel* (Beriut: Annahar Publishing, 2002), 50–53, cited in Rita Stephan, "Women's Rights Activism in Lebanon," Arenfeldt and Al-Hassan Golley, *Mapping*, 116.
16 Laure Moghaizel, *al-Mar'a fi-l-tashri` al-lubnani fi daw' al-ittifaqyiyat al-duwaliya ma` muqarana bi-l-tashri`at al-`arabiya* (Beirut: Institute for Women's Studies in the Arab World, 1985), 105 cited in Stephan, "Women's Rights Activism in Lebanon," 116.
17 Ibid.
18 Kari Karamé, "Maman Aida Lebanese Godmother to the Combatants, Fighting Without Arms," in *Women and War in Lebanon*, Lamia R. Shehadeh, ed. (Gainesville: University of Florida Press, 1999), 201.
19 Jennifer Eggert, "Female Fighters and Militants in Lebanon's Civil War: Individual Profiles, Pahtways and Motivations," *Studies in Conflict and Terrorism* (2018), 1–30.
20 Women also taught other women home economics, handiwork, and other elements of religion. Shahadeh, *Women and War*, 152–154. According to Schulze, some women were trained to fight in Hizbollah but were not used in combat, aside from a lone suicide bomber in 1985. "Communal Violence," 136.
21 Jocelyn Kweiri, "From Gunpowder to Incense," in *Women and War in Lebanon*, 209–210.
22 Zeina Abirached, *A Game for Swallows*, trans. by Edward Gauvin (Minneapolis: Graphic Universe, 2012), 16–17.
23 Darina al-Joundi with Mohamed Kacimi, *The Day Nina Simone Stopped Singing*, trans. by Marjolijn De Jager (New York: Feminist Press, 2011), 11–12, 26–27.
24 al-Joundi, *The Day Nina Simone Stopped Singing*, 74–76, 43.
25 al-Joundi, "The Day Nina Simone Stopped Singing," 1.
26 Chkeir, *Nisa'fil-imra'a*, 161, cited in Arenfeldt and Al-Hassan Golley, *Mapping*, 117.
27 Maya Mikdashi, *Sextarianism: Sovereignty, Secularism, and the State in Lebanon* (Stanford: Stanford University Press, 2022), 32.
28 "Taif Accords," (November 4, 1989), https://peacemaker.un.org/sites/peacemaker.un.org/files/LB_891022_Taif%20Accords.pdf.
29 Al-Joundi, *The Day Nina Simone Stopped Singing*, 114–115.
30 Rita Stephan, "Leadership of Lebanese Women in Cedar Revolution," in *Muslim Women in War and Crisis*, Faegheh Shirazi, ed. (Austin: University of Texas, 2010), 176–177.
31 Ziad Abu Rish, "Garbage Politics," *MERIP* 277 (2015), 36–37.
32 Joanne Nucho, "Garbage Infrastructure, Sanitation, and New Meanings of Citizenship in Lebanon," *Postmodern Culture* Vol. 30, No. 1 (2019). doi:10.1353/pmc.2019.0018.
33 Lina Duque, "Lebanon's Protests Could Mark a Victory for Women," *CNN Commentary* (November 23, 2019) https://search.proquest.com/wire-feeds/lebanons-protests-could-mark-victory-women/docview/2316886326/se-2?accountid=10639; Amnesty International, "Protests in Lebanon Explained," (Updated September 2020), https://www.amnesty.org/en/latest/news/2019/11/lebanon-protests-explained/.
34 Human Rights Watch, "They Killed Us From the Inside," August 3, 2021, https://www.hrw.org/report/2021/08/03/they-killed-us-inside/investigation-august-4-beirut-blast.
35 The below information about Israel is taken from Dalia Scheindlin, "Feminism in Israel/Women in Israel—A Revolution Halted?," February 2018. https://fathomjournal.org/women-and-feminism-in-israel-women-in-israel-a-revolution-halted/
36 Dalia Scheindlin, "Feminism in Israel/Women in Israel—A Revolution Halted?," February 2018. https://fathomjournal.org/women-and-feminism-in-israel-women-in-israel-a-revolution-halted/
37 Dalia Scheindlin, "Feminism in Israel/Women in Israel—A Revolution Halted?," February 2018. https://fathomjournal.org/women-and-feminism-in-israel-women-in-israel-a-revolution-halted/

38 The below section on Israel is taken from Hanna Herzog "Feminism in Contemporary Israel," August 2021, https://jwa.org/encyclopedia/article/feminism-in-contemporary-israel
39 Judy Maltz, "the Original 'Wall of Moms': How Four Mothers Changed Israeli History, Haaretz" (English-language version), August 27, 2000.
40 http://www.womenwagepeace.org.il.
41 Diner and Toktaş, "Waves of Feminism in Turkey," 45.
42 Diner and Toktaş, "Waves of Feminism in Turkey," 46–47.
43 Yesim Arat, "Women's Rights and Islam in Turkish Politics: The Civil Code," *Middle East Journal* Vol. 64, No. 2 (2010), 241.
44 Diner and Toktaş, "Waves of Feminism in Turkey," 44.
45 Diner and Toktaş, "Waves of Feminism in Turkey," 49.
46 Leslie Lewis, "Convergences and Divergences: Egyptian Women's Activism over the Last Century," Arenfeldt and Al-Hassan Golley, *Mapping*, 53.
47 Margot Badran, *Feminism and Islam: Secular and Religious Convergences* (London: Oneworld Publications, 2009).
48 Saba Mahmoud, *Politics of Piety: The Islamic Revival and the Feminist Subject* (Princeton: Princeton University Press, 2004).
49 Katherine Zoepf, "Islamic Revival Lead by Women Tests Syria's Secularism," *Islam for Today*, August 29, 2006, http://www.islamfortoday.com/womansyria.htm cited in Pauline Homsi Vinson and Nawar al-Hassan Golley, "Challenges and Opportunities: The Women's Movement in Syria," in Arenfeldt and Al-Hassan Golley, *Mapping*, 78.
50 Hillary Kalmbach, "Social and Religious Change in Damascus: One Case of Female Islamic Religious Authority," *British Journal of Middle Eastern Studies* Vol. 35, No. 1 (2008), 19, cited in Homsi Vinson and al-Hassan Golley, "Challenges and Opportunities: The Women's Movement in Syria," 78–79.
51 Kalmbach, "Social and Religious Change in Damascus," 39, cited in in Homsi Vinson and al-Hassan Golley, "Challenges and Opportunities: The Women's Movement in Syria," 79.
52 Haya Al-Mughni, "Political Actors without the Franchise: Women and Politics in Kuwait," in *Monarchies and Nations: Globalisation and Identity in the Arab States of the Gulf*, Paul Dresch and James Piscatori, eds. (New York: I.B. Tauris, 2005), 205, cited in Tétrault, Rizzo and Schultziner, "Fashioning the Future," 261.
53 Tétrault, Rizzo and Schultziner, "Fashioning the Future," 262.
54 Ibid.
55 Pernille Arenfeldt and Nawar Al-Hassan Golley, "Arab Women's Movements: Developments, Priorities, and Challenges," Arenfeldt and al-Hassan Golley, *Mapping*, 21.
56 Lina Abou-Habib, "The Journey Began in 1995: How Beijing Shaped 25 Years of Feminist Action," *Gender and Development* Vol. 28, No. 2 (2020), 309.
57 Amrita Basu, "Introduction," *Women's Movements in the Global Era: The Power of Local Feminisms*, Amrita Basu, ed. (Boulder, CO: Westview Press, 2016), 5.
58 Stephan, "Women's Rights Activism in Lebanon," 126.
59 Al-Ashtal, "A Long, Quiet and Steady Struggle," 223–234.
60 Ibtesam al-Atiyat, "Harvests of Golden Decades: Contemporary Women's Activism in Jordan," Arenfeldt and Al-Hassan Golley, *Mapping*, 149.
61 Abou-Habib, "The Journey," 308.
62 Stephan, "Women's Rights Activism in Lebanon," 126.
63 Abou-Habib, "The Journey," 309.
64 https://www.idea.int/gsod/sites/default/files/2021-11/10%20progress-on-gender-equality-gsod-indices.pdf.
65 https://news.un.org/en/story/2020/09/1071722.
66 George W. Bush, cited in Lila Abu-Lughod, *Do Muslim Women Really Need Saving?* (Cambridge, MA: Harvard University Press, 2013), 29.

67 Arenfeldt and Al-Hassan Golley, "Arab Women's Movements," 7.
68 IRIN (Integrated Regional Information Networks), "Syria: Women's Rights Activists Face Resistance." Women Living Under Muslim Laws, March 21, 2006, http:www.wluml.org/node/2877, cited in Homsi Vinson and Al-Hassan Golley, "Challenges and Opportunities," 74.
69 Rita Stephan and Mounira M. Charrad, "Introduction: Advancing Women's Rights in the Arab World," in *Women Rising: In and Beyond the Arab Spring*, Rita Stephen and Mounira M. Charrad, eds. (New York: New York University Press, 2020), 4.
70 Stephan and Charrad, "Introduction," 7. See also https://www.pbs.org/wgbh/frontline/article/the-paradox-of-saudi-arabias-social-reforms/.
71 Bayat, "The Feminism of Everyday Life," 87–88.

10 Women and Work

Introduction

This chapter weaves together local production and global capitalism as those phenomena combined to change women's work lives beginning in the nineteenth century. Capitalist forms of production brought increasing numbers of women into a new kind of work place, one which was not immune to nineteenth- and early twentieth-century debates about the appropriateness of "female labor." The fact that women had always worked, even if they were not remunerated for their labor, was lost on Victorian-era industrialists and colonial officials for whom domestic work was less valuable than factory work, and according to whom the "weaker sex" belonged at home. Setting patterns that continue to this day, captains of industry and colonial officials gave female industrial workers the most menial tasks and the worst pay. Women were also given an earful about the potentially deleterious moral consequences of working in public for pay.

In modern capitalist societies, there is a clear distinction between work, home, and leisure. In premodern, precapitalist societies, these lines were not so easily drawn. In the Middle East, as discussed in Chapter 2, women and men of the peasant and artisan classes worked close to home. Pastoralists had shifting home sites; however, as in the case of farmers and craftsmen, the family was the unit of production. For fishermen and pearl divers, the household remained the unit of (re) production. The precapitalist rhythm of life and subsistence varied throughout the region. Although some sources report women working for wages as early as the sixteenth century, paid labor was not the norm, even for men.

With the rise of capitalism, however, the commercialization of agriculture and the rise of wage labor, major shifts occurred in people's understanding of the relationship between domestic and public labor. As industry emerged, domestic production was devalued. As work began taking women and men outside of the home, debates emerged about the appropriateness of women working to begin with. The backdrop of colonialism against which paid work emerged supported both the devaluation of domestic production and the "inappropriateness" of women working outside of the domestic realm.

The stigma attached to work outside the home is so engrained in Middle Eastern societies that virtually every study of women and work in the region begins with a discussion of how to accurately capture data about female workers. Over the last half century of research, it has become apparent that women do not "count" like men do in statistical surveys. The view of the wife as a helpmate blurs the lines between spouse, daughter, and worker.

Changing the questions we ask about women and work, however, yields vastly different results. The foremost authority on women and work in the Arab world found that the majority of men claimed that their wives did not work. When she rephrased the question as to whether they would have to hire someone in the absence of their wife's labor, a different picture emerged: the majority claimed that they would indeed need a replacement.[1]

This chapter discusses the "factory girl" as a labor phenomenon and as a lightning rod for debate. Next, the chapter covers the rise of professions for women beginning at the turn of the twentieth century, illustrating that women's participation in industrial labor resulted both in increasing numbers of women entering the workforce and in men's continued determination that there were "female-specific" professions. We then turn to "pink"-collar work, which challenges us to think critically about "men's" and "women's" work. Next, the chapter examines domestic service and its evolution over the last century. Finally, we look at cottage industries and informal economies as well as their intersection with small business ownership.

Factories

The earliest factories in the Middle East to hire women tended to observe gender and religious norms. Many were located close to the homes of workers and provided some form of segregation of the sexes. Evidence suggests that some factory owners attempted to facilitate male and female workers' transition to the new environment of the factory. Egyptian Viceroy Muhammad `Ali established his first factories in the 1820s. Women were important contributors to the Viceroy's endeavors to industrialize Egypt's textile industry: men worked the cotton ginning machines, while women and children did the messy work of cleaning and sorting the cotton and flax. This work, some of which could be done at home, required "nimble fingers" and "patience," and connected the sphere of the home to the industrial world, at once gendering and devaluing tasks that men were unable or unwilling to do.[2] Women who worked in the newly-established factories did so in segregated areas and using only a veil as a separation from male coworkers. Women were generally relegated to tasks requiring less skill, less automation, and smaller equipment than jobs assigned to men.

Women who were recruited to work in Muhammad `Ali's factories tried to avoid what was for them the equivalent of conscription by maiming themselves. To protest paltry pay, women and men alike participated in burning factories down.[3]

Women's factory labor elsewhere in the Ottoman Empire was the outgrowth of cottage industry. The first trades to be mechanized in the early nineteenth century were spinning, yarn-making, and rug-making. In the early decades of the nineteenth century, a pattern of a home industry network had become common among various kinds of textile production, such as the production of linen and cotton cloth. In some areas throughout Anatolia and the Balkans, textile-producing centers emerged in which both women and men worked. Sometimes, women did the spinning at home and men did the weaving in factories. In other cases, such as the silk-reeling factories of Bursa, Izmir, and Mount Lebanon, production centers appealed to a largely-unmarried female working population and to widows with no other means of employment. By the late nineteenth century, as women's participation in Ottoman factories expanded, dormitories for workers became part of the industrial landscape.[4] Conditions in Ottoman factories were less than ideal. A grievance from Turkish, Greek, Armenian, and Jewish women from the silk mills of Bursa in 1910 compiled a list of complaints, including long hours, low pay, sexual abuse, physical abuse, and poor working conditions[5] (see Figure 10.1).

In Mount Lebanon, European (mainly French) capitalists began opening silk factories (later to be replaced by tobacco). Women and children received a fraction of the pay of local men. Maronite Church leadership put pressure on factory owners to keep male and female workers separate. Church leadership was also successful in setting 13 as the age at which male and female workers needed to be segregated. Age-specific gender segregation also allowed factory owners to practice a sex-segregated system for silk production in which women were given the worst jobs.[6] The precedent set by sex segregation in silk factories laid the groundwork for later types of industrial enterprises.

Unmarried women formed the backbone of the silk workforce because men in the region of Mount Lebanon had difficulty adjusting to the idea of factory work. Men perhaps acclimated to the idea of women working because it spared them

Figure 10.1 Silk factory, Chouf, Lebanon. Maroun Rached/Alamy Stock Photo.

from having to leave the land from which they derived great honor. Instead, men allowed their daughters to work. Whereas women had previously given over their wages to their family, by the turn of the twentieth century, women were increasingly retaining their salaries for dowries, particularly as the pool of eligible males declined with increased emigration from Lebanon.[7]

As silk production declined at the end of the nineteenth century, many women turned to tobacco factories where once again factory owners valued "nimble fingers" but did not compensate them overly well. Women working in tobacco factories in Lebanon accounted for a steady 40% or more of the workforce in those establishments. In factories in Egypt and Lebanon, women did the dirty work of sorting, grading, and cutting tobacco. In Egypt, the rolling of cigarettes was deemed to be a "skilled" job and was assigned to foreign men (usually Greeks), although women did fold cigarette packets. In Lebanon, any task that lacked mechanization was labeled women's work, including the rolling and packing of cigarettes. Thus, by 1930, Lebanese women had become huge opponents of mechanization, which they equated with male competition (see Figure 10.2).[8]

Iran's first European-style textiles factory opened there in the 1850s and women formed a major portion of the Qajar workforce. Nevertheless, most textile production continued to be home-based cotton, wool, or silk spinning. Handicrafts and manufactures of such things as rugs were mainstays of the Qajar economy prior

Figure 10.2 Woman weaving a carpet, Anatolia. Günter Flegar/imageBROKER/Alamy Stock Photo.

to the discovery and production of oil (1908–1914). Women were essential to the handicrafts and manufactures sectors forming a "reserve army" of available labor.

Beginning in the 1920s, states and industrialists began opening new factories and updating old ones. State building demanded the participation of women and men in mostly state-run industrial enterprises. The burgeoning oil industry's high level of technical expertise and mechanization was deemed by men to be suited for them alone, and oil therefore remains outside of the accepted Gulf standards for female labor. Despite such restrictions, women throughout the 1920s Middle East were prominent in the manufacture of textiles, tobacco, pharmaceuticals, and food. For example, state centralization under British Mandate rule in Iraq created a 100% increase in date exports. This low-tech industry, characterized by seasonal manual labor, lack of health regulation enforcement, and poor working conditions attracted a largely female labor corp.[9]

Egypt experienced its second industrial revolution in the interwar period. In the 1920s, the Bank Misr Group funded a series of national industries. Women (and children) worked in these large establishments, as well as in smaller workshops, clocking long hours in textile production, averaging about 15 hours per day in the 1940s, even after the passage of legislation which reduced the working day to nine hours. Because being married was grounds for dismissal from their jobs, most female workers remained unmarried.

During the early reign of Muhammad Reza Shah in Iran, women's groups and labor groups advocated for changes to the conditions in which women worked. By 1946, the state passed a series of laws that improved the lives of urban working-class women and children. The state established a 40-hour work week and made overtime voluntary. It set the minimum age for child labor at ten years and their work day at six hours. Women were given 12 weeks maternity leave and a minimum wage based upon subsistence needs for a family of four.[10]

WWII necessitated greater female mobilization in the French mandates of Syria and Lebanon. Women's labor participation increased in tobacco, textile, and food processing plants, particularly in Lebanon. Mandate officials treated female workers as inferior to male workers who were heads of household, encouraging women to leave the labor force after they married.[11]

The state socialist revolutions at mid-century in Egypt, Syria, Iraq, and later South Yemen put in place regimes that encouraged participation of female workers. Legislation in these countries protected female workers from discrimination in the public sector, gave them maternity leave, job protection for pregnancy, and time off for childcare. These laws did not apply to private firms. Accordingly, women flocked to public sector jobs, whether in industry or elsewhere. While capitalist Lebanon did not adopt laws to give women rights, Régie, Lebanon's monopoly-holding tobacco industry, eliminated child labor by the 1960s. Children's jobs then went to women, who were paid less than men. Young girls skirted the new laws and gained employment by using the pictureless ID cards of their older sisters.[12]

Beginning in the 1960s, Turkey began an aggressive import substitution program fueled by its expanded industrialization. Turkey's industrialization was dependent upon a Fordist mass-production line using unskilled labor. Women as well as men were part of the new industrial workforce. Over the course of the 1970s, the system became more modernized and efficient, and many of the daughters and granddaughters of the production-line laborers were accordingly forced out of the industrial workforce. Women who remain employed in industry tend to work in textiles and clothing (59.5%), food (14.4%), or manufacturing (metal, equipment, machinery; 12.2%). The shift from rural to urban living in Turkey meant an overall decline in female labor-force participation from 72% in 1955 to 25.5% in 2005, both as women's (and men's) labor was replaced by technology and as women found other avenues for employment.[13]

In the 1960s, Muhammad Reza Shah pioneered his "White Revolution" in Iran. While increasing numbers of women entered professional fields (see below), it was the service and industrial sectors where women's numbers rose sharply. Participation in agriculture remained the most significant work for women, even if that labor was not remunerated and therefore not counted by statisticians. Nonetheless, in 1972, half a million women were involved in industry, mining, or transportation. These women represented two-thirds of the paid (and accounted for) labor force in Iran.[14]

Economic reorganization, revolution, and war have all affected female labor-force participation, as have Islamic trends (see Chapters 12 and 13), which have supported a "stay-at-home" ideal for women. In Egypt, Sadat's *infitah* or open-door economic policy, which blossomed into privatization under Mubarak, began a process in which women were wedged out of the workplace. Sadat's 1971 Constitution included a clause guaranteeing women's equality, contingent upon women balancing home and work demands. This distinction was quite different from Nasser's 1956 Constitution, which had guaranteed men and women the same workplace rights. In the post-Mubarak era, the 2012 and 2014 Constitutions replicated the language of the 1971 Constitution.[15]

Sadat also made structural adjustments to the economy at the request of the International Monetary Fund, including gradually ending subsidized bread, an act that incited riots in 1977. Working men and women participated in the riots to protect the affordability of the literal staff of life. This strike marked the beginning of women's increased labor activism, particularly in the field in which they were most dominant: textiles. From the late 1990s to 2010, between 3,000 and 4,000 strikes took place in Egypt. Most notable were the strikes which took place between 2006 and 2008 in Mahalla al-Kubra, the textiles manufacturing district between Cairo and Alexandria, in which women played a prominent role.[16] The 2008 demonstrations were linked to pro-democracy groups, which had begun agitating for increased political participation, paving the way for the 2011 Revolution (see Chapter 14).

Since the Revolution of 2011, labor activism has been prominent in Egypt. The regime of General Abdel Fatah al-Sisi (r. 2013–) has implemented new, stricter bans against strikes. It has also passed anti-protest laws to discourage labor action. Nevertheless, in 2015, women and men from the textile factories at Mahalla al-Kubra demanded the 10% cost of living increase that Sisi's regime had promised them. Their protests were followed by a round of demonstrations by the workers at factories in Kafr al-Dawar. The government was consequently forced to give in to the workers' demands and preemptively offer the same raise to all workers in state-held companies.[17]

The backdrop for nearly three decades of Egyptian female labor activism has been a shrinkage of the public sector, a push for early retirement for women, and a lack of female leadership. In 1994, the government set up holding companies to replace public-sector ownership and management. Women were particularly susceptible to Mubarak's subsequent campaigns in favor of early retirement. Anxieties in female workers' lives have been fueled by long working hours, exhausting commutes, challenges in providing daycare, sexual harassment, and the overwhelming feeling of being scrutinized by neighbors, relatives, and male coworkers for impropriety. These sources of anxiety and increased Islamist rhetoric encouraging women's domesticity combine to entice women to take early retirement packages. This trend has also been fueled since 2006 by women's prerogative to retire at 45. An exception to the trend of early retirement among women has been female heads of household who, like men, have also viewed the terms of early retirement as insufficient for paying bills.[18]

In Iran, after the 1979 Revolution, several factors had an impact on women's industrial labor-force participation: changes in economic policy, Islamist discourse, the Iran-Iraq War, and greater educational opportunity for both sexes. Under the Shah, industry was highly dependent upon import substitution and upon production centered on consumer goods. The revolutionary government took a heavier hand in the industrial process, restricting foreign imports by imposing high tariffs. Initially, these policies led to a decline in female industrial employment and in overall female employment.[19] At the conclusion of Iran's eight-year war with Iraq, it became apparent to the regime that women needed to return to the workforce. The government therefore reoriented its economy again, slowly rebuilding the private sector. On the eve of the 1979 Revolution, women comprised about 38% of the manufacturing workforce, mainly in carpets and textiles. As the result of wartime policies, this figure had dropped to nearly 15% in 1986. A decade later, the number of women working in manufacturing had climbed again to almost 23%. This number dropped to 18.7% in 2006, however, as urban women became increasingly educated and as competition with China for these manufactures increased.[20]

The war with Iran brought Iraq's 1970s oil-driven economic boom to a halt. Over the course of the 1970s, the Baath passed a series of laws designed to encourage women's participation in the public sector. The 1970 labor law assured good working conditions for women, provided childcare at worksites, and offered generous maternity leave. Accordingly, Iraq's labor force more than doubled: by the end of the 1970s, the number of women who worked in Iraq's public sector had increased to 17.5%, up from 4% in 1967. Statistics show that on the eve of the war with Iran, Iraq's female labor force was active in work related to infrastructure (water, electricity, and construction) and production (agriculture, manufacturing, and mining).[21]

As the numbers of Iraq's fallen soldiers increased, however, the regime once again encouraged women to embrace motherhood; by increasing Iraq's population, women would save their nation from Iran, whose citizenry was far greater than Iraq's.[22] By 1987, the number of women in Iraq's labor force had therefore fallen substantially (from 17.5% in 1977 to 6.7%), while women's unemployment increased.[23]

Operation Desert Storm (1991), the 13 years of sanctions that followed it, and the American-led invasion of Iraq in 2003 accelerated Iraq's economic difficulties. The wars destroyed Iraq's infrastructure, resulted in high rates of unemployment, and gave rise to heated discussions about working women "taking" available work away from men. Salaries for work in the public sector—still the largest employer of women—dropped substantially over the 1990s. By 1996, Iraqi women's employment levels were at the lowest levels since the early 1970s.[24]

Like war, economic sanctions, which were put into place by the UN immediately following Operation Desert Storm, have brought women untold hardships in the workplace. Saddam Hussein's regime discontinued its practice of compensating women for work-training programs. Salaries for public sector jobs decreased substantially. Consequently, many women left public-sector work. Women have therefore had to be very creative in order to maintain their livelihoods. Under the UN-imposed sanctions regime, many Iraqi women resorted to selling other people's castoffs—a profession long seen as unfit for women—in street markets in order to survive. Others earned their living sewing clothes, cooking food, baking cakes, cleaning houses, raising chickens, and "reading" coffee cups and other kinds of fortune telling. Surviving the sanctions regime, for both women and men, became a sign of heroism among Iraqis.[25]

After the US-led invasion of 2003, Iraq quickly descended into violence, leading to a sectarian civil war. Armed militias have been the most influential force on Iraq's streets. As Iraq became a magnet for terrorists, its fledgling state was left to contend with its own sectarian violence and with the advent of ISIS (Islamic State of Iraq and Syria) in 2014. With security in the hands of militias, Iraq's industry has been slow to rebuild and unemployment accordingly remains high.

While Syria managed to limit confrontations outside its borders until its own Civil War in 2011, it nonetheless has witnessed a decrease in overall female labor participation. The peak in female labor participation came in 1996 at 23.3% and had dropped to about 13% just before the war. This decrease can perhaps be attributed to women's overrepresentation in agriculture and underrepresentation in modern sectors of the economy. As agriculture has become more efficient, requiring fewer individuals, women have either not been employed or have not been counted in official labor statistics. Industrial participation in Syria has also been hampered by regulations that prohibit women from doing work the government deems hazardous or immoral. Syria's economy, which relies on oil in limited measures has not been conducive to female participation.[26] Regardless, Syria has lost a half million of its citizens in the Civil War that broke out in 2011 and seen another five million of them displaced. The country's economic infrastructure has been destroyed, and the civil war's cost to the economy is immeasurable.

Palestine has had much lower industrial labor-force participation than other parts of the region because of its underdeveloped economy. Large-scale Jewish settlement, the creation of a Jewish state in 1948, occupation by Jordan and Egypt until 1967, occupation by Israel thereafter, the settler movement, and the building of a separation wall have all hindered Palestinian economic development. In the period between 1967 and the Oslo Accords of 1993, Palestinian men served as a pool of cheap labor for the Israeli economy; however, women were excluded from that pool by Palestinian men, for both political and cultural reasons. Palestinian women are underrepresented in the region as a whole with only 16% participation overall.[27]

The Professions

Although the ideal "New Woman" was a stay-at-home mother-educator, this goal was not achievable without a corps of female teachers. State-sponsored education for women began in the mid-nineteenth century in Egypt, the Ottoman Empire, and in a more limited fashion Qajar Iran (Chapter 4). State efforts were supplemented by the educational endeavors of foreign missionaries. Nevertheless, by the turn of the twentieth century, nationalists across the region came to view foreigners as less than ideal for producing mother-educators. The need for teacher education programs therefore increased along with the demand for girls' education.[28]

Medicine is a profession that first gained acceptance for women in various parts of the region in the early decades of the twentieth century, and women were increasingly trained to be doctors, midwives, and nurses. Nevertheless, in some parts of the region, even to this day, the nursing profession remains taboo for women. Gulf countries generally outsource this profession to foreign females. Nevertheless, the historic requirement for same-gender health care and higher standards of public health has necessitated training women in these fields.[29] Holding a profession has gained greater acceptance for women since WWI as the result of women's participation in social and political mobilization.

Women were most seamlessly integrated into the professions in the authoritarian dictatorships of Turkey and Iran, where some educational infrastructure existed. Similarly, Egypt has encouraged the participation of women in public life and maintains an educational system to support women's training. Through the state socialist organization and oil money, Iraq was able to place great emphasis on women's education. Prior to decades of war and sanctions, Iraqi women had high levels of participation in educational and professional life. Syria and Lebanon, while long providing education for women, were slower to provide opportunities for women to put their education to work. Palestinians in the territories lag behind the region at 16% overall labor participation; however, their high level of education means that women make up 43% of the professional class in the West Bank and nearly 26% in the Gaza Strip.[30]

The slow governmental independence of the Gulf and its subsequently-delayed national system of education has meant that women there have lagged behind the rest of the region in professional development. In order to maintain gender-segregated systems of health, education, and welfare, the Gulf countries have relied heavily on foreign professionals. The desire of many Gulf countries to replace foreign labor has meant a stepped-up effort in recent years to educate women and get them into the workforce. Jordan's slower development of female education, high fertility rates, and its dependence of male worker remittances from abroad meant that it did not become dependent upon female labor until more recent fluctuations in oil prices and market instability sent foreign workers home from the Gulf.

In Turkey, Atatürk upheld a belief in Republican "superwomanhood," in which women were encouraged to embrace both the mother-educator ideal and seek work outside of the home. Atatürk acknowledged a natural division of labor between the sexes. But he also insisted that "domestic duties are not necessarily the most important" thing for women to undertake. Atatürk emphasized women's role in educating their children. At the same time, however, he acknowledged that in order to shape the next generation, women would need to become "more enlightened, more educated and more able than our men."[31] Atatürk lived up to this ideal in his own home. He had no children of his own; however, he adopted or protected several, including Sabiha Gökçen, whose career as an aviator embodied the ideals of public womanhood for Atatürk. Atatürk cleared the way for women to gain professional degrees at the university level, which had only been open to them since 1916. Women consequently began to pursue careers in medicine, law, engineering, literature, music, anthropology, higher education, science, and politics. Between 1920 and 1938, approximately 10% of all university graduates were women.

The migration of villagers from the Turkish countryside to the city has had a profound impact on education and the professions. Migrant women in many cases have refused the trappings of secular, republican Kemalism and have demanded the right to wear the headscarf at the university and in public spaces (see Chapter 12). Nevertheless, migrant women have not disavowed careers. In 1973, women represented 17.5% of students in medicine and 9.7% of those in engineering. By the turn of the twenty-first century, those percentages had increased to 40.3% and 20.3%, respectively. Turkish women currently represent a significant proportion in certain fields: 60% of pharmacists, 19% of physicians, 30% of dentists, 34% of lawyers, and 23% of professors. While women are much less likely to be in management and to experience hitting the glass ceiling, their accomplishments since WWI have been remarkable.[32]

Under Reza Shah, the Iranian state's mandate for education, in particular higher education, increased considerably. By the 1930s, women began to enter higher education, and the Pahlavi regime found a place for women not only as mother-educators, but as well-compensated professionals—mainly teachers, professors, and civil servants.[33] The numbers of such educated women were low: the vast majority of Iran was still agricultural and these changes affected just a small percentage of the middle class. Nevertheless, the impact on girls' education was undeniable. The number of girls' schools in Iran in 1910 was just 41, and by 1933 that number had reached 870.[34]

Muhammad Reza Shah largely continued the policies of his father, and as Iran's oil economy developed after the 1953 coup, women became more marginalized in the economy and more dependent upon work in the pink-collar sector (see below). At the same time, however, the idea of women working had achieved greater acceptance among Iran's upper classes by the 1950s, and therefore more educated women were entering the professions. The Shah's White Revolution (see Chapter 8) brought some educational and professional gains to middle- and upper-class urban women.

While the 1979 Revolution initially had a negative impact on Iran's overall female labor force participation, by the mid-1980s, women had reentered the workforce. Between 1986 and 1996, women's participation in civil service increased from 30% to 38%. The large and increasing number of women in government service may be attributable to the increasing opportunities for men in the private sector. The expansion of educational opportunities for women and the nation's large population under the age of 30 have meant that there is a disproportionate number of unemployed or underemployed young, Iranian women.

Egyptian women's professional labor-force participation dates back to the nineteenth century. Women began to enter the professions only after women's participation in the 1919 Revolution, the state's expansion of its educational system, the establishment of compulsory elementary education, and the admittance of women to the university. The first generation of educated women served as administrators in women's schools. Women in the interwar period were slowly introduced into new professions, like veterinary medicine and architecture. Women became valued in fields that reinforced a nurturing role for women, such as pediatric medicine, gynecology, social work, and education. By the time of the Revolution of 1952 and the nationalization of the Suez Canal four years later, women benefited from an increased demand for their professional services. While women benefited from Nasser's form of state socialism, they also felt its burdens: on the eve of Khrushchev's visit in 1964, Nasser released a large number of prisoners of conscience. Among them was Communist Fatma Zaki, one of the first women to study science at the university level. After her release from prison, however, the Nasser regime stripped Zaki of her teaching credentials.[35] Nevertheless, state socialism and the expansion of education in Egypt guaranteed free education at all levels, with the gender-blind General Secondary Exam largely determining a student's course of study.

Lebanon's Civil War (1975–1990) (see Chapter 9) helped to pull women into the labor force. Like Egypt, Lebanon has a longstanding history of girls' education and an even lengthier connection to missionary education. Lebanon's integration of women into professions, however, has been slower and its educational system somewhat less gender-neutral than other Middle Eastern nations. Lebanese women have been more likely to study arts and humanities than science, for example. Even in the twenty-first century, when women outnumber men 54%–46% at the university level, they still make up only 26% of the (total) labor force. When Lebanese women are able to venture into fields such as finance or banking, they often find that their careers ultimately hit a glass ceiling.

Lebanon accepted CEDAW (Convention on the Elimination of all forms of Discrimination Against Women) in 1997. This international treaty originated in the UN in 1979, and beginning in 1981, it emerged as an international bill of rights for women. To date, 189 countries have adopted CEDAW.[36] Despite the passage of CEDAW in Lebanon, women still face disadvantages, such as unequal access to welfare rights and women's ability to retire upon marriage with life insurance. These laws discourage women's participation and advancement in the professions and encourage women's dependence upon men.[37]

While Jordan lacks the prestigious history of girls' education that exists in Lebanon, Syria, and Egypt, it invested heavily in education for both sexes beginning in the 1970s. When the oil boom hit (see below) and large numbers of Jordanian men went to work in the Gulf, more Jordanian women entered the workforce. Although it currently has one of the most educated female populations, Jordan has lower female labor-force participation (not counting the Gulf) than the rest of the region at 25%. Professional Jordanian women are most likely to work in the public sector in the fields of education or health care. The return of men from the Gulf, the influx of refugees from Iraq and Syria, and outdated laws inhibit women's full integration into the labor force.[38]

Oil and labor migration have had a direct and indirect impact on professional women in the Middle East. The paucity of skilled (and unskilled) labor, male and female, in the Gulf prior to the first Gulf War paved the way for the Gulf states' extreme dependence on outside labor. Many men but also some families from around the region went to the Gulf to work. Foreign professionals helped to build not only the petroleum industry, but also modern infrastructures for health, education, and welfare in the Gulf states. The conservatism of the Gulf countries and their desire for gender-segregated education have opened opportunities for professional women from other countries. Leila Ahmed, an Egyptian educated in Britain, traveled alone to Abu Dhabi a few years after its independence (1971) to help build its educational system, for example.[39] More common, however, was for families to travel to the Gulf together, whether for a limited period of time to save for a home (in the case of many cash-strapped Egyptians) or to relocate there semi-permanently (in the case of Palestinian refugees, some of whom had Jordanian citizenship by the 1970s). The Gulf states benefited from an oil boom that began in 1973 after two Arab-Israeli wars took place in six years. The first of those wars resulted in the loss of significant Palestinian territory and created more refugees, some of whom ended up working in the Gulf.

In the twenty-first century, 90% of the Gulf Cooperation Council (GCC) population (aside from Saudi Arabia) is urban. This phenomenal urban growth over the last three or four decades could not have taken place without an educated labor force from elsewhere in the region. For women, this growth has created a multitude of opportunities. Medicine has come to be accepted as a field of study; Egyptian and Filipina women fill nursing positions in the Gulf states. South East Asian labor has slowly come to replace Arab labor because the Gulf elites view Southeast Asians as more docile and more easily replaceable than Arabs (see below). Meanwhile, high-level administrative positions are more likely to go to Americans or Europeans than to Gulf women or men.[40]

Since the 1990s, programs of so-called "Omanization," "Saudization," and the like have been in place to replace foreign workers with nationals. Gulf women have been attending university in ever-increasing numbers, and in many countries such as Qatar, women are, in fact, far more likely to attend university than men by a ratio of 55%–45%. Nevertheless, women who want to work still face a number of obstacles. Many women prefer to work in a segregated environment and to wear some form of traditional clothing, options which are not always available to them. In countries where women are able to easily enter fields like engineering and medicine, they often find resistance from men. In the early 1990s in Oman, despite efforts to open universities to women based only on entrance exams, the first class of medical students to include women named "three" outstanding students of the year so that a man would be included in the group. Beginning in 1986, women were allowed in the Faculty of Engineering; however, protests from certain groups among Omani society denied access to women for a number of years. It is still the responsibility of the employer to convince the Ministry of Manpower that hiring a woman is necessary.[41]

Pink-Collar Work and Service Work

In both labor and gender studies, the term "pink-collar" work has been used to refer to female-dominated professions.[42] A number of the fields that are classified as "pink collar" in the West, such as secretarial work, either began as male- or mixed-gender work in the Middle East. In the Middle East, such work also carries a class distinction: pink-collar labor requires some type of skill, training, or language proficiency. Such skills give the jobholder a foot in the middle class. These occupations cross boundaries of public sector (clerks); service sector (beauticians, baristas, and tour guides); and private sector (technicians, secretaries, and switchboard operators).

One of the first pink-collar professions to surface on the perimeter of professional life in the Middle East was the store clerk. Store owners in Cairo and Istanbul ca. 1900 hired a wide variety of ethnic and religious groups. Shop girls had to hold the right credentials: they had to come from good families and they had to speak more than one language. While the age of the foreign-owned department store faded in the era of Atatürk in Turkey and the age of Nasser in Egypt, the pink-collar worker endured. As both Turkey and Egypt moved toward economic liberalization in the late twentieth century, women with proficient language skills once again found work as tour guides, coffee shop baristas, and in a whole host of service industries catering to foreigners and local elites. Tour companies specializing in "women only" tours are conducted by women and give tourists an idea about traditions, culture, and food, breaking stereotypes and misconceptions—a reversal of the harem tour of Chapter 3.[43]

Offices and bureaucracies throughout the region have been staffed historically by an army of women who have some degree of education and perhaps some level of skill, such as typing, shorthand, and, later, word processing. As women entered these professions, mixed-gender office environments created a new arena for the "Woman Question" to resurface in the press. In Iran under Reza Shah, for example, the tension surrounding women in public space heightened as women joined the ranks of the growing bureaucracy.[44]

Advertisements in the interwar press in Egypt encouraged men and women to earn the skills necessary to enter the pink-collar middle class. Correspondence schools, language schools, and vocational schools allowed both women and men who were on the margins of the middle class to gain the skills necessary to work in expanding the government bureaucracy or private enterprises. Egyptian men and women could advance their skills at home, at night, or outside of the classroom. Berlitz language schools offered classes at different times of the day, with male or female teachers, individually or in a group setting.[45] The Egyptian Correspondence Schools advertised their flexibility: students could work at their own pace, without leaving home, at about a quarter of the cost of traditional schools.[46] The Faks School, for example, offered language, shorthand, commerce, and accounting: career-advancing skills.[47] Advertising heralded the availability of jobs for people with such skills. Women were specifically targeted for clerical positions.[48]

The success of women entering the workforce in the interwar era was due both to the necessities of war and to the introduction of the typewriter. At the turn of the twentieth century, Theodor Herzl, journalist and founder of modern Zionism, presented Sultan Abdül Hamid II with a typewriter adapted to Arabic script and to the necessities of typing from right to left. Once Turkey's alphabet was Romanized in 1928, use of the typewriter spread through the region. Vocational education facilitated the typewriter's spread in the Arabic-speaking regions, as did the expansion of education in Iran.[49]

The ranks of the secretarial class grew throughout the region over the course of the first half of the twentieth century. By the mid-1950s, there was even a short-lived magazine in Turkey titled from the French words for secretary and typist: *Sekreter Daktilograf*. To encourage a good work ethic, governments and businesses sponsored speed-typing competitions.[50] To the present day, Turks dominate world keyboard competitions.[51]

The rise of personal computers ca. 1980 required new skill sets of the clerical class. Women across the region who worked in the public sector were more likely to be using outdated equipment and less likely to receive training in the use of computers. Women looking for private sector jobs as secretaries and administrators faced further obstacles, as classified advertisements sometimes list age, marital status, or appearance requirements that are illegal in many Western countries. A recent World Economic Forum study cited low female workforce participation as a general trend in the region. Consequently, the Forum recommended investing in digital literacy to prepare a new generation of workers—especially women who lag behind men in computer literacy—for what they call the fourth industrial revolution.[52]

Domestic Service

Domestic service is considered to be part of the informal economy. Nonetheless, it deserves special attention in any discussion of women's work. Domestic service in the Middle East had its roots in slavery (see Chapter 2). The abolition of the slave trade in the late nineteenth century led to a demand for cheap domestic labor.

Duties attendant to the home were ever-expanding in the late nineteenth century, as new schools for girls and new women's journals espoused the duties of domesticity to a growing middle class (see Chapters 4 and 6). The pool for this labor grew as conditions in the countryside worsened in the late-nineteenth and early twentieth centuries, the product of new private property laws, corresponding land scarcity, and the emergence of waged labor in the countryside.

"Adopting out" their daughters to train and work as domestic service became a solution for those struggling to survive. Peasant families in Egypt, greater Syria, and other parts of the Ottoman Empire found it increasingly difficult to feed, clothe, and house all their children—particularly female children. Elite and middle-class families therefore "adopted" peasant girls, providing them with food, lodging, clothing, a small salary, and sometimes even a bit of education in exchange for housework. These arrangements ranged from family-like conditions to situations of extreme physical and sexual abuse. Old Egyptian movies, often based on literature, vividly depict the miserable life of these women. *The Nightingale's Prayer* (1959), based on Taha Hussein's book by the same name (1934), highlights the misfortune of a Bedouin woman, Hanadi, who dreams of a better life and falls victim to the sexual predations of her employer. Hanadi's uncle carries out an honor killing in revenge.

Due to the persistence of slavery there, domestic service arrived in the Gulf somewhat later than it had in other parts of the region. It was not until the 1950s, and even early 1960s, that slavery was fully eradicated in the Gulf states. Domestic slaves therefore continued to function in elite homes until that time. Furthermore, after independence (which for many Gulf nations did not occur until 1971), oil wealth spread through the Gulf states more deeply than it had elsewhere. Post-independence, domestic labor first became an option for wives of unskilled Arab laborers who arrived in the Gulf after the oil boom.

The existence of inexpensive domestic labor facilitated women's entrance into the workforce as well as elite women's participation in various forms of charitable activities (described in Chapter 7). Textbooks and women's magazines from the early twentieth century onward emphasized the importance of governing the household as if it were a kingdom and of inspecting the work of their subjects: the domestic servants. While the stay-at-home mother-educator could watch her domestic servants' every move, the new corps of female professionals in the Middle East had to try as best they could to keep even a general accounting of their domestic help.

In many parts of the Middle East, it is only marginalized or refugee women who work as domestic servants contemporarily. In some cases, deeply underprivileged women hide the domestic labor that they perform because of the stigma that is attached to laboring. Historically, in Lebanon, for example, domestic work has been the domain of three underprivileged groups: Shiites, Kurds, and Palestinian refugees. During the Lebanese civil war, working-class women had to put themselves at great personal risk, crossing political lines and constantly recalculating the routes they took to get to their work sites (see Chapter 9). Currently, Syrian refugees constitute the newest pool of inexpensive labor across the region. In Egypt, it is Sudanese emigrants, male and female, who currently find work as domestic servants. Unlike the past, where women stayed close to home, living in the homes in which they worked, women currently have to either hold multiple day jobs, live off the limited income from a single job, or work part time.[53]

In the Gulf, women represent about 11% of all labor migrants, and the vast majority of these women work as domestic servants or nannies. The current trend among Gulf families has been to hire Asian women, 90% of whom work in the service sector, mainly in domestic service. In the last decade, there has been wide press coverage about the miserable working conditions in which these women labor. These women's complaints include long working hours with no days off, physical abuse, sexual abuse, and underpayment. Because employers are responsible for the "behavior" of their workers in the country, they retain their employees' passports, giving employers great power over their workers.[54]

In Iran, between the downfall of the Qajars and Reza Khan's ascension in 1925, domestic servants constituted one of Iran's 32 existing labor unions. At that time, one quarter of Iran's unions represented unskilled labor, whereas less than 19% represented modern wage earners, demonstrating the underdevelopment of the Iranian economy.[55] After his self-coronation in 1926, Reza Shah clamped down on the Central Council of Federated Trade Unions (CCFTC). Although he impeded the growth of the labor movement, in which the traditional professions were well represented, Reza Shah did support the creation of a new industrial class (see above). As more Iranian women began working in manufacturing and in the professions, opportunities for domestic labor expanded. Women's participation in Iran's workforce continued apace until it was temporarily interrupted by the Iranian Revolution, and as more and more women worked outside the home, the need for domestic labor increased. Domestic labor, whose official numbers are not recorded, is intimately tied to the numbers of women employed outside of the home, as few others can afford the luxury of hiring servants.

Cottage Industry and Informal Economy

The informal sector is the portion of the economy which is not monitored, measured, or taxed by the government. The informal sector unites a number of categories of work, including cottage industry, as well as the service industry, and it ranges in composition from desperately unskilled to highly-skilled workers. What unites the women who work in the informal sector across the region is their entrepreneurial spirit and desire to contribute to their families' economy. The cottage industry in which women participate includes various forms of piecework, tailoring, jewelry-making, and craft production. Women can work for themselves or subcontract for others, whether weaving baskets for tourists in Fayoum, Egypt, hand-beading jewelry for a small shop owner in Beirut, or weaving rugs in Tehran. Women produce these goods at home, where they can take care of their children, or in small workshop environments. Women in the service sector include taxi drivers, beauticians, wedding planners, middlewomen, caterers, daycare operators, and street vendors—any type of service that can go unreported and untaxed. Service workers who command a higher salary due to their education include computer programmers, designers, and tutors. While vast educational and class differences may exist among these women, some of whom may receive government aid, what unites them is that they generally do not have access to social insurance.[56]

In occupied Palestine, particularly after the first *intifada* in 1987, economic self-sufficiency has been a hallmark of women's experience (see Chapter 13). Women's informal economic networks of gardens, craft production, home food industries (jam, cheese), and bakeries have allowed them to continue to boycott Israeli goods, a practice born during the first *intifada*. In the absence of a full-fledged Palestinian state, the activities of production and reproduction that women do at home, such as childcare, elder care, and food production, make it difficult to separate the domestic economy from the formal economy. Furthermore, the Israeli tightening of tax laws and the closing of borders to day workers have forced more Palestinian men and women into the informal economy.[57] The general decline in the Palestinian economy after the 1993 signing of the Oslo Accords, a decline that continued after the second *intifada* (2000–2005), has added growing importance to women's informal economic activities.

In Egypt, an estimated 3.1 million female laborers in the informal economy represent 31% of women's total employment.[58] As agriculture has become more efficient, fewer women have been needed for the staple occupation. With migration to cities, some women found work in industry and in the professions; however, even in the late twentieth century some women remained undereducated or underskilled. Even women with little education and few skills can be involved in complex international market relationships, however. Imagine a woman, among the under-schooled from a Delta village, relocated to a working-class neighborhood in Cairo. She is married with several adult children and a husband working in the Gulf. She participates in a cooperative to earn some extra cash. When she receives her payment, she invests it in homemade cheese and other products from her village, bringing them back to her neighborhood and selling them at a profit. Through the connections she establishes while selling cheese, this woman is able to facilitate a job for her son in Saudi Arabia (from which he will, in turn, send her remittances) and a housekeeping job for her daughter in a wealthy neighborhood.[59]

At the other end of the spectrum, one might find the ambitious, well-educated, stay-at-home mother who earns extra cash by tutoring her neighbor's child while tutoring her own in a difficult subject. She has no "extra" work, but receives a steady income from her tutoring. As word of her skill spreads, she may choose to expand her business based on her time constraints and on her financial need.

Straddling the formal and informal economies are small-business owners, who require a small outlay of capital to begin their business, such as wedding planning or opening an atelier. A woman might begin by taking piecework in her home for many years, while her children are young, until she can afford to rent or buy an establishment where she can meet customers. Finally, after her children finish high school, she might have her own boutique where she designs gowns and dresses of all sorts, hires extra staff, and helps brides plan the details of their weddings. The greatest number of such small businesswomen in the Middle East of approximately

35% is between 55 and 60 years of age. A smaller percentage of women, 23%, are between 40 and 45, illustrating the time it takes for female entrepreneurs to acquire capital and to raise children.[60]

In Iran, just after the turn of the twenty-first century, official labor statistics estimated the activity of females over ten years of age in the labor force since the Revolution to be 10%. These statistics grossly under-enumerate women's work, much of which is in the informal sector. Informal labor in Iran conforms to patterns that we see in other countries. Undereducated women, relocated from the countryside to the city, fit the pattern of Palestinian women and working-class Cairene women: they assemble piecework in their homes, they process food products, or do traditional weaving. Often, these women are part of the intricate trading networks that connect multigenerational households or neighborhoods to a larger capitalist network. In service work, they are day-care providers, house cleaners, and beauticians. Women also labor in small workshops where toys, clothing, and other products are assembled. Many highly-educated women are also part of the informal sector. Computer programming, software design, interior design—any business that can run under the radar of taxation is part of the informal economy as are small businesses in their infancy.[61]

In Turkey it is women with few choices who comprise the informal sector. Women are more likely than men in Turkey to participate in the informal sector, whereas in Egypt and Iran participation by both women and men is both heavy and under-enumerated. In Turkey, women make up 65% of the informal sector. Like women across the region, Turkish women create a variety of handicrafts, lace, embroidery, rugs, and food products. There are also a number of industries in Turkey that allow women to finish work at home, such as sewing zippers, cleaning seams, or assembling equipment.[62]

Conclusion

Women's work is less likely to be enumerated, valued, or compensated than that of their male counterparts in the Middle East as in many other parts of the world. Throughout the region, women have flocked to the public sector over the private sector, which has afforded them greater opportunities and more benefits. Whether in the public or private sector, however, women have been a reserve pool of inexpensive labor for manufacturing and industry. In these areas, women have been given the least desirable jobs with the worst equipment for doing them.

An enormous gulf emerged between the mother-educator ideal portrayed in the press and in textbooks and the reality of women who worked outside the home. Access to domestic workers has enabled the professional class of women to achieve success both inside and outside the home. Working-class women, however, have the double burden of work both inside and outside their homes. Between the two extremes exists a pink-collar class that aspires to being middle class. Crossing all of these boundaries are women in the informal sector who desire the flexibility to work from home or in unconventional settings in order to provide income for their families. In some cases, informal work simply provides women with supplemental pocket money. In other cases, women who work in the informal economy are heads of household who provide their families with crucial earnings.

The creation of the household will be the topic of the next chapter, as we explore sexuality, marriage, and the family.

Notes

1 Nadia Hijab, "Women and Work in the Arab World," in *Women and Power in the Middle East*, Susan Slymovics and Suad Joseph, eds. (Philadelphia: University of Pennsylvania Press, 2001), 41.
2 Malek Abisaab, *Militant Women of a Fragile Nation* (Syracuse: Syracuse University Press, 2010), 30.
3 Helen Rivlin, *The Agricultural Policies of Muhammad Ali* (Cambridge: Harvard University Press, 1979), 184–185; Mona Hammam, "Women and Industrial Work in Egypt: The Chubra al-Kheima Case," *Arab Studies Quarterly* Vol. 2, No. 1 (Winter 1980), 52.
4 Donald Quataert, *Ottoman Manufacturing in the Age of the Industrial Revolution* (Cambridge: Cambridge University Press, 1993), 82–83, 127–129.
5 Donald Quataert, "Ottoman Workers and the State, 1826–1914," in *Workers and the Working Class in the Middle East*, Zachary Lockman, ed. (Albany: New York University Press, 1994), 36.
6 Abisaab, *Militant Women*, 5–10.
7 Akram Fouad Khater, *Inventing Home: Emigration, Gender and the Middle Class in Lebanon, 1870–1920* (Berkeley: The University of California Press, 2001), 20–21, 31–33, 35–36.
8 Joel Beinin and Zackary Lockman, *Workers on the Nile* (Princeton: Princeton University Press, 1988), 51–57; Abisaab, *Militant Women*, 16–17, 29.
9 Samira Haj, *The Making of Iraq, 1900–1963* (Albany: SUNY Press, 1997), 59–60.
10 Elaheh Rostemi-Povey, "The Women's Movement in Its Historical Context," in *Women, Power, and Politics in 21st-Century Iran*, Tara Povey and Elaheh Rostami-Povey, eds. (London: Routledge, 2012), 20.
11 Elizabeth Thompson, *Colonial Citizens* (New York: Columbia University Press, 2000), 238–241.
12 Abisaab, *Militant Women*, 128.
13 Kamil Yilmaz, "Industry," in *Routledge Handbook of Modern Turkey*, Metin Heper and Sabri Sayari, eds. (London: Routledge, 2012), 343–344; Yildiz Ecevit, "Economics—Industrial Labor—Turkey," in *Encyclopedia of Women in Islamic Cultures* Vol. 4, Suad Joseph, ed. (Leiden: Brill, 2006), 180–182.
14 Hammed Shahidian, *Women in Iran* (Westport: Greenwood Press, 2002), 40.
15 Ellen McLarney, "Women's Equality: Constitutions and Revolutions in Egypt," *Women and Gender in the Middle East Politics Workshop* (March 11, 2016), http://pomeps.org/2016/04/28/womens-equality-constitutions-and-revolutions-in-egypt/.
16 Wanda Krause, *Civil Society and Women Activists in the Middle East* (New York: I.B. Taurus, 2012), Chapter 3.
17 Mona El-Fiqi, "Ghazl al-Mahalla: A Revamp," *al-Ahram Weekly* (December 17, 2015) http://weekly.ahram.org.eg/News/15052/18/Ghazl-Al-Mahalla--Revamp-needed-.aspx.
18 Fatima El-Hamidi, "Early Retirement in the Government Sector in Egypt: Preferences, Determinants, and Policy Implications," Working Paper No. 0721, Economic Research Forum, 2007, 2, 4, 7, 14.
19 Valentine Moghadam, "Women's Economic Participation in the Middle East: What Difference Has the Neoliberal Policy Turn Made?," *Journal of Middle East Women's Studies* Vol. 1, No. 1 (2005), 116.

20 Roksana Bahramitash and Hadi S. Esfahani, "Nimble Fingers No Longer! Women's Work in Iran," in *Contemporary Iran*, Ali Gheissari, ed. (Oxford: Oxford University Press, 2009), 90.
21 Yasmin Hussein al-Jawaheri, *Women in Iraq: The Gender Impact of International Sanctions* (Boulder: Lynne Reinner, 2008), 24.
22 Nadje Sadig Al-Ali, *Iraqi Women: Untold Stories from 1948 to the Present* (London: Zed Books, 2007), 148–149.
23 Al-Jawaheri, *Women in Iraq*, 26.
24 Al-Jawaheri, *Women in Iraq*, 31.
25 Dina Rizk Khoury, *Iraq in Wartime: Soldiering, Martyrdom and Remembrance* (Cambridge: Cambridge University Press, 2013), 12.
26 "Syria Female Labor Force Participation," http://www.theglobaleconomy.com/Syria/Female_labor_force_participation/; Valentine Moghadam, *Modernizing Women*, 2nd ed. (Boulder: Lynne Reinner, 2003), 39–40.
27 Shuaa Marrar, "Report on Labour and Economy in the Palestinian Territory: A Gender Perspective," Riyada Consulting (2009), 7, 15, 26, http://www.riyada-consulting.com/files/server/Riyada%20Consulting%20-%20Women%20in%20Labor%20Force%20-%202009.pdf.
28 While teaching has been considered a pink-collar job in the US, in the Middle East, education at all levels historically was dominated by men.
29 For the purposes of this chapter, nursing will be considered "white collar," although it has been dominated by women. Recently men have started in nursing programs in the region, and in certain hospitals in the Gulf, they have been replacing a small portion of the foreign female nurses. Their attributes include Arabic language skills, ability to cater to men who desire same-sex care, and strength for performing tasks, for example, lifting bodies or CPR.
30 Marrar, "Report on Labour and Economy in the Palestinian Territory," 37.
31 Faith Childress, "Creating the 'New Woman': The Contributions of the American Collegiate Institute and the American College for Girls," *Middle Eastern Studies* Vol. 44, No. 4 (July 2008), 553.
32 Hayat Kabasakal and Idil Evcimen, "Economics—Professional Occupations—Turkey," *Encyclopedia of Women in Islamic Cultures* Vol. 4, Suad Joseph, ed. (Leiden: Brill, 2006), 238–240.
33 Camron Amin, "Propaganda and Remembrance: Gender, Education, and 'The Women's Awakening' of 1936," *Iranian Studies* Vol. 32, No. 3 (Summer 1999), 351, 361, 363–365, 377, 379.
34 Rostami-Povey, "The Women's Movement in Its Historical Context," 20.
35 "Red Rose of Cairo," *al-Ahram Weekly*, April 22, 2004.
36 "Convention of the Elimination of All forms of Discrimination Against Women," http://www.un.org/womenwatch/daw/cedaw/.
37 "Mideast Women Beat Men at Education, Lose Out at Work," *Inside the Middle East* (June 6, 2012), http://www.cnn.com/2012/06/01/world/meast/middle-east-women-education/.
38 Hijab, "Women and Work in the Arab World," 48; Taghrid Khuri, "Laboring Practices—Jordan," in *Encyclopedia of Women; Islamic Cultures* Supplement V, Suad Joseph, ed. (Leiden: Brill, 2012). http://dx.doi.org/10.1163/1872-5309_ewic_EWICCOM_001426
39 See Leila Ahmed, *A Border Passage* (New York: Penguin, 2000).
40 Edward Malecki and Michael Ewers, "Labor Migration to World Cities: With a Research Agenda for the Arab Gulf," *Progress in Human Geography* Vol. 31, No. 1 (2007), 467–484.
41 C. Berrebi, F. Martorell, and J. Tanner, "Qatar's Labor Markets at a Crucial Crossroad," *Middle East Journal* Vol. 63, No. 3 (Summer 2009), 421–442; Dawn Chatty, "Women Working in Oman: Individual Choice and Cultural Constraints," *International Journal of Middle East Studies* Vol. 32, No. 2 (May 2000), 241–254; "Women Blazing Trail in Middle East Marine Engineering," http://worldmaritimenews.com/archives/141247/women-blazing-trail-in-middle-east-marine-engineering/.

42. See Louise Kapp Howe, *Pink Collar Workers: Inside the World of Women's Work* (New York: G.P. Putnam's Sons, 1977).
43. "These Female-Only Tours in the Middle East Let You Bond with the Women Who Live There," *Travel and Leisure* (March 23, 2018), http://www.travelandleisure.com/trip-ideas/women-only-tours-to-middle-east-morocco-jordan-iran.
44. Camron Amin, *The Making of the Modern Iranian Woman* (Gainesville: University of Florida Press, 2002), 217, 220–221.
45. Advertisement in the Egyptian periodical *New Woman* (*al-Mar'a al-jadida*), November 6, 1924.
46. Advertisement in the Egyptian periodical *Riyada Badaniya*, August 1, 1931.
47. Advertisement in the Egyptian periodical *al-Ithnayn wal-dunya*, July 22, 1935.
48. Thompson, *Colonial Citizens*, 239.
49. Uri Kumpferschmidt, "'Small' Technologies and Consumer Goods," in *A Global Middle East*, Liat Kozma, Cyrus Shayegh, and Avner Wishnitzer, eds. (New York: I.B. Taurus, 2016), 237–239.
50. Kumpferschmidt, "Small Technologies," n49, 253.
51. "Record Breaking Turkish Typist Brings Home Two World-Class Medals," *Daily Sabah Life* (August 7, 2017), https://www.dailysabah.com/life/2017/08/08/record-breaking-turkish-typist-brings-home-two-new-world-class-awards.
52. Richard Samans and Saadia Zahidi, "The Future of Jobs and Skills in the Middle East: Preparing for the Fourth Industrial Revolution," *World Economic Forum* (May 2017), iii, 9, http://www3.weforum.org/docs/WEF_EGW_FOJ_MENA.pdf.
53. Annelies Moors, "Economics—Paid Domestic Labor—Central Arab States, Egypt, Yemen," *Encyclopedia of Women in Islamic Cultures* Vol. 4, Suad Joseph, ed. (Leiden: Brill, 2006), 220–222.
54. Nasra Shah, "Gender and Labour Migration to Gulf Countries," *Feminist Review* No. 77 (2004), 183–185; Rima Sabban, "Economics—Paid Domestic Labor—Gulf States," in *Encyclopedia of Women in Islamic Cultures* Vol. 4, Suad Joseph, ed. (Leiden: Brill, 2006), 222–224.
55. Ervand Abrahamian, "The Strengths and Weakness of the Labor Movement," in *Modern Iran*, Michael Bonine and Nikki Keddie, eds. (Albany: SUNY Press, 1981), 213.
56. Moghadam, "Women's Economic Participation," 112, 128.
57. Marrar, "Report on Labour and Economy in the Palestinian Territory," 24.
58. Mariz Tadros, "Economics—Informal Economy—Egypt," in *Encyclopedia of Women in Islamic Cultures* Vol. 4, Suad Joseph, ed. (Leiden: Brill, 2006), 252–253.
59. See Evelyn Early, "Getting It Together, Baladi Businesswomen of Cairo," in *Arab Women: Old Boundaries, New Frontiers*, Judith Tucker, ed. (Bloomington: Indiana University Press, 1993), 84–99.
60. Mariz Tadros, "Economics—Small Businesses—Egypt," in *Encyclopedia of Women in Islamic Cultures* Vol. 4, Suad Joseph, ed. (Leiden: Brill, 2006), 252–253.
61. Fatimeh Moghadam, "Economics—Informal Economy—Iran," *Encyclopedia of Women in Islamic Cultures* Vol. 4, Suad Joseph, ed. (Leiden: Brill, 2006), 183–185.
62. Sibel Kalaycioğlu, "Economics—Informal Sector—Turkey," *Encyclopedia of Women in Islamic Cultures* Vol. 4, Suad Joseph, ed. (Leiden: Brill, 2006), 194–196.

11 Sexuality

Introduction

Western stereotypical misperceptions about sexuality in the Middle East share some interesting similarities with traditional Islamic views about gender and sexuality. Western media has portrayed Muslim women generally and Middle Eastern women in particular as submissive, frigid, and dominated by their husbands and fathers. Conversely, Middle Eastern men have been portrayed as domineering and oversexed. In a similar vein, traditional Muslim views portray women as a source of *fitna* or chaos—beings capable of bringing about social disorder and discord through their sexuality and sexual energy. This energy, according to such interpretation, needs appropriate channeling through the licit sexual relations that are provided by marriage. According to such views, because they have multiple outlets for satisfying their sexual needs, men are less threatening to social harmony than women are.[1]

Far more nuanced views of sexuality than these have existed in the Middle East historically. Regarding what we would now refer to as "gay," for example, some Sufis in the medieval and early modern worlds extolled the beauty of beardless males. In the same eras, legal scholars dismissed same-sex female activity because it did not specifically violate any Quranic injunctions. Such fluidity of sexual practice and desire in the medieval and early modern worlds complicates modern discussions of sexuality, which utilize Western paradigms, terms, and categories of identity.[2] (Categories such as "gay" or "lesbian" are relatively new in the West, historically speaking, even while same-sex desire is not.) As vocabulary for describing same-sex desire and relationships emerges among the still relatively small group of individuals who adopt a "gay" identity in the Middle East (see below), some confusion remains among the wider population. Aside from the term *shadh*, meaning deviant, which has been in usage since the mid-twentieth century, most of these new terms, similar to Western terms, inspire confusion and even laughter among the general population. Some in the small population that adopts a "gay/lesbian" identity want to reclaim *shadh* in the same way that "queer" has been positively reaffirmed by the gay/lesbian community in the West. Nevertheless, the word's association with perversion and deviance make it too difficult for many to embrace.[3] Because of these linguistic ambiguities, many intellectuals and self-identified gays and lesbians in the Middle East prefer to use English or French when discussing sex, desire, or sexual identity.[4]

This chapter addresses same-sex desire historically, along with marriage. We also examine portrayals of same-sex desire in film. Finally, we return to the group of people who self-identify as LGBT in the Middle East and close with queer interpretations of scripture. In each case, our goal is to illustrate the great fluidity that has defined desire and sexuality historically, defying the rigid binaries through which "Middle Eastern sexuality" has been categorized and understood in the modern era.

Sexuality, Gender, and Desire Historically

While marriage and the production of children have been the standard for men and women across the region historically, same-sex desire has not been uncommon. In Ottoman Anatolia and the Arabic-speaking provinces, men lauded and celebrated the beauty of beardless young men. "Gazing" at male beauty did not constitute homosexuality as we now understand it. (Modern states often legislate against same-sex relationships because that lifestyle challenges the monogamous, heterosexual union that forms the basis for the contract between those states and their citizens.[5]) Rather, gazing at and praising the beauty of male youths formed the heart of several cultural and religious conventions which, while not seeking to displace the Islamic injunction to marry and procreate, nonetheless shaped popular culture in the early modern Middle East. This is not to say that same-sex unions did not exist outside of the literary, theatrical, and Sufi practices in which homoeroticism was limited to gazing. Rather, it is to suggest that the rigid proscription against same-sex relationships that defines the relationship between modern, Middle Eastern states and their citizens does not have its roots in the empires of the region in the early modern era.[6]

Homoeroticism between males found its place in early modern Sufi practices, in poetry, and in theater. In urban centers in the Ottoman Empire, where Sufism was popular, sexuality and spirituality were connected. Sufis asked how humans could possibly perceive attributes of the divine. Their answer suggested that perceiving human beauty helped humans to understand the divine. Identifying God as male, some Sufis argued that gazing at male beauty (understood to mean the beauty of beardless, male youths) helped humans to bridge the gap between the profane and the divine. While Islamic reform movements in the eighteenth century worked against such practices (just as they worked against men gathering in coffee houses, using tobacco, and practicing saint worship), gazing at men nonetheless formed part of religious popular culture for centuries.[7] Throughout Ottoman territories, men, including conservative members of the ulama, wrote love poetry to other men, frequently exalting—as did the Sufis—the beauty of beardless youths.

In the popular Karagoz puppet theater that was enjoyed in Turkish-speaking Ottoman urban centers, sexual promiscuity and lewd sexual behavior involved same-sex as well as opposite-sex encounters. Conservative ulama were as critical of the Karagoz theater as they were of Sufism; nonetheless, puppet theater was the most popular form of entertainment in the eighteenth century.[8]

In art from early Qajar Iran, beauty was not represented or distinguished by gender. Qajar-era artists depicted men and women with similar bodies and similar features. Men desired men who would, in today's world, be considered "feminine": young and beardless, rose-faced, and tulip-cheeked.[9] Adult men considered other men with beards to have reached full manhood. As such, bearded men were considered to be desiring subjects, not objects of desire. Adult men who shaved their beards therefore demonstrated their willingness to be desired by other men. As in other parts of the Middle East, Iranian men were known to marry women and to gaze at beautiful men. Ca. 1800, the Qajar police mentioned the indiscretions of men with women but did not mention similar relations between adult men and beardless youths.[10]

Islamic law (all four schools of Sunni law as well as that of Twelver Shi'ism) prohibits anal intercourse between men and understands penetrative sex outside of marriage, including sodomy, to be an abominable sin. But gazing, like writing love poetry, was understood to be a far cry from sodomy. Falling in love with a man, or expressing love to a man in the form of poetry, was not understood to be sinful in the eighteenth century. Because they were more beautiful than females, some jurists suggested, young boys were more tempting to those who gazed at them. Others advised their communities to resist gazing altogether. Most jurists permitted gazing in the absence of lust.[11]

Being the active partner in sex between two men did not violate cultural understandings of passivity, which were historically linked to femininity.[12] In popular culture, the penetrator left such an encounter with his honor unchallenged; in Islamic law, however, he was guilty of sodomy. Religious scholars were indifferent to women's same-sex activities, which were devoid of penetration and, therefore, licit. A few scholars, for example, al-Mashtooly (sixteenth century), explicitly condemned "grinding" by likening female genitalia to male genitalia, based on what he considered to be the Prophet's own words (*hadith*). Nevertheless, most scholars consider the *hadith* to which Mashtooly referred to have been fabricated.[13]

The medieval and early modern social order was clearly regulated by gender distinction. An individual born with male and female sex organs, or intersex (*kuntha*), was socialized in the Islamicate social order through a series of tests which determined which urinary orifice the individual best used. By resolving this question, jurists could determine social, economic, and mundane matters, for example, who (s)he would marry, where (s)he would pray, how much (s)he would inherit, and how (s)he would be buried.[14]

Blurred gender boundaries were tolerated, if not always appreciated, in early Islamic societies; among early communities of Muslims in the Arabian Peninsula and later in the Abbasid court, for example, "effeminate" men, or *mukhannathun*, were known figures. *Hadith* exist condemning both effeminate men and mannish women; reportedly, both Muhammad and Umar (the third Caliph) banished at least one such individual. Nonetheless, in this early period, the *mukhannathun* were given access to women's quarters. By the fourteenth century, *mukhannathun* had become associated with musical talent and a quick wit—positive attributes of the day—and with cross-dressing, which did not appear to have had the kinds of negative associations that it does in the contemporary era. During that period, however, the *mukhannathun* were also known for seeking the passive role in homosexual liaisons.[15]

Some scholars connect the practices of the *khanith* in Oman today with traditions that date back to this early period in Islamic history. The *khanith* have been described variously as constituting a "third sex," as transvestites, as prostitutes, and as existing in a transitional phase between youth and manhood. They occupy a liminal space in between the rigid binaries touted by the religious establishment: their hair is neither short nor long: it is styled in a fashion neither masculine nor feminine. Their heads are uncovered—atypical for Omani society. Their tunic is white and shaped like men's clothing; the cinched waist of their garb is all that reveals their attire as feminine (see Chapter 12). Some *khanith* adopt the mannerisms of women. Some provide sexual services to other men. Like the *mukhannithun* before them, *khaniths* are allowed to enter female-only space. Some scholars connect the *khanith* to descendants of former slaves. Just as emancipation from slavery meant entrance into domestic service, *khanith* can become "real men," marry, and have children.[16]

Similarly, among the marsh Arabs in southern Iraq, women who choose not to marry are known to become surrogate men (*mustarajil*). They dress in men's clothing, carry arms, and join the men's world of public affairs. Some make this choice as girls, while others make the decision after their first period, as the prospect of marriage looms on the horizon. Still others make this strategic choice out of economic necessity. Other women might don men's clothing after the death of their husband in order to protect their children or claim property. These women still veil, viewing obligations to God in specifically female terms. These "surrogate men" do not enjoy the status of cisgender males in Iraq: they neither hold the legal status of men nor could they choose a female partner.[17]

Marriage

Marriage in Islamicate societies begins as an agreement between two families. Historically, a father or other suitable guardian would contract the marriage for both his sons and daughters in their minority (below legal age of marriage). Historically, the Islamic ideal was for a couple to be similar in social standing, background, occupation, and outlook in order to provide the basis for a stable marriage. The marriage contract stipulated a *mahr* (dower) that the groom paid to the bride in two parts. The initial payment of money, land, or goods is made up front. The deferred portion of the *mahr* was paid upon termination of marriage by death or divorce. Brides have historically been expected to bring a trousseau (*jihaz*) to the new household, of clothing, cooking vessels, and other household items. If knowledgeable about the law, a woman could put conditions in her marriage contract, for example, the ability to divorce a husband who takes a second wife. Consequently, Jewish and Christian women in various parts of the Ottoman Empire used Islamic law courts to register stipulations.[18] Once married, it was the husband's responsibility to support his wife in the manner to which she was accustomed. In turn, it was the wife's responsibility to obey her husband. Both husband and wife had the right to sexual satisfaction. While the husband had more options for divorce than his wife did, the wife nonetheless had recourse to court for an annulment or a termination of the marriage.

The marriage of cousins through the paternal line remains extremely common in the Middle East. Many view marriage to someone who is known and from a good family as preferable to marriage to a "stranger" (e.g., if treated poorly, a woman has recourse to her family). It has only been slowly that, with growing awareness of the diseases associated with consanguineous marital practices, these unions are starting to decline.

Despite the spread of companionate marriage and free choice of one's spouse, many young people still rely upon family and friends to find potential marriage partners. Among Muslims, the idea of dating was unheard of until quite recently and remains unevenly accepted across classes and regions. In Turkey, for example, it is not uncommon for university students to date, while the practice is less common among their counterparts in the countryside and even less so among university students in the Gulf.[19]

Once two young people have become a couple, engaged or otherwise, they are not likely to engage in premarital sex, although sex between them is not out of the question. Men and women alike place a high value on virginity at the time of marriage. Increasing numbers of women will engage in some sexual activity short of penetration to maintain their virginity. While the days of having the midwife demonstrate a bride's virginity or showing the bloody sheet of a newlywed are largely over in the region, the technological next generation has come: texts from inquiring parents in conservative families request information about the wedding night.[20]

There are religiously-sanctioned ways to navigate physical relationships and marital sanctity without the formality and expense of traditional marriage. One way is *urfi*, or customary marriage, which requires only two witnesses. Customary marriage provides couples the alternative of having guilt-free sexual liaisons without the hassle of parental interference or the expenses associated with setting up households. *Urfi* marriage is sometimes used by Gulf travelers to-Egypt and other parts of the Middle East as a means of obtaining a temporary bride. Since the start of the civil war in Syria, *urfi* and ordinary marriage of underage refugee girls has become more common in surrounding countries, such as Jordan.[21] Typically, a legal condition prohibits procreation in these unions. In reality, temporary marriage is an agreement that gives the man sexual pleasure and provides the woman's family, who create the terms of the bargain, with economic resources until the man grows tired of the union. The more fortunate are formally divorced by their husbands and are thus able to remarry.[22]

Feminists are of two minds on the topic of *urfi* and temporary marriage. On the one hand, through such marriages, women have more sexual freedom and (in some cases) greater personal choice with respect to a partner without interference from family. The temporary marriage arrangement liberates women sexually and provides the couple with greater economic freedom in terms of eliminating the formalities of an expensive wedding and setting up a household. On the other hand, such practices allow men to have four wives and to contract any number of traveling, temporary, or customary marriages where these are allowed. While it is not common to do so, it is not out of the question for a wealthy Gulf man to have four wives, a *misyar* (traveling) wife, and two *urfi* wives.

Sexuality, Desire, and Identity: Passion on the Silver Screen

The long-standing traditions of same-sex desire that were celebrated in the medieval and premodern world caused enormous anxiety in the age of colonialism.[23] Nineteenth-century Westerners commenting on the sexual customs of Middle Easterners tended to fall into one of two categories: the condemning Victorian or the curious tourist. Both depicted habits of Middle Easterners as lust-driven: outside the pale of what could be found back home in Europe. The reaction to Europeans by local intellectuals, even as they celebrated poetry and traditions from the golden age of Islam, was to suppress not only (male) same-sex desire, but also all forms of sexuality and desire that were deemed deviant by Europeans.[24]

These tensions were often worked out on-screen, on stage, and in literature through reproduction of proper heterosexual unions. But tensions regarding sexuality uncovered a range of desire, sexuality, and boundaries. Humor and

Figure 11.1 Advertisement for *Midnight. al-Ithnayn wal-dunya* March 1949.

cross-dressing have allowed filmmakers to present transgressive boundaries in Egyptian films, the leader in regional film production and distribution historically.[25] An early demonstration of cross-dressing occurred in *Daughter of the Pahsa* in *Charge* (1938). In this film, Assia Degher stars as a woman replacing her brother Hikmat as a tutor on a wealthy estate. To do so she dresses as a man. One of the Pasha's daughters, Badria, tries to seduce Hikmat in an erotic scene that is only interrupted by the sudden arrival of a family member. One scholar calls it is "one of the most erotic portrayals of two women" in Arab cinema.[26] Yet, one did not have to look too far (or even see the movie) to find another such portrayal: the advertisement for *Midnight* (1949) portrays Camellia, a famous Egyptian actress, about to kiss another woman, Huda Shams al-Din. The headline for the advertisement reads: "Not an American film!"[27] Such instances of tension, flirtation, and glances appear often in films. Frequent Eastern dance sequences (belly dancing) similarly showcase moments of same-sex desire.[28]

In *For Men Only* (1964), two legends of the screen, Soad Hosni and Nadia Lutfi, portray geologists looking to take advantage of posts in the Sinai, only to find that the jobs were (as the title would indicate) for men only. Ready to accept the challenge, the women dress as men and relocate to the job site, where they encounter a pair of male geologists who enthusiastically introduce their new colleagues into camp life. The film provides multiple opportunities for homoerotic, albeit comedic, encounters, including cheek to cheek dancing, a come-on by a Bedouin woman (nearly followed by an honor killing), and pillow fighting. Predictably, by the end of the film, the female geologists' guise is made known, the women have fallen for men, heterosexual pairings have taken place, and, symbolically, oil gushes forth from the earth.[29]

The (relatively) new technology of sex reassignment surgery (SRS) provided the context for *A Girl Named Mahmud* released in 1975.[30] Hamida, the protagonist, wants to attend university, much to the dismay of her father, who would rather see her married—and to a groom of his choice. As Mahmud, Hamida can attend university and successfully run her father's business. The film provides multiple opportunities for homoerotic tension: "Mahmud" makes out with her boyfriend Hassan; fearing his son's lack of masculinity, the father hires Mahmud an aggressive cabaret entertainer to tutor him, unwittingly pairing his "daughter" with a woman. All ends well, however, as Hamida is revealed to be a woman, dressed in a wedding gown, and about to marry a man.[31]

Youssef Chahine (1926–2008) was one of the first filmmakers to offer more nuanced and sympathetic depictions of gay characters. In his semi-autobiographical *Alexandria, Why?* (1978), set in WWII Egypt, it was the love of a drunk, English sailor that kept protagonist Adel from murdering an Englishman. Tommy similarly helped Adel take a stance against the Allied occupation of his country.[32] While other Egyptian filmmakers have followed Chahine's lead in developing characters beyond stereotypes, Tunisian filmmakers have been at the forefront of the region. Tunisian filmmaker Nouri Bouzid is credited with first creating scripts centered on characters dealing with crises stemming from sexual identity. Bouzid also addresses the long-term ramifications of sexual harassment, molestation, and sex work in his films.[33]

Fewer depictions appear of same-sex desire between women, however. If such desire is depicted at all, it is likely to appear in films made in partnership with foreign film companies. In the regionally-produced *Dentelle (Lace)* (Egypt; 1993), director Inas Degheidi presents female same-sex desire through subtext and inference. *Dentelle* follows the story of two lifelong friends and roommates whose intimacy is challenged by their shared love for the same man. The two women ultimately reconcile and even raise a child together, but the nature of their almost erotic relationship is never explicit.[34] By contrast, Jordanian-Palestinian producer Hanan Kattan's *I Can't Think Straight*, produced in the UK in 2008, requires no such subtleties.[35] Jordanian-Palestinian Tala, who is to travel to Jordan to get married, falls in love with a woman. Both films privilege plot and character development over reliance on stereotypes.

Such movement away from stereotyping is also evident of more recently-released films about same-sex between men; themes such as coming out to family, pressure to marry, losing boyfriends to marriage, pressure to declare oneself "gay," and confrontation with authoritarian regimes are included in *All My Life* (Egypt, 2008), *The String* (Tunisia, 2009), and *Salvation Army* (Morocco, 2013).[36] (Of the latter titles only *Salvation Army* has had a release date in the region listed on IMDb; the others have only been screened abroad) At the time of the film's release, the Grand Mufti of Egypt proclaimed that *All My Life* should be burned immediately, viewing the film as a "gateway to debauchery … [and] deviant social behavior."[37]

The "Gay" Life: Those Who Accept the Identity

The complexity of life demonstrated in recent films highlights problems encountered by men and women in the region who do not necessarily fit the mold of heterosexual, cisgender identities.[38] *All My Life* is a good starting point for some of the problems faced by men. At the start of *All My Life*, the audience meets Rami, a well-educated, cultured Egyptian, who works by day in an office and studies dance in his free time. His love interest, Walid, breaks up with him in order to marry a (female) coworker. Rami looks for companionship in various places: random hookups, a foreign tourist, chatrooms, and a relationship with a coffee shop worker, Atef, who seeks him out. Atef lacks education, class-standing, and cultural capital, but is smitten with Rami, despite their class and cultural differences: Atef is unable to understand the language of elites just as he does not understand the term "gay" (pronounced as in English), an identity which Rami proclaims.

All My Life takes place against the backdrop of the Queen Boat raid carried out by the Egyptian government in May 2001, in which 52 men were arrested for debauchery. At the trial in November of the same year, 29 men were acquitted and 23 convicted.[39] The film covers the mood in Egypt during that time. The public voraciously consumed news of the arrests, replete with images of the accused and reports of forensic testing (for sodomy) and testing for HIV. Many in the small gay(-identifying) community wanted to leave Egypt. While Rami was not caught up in the Queen Boat arrests, his forays into chatrooms ultimately lead him into police entrapment. Unable to claim the most basic civil rights, he is charged with habitual debauchery and after two rounds of torture submits to a guilty plea.

Not appearing "gay" is important even for men who accept the moniker of gay: they worry not only about their own fate, but that of their family. One individual's shame reflects back upon his parents and siblings (and their children) and threatens their family members' marital prospects. With such emphasis on appearances, some men aspire to be "bears," to acquire high degrees of masculinity (hairy, muscular) in order to survive in a heteronormative culture.[40] In interviews, men of different classes repeatedly relate that they will leave venues that become too "gay" for fear of association or arrest. Furthermore, there are men who explicitly seek out "straight" (looking) men in online forums. Transgressive appearance, even long hair, in post-2003 Iraq can be cause for death.[41]

For women, gender performance also creates tension and anxieties. In Iran, girls with boy-like characteristics are praised or encouraged rather than scolded for having these qualities. It is only when they reach a certain age in their 20s and resist marriage that perceived masculinity becomes a problem. At this point, a young woman might be forced to move out and live on her own. While this ultimatum might sound appealing to some readers, such a young woman would face tremendous difficulty finding employment and housing on her own.[42] She might choose to live and work as a man—an option that would not be out of the question even for a straight woman faced with the task of supporting a family, given high unemployment rates (among youth and among women).[43] In Dubai (UAE), undercover policewomen keep an eye out for *boyat*, girls who dress or behave as boys, in public spaces. To avoid this scrutiny, other Gulf countries' *boyat* fill cyberspace on social networking sites, where they proudly display symbols of national and cultural identity—flags, hats, sunglasses, and other cool things. Across the region, the phenomenon of *boyat* (and boys who are non-gender conforming) has created a market for all manner of therapies for social rehabilitation. These methods, not entirely different from evangelical Christian "gay conversion," hope to offer the same outcome. Even in Iran, which has greater leeway for transsexualism (see below), some therapists use a bullying method to determine whether or not a patient is really a candidate for SRS.[44]

Finding partners can be fraught with difficulties, especially for the working classes. Throughout the region, wealthy individuals can afford to attend and create spaces that the police will not raid (clubs, restaurants, upscale coffee shops, bars, etc.), while the lower-middle and working classes do not have such a luxury. They are confined to public spaces, known corners, parks, ordinary coffee shops, knowing glances, and catch phrases. In some circles in Beirut (or Cairo, Istanbul, etc.), one must know French or English in order to participate in LGBTQ-friendly settings. Furthermore, (in Beirut) marginalized groups, for example, Palestinians, South Asian domestic workers, or Syrian refugees, lack access to the venues frequented by elite Lebanese or foreign tourists. Indeed gay-friendly is often synonymous with more expensive.[45]

The existence of "gay-friendly" sites throughout the Middle East is both a cause and a byproduct of gay tourism, which has brought income into the region for decades. Morocco, Egypt, Lebanon, and Israel have all been popular "gay tourism" destinations; however, only in Israel, Lebanon, Iraq, and Jordan is it legal to engage in same-sex activities. It was only in July of 2018 that Lebanon repealed Law 534, covering sexual relations "contrary to the laws of nature," which was sufficiently vague to handle any morals violation.[46] The rebuilding of Lebanon after its civil war (1975–1990) and the growth of the regional tourism industry spawned a gay and lesbian tourism niche, the former of which has been the subject of more academic study than the latter. Lebanon contends with Israel in the global economy for "pink" tourism dollars. In recent years, Israel has tried to brand itself as a haven for gay and lesbian vacationers in order to attract not only tourism dollars, but also venture capital more generally.[47] Nonetheless, much like the Victorian-era tourists described in Chapter 3, contemporary "pink tourists" often arrive in the region with a distorted sense of the region's culture, which does not always align with the practices of gay outsiders. [Male] visitors arrive with expectations of finding a "new gay Middle East" on tours, which are marketed and scripted to match those desires. Some "pink tourists" both long to find (and fear discovering) the unbridled lust, anger, and hypermasculinity of stereotypical Arab men.[48]

Across the region, government repression of the LGBTQ community has become more visible through social media. The same internet tools which advocate use to heighten awareness, meet like-minded comrades, or to simply hookup have also been used by police to entrap and brutalize, particularly gay men. Between late 2003 and spring 2004 alone (in Egypt), some 40 men were detained and charged with debauchery, a crime which dates back to the criminalization of prostitution and which has a gendered aspect.[49] The 1961 law, upheld by a 1975 Cassation court ruling, separates "debauchery" (transgressive sex) from prostitution (sex for monetary gain). According to this ruling, in the same manner that a "John" is not prosecuted, but a prostitute is charged with solicitation; a penetrator is not charged, but a passive male partner can be charged with *fujur* (debauchery).[50] Since there is no explicit definition of what constitutes *fujur*, therefore there is no defense in the face of criminal charges. General religious and social biases likewise make a debauchery charge difficult to defend. In Egypt, *fujur* appears to be a category under expansion; since the time of the Queen Boat raid in 2001, both active and passive partners now seem to be equally culpable. But the distinction between the culpability of the passive partner and the innocence of the active one remains in other parts of the Middle East. In 2016, for example, Islamic State officials threw a 15-year-old (boy) off a building because he had been raped by a senior commander. While the younger passive male was sent to his death, the other man was flogged and sent to the front.[51]

Where satellite TV and the internet have made them available, gay and lesbian characters from European and American television series have helped some individuals with same-sex preference to choose to identify as gay/lesbian and, later, to mobilize in various forms of activism.[52] Studies of gay and lesbian blogs in Egypt demonstrate differing needs and agendas among communities of self-proclaimed gays and lesbians. Acknowledgment of the violence perpetrated against men's bodies, along with the atmosphere of shame and injustice surrounding same-sex identity are common topics in gay male cyberspace. Women's blogs characteristically focus on romance and creativity.[53] In either case, new spaces for expression have given rise to new types of mobilization and activism, not only for LGBTQ rights, but for human rights in general.

Ca. 2001, the confluence of the spread of the internet, the Queen Boat raid, Israeli policy toward its neighbors, and the US war on terror all combined to mobilize a variety of human rights groups. In Lebanon in 2003, Hurriyat Khassa, a group aimed at eliminating governmental influence in the lives of Lebanese citizens, emerged from this activism. The following year, HELEM (the acronym for Lebanese Protection of Gays/Lesbians [literally means dreams]) voiced similar concerns for members of the LGBTQ community. HELEM's outreach is also quite practical. It has created a clinic (marsa) that provides a wide variety of sexual health services for men and women regardless of sexual orientation. HELEM has splinter groups, including Meem, a support group specifically for lesbians. Meem often works through existing organizations that tackle women's issues, for example, domestic violence or drug addiction. The work of HELEM and Meem has inspired like-minded organizations across the Middle East, some of which may exist only in cyberspace and others which work in conjunction with NGOs on the ground to prevent HIV and advance sexual health: Kifkaf (Morocco), Abu Nawas (Algeria), Bedayaa (Egypt), Iraqi LGBT (London-based), and Aswat and Al Qaws (Palestine).[54]

The only countries to successfully hold Gay Pride events have been Turkey and Israel; however, such events have been planned across the region at various points, in particular, in the heyday of the Arab Spring. The beginning dates of both Istanbul and Tel Aviv Pride have political significance: 2003 and 1996, respectively, marking a changing political landscape. Because Israel has marketed itself as an LGBTQ tourist destination, the explosive politics of its Pride events have calmed significantly. Nevertheless, a faction of activists demonstrates annually, using Pride as an occasion on which to erect barriers around the marchers in order to physically and metaphorically demonstrate that there is no pride in the Israeli occupation of the West Bank. Jerusalem's pride events have a history of violence and mar the country's pink image. The same ultra-Orthodox (Jewish) man attacked the parade in 2015, after having served a ten-year sentence for attacking it in 2005.[55]

By 2014, Istanbul's Pride event had come to be the biggest event of its kind in the Muslim world and continued to draw ever larger crowds (up to 100,000 by some estimates). That year witnessed the last parade without government interference, however. Since that time, the Turkish government has banned the parade and used plastic bullets and tear gas on crowds that now number in the hundreds. In Lebanon, in 2017 and 2018, Beirut pride week activities were planned, culminating in a parade; however, the government blocked the parade both years, taking the additional step of arresting the parade's organizer in 2018, effectively ending the activities.[56]

Reports about gay and lesbian life in the Gulf are limited and sometimes fraught with inaccuracy. Reliable scholarly sources are scarce. A 2014 news report from Saudi Arabia claimed that a man was flogged 450 times and given a three-year sentence for tweeting about his gay life. The Tweet was supposedly translated from *al-Watan* and reported in *Gulf News*; however, the location for the event was Manama, a city in Bahrain—thus one wonders about the accuracy of the rest of the report.[57] Individuals from outside Saudi Arabia, who come for work, study, or family commitments, write about the vividness of the "gay" culture there, repeatedly using the term "underground." Underground means several things simultaneously. Sexual segregation enhances single-sex interaction, and *de facto* there are spaces for "families," "men," or "women." Appearance matters in the Gulf. It is less difficult to arrange a same-sex encounter than it is for an unmarried man and woman to take a walk together or to sit and chat in a car without a chaperone. Many Gulf men and women with same-sex preference do not identify as gay, and in particular, men who seek "top" positions only consider "bottoms" gay. Even youthful time spent as a "bottom" is not necessarily considered gay. The large number of rules governing licit sex among the devout, for example, the prohibition against intercourse during a woman's menstrual cycle, also affords men (in their minds) the opportunity to seek out liaisons beyond the confines of marriage. The religious police seem most concerned about individuals who violate basic dress and hygiene rules: men with long hair, makeup, and jewelry and women whose clothing is deemed disrespectful are most likely to be stopped by the police, which helps to explain crackdowns on transgender individuals in the Kingdom and the Gulf (see below).[58]

Lesbians in Saudi Arabia report a vibrancy to the same-sex scene. Lamia, a Lebanese student who grew up in Saudi Arabia, claims she encountered "lots of gays and lesbians in Riyadh." Some engage in same-sex practices due to social isolation, but others just prefer same-sex activity. Lamia suggests that lesbians in Saudi Arabia live normal lives. Some choose to get married and some do not. She never felt "different" in Saudi Arabia. The homosocial environment was emotionally supportive to her needs. In Saudi Arabia, like elsewhere, some girls begin to experiment with same-sex liaisons in high school and university. At certain schools, bathrooms and other areas of campus are known to witness sexual activity. Not everyone approves of this behavior, however, and bathroom stalls are covered with graffiti that offer social and religious advice: "she doesn't really love you no matter what she tells you." Lamia's account is consistent with the fictitious one in *Girls of Riyadh*: Sadeem is warned by her friends to stay away from Building No. 4 (at the university), the hunting ground of Arwa, the charismatic, attractive (but masculine) woman who stalks other women.[59]

Identity, Modernity, Media, Homosexuality, and Transsexuality

The reluctance to take the identity of gay or lesbian, and the more recent adoption by some individuals of new identities, is a specifically modern phenomenon, one related to modern state building, the rise of the modern press and, later, of television and social media. For individuals who did not "feel" the way other boys and girls did, reading stories in the press, seeing role models in the theater and on TV, and later becoming part of a cyber community have all been crucial elements in understanding difference.

Gender-bending (and straight) performers have often been role models for young people who felt that they did not conform to the norm. Saleem Haddad (b. 1983), author of *Guapa*, drew inspiration from characters on television. He recounts that watching the female Egyptian dancer Sharihan, a woman known for her flair and for her marvelous array of costumes, inspired "the seeds of his gay identity" as he watched her perform in a Ramadan television special.[60] Zeki Müren (1931–1996), who became a sensation on Turkey's radio airwaves in the early 1950s and popular on the radio, later took to stage and film, becoming famous for his outlandish costumes, makeup, and carefully-coiffed pompadour. Decades after his death, at Istanbul pride celebrations, Müren is still an icon of nonconformity.[61] In Egypt, it is Hanan al-Tawil (1966–2004) who serves as such an icon. Born male in Egypt, Tawil underwent SRS in Europe, returned to her home country, and began a successful, if short, career as a transsexual actress, appearing both in film and on stage. Tawil's life, which apparently ended in suicide in 2004, has been commemorated by the LGBTQ community in the form of a documentary film.[62]

At the same time, however, individuals born in the mid-late twentieth century have been socialized against the backdrop of heteronormative images: in textbooks as a child, in popular magazines as a youth, and as an adult through film and television. Across the region, the modernizing project has been based upon the nuclear family. Modernization has drawn on modern medicine to solve social ills, combat deviancy, and develop new categories. Many of the stereotypes about so-called social ills in Middle Eastern societies have been in circulation since the early twentieth century. Even self-identifying gay authors struggle not to fall into the trap of linking homosexuality to such alleged causes as parental misconduct, marital discord, corrupting influences, and folk superstitions.[63]

Major cities in the Middle East offer plastic surgery and are home to skilled surgeons who can provide some of the services required for SRS; however, early on, most individuals desiring SRS went to Europe, the US, or Thailand. By the 1970s, however, a handful of hospitals in Tehran and at least one in Shiraz were regularly performing sex surgeries, some of them related to sex-disambiguating for intersex individuals. With increasing frequency, those hospitals began to offer SRS. As the number of such operations increased and as stories about people who got them circulated, SRS was no longer associated with intersexuality. Rather, the surgery came to be associated with homosexuality. In 1976, the Medical Council of Iran (MCI) determined that SRS was only ethically allowed in cases of inter-sexism. This ruling held for over a decade.[64]

While it must be acknowledged that Ayatollah Khomeini wrote about the permissibility of sex reassignment as early as 1964, it is nonetheless important to note the remarkable role of transgender individuals in Iran in achieving change. Due to the advocacy of a transwoman, for example, Khomeini reissued his opinion regarding SRS. The process through which Iranian citizens can currently seek SRS is the result of cooperation between the state, the religious establishment, legal experts, and biomedical authorities, which extends back to the 1980s. The implementation of SRS in Iran has not always been a smooth process. After the rigid sartorial changes (see Chapter 12) put in place after the 1979 revolution, for example, woman-presenting males were expected to dress as men. The Iran-Iraq war created a tense atmosphere of nationalism, panic, and intense moral scrutiny. Thus, "men" were expected to conform; what had been acceptable in the 1970s was now viewed as unacceptable Westoxification. Nonetheless, Khomeini's rule has been supported by Khamenei, and the Iranian state has maintained the infrastructure for supporting transgender individuals.[65]

What Iran does not support, however, is homosexuality. Same-sex relations run the risk of capital offense, and it is therefore possible that some individuals seek to escape the condemnation of the state and the religious establishment by opting for SRS. The author of the most thorough study of transsexuality in Iran found that the Iranian establishment had not engaged in a mass campaign to use SRS to purge Iran of homosexuality, however. Rather, a community of empathetic, dedicated Iranian medical professionals works for the best outcome for their patients through screening, counseling, treatment, and follow-up care.[66] At the same time, however, hundreds of Iranian refugees are currently in Turkey, where they took refuge from fear and from the pressure placed on them by their families to undertake SRS.[67]

Regardless of the intentions of the religious authorities, however, treatment of trans people across the region runs the gamut from discriminatory to hostile, particularly for transwomen. Even in Lebanon, a country with support organizations and services, a recent survey indicated that 80% of the population finds cross-dressers to be "perverts." Similarly, 18% of the population report that they would consider being physically or verbally abusive to a man dressed as a woman. The idea that men have voluntarily given up their masculinity strikes some (men and women) as difficult to grapple with. Several categories of trans people exist: those who have had complete SRS, those who have had some procedures but not complete SRS, those who simply take hormones, those who live and dress as the gender to which they identify, and those who choose not to identify with a single (or either) gender (and who may choose any number of cosmetic or medical options). Only in Iran, Lebanon, and Bahrain (by court order) is sex-change acknowledged legally. In Turkey, prior to 2018, an individual seeking SRS had to be rendered infertile.[68] Still, only those who have reached the age of 18 qualify for the procedure in Turkey. Thus, regardless of phase or type, trans people are subject to humiliating abuse at airports and other venues, where their personal identification cards are required for passage. These same identification cards are necessary for school matriculation, job application, land purchase, building permits, and so on.

Consequently, it can be difficult for transgender people to find employment. Put in this predicament, many work in the informal economy (see Chapter 10). Because many of these individuals have suffered the largest crisis of identity during their adolescence, when their focus might otherwise have been on education or job training, their struggle to find work has been compounded. Some find sex work as an alternative and evidence suggests that demand for transwomen (male to female) is particularly high, especially in the Gulf. At the same time, Saudi Arabia, Kuwait, Qatar, Oman, Bahrain, and the UAE have enacted extremely strict regulations to restrict the entry of transgender people into their countries and to criminalize behavior that crosses boundaries of the sex into which one is born. For example, in 2007, Kuwait enacted legislation that criminalized behaving like the opposite sex. Despite the fact that the country had recognized gender dysphoria as a medical condition (paving the way for individuals to have SRS), there was no legal mechanism to record the change on one's identification. Transwomen in Kuwait have therefore been arrested for charges as simple as having "smooth skin" or a "soft voice" and then subjected to blackmail, rape, and beating by police. Others have been punished and defeminized by having their heads shaved. In 2010, the UAE enlisted the help of its civilian population by activating a hotline to report cross-dressing individuals. Press reports indicated that individuals arrested were all either transwomen or men cross-dressing as women—none were transmen or *boyat*. Notably, the *boyat* tend to be arrested for behavioral issues, public disturbance, aggressive behavior rather than dressing like a man. Backlash has also fallen heavily on foreign nationals. In a number of Gulf nations, for example, Dubai, migrants make up 90% of the labor force.[69] In the same way that *fujur* crimes were prosecuted prior to 2001 in Egypt, the soliciting transwomen bear the brunt of the blame.

Conclusion

While marriage is a social norm, desire takes multiple forms and cannot be measured solely through the boundaries of marriage. As we have seen, married men and women have historically found ways to express desire for those to whom they are not married, all the while remaining safely within the realm of licit behavior. Gazing at beardless youths and viewing theater and films, for example, provide contact with desires that fall outside of the marital union, if not the consummation of those desires. And, as we have also seen, sex happens outside of marriage, sometimes with partners of the same sex. In a word, marriage is not always what it looks like.

Similarly, we have seen that while marriage is the normative union between men and women in the Middle East, boundaries separating "man" and "woman" have not always been easily kept. Cross-dressing in real life and the arts turns one sex into the other in the blink of an eye, widening avenues for licit desire (and for potential transgression). Transvestitism and transsexualism have also allowed men and women, when taking on the role of the other, to participate fully in the social order, as when a woman dresses and behaves as a man in order to make a living or to protect her family. Simply put, "men" and "women" are not always who they appear to be.

Fatima al-Qadiri's "Dala3 in Vegas" illustrates the mirage of sex and marriage. "Dala3 in Vegas" is at first glance a photograph of a young man and woman, a young couple, perhaps on their honeymoon in Vegas. She wears a dress and a modern Fedora; he sports a long-sleeved tee shirt, jeans, and a cap. Married or not (we don't know), the pair represent the sought-after union of male and female. Upon closer inspection (and with the help of cultural critics), we discover that "he" is a *boyah*: a female dressed as a male. Both the *boyah* and his/her ultrafeminine counterpart are intended to be critiques of gender roles in contemporary Arab society (she of Arabs' current, idealized "femme" and "he" of the relationship between masculinity and consumption, muscle car and all).[70] But what we see is a couple. And we assume that their union is licit and that they desire each other.

Reactions to *boyat* in the region (the young women who dress as boys and wear pixie haircuts have been labeled "alien," "shameful," and "disgusting," among other things) suggest that this photograph depicts a transgression against the social order, not because it is absent a "male" but because it hints at desires not so easily categorized.[71] Does she desire a man? A beardless youth? A woman? If so, is she a lesbian who might rebel against the social order by not marrying despite the suggestion that she is married? Does "his" desire for this woman define "his" masculinity? Or can "he" be masculine enough without desiring her, relying instead on "his" expensive watch, clothing, and car? Does this *boyah* transgress because she desires a woman or because she masquerades as a man?

Some observers of the *boyat* (plural of *boyah*) phenomenon regard it as a sexual transgression, translating *boyah* not as tomboy (the word is an Arabized version of the English word for boy) but as transsexual and have therefore called for the death penalty for those who partake in such gender-bending. (Qatar has a rehabilitation center for *boyat*.) Others see young women dressing as men as a sartorial transgression, threatening femininity and with it, the social order. The Arab Emirates launched a campaign against the habit, called "Excuse Me, I'm a Girl," stressing the dangers to the social order of women dressing as men.[72] In the following we chapter, we examine how modern states (and their rulers) have used clothing to mold political, social, and religious agendas, as well as changing conceptions of beauty.

Notes

1 Fatima Mernissi, *Beyond the Veil* (Bloomington: Indiana University Press, 1987 [1975]), 31–45.
2 Sex is a biological determination and desire is a personal preference. The standard Western bifurcation of desire between heterosexuality and homosexuality (with the nuance of bisexuality) is a categorization many in the Middle East reject. Thus, the term same-sex preference or desire is used throughout this chapter.
3 Gabriel Semerene, "The Words to Say It," https://www.mashallahnews.com/language/words-to-say.html.
4 Semerene, "Words."
5 Khaled el-Rouayheb, *Before Homosexuality in the Arab-Islamic World, 1500–1800* (Chicago: The University of Chicago Press, 2005), 153–156.
6 Dror Ze'evi, *Producing Desire: Changing Sexual Discourse in the Ottoman Middle East, 1500–1900* (Berkeley and Los Angeles: University of California Press, 2006), Introduction.
7 See Rouayheb, *Before Homosexuality*, for examples, 65.
8 Ze'evi, *Producing Desire*, 130.
9 Afsaneh Najmabadi, *Women with Mustaches, Men Without Beards* (Berkeley and Los Angeles: University of California Press, 2005), 11.
10 Najmabadi, *Women with Mustaches, Men Without Beards*, 16, 23.
11 El-Rouayheb, *Before Homosexuality*, 3, 113–116.
12 El-Rouayheb, *Before Homosexuality*, 12.
13 Samar Habib, *Female Homosexuality in the Middle East* (New York: Routledge, 2007), 58; Sahar Amer, "Medieval Arab Lesbians and Lesbian-like Women," *Journal of the History of Sexuality* Vol. 18, No. 2 (May 2009), 223.
14 Paula Sanders, "Gendering the Ungendered Body: Hermaphrodites in Medieval Islamic Law," in *Shifting Boundaries in Middle East History*, Beth Baron and Nikki Keddie, eds. (New Haven: Yale University Press, 1991), especially 74–76, 88–89.

15 Everett Rowson, "The Effeminates of Early Medina," *Journal of the American Oriental Society* Vol. 111, No. 4 (October–December 1991): 671–693.
16 Uni Wikan, "Man Becomes Woman: Transsexualism in Oman as Key to Gender Roles," *Man* Vol. 12 (1977), 304–319, and discussions that followed in *Man* Vol. 13 (1978), 473–475, 663–661; Stephen Murray, "The Sohari Khanith," in *Islamic Homosexualities*, Will Roscoe and Stephen Murray, eds. (New York: Routledge, 1997), 244–255.
17 Sigrid Westphal-Hellbusch, "Transvestiten bei arabischen Stämmen," *Sociologus* Vol. 6, No. 2 (1956), 129, 131, 132, 137.
18 Judith Tucker, *In the House of Law* (Berkeley: University of California Press, 1998), Chapter 2; on Coptic women, see Mohamed Afifi, "Reflections on Personal Status Laws of Copts," in *Women, the Family, and Divorce Laws in Islamic History*, Amira Sonbol, ed. (Syracuse: Syracuse University Press, 1996), 204.
19 Shereen El Feki, *Sex and the Citadel: An Intimate Life in a Changing Arab World* (New York: Random House, 2013), 50.
20 El Feki, *Sex and the Citadel*, 128–129.
21 Dominique Soguel, "Syrian Refugee Crisis Fuels Underage Marriage in Jordan," *Women's e-News* (February 12, 2014); http://womensenews.org/2014/02/syrian-refugees-fuel-underage-marriage-in-jordan/.
22 "In Jordan, Fatwas Differ on 'Misyar' Marriages and Women Suffer," *Arab Reporters for Investigative Journalism* (March 23, 2013); http://en.arij.net/report/in-jordan-fatwas-differ-on-misyar-marriages-and-women-suffer/.
23 See, for example, Afsaneh Najmabadi, *Women with Mustaches, Men Without Beards*, Chapter 2, Joseph Massad, *Desiring Arabs* (Chicago: University of Chicago Press, 2008), Chapter 1.
24 Massad, *Desiring Arabs*, 1.
25 Garay Menicucci, "Unlocking the Celluloid Closet: Homosexuality in Egyptian Film," *MERIP* No. 206 (Spring 1998), 32–36; Samar Habib, "Notes on Crossdressing in Early Egyptian Cinema," (July 31, 2016); http://samarhabib80.blogspot.com/2016/07/in-spring-of-1998-middle-east-report.html.
26 Menicucci, "Celluloid Closet," 32. For a clip (not subtitled), see https://www.youtube.com/watch?v=bm3skKuNlR8&feature=youtu.be.
27 Advertisement for *Midnight, al-Ithnayn wal-dunya* (March 14, 1949), 41.
28 See, for example, actress Kariman's response to Huda Shams el-Din in *An American in Tanta* (1955); https://vimeo.com/103306710.
29 Menicucci, "Celluloid Closet," 32–33.
30 Niazi Mustafa, Director, 1975.
31 Habib, *Female Homosexuality*, 126–129; Menicucci, "Celluloid Closet," 33.
32 Joseph Boone, *The Homoerotics of Orientalism* (New York: Columbia University Press, 2015), 245.
33 Menicucci, "Celluloid Closet," 36.
34 Samar Habib, *Female Homosexuality in the Middle East*, 116.
35 *Dentelle*, Director Inas Dedheidi, 1993 (Egypt); *I Can't Think Straight* was based on the novel by Shamim Sharif, who also directed the film (2008).
36 *Tul Omri*, Director Maher Sabry, 2008 (US, Egypt); *Le Fil*, Director Mehdi Ben Attia, 2009 (Tunisia/Algeria/France/Belgium); *L'armée de salut*, Director Abdellah Taia, 2013 (Morocco, France, Switzerland).
37 Quoted in El Feki, *Sex and the Citadel*, 255.
38 Cisgender refers to those whose gender identity corresponds with their birth sex. It does not suggest sexual preference.
39 "In a Time of Torture," https://www.hrw.org/reports/2004/egypt0304/3.htm. In fact, 60 men were arrested and 54 incarcerated, but the wealthiest and most well connected were not charged.

40 Jared McCormick, "Hairy Chest Will Travel: Tourism, Identity, and Sexuality in the Levant," *JMEWS* Vol. 7, No. 3 (Fall 2011), 86.
41 El Feki, *Sex and the Citadel*, 229; Mathew Gagné, "Queer Beirut Online: The Participation of Men in Gayromeo.com," *JMEWS* Vol. 8, No. 3 (Fall 2012), 131; Sofian Merabet, "Disavowed Homosexualities in Beirut," *MERIP* No. 230 (Spring 2004), 30–33; https://www-jstor-org.jproxy.lib.ecu.edu/stable/pdf/1559293.pdf; Amrou al-Kadhi, "As a Gay Man Born in Iraq ..." *Independent* (July 5, 2017); https://www.independent.co.uk/Voices/iraq-actor-karar-nushi-war-homosexuality-lgbt-home-office-western-intervention-gender-a7824881.html.
42 "Iran's Women Labor Force Participation Lowest Worldwide," *Financial Tribune* (December 26, 2017); https://financialtribune.com/articles/economy-business-and-markets/78671/iran-s-women-labor-force-participation-lowest-worldwide.
43 Najmabadi, *Professing Selves*, 152, 271. An internet story appeared about an Egyptian woman Bahia Suleiman working as a tuk tuk driver and construction worker to support her family. "This Egyptian Mother Lived for Five Years as a Man"; https://www.facebook.com/Vocativ/videos/1680578931954335/.
44 El Feki, *Sex and the Citadel*, 237–238, 272–273; Najmabadi, *Professing Selves*, 41–42; Noor al-Qasimi, "Boyah and The Baby Lady: Queer Mediations in Fatima al-Qadiri and Khalid al-Gharaballi's Wawa Series (2011)," *JMEWS* Vol. 8, No. 3 (Fall 2012), 139–140.
45 Moussawi, "Queer Exceptionalism." For example, Arabic is not one of the languages available on GayRomeo, and even the ability to use certain dating apps is contingent upon having a smartphone. Gagné, "Queer Beirut Online," 119; Mathew Gagné, "Nadir's Intimate Biography," *Middle East Journal of Culture and Communication*, Vol. 9, No. 2 (2016), 165–181; Massad, *Desiring Arabs*, 182.
46 "Avancée historique au Liban: l'homosexualité n'est plus un crime," *Newsmonkey* (July 15, 2018); http://m.fr.newsmonkey.be/article/25243?utm_source=Facebook&utm_campaign=SocialMedia&utm_medium=PostContent.
47 Tallie Ben Daniel, "Branding Israel: Queer Markets in San Francisco and Tel Aviv" (PhD Diss., University of CA-Davis, 2014), 37.
48 McCormick, "Hairy Chest Will Travel," 72, 79, 82.
49 Hossam Bahgat, "Egypt's Virtual Protection of Morality," *MERIP* No. 230 (Spring 2004), 24.
50 "In a Time of Torture," Section II.
51 Tim Teeman, "The Secret Hypocritical Gay World of ISIS," *The Daily Beast* (January 6, 2016); https://www.thedailybeast.com/the-secret-hypocritical-gay-world-of-isis.
52 Serkan Gorkemli, "Coming Out of the Internet: Lesbian and Gay Activism and the Internet as a 'Digital Closet' in Turkey," *JMEWS* Vol. 8, No. 3 (Fall 2012), 73.
53 Grant Walsh-Haines, "The Egyptian Blogosphere: Policing Gender and Sexuality, the Consequences of Queer Emancipation," *JMEWS* Vol. 8, No. 2 (Fall 2012), 57.
54 Ghassan Makarem, "The Story of HELEM," *JMEWS* Vol. 7, No. 3 (Fall 2011), 102, 104, 105, 107–110; El Feki, *Sex and the Citadel*, 261, 266.
55 Sahar Amer, "Can the 1/11 Revolutions be Rainbow Revolution" (Presentation Annual Meeting MESA, 2011); Ilan Lior, "Tel Aviv Gay Pride Draws 200,000—Including 30,000 Tourists," *Haaretz* (June 9, 2017); https://www.haaretz.com/israel-news/MAGAZINE-tel-aviv-s-19th-pride-parade-draws-200-000-1.5482374.
56 Juliane Helmhold, "Turkish Police Clash with LGBT Crowd After Parade Canceled," *Jerusalem Post* (July 2, 2018); https://www.jpost.com/Middle-East/Turkish-police-clashes-with-LGBT-crowd-after-official-Pride-parade-banned-561322; "Beirut Pride Canceled After Organizer Arrested," *BBC News* (May 16, 2018); https://www.bbc.com/news/world-middle-east-44141603; "Jerusalem Gay Pride Stabbing: Yishlai Schlissel Jailed for Life," *BBC News* (June 26, 2016); https://www.bbc.com/news/world-middle-east-36634148.

57 Habib Toumi, "Gay Man Sentenced For Twitter Debauchery," *Gulf News Saudi Arabia* (July 23, 2014); https://gulfnews.com/news/gulf/saudi-arabia/gay-man-sentenced-for-twitter-debauchery-in-saudi-arabia-1.1363181?.
58 Nadya Labi, "The Kingdom in the Closet," *The Atlantic* (May 2007); https://www.theatlantic.com/magazine/archive/2007/05/the-kingdom-in-the-closet/305774/. Only in March 2018 did the kingdom relax rules for women's dress stating that the *abaya* and specific head covering were no longer necessary.
59 Haddad, "Myth of the Queer Arab Life."
60 Cara Giaimo, "Before Bowie or Prince There was Zeki Müren—Turkey's Gender-Bending Rock Star," *Atlas Obscura* (May 9, 2016); https://www.atlasobscura.com/articles/before-bowie-or-prince-there-was-zeki-murenturkeys-genderbending-rock-star;
61 "Video Documenting the Life and Death of Egypt's First Transsexual Actress Goes Viral," *Cairo Scene* (February 13, 2017); http://www.cairoscene.com/ArtsAndCulture/Video-Documenting-the-Life-and-Death-of-Egypt-s-First-Transsexual-Actress-Goes-Viral.
62 On gender and textbooks, see Russell, *Creating the New Egyptian Woman*, 145–146, 153–154; on popular magazines, see Wilson Jacob, *Working Out Egypt* (Durham: Duke University Press, 2011), 156–185; Najmabadi, *Professing Selves*, ch. 3; Liat Kozma, "Sexology in the Yishuv," *International Journal of Middle East Studies* Vol. 42, No. 2 (May 2010), 240–242; and on the medical profession, see Najmabadi, *Professing Selves*, 84–87.
63 Najmabadi, *Professing Selves*, 67–69.
64 Najmabadi, *Professing Selves*, 20, 187–189.
65 Najmabadi, *Professing Selves*, 315, Chapter 1.
66 Carmel Kilkenny reports 471, many awaiting the next leg of journey to the US or Canada; however, with the travel ban in the US, they are stranded. "LGBTQ Refugees from Iran Stranded in Turkey" (September 4, 2017); http://www.rcinet.ca/en/2017/09/04/lgbtq-refugees-from-iran-stranded-in-turkey/.
67 Many countries require infertility and obviously some procedures necessitate it, while others do not. "The Constitutional Court's Changes to Article 40 Now in Effect," *LGBT News Turkey* (March 20, 2018); https://lgbtinewsturkey.com/2018/03/23/the-constitutional-courts-changes-to-article-40-are-now-in-effect/.
68 Sulome Anderson, "Ladyboys in the Gulf," *Foreign Policy* (October 19, 2012); https://foreignpolicy.com/2012/10/19/ladyboys-in-the-gulf/; Brian Whitaker, "Transgender Issues in the Middle East: Part One—Crossing Lines" (July 26, 2016); https://medium.com/@Brian_Whit/transgender-issues-in-the-middle-east-1-crossing-lines-2cbfbbd29e93.
69 Noor al-Qasimi, "The 'Boyah' and the 'Baby Lady,'" *Journal of Middle East Women's Studies* Vol. 8, No. 3 (Fall 2012), 139–142.
70 *The Middle East Times*, December 6, 2012; Mideast-times.com/left_news.php?newsid=2904.
71 "A Debate About Fashion in Qatar: Cross about Cross-Dressing," *The Economist*, January 28, 2010.

12 Fashion, Clothing, and the Body

Introduction

In this chapter, we examine the multiple gendered meanings of various types of clothing associated with modernity. We analyze the history of grooming and of sumptuary laws in the region during the era of modernization and Westernization, illustrating how political exigency, economic tensions, and laws regarding dressing oneself have historically gone hand in hand. We will then turn our attention to more recent trends, including "reveiling," Islamic fashion, and cosmetic enhancement, to show that men and women make sartorial choices (or have those choices made for them) due to complex combinations of local and international politics, economic conditions, and personal decisions regarding piety. Next, we will examine one of the pivotal items from which Middle Eastern girls (like girls elsewhere) learn standards of beauty and fashion: their dolls. We conclude with a brief section on the trend toward "unveiling." In each case, our goal is to illustrate that clothing in the modern Middle East has been a marker of tradition and of modernity, of subjects' and citizens' relationship to the nation-state, and an expression of individualism. Far from being a stand-in for religion, as it is often viewed in the West, clothing choices (and edicts) in the Middle East are palimpsests for the complexities and challenges that have faced the region in the modern era.

Covering, Uncovering, and Modernity

In the Western imagination, no article of Middle Eastern clothing has received more attention or condemnation than the veil. Outside the Islamic world, emotions about the veil run the gamut from fascination to outright hatred. There is little understanding of the range of practices that fall under the category of veiling. Nor is there awareness that the reasons for donning or doffing "the veil" have changed over place and time. Veiling predates Islam, and it connects to a variety of religious traditions for men as well as for women. Sumptuary laws, issued by rulers and religious authorities in various times and places across the region, have carefully delineated a negotiation of class and rank from the top down, starting from the state and elites to subjects and citizens, as seen in Chapters 4 and 7. Similarly, clothing and its customs have been a means through which religious, occupational, and ethnic groups negotiate upward with the state.[1]

In many cases, however, women's decisions regarding dress have been made in total disregard for the state or for religious elites. In 1923, the Egyptian feminist Hoda Shaarawi famously removed her "veil" after returning to Egypt from an International Women's conference in Rome at a time of national upheaval in her country. The "veil" in question was a *yashmak*: a flimsy, translucent piece of material worn across the face of elite and middle-class women, in addition to a headscarf and an outer garment that concealed the figure. Shaarawi continued to wear her headscarf for a number of years after her historic removal of the *yashmak*. Journals generally depict her with her face uncovered and head covered. Similarly, Doriyya Fahmy, the first Egyptian woman to study in France, recollects removing her *yashmak* on board a ship en route. She did not find it significant to discuss whether or not she wore a headscarf.[2] She wanted an advanced education, and she wanted to work, with or without her family's approval.

Both instances reflect the education and orientation of women whose sartorial decisions were made independently. They differ from Atatürk's 1925 ban of Islamic clothing and from the Turkish government's forced removal of the *hijab* in public spaces between 1982 and 2017. They also differ from those of Reza Shah Pahlavi, who forced the removal of the veil in public spaces in Iran (see Chapter 8). And all of these cases differ from later acts of defiance and "bad *hijab*" as practiced in Iran from the late 1990s, in which women not only let portions of their bangs or hair fall out, but flaunt capri pants, sandals, and brightly-colored nail polish, lipstick, dramatic colors, cosmetically-altered features, piercings, and tattooing eyeliner.[3] Whether individually-inspired or state-mandated, each act of donning the "veil" or its removal has a context.

Similarly, donning the veil has had different (and perhaps) overlapping meanings, historically. Some interpret the verse regarding the *hijab* in the 33rd chapter of the Quran within the context in which it was revealed.[4] "Believers do not enter the Prophet's apartment for a meal unless you have permission to do so. ...When you ask his wives for something, do so from behind a screen; this is purer for your hearts and for theirs" (33:53).[5] In this context, *hijab* refers to a separation between the Muslim community and the wives of the Prophet Muhammad. According to this interpretation, the "veil" is only prescribed for his wives. For others, the context in which the verse was revealed is less important than the injunctions to modesty and separation of men and women.

Scholars and believers also differ in opinion about the verses in the Quran that deal with modesty (33:53, 33:59–60, 24:30–31). Chapter 33, verse 59, for example, reads: "Prophet, tell your wives, your daughters and female believers to make their outer garments hang low over them so as to be recognized and not insulted."[6] For some, the verse indicates that the responsibility for modesty lies on women's shoulders alone. Feminist and conservative interpretations suggest that both men and women need to be modest in conduct and that women's burden is greater than men's when it comes to clothing and modesty. The meaning of that burden, however, is vague.[7]

Outsiders consider women's clothing to be conservative in the Persian Gulf. In actuality, there is a great variety among Gulf countries and even within them. Saudi Arabia mandates wearing an *abaya* or cloak, while in Dubai, UAE, clothing preferences range from conservative to the latest in Western fashion. Saudi Arabia has a morals police, yet there are differences in the application of law within the country itself. Saudi Arabia is equated with dark colors and the face-covering *niqab*, but neither is mandatory. Women on the western coast routinely wear brighter colors and long jackets rather than traditional garb. Saudi women are well known for accessorizing with designer sunglasses, handbags, and shoes, as well as for wearing their own styles at home and abroad. The ritual of shedding or donning the *abaya* on the plane is part of Saudi culture

It is not only Middle Eastern women who cover their heads. The *keffiyeh* has been well known as the symbol of male Palestinian resistance since the 1930s. It has gained worldwide cachet since the 1980s, booming in various fashion circles in the 2000s[8] (see Figure 12.1). Israeli and European designers have integrated the black- and white-squared headscarf into fashions such as dresses and skirts, to the extent that contemporary Palestinian women are fighting to reclaim an industry that they see as their own. In the West Bank town of Hebron, for example, a women's cooperative rallies against "made in China" *keffiyehs* that have flooded the world market.[9] At the same time that Palestinian women fight to save their national garment, an Israeli designer has appropriated the *keffiyeh* to make expensive dresses, with a line beginning at USD 150.[10]

The nationalist symbolism of the *keffiyeh* has some similarities with the *chador*, the traditional, Iranian head and body covering for women. The *keffiyeh* was a resistance symbol during the 1936–1939 Palestinian rebellion against the British Mandate and has subsequently been incorporated into the Palestinian *intifadas* of the late 1980s and the early twenty-first century. After the first *intifada* (1987–1993), the wearing of Islamic dress, particularly in Gaza, was also a sign of dedication to the Palestinian cause within the territories and solidarity outside of them. In Iran, in the era just prior to the 1979 Revolution, wearing a *chador* or even a headscarf was a sign of resistance to the corrupt rule of Muhammad Reza Shah Pahlavi. Nevertheless, the same women who took to the streets to bring down the Shah would have had no way of knowing that the new Islamic Republic would institute a dress code in 1983.

These examples are quite different from the women who have returned to "the veil" in a variety of forms as part of the "piety movement." Their garb ranges from small snoods to designer silk scarves to long, dark, shapeless *khimars* to full-scale *burq'as*, never worn before by women in many of their home countries until relatively recently. In Egypt, the failure of pan-Arab secularism, the rise of petrodollars fueling *salafi* forms of religion, Sadat's support of Islamic groups to counterbalance Nasserists, and Egyptians' disgust with the colonial legacy led to a resurgence of religiosity. For middle- and upper-class women who desire advanced education and a hassle-free workplace environment, the return of the veil is a welcome expression of piety, authenticity, and modernity all at the same time (see below).[11]

Figure 12.1 Palestinian women sport *keffiyehs* at protest. Jenny Matthews/Alamy Stock Photo.

For men, one of the most charged sartorial symbols of the last (nearly) 200 years has been the *fez* or *tarboosh*. Mahmud II, who introduced the brimless headgear to his military in 1826, saw the fez as an instrument of modernization. Then, in 1829, the Sultan decided that every civil servant would wear the exact same headgear. He therefore created 17 different types of clothing for religious and civil officials, taking clothing decisions out of the hands of communities who had traditionally conferred their own attire and headgear. Furthermore, the Sultan wanted clothing changes to be mirrored by society as a whole. Those who did not want to give up their distinctions from other religions and classes continued to wrap cloth around the fez in the style of a turban.[12] Nonetheless, the fez became the marker of the male educated classes ca. 1900.

After Atatürk's ban of Islamic dress, the headgear grew in popularity. For men, a *tarboosh*, a suit, and a shaved beard were the sartorial markers of the *effendiyya* (middle class) and were required for admission into wealthy shopping districts, sporting clubs, and new forms of recreation. Yet, after the rise of Nasser, the *tarboosh*, as the fez is also known, was once again deemed taboo: Nasser banned the hat in 1954 and associated it with the old regime. Nasser's charisma and the politics of the era (see Chapter 8) ensured the *tarboosh*'s relegation to old movies, tourist trinkets, and hotel doormen.

In all these cases, the rhetoric surrounding clothing choices is that of social progress. Historically, minority groups were typically the focal point of clothing laws, but as the Middle East integrated into the world economy, women increasingly became targets as well. Women have been active agents in generating change. Nonetheless, they have also been the focus of state-sponsored changes, and they have been targets of male-sponsored Islamic-reform campaigns.

Grooming, Clothing, and Sumptuary Laws in the Era of Reforms

In the era of reform, changing patterns of consumption, the result of the Ottomans' continued opening to the West and its goods, resulted in sumptuary laws aimed at women and minorities. In the eighteenth century, Muslim women had begun adopting the outer coats and headgear of European Christian women. Critics suggested that the garments of these "immoral" women represented a threat to public and to their husbands' finances. (They were also seen as threat to the economy as women no longer shopped from used garment salesmen.) Both men and women of non-elite backgrounds were therefore forbidden from wearing ermine fur, a longtime status symbol of Ottoman royalty.[13] Finally, there was a concern that turban-makers were making headgear for Muslim men that looked too much like that of their Jewish counterparts. In all these cases, boundaries had been crossed—religions confused, women imitating foreigners, and subjects behaving like rulers—and sultans put sumptuary laws in place to relieve anxieties.[14]

Over the remainder of the eighteenth century, as Europe's economy and military power remained ascendant and as power shifted away from the imperial court to bureaucrats and from bureaucrats to non-Muslim traders, sumptuary laws continued to reflect tensions in Ottoman society. Osman III (r. 1754–1757) was noteworthy for his obsession with sartorial reforms. He took it upon himself to patrol the streets in disguise, attacking women for clothing he deemed inappropriate or ill-fitting, while rebuking men for living beyond their means and for using luxurious threads or fabrics in their clothing. Mustafa III (r. 1757–1777) took a similar approach to order and clothing. He felt it necessary to reiterate fur laws for men and women and to regulate the height of women's headdress.[15]

Despite the sultan's obsessions with sumptuary laws, men's and women's clothing had not changed significantly over the course of the eighteenth century; however, by the turn of the nineteenth century, change had become more visible. Women's bodice necklines were beginning to plunge and their headgear heighten. But it was hard to know if Europeans were borrowing from Ottomans or Ottomans from Europeans, as elements of Turquerie were being adopted in Europe at the same time.[16] It was only in the late eighteenth and early nineteenth centuries that Europeans living and working in the empire began to wear European clothing. This is why headgear, coat length, and colors worn were particularly important identifiers of non-Ottoman and non-Muslim residents.

As Selim III (r. 1789–1807) worked to modernize the Ottoman military, he also passed laws reflecting a preoccupation with his subjects' clothing. External wars, internal rebellions, inflation, and currency devaluation led him to emphasize the local: Selim viewed consumption of foreign goods as a form of moral treason. He criticized statesmen who wore Iranian and Indian-made clothing as opposed to clothing made in Istanbul or Ankara, preaching economic reform and arguing for national industry.[17] At least one foreigner viewed him as ruthless in his enforcement of sumptuary laws, claiming that he would even cut off the hands of offenders.[18] Selim laid the groundwork for the more comprehensive changes in clothing and centralization that would come under Mahmud II and the *tanzimat* reforms (see Chapter 4).

In the nineteenth century, fashion in the Ottoman Empire underwent enormous change. *Tanzimat* reforms eliminated distinctions that had existed between religious groups and centralized state authority. Europeans who arrived and took up residence in the Ottoman Empire brought sewing patterns, journals, and new stores with them. By the turn of the twentieth century, European women influenced the consumer habits of upper-class women. New technologies, such as photography, the sewing machine, and print capitalism, helped to spread fashion trends across the empire more rapidly.[19]

In Qajar Iran, the royal family set fashion trends through portraiture, ritual, and, later, photography. Royal men shifted their taste toward Europeanized fashion, hairstyles, and grooming over the course of the nineteenth century—aside from the manly moustache that distinguished them from women. The Qajar official who adopted European clothing and habits in a bow tie, with form-revealing pants, was, however, a subject of fascination, satire, and scorn. New laws restricting fashion came from clerics who saw European clothing and grooming as a threatening the feminization of society. Some laws outlawed not only the shaving of beards (for which there was religious precedent), but also the wearing of ties. Clerics also issued laws against women wearing shoes with stiff backs.[20] Parliament enacted sumptuary laws aimed not at the people, but rather at the extravagant spending habits of the ruling family.

Both Reza Shah and Atatürk mandated changes that privileged Western clothing, and those who wore it, over those who wore traditional clothing. While the kinds of morals police that existed in Saudi Arabia and Iran at the turn of the twenty-first century did not exist in post-WWI Turkey and Iran, Western appearance was required in public space and for advancement in anything that required government assistance. Reza Shah's ban on the *chador* was only an issue if a woman wanted to attend school, go to an office, ride public transportation, or appear "publicly" in urban spaces. Women who lived the countryside could continue to dress as they pleased. Men had to wear suits to the office and hats when entering court houses. Villages therefore purchased collective fedoras for doing government business. Atatürk privileged the suit and expected civil servants and their wives to model the behavior that he and his wife Latife displayed (during the two and a half years that they were married). Owning a suit became the marker of being an educated member of the middle class throughout the Middle East.

The Body

The interwar era brought new anxieties for both men and women's bodies. There were new sporting clubs, fitness institutes, specialized magazines, products, clothing, and new role models—movie stars from both regional and American cinema. Westernized schools emphasized sports and fitness in ways that the traditional religious school system did not. Sporting Clubs imported to the region by foreign officers were soon copied by locals. At Sporting Clubs, women and men were introduced to new types of clothing for golf, tennis, swimming, and other activities. By the interwar years, the regional press was filled with advertisements for weight-loss pills, self-defense courses, gymnasiums, sexual-vitality pills, and a host of products with a new body type: the fit, masculine man and the slender, feminine woman. In the 1920s and 1930s, advertisers used bathing suits, which would not become trendy until the 1940s, to create a fear of being fat among women. By the time women started wearing bathing suits, Egyptian actresses and dancers, such as Leila Murad and Samia Gamal, evoked familiar Hollywood images of Rita Hayworth and Esther Williams, who were also popular in the region and whose body types defined the fashion norm.

The move from idealized plumpness to lean as a favored figure did not take hold immediately throughout the entire region, nor did it move from urban to rural until the late twentieth century with the spread of satellite television. Regardless, fitness, vitality, and fashion came to have new meanings beginning in the interwar period for urban, literate women and men. Specialized magazines, some more expensive with splashy pictures and others small and inexpensive, were aimed at a variety of audiences: middle-class women, girls, elite women, young men, upper-middle-class men with varying tastes and interests—fashion, sports, cinema, and even matters of sexuality. Through the circulation of these magazines, the body, its form, its clothing, and its function became topics of interest.

As a wave of revolutions hit the mid-twentieth-century Middle East, the bourgeois obsession with the body was replaced with a state obsession with the body. Fitness was the new word. Sporting clubs were now accessible to the ever-increasing ranks of the middle classes. New clubs emerged associated with professional syndicates and workers' groups, which may have lacked the golf and polo fields of the elite clubs, but nonetheless offered members a wide range of activities such as swimming, tennis, soccer, and martial arts. Fitness for duty also became part of state curriculums, even girls in state schools in Syria, for example, would learn how to do military drills.

Recent Trends: Pious Fashion, Resistance, Islamic Chic, and Cosmetic Enhancement

In the 1970s, the movement toward religiosity in Egypt was not limited to women or to Muslims; however, the large numbers of women taking up *al-ziyy al-Islami* (Islamic fashion) was physically more noticeable on college campuses, especially after the 1973 war. Not simply covering their heads, these women wore full length robes with long sleeves and high necklines, accompanied by an opaque head-covering that concealed all hair, neck, shoulders, and sometimes the entire bosom, in neutral colors without prints. The most conservative even concealed their faces (*niqab*), hands (gloves), and feet (opaque socks or closed shoes). While Egyptian men were joining the same Islamic groups and following some Islamic grooming habits, such as growing an Islamic beard (shaven cheeks and groomed jawline), their new habits were not nearly as visible. Furthermore, men were less likely to adopt Islamic clothing. For example, a *gallabeya* conveyed ambiguity in its sartorial statement: it could mean religiosity but could also mean backwardness or "country" origins.[21]

The promises made by various states in the region during the 1960s to extend education (see Chapter 8) at all levels to all citizens resulted in an increased demand for schooling in cities like Cairo, Damascus, and Istanbul by the 1970s. Women who succeeded in national exams found themselves for the first time in large cities, ready to enter universities but uncomfortable with the negotiation of urban spaces. Even women who were second-generation city folk found it difficult to manage the crowding, the public transportation, and the mixtures of Western and local fashions that presented themselves in large cities of the Middle East. Additionally, classrooms were jam-packed with women and men. In Egypt, the numbers of men and women enrolled in universities rose from under 200,000 in 1970 to over half a million in 1977. As women found themselves disheartened by the country's political situation and personally challenged in new living and academic situations, Islamic organizations offered practical solutions and a self-sustaining identity for them. Sadat began to support Islamic student groups over Nasserist and other leftist groups in a bid for his own personal success. By the mid-1970s, Islamic groups had taken control over all important resources on Egyptian campuses. Islamic groups created their own transportation networks, classroom sections for women only, and other practical solutions for students who were inclined to Islamist beliefs.[22] For women, the admission ticket to these perks was *al-ziyy al-Islami* or Islamic dress. Alternatively phrased, without Islamic dress, women would not have access to the benefits offered by Islamic student groups.

It was not merely material benefits that Islamic student groups offered. Rather, these groups provided women with the emotional and spiritual nourishment that was lacking in the post-1973 environment of humiliation and corruption. In 1981, Fadwa El Guindi rather perspicaciously referred to the veiled woman as the "new Egyptian woman," a term reserved for women at the turn of the twentieth century, connoting modernity, "advanced views," and "the defiance of convention."[23] Indeed, by the 1970s, the politically conscious saw the veil as a form of *da'wa* or mission. The percentage of women who viewed themselves in such political terms is unknown.

In Turkey, the large-scale migration of women from rural to urban areas in the 1970s brought women who had never stopped veiling or who came from families where women had never stopped veiling into greater view. By the 1980s, the pressure on the Turkish system of higher education from increased numbers of students from the countryside led to an expansion of the whole university system (from eight in 1980 to 29 in 1990 and to 73 by 2000). Female students were knowledgeable about religion. And they linked the practice of religion to the political process. Thus, the secular Turkish government of the time was faced with ever larger numbers of visibly-veiled women, who were distinct from their working-class counterparts on the margins of urban society. The government dubbed the demands of these women the "turban movement" (rather than *hijab* or scarf) to connote what it saw as transgressive behavior on the part of religiously-inspired women specifically and its dim view of Islamism more generally.[24] The government responded to women's increased demands for space at Turkey's universities and to their insistence upon sporting traditional clothing by banning the *hijab* on university campuses in 1982. The ban led to a decades-long confrontation over dress in public space. Women continued to demand their religious freedom and the government insisted upon secularism—symbolized as an unveiled woman—as the basis for democracy. Between the ban in 1982 and its repeal in 2013, there were numerous court cases, attempted repeals, and acts of resistance by Turkish students, including the wearing of wigs in place of veils and the use of hats to conceal headscarves.

The Iranian Revolution of 1979 marked a watershed moment in the region as the veil became a symbol of revolution in the name of Islam, of anti-colonialism, and of anti-Westernism. Veiling after 1979 also created a battle within Iran over personal freedom for women. There was precedent in Iran for bringing out the traditional garment once banned by Reza Shah. Women, for example, had taken to the streets in *chador* during the oil nationalization crisis between 1951 and 1953. During the revolution of 1979, the veil was a powerful and visible marker of what revolutionaries referred to as authenticity, and it became a hallmark of the revolutionary era. Nevertheless, not all Iranian women wore the chador during the Revolution, nor did those who wore it believe that veiling would become mandatory. On the eve of International Women's Day in March 1979, however, Khomeini's new regime issued "reveiling" orders that spawned protests against the chador. The spring of the following year also witnessed a similar round of *chador* orders and protests. It was not until 1983 that it was actually written into the Constitution that women could not appear in public without Islamic dress.

A similar compunction to wear the *hijab* came after the outbreak of the first *intifada* in the Palestinian territories, particularly in Gaza, in 1987. For women, clothing in the territories had been a mix of traditional attire and Western clothing. In the 1970s, a few women associated with political Islam, particularly the splinter group of the Muslim Brotherhood that would later become HAMAS, adopted *al-ziyy al-Islami*. Over the 1980s, Islamic dress became location-specific: in the workplace, the Islamic university, and among religiously-conservative families. A year after the outbreak of the first *intifada*, in Gaza, it became intolerable for women to wear anything other than Islamic dress, due to pressure from (male) youth and religious groups. By 1989, the campaign in favor of Islamic dress had spread into the West Bank: women who did not wear the *hijab* or did so only out of fear were concerned about the dangerous political consequences, such as the rise of an Islamic state (see Chapter 13).[25] Clothing choices spelled danger for both the veiled and the unveiled: Politically-active unveiled leftists were often known to

(Israeli) soldiers and thus vulnerable. Other women who chose to remain unveiled were preyed on by assertive youth. Women who chose not to veil as a political statement against HAMAS voted with their clothing about the nature of their preferred form of government.

By the 1990s, Islamic fashion and Islamic revivalism both increased. In Egypt, generations of university students from the 1970s and 1980s had now risen in their professions and many of the leading professional syndicates had taken on an Islamic element. Islamic organizations flourished in a period of economic privatization as the government abandoned its social contract with the people. Islamic social welfare societies filled the gap by providing health, education, and welfare services. Only a small minority of the groups were radicalized. All, however, believed that women should wear traditional Islamic dress. Women themselves proved quite formidable to the movement, convincing other women to veil, advancing arguments in favor of veiling, and even providing garments to other women. Charismatic imams were pivotal in convincing women to go above and beyond the *hijab*, to the face-covering *niqab*.[26] For working-class women, it was simply more cost-effective to wear Islamic dress. Women were less likely to suffer harassment on public transportation and more likely to be respected in the workplace (with fewer outfits).[27]

At the same time, however, as more women veiled for a multiplicity of reasons—including not having to do their hair—new options for Islamic fashion emerged. A burgeoning local textile market produced Western clothes for export and ethnic chic for local consumption. Stores with names like "Hoda's Clothes for Veiled Women" opened to cater to a new market, particularly as the Islamic trend spread upwards in terms of class and age. There was a ready market for women who wanted to wear Islamic clothing but wanted style and fashion—clothes for everything from business suits to wedding attire to Islamic bathing suits. No longer would women be limited to drab colors, lack of prints, and ordinary fabrics. Conservative critics, male and female, complained that such dress defied the principles of *al-ziyy al-Islami*.

While the government maintained a critical distance from men in Islamic dress in public spaces such as offices and universities, the notion of the respectable Egyptian woman demanded new representation, and the new Islamic chic fit this mold.[28] The notion of reveiling for many years was reviling to the Western-oriented regimes of Sadat and Mubarak. Their first ladies adhered to Western convention in unveiling, style, and skirt length, but they usually wore long sleeves and a conservative neckline. The 1971 and 1980 Constitutions made *sharia* first "a principal source" and then "the principal source" for law, Mubarak, nonetheless waffled on how to enforce this state directive. Sadat and Mubarak seemed to move against the current fashion trends. Under both men, not only were Egypt's newscasters unveiled, they *had* to be unveiled. At the same time, however, Islamic-chic or Western-conservative became the trend for women in government offices, from low-level clerks to cabinet ministers.

In the 1980s and 1990s, Turkish university women were at the forefront of change, yet their bodies were appropriated by male secularist and Islamist politicians as embodiments of what the Turkish nation should be. Religiously-conscious students not only insisted upon wearing the banned headscarves, but they also refused to have pictures taken for identification, touch cadavers in medical training, wear shorts at national sporting events, or sketch nudes in art class.[29] Recent Turkish literature has contrasted images of women within the same family, unveiled and veiled, as relatively insignificant in the larger landscape of problems. Nowhere is this more evident than in Orhan Pamuk's *Snow*, in which the "headscarf" issue is actually highlighted. *Snow* contrasts sisters Ipek and Kadife and a portion of the novel's plot deals with the protagonist investigating the suicide of university students who insist upon wearing the veil. Elif Shafak's *Bastard of Istanbul* centers similarly upon a matriarchal family, divided between fervent Kemalist secularists and devout Islamists. In both texts, the reader is left with the sensation that women's bodies are battlefields for larger issues in Turkish society, including identity, the role of government, and poverty.[30]

Like the stylish Egyptian consumer, some Turkish and Iranian women began to move toward stylish Islamic consumption in the 1980s and 1990s, which was not necessarily limited to clothing but could also include products as diverse as toothpaste, chocolate, magazines, social networks, and dolls (see below).[31] At the turn of the twenty-first century, women in both of these countries abandoned the long, "boxy"-style coats of their mothers, grandmothers, and aunts in favor of more colorful, shorter, tailored looks. Before these changes, there was a bit more flexibility in Turkey, which had no clothing requirements and a vibrant textiles industry, including patterned scarves. There was less flexibility in Iran in the early years of the Islamic Republic.

A variety of Turkish companies produced the *tessetür*, the Turkish overcoat, and these companies emerged in the context of an Islamically-conscious local bourgeoisie and an eager handful of multinationals.[32] By the late 1990s and early 2000s, the coats were shorter, tighter, and more colorful and the headscarves much smaller. Nevertheless, focus groups have shown that the companies have tried to weave the notion of piety and consumption in marketing.

The success of the Justice and Development Party in Turkey has, since 2002, facilitated a number of changes in fashion. Although the Party rejects the moniker of religious or Islamist in favor of conservative democracy, its platform has consistently supported a moderately Islamist agenda. This platform worked in favor of students and government workers seeking to wear the headscarf as the party finally ended the ban in 2013. The wife of former Prime Minister (later President) Erdoğan, also set an example for conservative fashion, as she is always dressed in colorful *tessetür* and Ottoman-style scarf, complete with back-end bump. Her image has been frequently captured on social media, on sites such as Pinterest, Twitter, and Instagram.

In Iran, female entrepreneurial spirit has been at the forefront of health, beauty, and fashion change since the late 1990s. Iran went through a period of reform after the election of Muhammad Khatemi in 1997 (see Chapter 13) and witnessed student protests in 1999. "Bad *hijab*" practices inaugurated radical changes in clothing in Iran. "Bad *hijab*" was not necessarily a bold feminist statement, but rather an assertion of individuality in a country in which 70% of the population is under 30 and in which unemployment is high. Iranian-American Azadeh Moaveni, who visited Iran in 2000, links women's exchange of the *chador* for the new, more colorful *roopoosh* or *manteaux* (overcoat) to the election of the reform-minded Khatemi and the concomitant relaxing of old clothing regulations. She recollects meeting a male tailor and a female designer who were both taking advantage of the demand for new fashion.[33]

Scholars, journalists, and visitors to Iran have all observed the emergence of the female-run health-fitness industry. Elaine Sciolino, a noted journalist, highlighted the importance of the aerobics studios as one of "repose," in which female customers blur the lines between forbidden (dance) and allowed behaviors (exercise). Moaveni similarly describes the clientele at a high-end fitness center for women—whose concern for hygiene is greater than concern for disciplined exercise—lined up on the treadmills and ready for gossip, their bangles clanking. As for aerobics, Moaveni described the class she attended as solving the perennial problem of exercise, normally carried out in heat (or cold) of the outdoors in a headscarf, now done bareheaded in a climate-controlled environment with the fringe benefit of gossip.

A tremendous rise in plastic surgery for women and men accompanied Iran's reform movement in the 1990s. In fact, Iran has the highest per capita rate for rhinoplasty in the world. Not only do Iranians get one nose job: women often go under the knife two or three times before they get the nose of their dreams. Middle-aged men see the nose job as a means of looking younger, modern, and wealthy. Even office workers and students with modest incomes seek surgery and wear a bandage long after it is necessary to demonstrate their new beauty with pride. Even members of the most conservative families attest to having sought the skills of a plastic surgeon. The wife of a foreign policy adviser to the supreme leader, Ayatollah Khamenei, died due to complications from her liposuction. The stereotypical vain Tehrani woman is said to sport a "bumpit" in her hair, which she loosely covers with a designer scarf. She is alleged to wear layers of makeup, to sport tattooed eyebrows, a button-nose, and collagen-injected lips. Finally, she completes the picture by wearing colored contact lenses to match her ensemble.

As Iranian women move in extreme directions, the Revolutionary Guard has looked for someone or something to blame for women's behavior. Barbie has been a favored target (see below); however, more recently social media and Kim Kardashian have been the outlets for the Guard's outrage. A spokesperson for Iran's Organized Cybercrime Unit alleges that Kardashian wants to lure Iranian women into her extravagant lifestyle, one that Unit members claim is at odds with Islam.

She is part of a larger investigation by the Cybercrime Unit into Instagram and Facebook accounts which are allegedly guilty of "promoting a culture of promiscuity, weakening and rejecting the institution of family, ridiculing religious values and beliefs, promoting relationships outside of moral rules and publishing pictures of young women."[34]

Plastic surgery is also becoming more common elsewhere in the region, particularly in the wealthy Gulf states. By 2009, there were about 35 clinics in Riyadh alone. The increase can be attributed to the mutual consultation between doctors and religious authorities in 2006. Saudi clerics left open a wide range of pretexts for procedures, from medical necessity to problems stemming from accident or injury to problems that would cause a patient personal grief. At the same time, however, religious authorities were clear that cosmetic surgery should not be performed where it was not necessary or when a patient sought surgery in imitation of celebrity trends. Among the most common treatments in Saudi Arabia has been laser skin whitening, which achieves the age-old standard of fairness in beauty. Liposuction is also a common practice in Saudi Arabia, allowing women (and men) to achieve newer standards of slenderness.[35]

Beirut has been a destination of choice for generations of Middle Eastern women seeking beauty treatments. Since at least the 1930s, the wives of the wealthiest capitalists and politicians, actresses and actors have sought out specialists in Lebanon. Thus, it is not surprising that Beirut clinics are still perceived by many in the region to be the most experienced. Image Concept is the first "cosmetic tourism" company in Lebanon. The clinic combines privacy, wide-ranging vacation options, such as Lebanon's beaches, mountains, and historic sites, with an array of surgical procedures. The Dubai-based company, founded by Zeina El Haj in 2009, packages what people had been doing for years: going to Lebanon during their holidays to connect with its many experts on plastic, orthodontic, fertility, and aesthetic procedures. While Image Concept's webpage indicates that its clientele is mostly Gulf-based, it offers its services to clients from around the world. As obesity in the Gulf increases, men are more frequently undergoing breast reduction and liposuction at the clinic.[36] As time passes, more facilities like Image Concept are becoming available in the Gulf, with Dubai leading the way.

Egypt, home to the region's first film industry, has also been a leader in the plastic surgery industry. Since the 1990s, Egypt has been a sought-after center for cosmetic tourism. Cosmetic tourists in Egypt have generally hailed from outside the region, particularly Europe and the US. As in Lebanon, customers seek Egypt's beach resorts and other destinations such as the pyramids, in addition to the skilled hands of their surgeons. Perhaps what is most notable about Egyptian plastic surgeons is their reputation for charitable surgery. A forerunner of this trend began more than 20 years ago by donating his skills to children of garbage collectors, who are often engulfed by fire due to non-flame-retardant clothing. The surgeon uses some of the riches acquired by his wealthy clientele to treat the young burn victims. Now, others have followed this surgeon's lead, and it is common for surgeons to fix botched jobs of unlicensed hacks or simply aid those who find cosmetic surgery out of their reach, be they "[i]lliterate housewives fearing abandonment, soldiers mocked for having a flabby chest, or overweight women struggling to find a husband."[37]

Beauty Learned

An iconic doll can tell us quite a bit about a country's standards of beauty, its customs, and its social mores. Furthermore, changes in the doll are evidence of changing times and tastes. *Time Magazine* recently chronicled the birth of Barbie and the challenges she has faced since her introduction in the US in 1959. Barbie was an instant success in the US. Over the years, however, she has faced periodic criticism for her standardized beauty, conformity to gender stereotypes, and vacuous remarks, such as "Math class is tough." While battling charges of vacuity, Barbie has also had numerous cutting-edge careers in fields ranging from surgery to space to politics, in addition to fulfilling more traditional female roles as babysitter, teacher, and nurse. Her long-term relationship with Ken never culminated in marriage and ended in 2004; however, the two reunited in 2011. By the early twenty-first century, Barbie's market share in the US was eroding in younger markets to princess dolls and in older demographics to trendy, web-friendly Bratz.[38]

Just as the piety movement had taken hold of the Middle East and Islamic fashion had become a household word, conservative governments, particularly Saudi Arabia and Iran, took aim at Barbie for being an alleged vessel of senseless sin and consumption. For extreme religious conservatives, Barbie dolls are a form of idol worship unless they are maimed or deformed in some way. Thus, in 1994, a Kuwaiti official warned that Barbie should be banned from Kuwait's marketplaces because of the potential of the doll's fully-developed figure to warp children. Iranians viewed Barbie and her potential to harm Iranian children in more metaphorical terms, referring to her as a "Trojan Horse," more powerful than an American missile. The Iranian government began efforts to remove Barbie dolls from the shelves in the mid-1990s and to replace her (and her morally-corrupt boyfriend, Ken) with alternatives.

Iranian-produced "Sara and Dara" dolls therefore made their appearance on the Middle Eastern market in 2002, developed by the Institute for the Intellectual Development of Children and Young Adults. Sara and Dara are sister and brother, who seek wisdom from their parents. They are about eight years old, so there is no need for worry about covering Sara's head—although all versions of Sara come with a head covering of some sort. While Barbie has been banned in Iran since 1996, she has nonetheless continued to be a bestseller among Iranian girls aged four to ten. Iran's morals police periodically raid toy stores to either remove the dolls or cover inappropriate displays of Barbie's flesh with black stickers on boxes. Such raids take place particularly when relations with the US are strained.[39] While Barbie might therefore be losing cachet to edgier dolls in the American market, she is still the doll of favor across the Middle East, even in Iran where a black-market doll fetches a price three times higher than her more pious, younger competitors Sara and Dara.

As the anti-Barbie hype intensified across the region in the late 1990s, Egypt boldly announced its intentions to create a "Laila" doll, with wavy dark hair, dark eyes, and full lips, what an Arab League official proclaimed to be "a representative Arab girl." Laila, would be somewhat older than Iranian Sara, but at 10 or 12, would still wear children's underwear, a signal of her prepubescent body. "Laila" was carefully selected as a name that would suit Christian and Muslim households alike; she would have a variety of different "traditional" costumes from which to choose. Some prototype of "Laila" was tested in the 22 member-states of the Arab League; however, the actual doll herself was kept top secret until her market release.

"Laila" was touted as a guaranteed success at a quarter of the cost of an imported Barbie.[40] But Laila was hardly a success. Despite her touted arrival in 1999, "Laila" seems to have stayed on the design-room floor. One can speculate that Laila was left behind due to delays in production, lack of agreement among the Arab League participants regarding "Laila's" features or her cost, or the regional instability that resulted from the American occupation of Iraq in 2003.

Or perhaps Laila was afraid to tackle the competition of "Fulla," who first hit Syrian shelves in late 2003. "Fulla" is the marketing genius of New Boy Designs, originally headquartered in Syria and now operating in Dubai. The first real threat to Barbie, Fulla has been sold across the Middle East, North Africa, and in other Islamic markets. Fulla is the Islamic version of Barbie available in a variety of skin tones, hair colors, and costumes to meet the needs of those markets.

While Fulla appears more concerned with religion and family than Barbie, she bears some similarities to her American counterpart. She is a savvy consumer, defined by delicate features, and she displays only a slightly less voluptuous figure than Barbie, sporting the same 11½-inch body. Rather than bikinis, miniskirts, form-fitting clothes, and high heels; however, Fulla sports a full-length coat for wearing outdoors. In Saudi Arabia and other conservative Gulf countries, Fulla has a cloak, an *abaya*, and in more liberal countries she wears a light-colored coat and white scarf. Like the Iranian Sara, Fulla's companions are her siblings rather than a boyfriend. According to one Syrian toy store manager, "Fulla is one of us. She's my sister. She's my mother. She's my wife. She's all the traditional things of Syria and the Middle East." In fact, other store owners, managers, and company officials repeat this stock phrase whenever they are interviewed about Fulla (with some slight variation), suggesting that such sentiment about Fulla must be part of a marketing strategy.

And yet Fulla is not wholly distinct from Barbie. Under pressure, Fulla has been given some friends, Yasmine and Nour, who notably have lighter hair color. Fulla is also a consumer, who buys the products that are available for her, such as multiple headscarves, handbags, and, of course, her prayer mat. Aside from her bathing suit,

234   *Fashion, Clothing, and the Body*

she does not wear sleeveless outfits. She does have different outfits to wear indoors, however, including skirts that hit her just below the knee.

Fulla's likeness is tied to items of ordinary consumption aimed at nearly all classes, such as chewing gum, stationary, and cereal. Other items are targeted to the middle and upper classes; even the most pious parents might have difficulty saying no to the matching Fulla prayer mat, skirt, and scarf designed to facilitate girls' regular and enthusiastic participation in prayer rituals. And what middle-class parent could say no to a Fulla backpack when every other girl in school has one? If Fulla is on it, it will sell. More elite parents can shower their daughters with CDs, inline skates, a bicycle, beach ball, or any of the 180 licensed items offered in the Fulla catalog (see Figure 12.2).[41]

Since the emergence of Fulla, similar dolls like Saghira (Morocco), Razanne (North America), and Jamila (Germany) have also become available worldwide. Each has hoped to command Fulla's market share not only in the Middle East but across the Islamic world. Saghira, Razanne, and Jamila all share a similar look, wear similar clothing, and are marketed in the same way. All the dolls have similar features, even as some of the dolls' models possess a greater range of hair color or skin tone. The dolls are all marketed as Muslim, family-loving, pious, and modest—lacking Western values.

The war in Iraq helped to fuel anti-American sentiment, in general, and icons of American culture such as Barbie, in particular. Barbie had been a target of scorn in the region since the 1990s. Nonetheless, a few months after the start of the Iraq War, in September of 2003, a Saudi spokesperson for the

Figure 12.2 Fulla bag, Alexandria, Egypt. Jeremy Graham/Alamy Stock Photo.

Committee for the Propagation of Virtue and the Prevention of Vice renewed attacks on Barbie, disclosing what he described as her "Jewish" origins—origins which, he claimed, made her "offensive to Islam." Exactly how Barbie became Jewish is unknown. Whether it was the religion of her American creator or the conflation of her adult and German origins with anti-Semitic claims is unclear. The timing, however, was uncanny. In addition to its anti-Jewish elements, the anti-Barbie campaign was accompanied by an education program, which targeted school classrooms to educate children about the dangers of playing with Barbie. The campaign included a poster called "A Strange Request," showing Barbie in her skimpy clothing alongside a Saudi child requesting that she be given a similar outfit. The cultural offensive came just before the introduction of Fulla in November of the same year.[42]

If Barbie posed such a great threat to the moral and social fabric of the Middle East, then why do the dolls of the Middle East look so much like Barbie? Much in the same way that African-American Barbies look like white Barbies with only minor variations, the Islamic dolls have not strayed far from Barbie's standard of beauty. Only Sara and Dara have completely moved in another direction, and their sales do not come close to competing with the outlawed Barbie doll. Critics inside and outside the Middle East are quick to point out that locally-produced dolls have Barbie's familiar facial features, hair textures, and body type, and that even Fulla dolls therefore leave girls striving to achieve something that they will never be. Supporters of Barbie and her Middle Eastern sisters, however, remind us all that as a vehicle for imaginative play, a doll can be anything a girl (or boy) chooses her to be. To quote an Egyptian filmmaker (responding to the creation of Laila), "What was nice about Barbie was that she didn't look like me ... I will never have this car or this pink house which is all so perfect but it takes you out of reality into a fantasy life. Kids need make believe."[43]

The Veil Revisited in Egypt

The commitment to veiling is understood to be lifelong whether a woman has had veiling chosen for her or has made a personal decision to do so. At the time of the 2011 Revolution in Egypt, estimates were that almost all adult women veiled, aside from Copts (Christians) and a handful of nonconformists, such as intellectuals, activists, feminists, and performers. What had been an oddity in the 1970s, the veiled woman, was now the expectation, as was politically confirmed in the first truly democratically-held election in Egypt's history in June 2012. This election brought Islamist Mohamed Morsi to the presidency. Morsi's presidency was marked by authoritarianism and by the promulgation of a constitution which neglected women's rights in a fashion reminiscent of the 1923 Constitution. Within a few months after Morsi's ouster by the military, a trend began in Egypt whereby women began to renegotiate the use of the veil. Some who wore the *niqab*, scaled it down to just a *hijab*; and some *hijab* wearers discarded the garment entirely. In the words of one veil remover, "[t]wo things are making us do this: revolution and the Islamic current. The revolution taught us the idea of rebelling and protesting ... [a]nd the Muslim Brotherhood made us think differently about religion ... We looked for our own answers." These women are also careful to note that they are no less pious without the garment. Many of these women are the generation after the generation that retook the veil. They have given themselves permission to think about veiling without outside counsel. Others are women who made the choice themselves and have suffered the consequences of their choices. An Egyptian denied a job as a newscaster in Iraq in 2004 because she was veiled, for example, has the opposite problem now that she is back in Egypt where the veiling trend has been reversed from the days of Sadat and Mubarak.[44]

Conclusion

The Middle East's experience with modernity has often been dressed up and made visible in clothing. Beginning with sumptuary laws in the early modern era, both states and subjects have negotiated relationships with one another through careful attention to attire. The Ottoman state sought delineations between classes, sexes, occupations, and religions by issuing laws designed to make ranks visible. But the attire dictated by those laws was not static: styles changed and subjects rebelled against restrictions. Elites defied the law by wearing fur; laborers rebelled against the fez by wrapping a turban around it. In each instance, fashion indicated order just as it allowed for dissent.

In the modern era, heads of nation-states have also used clothing as means of modernizing, suggesting that, as did Atatürk, what was modern in one era (the fez) was a sign of ignorance in the next. In Nasser's Egypt, the very *tarboosh* that had guaranteed entrance to middle- and upper-class venues in earlier decades became a symbol of men's unwillingness to participate in a new order of things. Iranian women who donned the chador as a means of protesting the Shah's version of secular modernity were soon required to veil as a symbol of the Islamic Republic of Iran's new vision of modernity. Within the context of the modern nation-state, clothing reveals both the agendas of regimes and citizens' commitment to those agendas.

Outside of the context of state-mandated laws regarding clothing, men and women have donned and doffed hats, cloaks, ties, and veils to indicate satisfaction with the status quo and rejection of it. Women's choice to veil or unveil in the last two centuries has been the most obvious indicator of such sentiments. The veil has indicated women's regard for their own safety, has made crowded, urban living more manageable, and has served as a means through which women have expressed their professionalism and their autonomy. Women's decision to unveil similarly reflects dissatisfaction with contemporary politics. In each case, the decision to take the veil, remove the veil, or adjust levels of veiling is evidence of women having their say in decisions affecting not only fashion but religion, politics, and social change.

Men have similarly used clothing and grooming to indicate their regard for the status quo. Wearing a suit and tie, grooming a thick mustache, joining a gym or a sporting club, or getting a nose job have all been means through which men have expressed their relationship to modernity. Donning loose-fitting, ankle-length trousers and sporting long beards with clean-shaven cheeks can be seen both as a rejection of the West and as a preference for a different order of things. Like women, men vote with their clothing.

Notes

1 Donald Quataert, "Clothing Laws, State, and Society in the Ottoman Empire, 1720-1829," *International Journal of Middle East Studies* Vol. 27, No. 3 (1997), 406–407.
2 Mona Russell, *Creating the New Egyptian Woman* (New York: Palgrave, 2004), 92–93.
3 Elaine Sciolino, *Persian Mirrors* (New York: Simon & Schuster, 2000), Elizabeth Bucar, *Veiling: A Beginner's Guide* (Oxford: OneWorld, 2012), and Azadeh Moavini *Lipstick Jihad* (New York: Public Affairs, 2005).
4 Fatima Mernissi, *The Veil and the Male Elite*, Trans. Mary Jo Lakeland (New York: Perseus Books, 1992), 85–101; and Leila Ahmed, *Women and Gender in Islam* (New Haven: Yale University, 1992), 55–56. There are various verses regarding modesty (24: 30–31, 32: 32–33, 33: 58–59).
5 *The Qur'an*, M.A.S. Abdel Haleem, trans. (London and New York: Oxford University Press, 2010), 270.
6 *The Qur'an*, 271.
7 A discussion of these debates is outside the scope of this work. See Bucar, *Beginner's Guide*, or Saher Amer, *What Is Veiling* (Chapel Hill: UNC Press, 2014).
8 Ted Swedenberg, "The Keffiyeh: From Resistance Symbol to Retail Fashion Item," *Palestine Center* (April 8, 2010), http://www.thejerusalemfund.org/ht/display/ContentDetails/i/10733/pid/897.
9 "Women in Hebron: A Palestinian Women's Cooperative," http://womeninhebron.com/our-products/keffiyehs/.
10 http://www.dodobaror.com/.
11 Leila Ahmed, *A Quiet Revolution* (New Haven: Yale University Press, 2011); Fadwa El Guindi, *Veil: Modesty, Privacy, and Resistance* (Bloomsbury Academic, 1999); Sherifa Zuhur, *Revealing Reveiling* (Albany: SUNY Press, 1992); Arlene Macleod, *Accommodating Protest* (New York: Columbia University, 1991).
12 Quataert, "Clothing Laws in the Ottoman Empire," 403–425.
13 Quataert, "Clothing Laws in the Ottoman Empire," 409.
14 Fatma Müge Gőçek, *The Rise of Bourgeoisie, The Decline of Empire* (Oxford: Oxford University Press, 1996), 39.
15 Quataert, "Clothing Laws in the Ottoman Empire," 410.
16 Charlotte Jirousek, "The Transition to Mass Fashion System Dress in the Later Ottoman Empire," *Consumption Studies & The Ottoman Empire, 1550–1922* (Albany: SUNY Press, 2000), 217–218.
17 Quataert, "Clothing Laws in the Ottoman Empire," 411–412.
18 Alfred Slade claims that a Mr. Abbot wore a turban in his presence and was nearly decapitated. See his *Records of Travels in Greece, Turkey, &c.* Vol. 1 (Philadelphia: E.L. Carey & Hart, 1833), 179.
19 Russell, *Creating the New Woman*, 30.

20 Afsaneh Najmabadi, *Women with Mustaches and Men without Beards* (Berkeley: University of California Press, 2005), 137–146.
21 Andrea Rugh, *Reveal and Conceal: Dress in Contemporary Egypt* (Syracuse: Syracuse University Press, 1986), 153–154. Furthermore, there was greater governmental regulation regarding male dress in government offices and on university campuses.
22 Gilles Kepel, Trans. Jon Rothschild, *Muslim Extremism in Egypt* (Berkeley: University of California Press, 1985), 129–147.
23 Fadwa El Guindi, "Veiling Infitah with Muslim Ethic: Egypt's Contemporary Social Movement," *Social Problems* Vol. 28, No. 4 (April 1981), 483; Russell, *Creating the New Egyptian Woman*, 1–2.
24 Nilüfer Göle, *The Forbidding Modern* (Ann Arbor: University of Michigan Press, 1996), 5–6, 88–92.
25 Rema Hammami, *MERIP*, No. 164/165 (May to August 1990), 24–28, 71, 78. In this context, Hammami means a state administering Islamic law.
26 Carrie R. Wickam, *Mobilizing Islam* (New York: Columbia University Press, 2002), 119–149.
27 Homa Hoodfar, *Between Marriage and Market* (Berkeley: University of California Press, 1997), 196–199.
28 See Mona Abaza, "Shifting Landscape of Egyptian Fashion," *Fashion Theory* Vol. 11, No. 2/3 (2007), 282–298.
29 Göle, *The Forbidden Modern*, 84–86.
30 The exceptions in *Bastard of Istanbul* are the dual protagonists, Zeliha and her daughter Aisha, who rebel against both conventions (New York: Penguin, 2007). See also *Snow* (New York: Vintage, 2005).
31 Annelies Moors and Emma Tarlo, "Introduction," *Fashion Theory* Vol. 11, No. 2/3 (2007), 138.
32 Özlem Sandikci and Güliz Ger, "Constructing and Representing the Islamic Consumer in Turkey," *Fashion Theory* Vol. 11, No. 2/3 (2007), 190–194, 206.
33 Moaveni, *Lipstick Jihad*, 40, 156, 161–163. See also Sciolino, *Persian Mirrors*, 100.
34 Moaveni, *Lipstick Jihad*, 163; Elaine Sciolino, "Iran's Well-Covered Women Remodel a Part that Shows," *New York Times* (September 22, 2000); http://www.nytimes.com/2000/09/22/world/iran-s-well-covered-women-remodel-a-part-that-shows.html?pagewanted=all; "The Beauty Obsession Feeding Iran's Voracious Cosmetic Industry," *The Guardian* (March 1, 2013); http://www.theguardian.com/world/iran-blog/2013/mar/01/beauty-obsession-iran-cosmetic-surgery; Kia Makarechi, "Iran's Revolutionary Guard Accuses Kim Kardashian of Being a Secret Agent," *Vanity Fair* (May 16, 2016); http://www.vanityfair.com/news/2016/05/iran-kim-kardashian-instagram-agent.
35 Denise Chow, "Cosmetic Surgery Boom in Saudi Arabia; Clerics Consider Intersection of Religion and Beauty," *Daily News* (August 4, 2009); http://www.nydailynews.com/news/world/cosmetic-surgery-booms-saudi-arabia-clerics-intersection-beauty-religion-article-1.393888.
36 "Cosmetic Tourism Lebanon"; http://www.cosmetictourismlb.com/.
37 Sarah Mikhail, "Poor Egyptians Seek Better Life with Plastic Surgery," *Reuters* (November 24, 2010); http://www.reuters.com/article/us-egypt-plasticsurgery-idUSTR-E6AN2Y720101124; Mona Russell, *Egypt: The Middle East in Focus* (Santa Barbara: ABC-Clio, 2013), 368.
38 Eliana Dockterman, "A Barbie for Every Body," *Time Magazine*, Vol. 187, No. 4 (February 8, 2016), 44–51.
39 Amina Yaqin, "Islamic Barbie: The Politics of Gender and Performativity," *Fashion Theory* Vol. 11, No. 2/3 (2007), 175; Moaveni, *Lipstick Jihad*, 125.
40 See e.g. Douglas Jehl, "Cairo Journal; It's Barbie vs. Laila and Sara in Mideast Culture War," *New York Times* (June 2, 1999).

41 Yaqin, "Islamic Barbie," 175–179; Amany Abdel Moneim, "Move over Barbie," *al-Ahram Online* (June 12, 2006); http://weekly.ahram.org.eg/Archive/2006/797/li1.htm; "Fulla," http://corporate.newboy.com/en/Products.aspx?did=1&bid=PVvYRbRemfVAFGdMRnH1bQ%3d%3d.
42 "Barbie Deemed Threat to Saudi Morality," *USA Today* (September 10, 2003); http://usatoday30.usatoday.com/news/offbeat/2003-09-10-barbie_x.htm.
43 Mona Eltahawy, "Barbie Faces Rival for Arab Affections," *The Guardian* (June 7, 1999); www.theguardian.com/world1999/jun/08/04.
44 Sheera Frenkel and Maged Atef, "More and More Egyptian Women Are Casting Aside Their Veils," *Buzzfeed* (November 7, 2013); https://www.buzzfeed.com/sheerafrenkel/more-and-more-egyptian-women-are-casting-aside-their-veils?utm_term=.mgYdV0a#.uukw0K1.

13 Houses in Motion[1]

Women in War and Revolution

This chapter examines the extent to which upheaval—national, political, ideological—has shaped the lives of women in Iraq, Iran, and Palestine. In Iraq, decades of disturbance began with the consuming Iran-Iraq War (1980–1988) and continued with the Gulf War of 1991. The Gulf War was, in turn, followed by the enduring international sanctions, the American invasion of 2003, life under American occupation, and the chaotic conditions of the nation's transition to independent rule. For Iran, war with Iraq came quickly on the heels of revolution, and has been followed by intense and often rapid shifts in expectations from (and exclusions of) women. For Palestinian women, upheaval has been a constant: the loss of a state, life in exile, life under military occupation (for those who live in Gaza and the West Bank), and the transition from secular to Islamic rule in Gaza.

Like other women across the region, Iranian, Iraqi, and Palestinian women have navigated crisis and revolution within a discursive framework that links their homes to the success of their nations. In addition to upheaval, then, what sets these women apart is the extent to which these particular women have navigated crisis from homes (literal, national, and ideological) lost, destroyed, or replaced, and frequently reconfigured, discursively. To keep and to represent literal, national, and ideological homes have required women to negotiate terrains that have been neither stable nor fixed.

Because women in the Middle East are expected to carry the values of the home into the public realm, we also use "houses in motion" to suggest that we see women as such: the women who move through the public realm as revolutionaries, activists, soldiers, and civil servants are understood in the public realm as mother-activists, mother-soldiers, and so on. Crises and revolutions have freed women to act independently of their assigned domains, if for a moment. In the end, however, women act within the constraints of the domestic politics not only of their own homes but also those of the national communities within which they live. Those domestic politics, too, have been frequently in motion in Iran, Iraq, and Palestine.[2]

Finally, we use "houses in motion" to suggest that women in Iraq, Iran, and Palestine have brought the domestic realm into the public and political realms.[3] The influences of women on resistance movements and revolutionary agendas, and on the state programs into which women are mobilized, illustrate that just as the political has defined the domestic, so too has the domestic shaped the political.

Iran

In the years leading up to the 1979 Revolution (see Chapter 8), tensions between "modern" and "traditional" in Iran were quite visible among women. By the 1970s, the Pahlavi regime had produced plenty of "New Women," who benefited from the regime's prescription for modernization: education, professionalization, and visibility in public. These women inherited a legacy of middle- and upper-class women's activism, which had experienced a reflourishing in the years between Mohammed Reza Shah's ascension to power in 1941 and the early 1960s. On the lips of women who joined the rebounding women's movement were suffrage and reform to personal status laws.[4] On the heads of some them: the *hijab*, a practice once again taken up by women of the more comfortable classes and never fully abandoned by others.[5]

The shah did grant women the vote, just as he passed several woman-friendly legal reforms (see Chapter 8). In addition to advancing causes dear to female activists, however, the shah used the media to circulate images of Iranian womanhood that were tied to Western models of beauty and consumption habits. Women reported feeling less like modern citizens than sex objects and consumers (Figure 13.1). Taken as a whole, the shah's reforms had not provided women of any class with the legal, political, and social autonomy they desired.[6]

For women of the lower socioeconomic orders, the Pahlavi's "New Woman" was, while omnipresent, neither appropriate nor particularly relevant. Conservative families in both urban and rural areas were hesitant, if not unwilling, to send their daughters to state schools wherein unveiled girls sat side by side with boys, often in the presence of male teachers. The daughters of families who did relent recount

Figure 13.1 Shops on Jumhuri Avenue, Tehran. Wikimedia Commons.

being taunted on their way to and from home, traversing towns and cities in *hijab*, only to remove their headscarves when they arrived at school. Once inside, excitement over education was mixed with cultural alienation.[7]

Furthermore, the cultural circles in which women of Iran's lower socioeconomic classes moved were more likely to be religious rather than state-organized ones.[8] The sermons that women of Iran's traditional orders listened to and the rituals and observances they participated in focused not on the attributes and opportunities of the Pahlavi's "New Woman," but rather on praiseworthy women from the Islamic past. Most worthy of emulation by women of the rural and lower urban classes were Fatima and Zeynab, members of the Prophet Mohammed's family and central figures in the emergence of Shia tradition. To be like Fatima and Zeynab in Iran ca. 1970 was to play supporting roles to men through modest dress and devotion to home and family.[9]

Opposition to the shah came in various registers over the 1970s. The largest and ultimately the most effective voice demanding a change in regime, a rejection of Iran's emulation of and dependence on the West, and a return to a more Islamic and a more authentically-Iranian culture was that of Ayatollah Khomeini (see Chapter 8). His *Vilayet-e Faqih* (*Government of Jurisprudents*) outlined an alternative to Pahlavi modernization, one built upon Islamic law and tradition; his popularity lay not only in his condemnation of Pahlavi despotism but in his appeal to those Iranians—even Westernized elites—who resented the shah's marginalization of Iran's religious traditions in favor of the adoption of Western ones. Other voices joined in pitching political alternatives rich in the embrace of tradition, advocating for the reestablishment of a more culturally-authentic Iran.[10]

The anti-shah movement offered alternatives to Pahlavi womanhood. For the Marxist-Leninists, the future would be marked by full equality between the sexes. For revivalists like Ali Shariati, a "different but equal" approach suggested that women's ordained responsibilities to their homes would be protected by a commitment to equal rights. Khomeini's *Vilayet-e Faqih* portrayed a public realm in which women were absent. Nonetheless, he nodded approvingly as women became increasingly present in a public realm, now alight in protest. Veiled and unveiled women received his praise as they sought to right injustices wrought by imperialism and despotism.[11]

Legions of Iranian women joined supporters of Khomeini and others as organizers, demonstrators, leaders of strikes and boycotts, and guerilla fighters (see Figure 13.2). While women did not hold leadership roles in political parties, they nonetheless mobilized with them. Additionally, women organized their families, neighbors, and friends to attend rallies and demonstrations. They gave blood. They washed bedding for hospitals. Female doctors worked round the clock to attend to the wounded and dying. Women offered their homes as safe zones for fleeing demonstrators. They prepared and served food to militia members; they circulated

Figure 13.2 Women participate in the Iranian Revolution, 1979. Historic Collection/Alamy Stock Photo.

literature about the revolution. And they gave their lives. Women were among the victims of the fire in the city of Abadan's Cinema Rex in August 1978 which, once linked to the regime, triggered the uprisings now known as the Iranian Revolution. Women were killed on September 8, 1978, known as "Black Friday," the result of which the Revolution began its quick spread after riot police opened fire on protestors in Tehran.[12] Women did not necessarily mobilize around women's rights. Rather, they mobilized as political subjects, determined to fight for their full inclusion in Iranian society, public and private.

Khomeini had addressed the concerns of many Iranians when he suggested that the Islamic Republic would have room in it for everyone. But beginning in the spring of 1979, the regime rolled out a new gender order designed to get women to "go home" and to swap the behavior of the Pahlavi "New Woman" for that more akin to Fatima and Zeynab.[13] Married women were no longer allowed to attend university; those women who could attend found their curricula, like their aspirations, limited to nurturing careers such as teaching and social work.[14] In the workplace, women were purged from government offices and from professions through which they might have contact with men. Day-care centers were shuttered. Women were allowed to work only part-time and encouraged to retire after 15 years. In the workplace, men treated women as if they were a grand nuisance at best and as trespassers in the public realm.[15]

The regime's new gender order emerged against the backdrop of a war with Iraq, initiated by Saddam Hussein in the fall of 1980. In mobilizing for the "Sacred

Defense," Khomeini initially encouraged women to use their homes to protect Islam and the Islamic state. Their jobs? To bear children and to prepare themselves to sacrifice the lives of their husbands and sons to the war. The steady relegation of women to realms without men, against the background of war, turned the home into women's appointed place in the new Republic.[16]

During the war years, women also used their homes as volunteer bases of operations. A certain Umleila Hassanzdeh, for example, transformed her home on the Caspian Sea into a workshop from which she and other women made bandages, packaged vegetables, and knitted and sewed shirts, hats, and gloves. Similarly, women across Iran gathered in mosques and homes to cook and to prepare auxiliary supplies. Care packages for soldiers included notes written by women and children. While her son was mobilized, later to be martyred, Umleila corresponded with a number of mobilized soldiers, exchanging stories of sacrifice and duty with them. She was pleased when one of them called her a Zeynab of her times.[17]

Many women, however, took up defense of the nation. The regime quickly discovered that keeping women at home would not be a sustainable strategy. Khomeini accordingly used Shiite theology to mandate women's participation in fighting and services auxiliary to fighting as long as they were safe from the sexual dangers brought by proximity to unknown men—Iranian or Iraqi.

And fight they did. Some postponed marriage so that they could mobilize for war. Some were mobilized to the front by the state, serving as propagandists and photographers, or training other women in combat skills. Others volunteered for the Islamic Revolutionary Guards Corps. Others simply fought, some dying in defense of their besieged cities and towns. Women were dispatched to warn locals in advance of a launch of chemical weapons by the Iraqi army. Iraq's first Iranian prisoner of war (POW) was a woman. Iran officially counts 837,918 women who fought or who served at the front in an auxiliary capacity. Iran has also officially designated 6,428 of them as martyrs.[18]

Since the conclusion of the war in 1988, women have served from home as caregivers for the many husbands and sons who returned from battle as invalids. For many women, the patriarch has returned from battle, but is incapable of making a living. (Sometimes, he is equally incapable of making babies: chemical agents and radiation from the war years led to tremendous rates of infertility, miscarriage, and stillbirth). For these women, the nightmares of war have therefore been replaced by men with *posttraumatic stress disorder* (PTSD), men without limbs, men with colostomy bags. Many of these women are themselves unwell: a 1991 report by the CIA estimated that at least 50,000 Iranians were exposed to chemical agents by the Iraqi military, many of whom still require regular care.[19]

In Iran's official commemorations of the war, however, these women have not been counted as men have. In the nation's annual Sacred Defense Week, women are only acknowledged in their capacities as wives and mothers, Fatimas and Zeynabs, but not as equals to men on the front. Furthermore, women report that the state has failed to care for its female veterans—adding insult to the injury of nonrecognition.

Mateo Mohammed Farzaneh, who has collected and published the recollections of the women we read about here, concludes that Iranian women have, in peacetime, been as omnipresent and marginalized as they were in the state's recollection of the war.[20] The state's denial of women's active participation in Sacred Defense reflects the new regime's strategies for encouraging, if not forcing, women to embrace both their inferiority in the public realm and their hallowed role in the domestic sphere. This role has been reinforced by the regime's encouragement of women to have lots of children.

And yet, as the war with Iraq illustrates, the regime's illusion that theirs is a nation in which women do not participate in the public realm is just that. Iranian women use work as resistance. Segregation by sex and enforced *hijab* in schools have turned even the most conservative of parents into supporters of their daughters' right to partake of the substantial public education system, first established by the Pahlavi shahs and then maintained by the Islamic Republic. The state needed the millions of such women: two-thirds of Iran's provinces were destroyed after eight years of war. And women have found that they need to work, sometimes at more than one job, to keep pace with the inflation that accompanied the rebuilding of Iran and that has dogged the Iranian economy since the late 1980s, including years of crippling sanctions regimes imposed by the West[21] (see Chapter 10).

Because the new regime overturned the shah's commitment to providing day care, working women have brought their homes into the workplace by bringing their preschool-aged children to work with them. Even women who work in hospitals take their children to work.[22]

Women point to legitimate access to participation in street demonstrations as the most important legacy of 1979. They speak of a new attitude among their parents' generation: "Parents and husbands never allowed their womenfolk to participate in street demonstrations for any cause…After the Revolution, such barriers…were removed."[23] Subsequent generations of women understand that they can make a contribution in the streets.

Indeed, followers of Iranian politics can attest to the consistent and conspicuous presence of women in Iran's streets. Women have continued to mobilize against political corruption—their participation in the 2009 Green Movement in protest of government interference in elections, for example, was high profile. By the end of the uprisings, the state had made martyrs: out of 107 Iranians, 13 were female (Figure 13.3). The first woman to succumb to the regime's bullets was Agha Soltan, a 27-year-old university student.[24]

In the Iranian people's current struggle with the regime, triggered by the murder of 22-year-old Mahsa Amini for an alleged *hijab* violation, women have overrun the public realm in protest (see Figure 13.4). While those protests are, at the surface, about clothing laws and the hyper-surveillance of women's behavior, demonstrators—both male and female—have more than the policing of clothing and morals in mind. In the words of Shervin Hajipour, whose "*Baraye*" (Because) became the anthem of the uprisings that swept Iran after Amini's murder in September 2022, Iranians yearn for an ordinary life, for pockets that are not penniless, for clean air, for equitable child labor laws, for women's freedom, and for freedom from "rotted minds."[25] Ziba, a fan of the song and a participant in the uprisings, said: "The first time that I heard it…it was if all my cries of my last 30 years were being shouted by Shervin's voice. All the things I have not been able to do. All

246 *Houses in Motion: Women in War and Revolution*

Figure 13.3 Agha Soltan, 2009. 360b/Alamy Stock Photo.

Figure 13.4 Mahsa Amini mural, NYC. Erin Alexis Randolph/Alamy Stock Photo.

my feelings of being inferior in work and in the society. All the discrimination I encountered."[26]

If we were to conclude, however, that women's presence in the public realm as workers, politicians, commuters, businesswomen, and protesters has liberated women from the roles they play and the responsibilities they bear in their homes, we would be mistaken. Family reigns supreme in Iran. It is written into the constitution of the Islamic Republic as the foundation of the state. Women learn from a young age that sublimating their individuality to the needs of the family is nonnegotiable. Some suggest that the discrimination they face at home is greater than that at work.[27] And we must not forget that the home is a place wherein women are themselves violated in a state that pays scant attention to domestic violence. The state itself is often the perpetrator of such violence: legions are the tales of the regime's security apparatus violating the homes of its citizens to arrest its suspected male and female opponents.[28]

Iraq

In the stifling heat of late summer 1980, the rhythms that had shaped Iraqis' lives over the course of the 1970s—the state's devotion to development that had resulted in the "days of honey"—began to change as Saddam Hussein mobilized the country for war against neighboring Iran. Work and school, the very hallmarks of the Baath's social and economic agendas, began to shift along with men's and women's daily routines, as the state mobilized young men and requisitioned factories and goods for war.

Just as Iraq's mobilization to war brought the "days of honey" to an end, it also quickly brought suffering to Iraqis, both on and off the battlefield. "A few months after full mobilization, our lives are transformed into mere fragments of the lives we had before the war."[29] Iraqi women learned to sew cotton bandages and to prep their homes for bombing raids. They descended on food shops and stood in long lines for supplies, panicked by sudden shortages. As the war dragged on, medicine became scarce, as did water and gasoline. Little of prewar civilian life remained. At parties, conversation tended to focus on the high price of food, lack of construction materials, and the paucity of opportunities.[30]

War brought about new categories of citizenship: whereas Iraqis of all kinds had once benefitted from the state, it was now only soldiers, martyrs, and their families who received the state's praises and rewards. Deserters and their families, by contrast, were punished. Consequently, it was only the "right women" and the "right men" who got to be included in and rewarded by the state. The best benefits went to the families of martyrs who had been Ba'ath state employees prior to the war and to their descendants.[31]

The "wrong" Iraqis were deserters, Kurds and Shiites—those who threatened the state's mantra about the war that all Iraqis were in it together.[32] Over the course of the war, Kurdish and Shiite opposition parties formed their own militias and fought alongside Iranian troops. Both groups suffered the agonies of the regime's revenge: Saddam Hussein used chemical weapons against the Kurds in Hallabja in 1988, in a brutal example of ethnic cleansing. In Iraq's southern regions, Shiite Muslims faced similar atrocities: Saddam Hussein deported approximately 400,000 Shiites of so-called Persian origin to Iran. Members of Shiite political parties were executed or exiled.[33]

To mobilize for war, to nurture those Iraqis who were regarded as "family members," and to keep track of who supported the war and who did not, the regime created an elaborate bureaucracy, one which transformed "war into the politics and practices of everyday life."[34] The Baath party grew in size and scope during the war years. By 1989, a party bureau could be found in almost every location in Iraq; the increased presence of the Baath was especially visible in Iraq's north and south, regions in which the state was most contested.

Party bureaus relied upon members of the state's Iraqi Women's League, now called the General Federation of Iraqi Women (GFIW), to assist the state in dividing "right" from "wrong" and to transforming "wrong" into "right" whenever possible. Ulama loyal to the regime formed a cadre of preachers who disseminated the state's vision of Sunni Islam, as did members of the GFIW. The state focused substantial resources in its bureaus in Najaf and Karbala, seats of Shiite learning and pilgrimage sites, directing party members to attend Shiite rituals and to encourage "correct" Islamic practices. GFIW members were sent to join them, to observe processions and rituals, and to suggest to Shiite women that their practices were harmful to the embattled Iraqi state, to women's health, and to the health of their children. GFIW members were also assigned the task of preaching about the backwardness of wearing the *abaya*. Similarly, GFIW women were tasked with lecturing Shiite women about the Baath's many accomplishments, particularly with regards to women's rights.[35]

As the numbers of Iraq's fallen soldiers increased and as demobilized men began returning to civilian life, the state's campaign to promote women's employment was replaced by one which encouraged women to go home: GFIW members encouraged women to have at least five children.[36] Pharmacies were prohibited from selling contraceptives. State television applauded and promoted early marriage and procreation, funding mass marriage ceremonies for willing couples. Colleges and universities gave special grants for willing brides and grooms.[37] By 1987, in a nation recently known for its high rates of women's employment, women made up just under 8% of Iraq's workforce.[38]

Subsequently, women were exalted, almost uniquely, as wives and mothers of martyrs. Women increasingly wore black and were introduced in social gatherings not by their given names but as the wife, sister, or mother of a martyr. "We have become accustomed," said one martyr's wife, "to death and its tales."[39]

The guns of war with Iran had hardly quieted before Saddam Hussein led the exhausted Iraqi populace into another war. Operation Desert Storm (1991), waged by the US and its allies against Iraq, and the 13 years of UN-imposed sanctions that followed it accelerated Iraq's devastation. A strict sanctions regime deprived Iraq of trade and financial resources, while allowing the tightly-regulated import of food and medicine. In 1991, the UN implemented its Oil for Food Program, designed to relieve the civilian suffering that had resulted from sanctions. The program was indeed successful at alleviating hunger, but less so at lessening Iraq's humanitarian crisis.⁴⁰ The years following the program's implementation witnessed increases in child malnutrition and mortality rates.⁴¹

Desert Storm destroyed Iraq's infrastructure (power, potable water, sewer, garbage collection), making tending to home a daily exhaustion of women's strength. Homes replaced hospitals as women took up the additional burdens of caring for their injured and their sick. Both Gulf War veterans and their children suffered from a chronic shortage of medicine. An alarming number of children born to Gulf War veterans have been born with birth defects and abnormalities, extending women's caretaking roles into a new generation.⁴²

As women spent increased amounts of time tending to their homes and to their wounded kin and to searching for scarce material and economic resources, participation in activism and volunteerism became a luxury that few women could afford. As women's access to the public realm became increasingly fragile, many stopped looking to education as a vehicle for change. Accordingly, illiteracy boomed, climbing from 8% in 1985 to 55% by the late 1990s.⁴³

The 160,000 America troops sent to Iraq in March 2003 were not sufficient to the task of sealing the country's borders, through which insurgents began flowing soon after the toppling of Saddam Hussein's regime. Former US ambassador L. Paul Bremer, head of the Coalition Provisional Authority (CPA) that ruled Iraq between 2003 and 2004, chose to dissolve Iraq's military and to de-Baathify the nation's governing institutions and bureaucracies, effectively leaving those capable of working with the CPA unemployed. Many of those men turned to the rule-by-militia that had become the order of the day in the months after the occupation. Iraqi women, under the alleged protection of coalition forces, were subsequently unprotected from increased lawlessness, rape, and violence by Islamist militias, including humiliations brought upon women at checkpoints, rape, and punishments over dress-code violations (perceived or otherwise).⁴⁴ As local and foreign-sponsored Sunni and Shia militias issued legal injunctions in favor of mandatory veiling and seclusion, women once again became stand-ins for the politics of would-be regimes. For most women, the years immediately following the invasion were not years spent debating the future of the Iraqi body politic. Rather, they were years spent making survival a priority.⁴⁵

In addition to militia-led violence, the results of American decisions led to widespread corruption as powerbrokers grabbed for stakes in Iraq's natural resources, particularly in the north and the south. The website for Iraq Body Count concluded that by the 2008 withdrawal of troops from Iraq, there had been approximately 90,000 deaths beyond Iraq's normal mortality rates since 2003. These figures are likely underestimates.⁴⁶

The five Iraqi administrations that have governed Iraq since 2004 have overseen a great deal of rebuilding. Women once again attend school and work outside their homes. But they do so in conditions hardly ideal to flourishing. Militias kill female students for going to school. They assassinate women who run for elections, just as they target women as they make their way to the polls. Women's participation in Iraq's associational life has nonetheless mushroomed: women work to ensure that Iraq's personal status laws, in place since the late 1950s, remain generous. And they work to maintain quotas for women's political participation—part of Iraq's new constitution. In a violent and uncertain public realm, however, women's participation in life outside the home takes place at their peril.⁴⁷

In addition to the dangers of the public realm, homelife presents its own challenges. Services once provided by the Baathist welfare state—food, water, medical care—are now privatized, unreliable, and expensive (as are food and medicine). For some women, homes remain hospice to yet another generation of war wounded. From home, women witness the frustrations of the generation of children born at the time of the occupation, many of whom attend university with the expectation of work that they cannot find. For that generation, promised democracy and opportunity in 2003, life stuck at home offers limited horizons.⁴⁸

Finally, Iraqi women are the mothers of children who grew up without a safe and secure childhood. Those children spent their formative years hiding, primarily at home. By 2006, as Iraq was engulfed in civil war, families began fleeing towns and neighborhoods dominated by "the other side," their houses in motion and their sense of a coherent, multicultural Iraq destroyed. In October 2019, these children were at the helm of an Arab Spring-like movement in favor of a better Iraq (see Figure 13.5). The uprisings were the largest grassroots demonstrations in Iraq's history, bringing hundreds of thousands to the streets in favor of an Iraq devoid of the politics and violence of militia rule. The central demand of October 2019 was a homeland. "I never felt any patriotism before. I was willing to die for a better Iraq. There were so many people just like me," said Fayhaa Khalid, who added that October 2019 "felt like a revolution." While that revolution was quickly put down

Figure 13.5 Demonstrators in the 2019 Iraqi October Revolution. Mondalawy/Wikimedia Commons, CC BY-SA 4.0.

Houses in Motion: Women in War and Revolution 251

by state security, it served to put militia leaders on the back foot and perhaps to inspire Iraqis of all generations to future action.⁴⁹

Occupied Palestine

In 1987, as women in Iran and Iraq found their worth as citizens to be increasingly limited to their homes, women in occupied Palestine—the West Bank and the Gaza Strip—gained substantial worth in the public realm. As activists and organizers of a popular, grassroots resistance movement against the Israeli military occupation and rule of the West Bank and Gaza—the *intifada* of 1987—women shared the reins of popular resistance with men. The *intifada* occurred on the heels of almost a decade of Palestinian, mass-based activism, during which traditional leadership had given way to youth groups, women's groups, student and trade unions, professional organizations, charitable organizations, and mosque and church communities. Reliance upon organized women had forced men to concede that home was no longer auxiliary to the struggle for nation.

Home is, in fact, central to Palestinian national identity. After the *nakba* in 1948, the homes of Palestinians who fled or were expelled from Israel were indeed houses in motion. As members of Palestinian households in exile, women—then and now—were the last vestige of honor for a nation now bereft of a homeland (see Figure 13.6). At women's tables, families shared memories of a lost nation, tasted the foods of that nation, and nurtured hopes for a more triumphant future for their children. In women's bodies—the virginity of their daughters and the honor,

Figure 13.6 Palestinian refugee camp, 1949. World History Archive/Alamy Stock Photo.

modesty, and obedience of their wives—Palestinian men maintained the honor of their lost homeland. By controlling women's dress, their activities and their movement, the Palestinian men who have failed—then as now—to restore Palestine, guard what honor is left to them.[50]

In the Palestinian resistance movement, particularly as it emerged after the establishment of the Palestine Liberation Organization (PLO) in 1964, women who dedicated themselves to the national cause by joining political parties did so largely from their homes or by attending to other women in their homes. Women in Palestinian refugee camps in Lebanon, for example, joined political parties dedicated to securing Palestine. But they did so under the leadership of men and not alongside them. As auxiliary rather than principal party members, women played support roles to male freedom fighters, tending to home and community while men struggled to secure the nation.[51]

Exiled Palestinian women who came under military occupation with Israel's victory in the Six-Day War of 1967 had been similarly linked to the resistance movement historically. Prior to the rise of the resistance movement in 1964, elite and middle-class women independent of politics continued, as they had historically, to draw on their material resources and their organizational skills to provide a modicum of welfare relief to their communities. With the establishment of the resistance movement, however, came the encroachment of men: political parties took over women's efforts and laid claim to representing Palestinian womanhood.[52] The General Union of Palestinian Women (GUPW), established by the PLO as an umbrella group for women's organizations in 1965, provided a framework within which women could actively contribute to the national cause. What the GUPW did not do, however, was elevate women's issues to a level of primary concern or to put women in leadership positions within the resistance movement.[53] This relegation of women's issues to a secondary tier was not remedied by the *intifada*. Nonetheless, the *intifada* did result in the transformation and normalization of women's public roles, however temporarily.

For the then 1.7 million Palestinians living in the West Bank and Gaza, the realities of the Israeli occupation were harsh, for women and for men. Obtaining endless permits exposed Palestinians to added burdens and humiliations. Checkpoints, roadblocks, and settler-only roads made movement within and between communities difficult (and often impossible), transforming the simple errands attendant to keeping home into endless waits and countless confrontations with Israeli soldiers. Arrests, imprisonments, and exile of their male kin left women as heads of householders and breadwinners, often with limited financial recourse. Israeli confiscations of land for the construction of settlements and the destruction of Palestinian homes as punishment for participation in the resistance robbed families of home and livelihood; Israel Defense Forces (IDF) raids of Palestinian homes exposed women and children to violence and, often, to arrest. Life at home exposed women to violence at the hands of male kin, often victims of Israeli violence themselves.

For many Palestinian women, the answer to a brutal occupation was increased political activism. Israel cracked down on the resistance by making political activity in the occupied territories punishable: arrests, interrogations, and imprisonment of suspected activists were common occurrences. Because that suspicion was largely of men; however, women found opportunity and took it. "The occupation won't end if we're afraid and stay home."[54] The outbreak of the *intifada* was spontaneous, but the resistance that nurtured it once it had begun was not.

The *intifada* started on December 8, 1987, after an accident in Gaza involving an Israeli military vehicle killed or injured several Palestinians. In response to a protest march by residents of the Jabalya refugee camp, the IDF shot into a crowd and killed several more. The population of Gaza consequently rose up in revolt. By January 1988, the uprising had spread to the West Bank, where protestors confronted Israeli authority by carrying and throwing rocks and gas bombs (see Figure 13.7). The *intifada* sustained itself through the cooperation of local committees and neighborhoods, each organized for mutual assistance, many organized by women. By January 1988, however, the PLO leadership in Tunis had issued its sponsorship of the movement and had joined the United National Leadership (UNL). The *intifada* continued through the fall of 1993, when PLO leader Yasser Arafat and Israeli Prime Minister Yitzhak Rabin signed the Oslo Peace Agreements in Washington, DC.

By late January 1988, the UNL had outlined the goals of the *intifada* through the publication of a 14-point manifesto. Among the Palestinians' demands were an end to the building of settlements, a cessation of the confiscation of Palestinian land, and an end to the daily bureaucratic obstacles placed on Palestinians by Israel. The manifesto called on Israel to recognize an independent Palestinian state led by the PLO. Tactics called for by the UNL included civil disobedience: demonstrations were designed to provoke violence from the Israeli government, grab

Figure 13.7 A Palestinian youth arrested by the IDF. John Chapman/Alamy Stock Photo.

headlines, and arouse outside anger and sympathy. The manifesto also called for strikes, which effectively reduced the Palestinian labor force in Israel. Boycotts of Israeli goods in favor of Palestinian-produced goods pinched at the Israeli economy. Grassroots politics had Palestinians of all ages and all classes more involved in their own self-governance than ever, and women were at the helm of the many committees supporting them. One woman reported that there were local committees for just about everything.[55]

Israel made a determined effort to stop the *intifada*, using tactics such as an increased military presence in the West Bank and the Gaza Strip, the imprisonment and the house arrest of both men and women, the deportation of Palestinian men, and the maiming of young male rock throwers. Israel combined increased military presence in the occupied territories with collective punishment, cutting off water and electricity to neighborhoods and villages suspected of harboring stone throwers; bulldozing the homes of participants; implementing long curfews; and shutting down schools and universities, sometimes for years. Far from shutting the uprising down, however, Israel's tactics united Palestinians in a common cause.[56]

The *intifada* also witnessed the rise of alternative political organizations to the PLO, namely the Islamic Resistance Movement or Hamas. Hamas leadership called for Palestinian resistance to Israel in Islamic, rather than secular, language. The ranks of Hamas included many young, university-educated Palestinians who had felt locked out of the elite-dominated PLO leadership. While Hamas was initially a Gaza-based phenomenon, the organization's influence had spread to the West Bank by the end of the 1990s. In both locations, Hamas brought charitable relief to those who had been hard hit by the *intifada*.

Amidst the rise of some political institutions and the failure of others, Palestinian women found great challenges and opportunities. Some found employment, often filling the void left by arrested and imprisoned men. Others increased their efforts in charitable work. Palestinian women used public space to their advantage during the *intifada*: stories abounded of women warning men of the impending arrival of Israeli troops, smuggling supplies and information to protestors, and protecting male activists whenever possible.

By the early 1980s, the pioneers of Palestinian women's charitable organizations had been joined by a new wave of feminists. In 1980, Palestinian women had formed the Palestinian Union of Women's Work Committees (PUWWC) as an alternative to their traditional alliances with the resistance movement's male-dominated parties. The PUWWC's strategy was to empower women to be self-sufficient. The establishment of the PUWCC resulted in an atmosphere in which party took a back burner to women's role in the national struggle.[57] By 1988, the overwhelming needs of Palestinian society had led the PUWWC to consolidate all of their committees into one, the Higher Women's Committee (HWC). The HWC played an instrumental role in organizing committees responsible for keeping classrooms open and providing first aid and to stockpiling food and medicine.[58] Members of the neighborhood committees provided critical and often life-saving care to wounded demonstrators, coordinated strikes and demonstrations, and worked with the UNL to provide uninterrupted education to Palestinian children during the uprising. Finally, the HWC took the initiative in formulating an agenda for the women's movement going forward and in increasing women's influence on the Palestinian nationalist movement.[59] A common women's slogan: "No Going Back."[60]

Palestinian society subsequently witnessed some relaxation of its historic gender norms. One mother reportedly allowed a young man pursued by the IDF to get into the shower with her daughter. Hiding him bore witness to her idea, shared by many, that women's honor was less critical than the struggle for Palestine at that particular moment.[61] Certain repressive gender dynamics waned during the *intifada*, including the prohibitive cost of weddings and arranged marriages themselves.[62] The *intifada* therefore brought women into a dual commitment to end the occupation and to continue the fight for gender parity in Palestine.[63]

By the early 1990s, Israel had clamped down on Palestinians' freedom of organization and had substantially curtailed the *intifada*'s leadership, including women's organizations. Palestinian frustration grew as the goals—and the successes—of the *intifada* appeared to vanish in the face of such restrictions. Men became more likely to speak out against women's gains in the public arena and less likely to support women's continued presence outside their homes. A region-wide recession caused by the Gulf War fueled a conservative backlash against the working women who appeared to be taking jobs from men. The atmosphere of growing conservativism in the West Bank and Gaza was also affected by Hamas' "*hijab* campaign," which both encouraged and coerced women into wearing Islamic dress. Women's access to education was blocked by Israel's strategy of closing schools and universities in the occupied territories, leaving many women with only one recourse: early marriage. Even as they continued to organize despite Israeli crackdowns on organizing, women lost the visibility in and access to the public realm.[64]

The *intifada* was nonetheless of substantial local and international consequence. In 1988, the PLO's then Chairman Yasser Arafat recognized Israel's existence. The result was a series of meetings between US officials and the PLO in Tunis, designed to outline a future role for the US as a broker between the PLO and Israel. Israel's intransigence regarding the status of the occupied territories combined with repeated Palestinian incursions into Israel led to the breakdown of the Tunis negotiations. In the aftermath of the Gulf War, however, US President George H.W. Bush was determined to harness war success to brokering peace. That determination led to the Madrid Conference of 1991, which, while bearing little fruit, brought Israelis, Palestinians, and representatives of Syria, Jordan, and Lebanon together in a dialogue about the future of the occupied territories. Israeli Prime Minister Yitzhak Shamir's refusal to yield on building settlements in the occupied territories brought the Labor Party and Prime Minister Yitzak Rabin back to power in the 1992 elections and, with them, a promise of "land for peace."

During the Madrid Conference, Hanan Ashrawi (1936–) was the official spokeswoman for the Palestinian delegation (see Figure 13.8). Ashrawi had been an active member of several popular committees during the *intifada*. What she took to Madrid was the voice of the *intifada*, the recommendations and demands of the

Figure 13.8 Hanan Ashrawi. Pictures From History/CPA Media Pte Ltd/Alamy Stock Photo.

many women whose experiences had shaped the Palestinian committee's negotiating points.[65]

In the summer of 1993, as the efforts of Ashrawi and her colleagues (including longtime women's activist Zahira Kamal) appeared to stall, Washington announced an agreement between Palestinians and Israelis, reached through secret, parallel negotiations between the two parties outside of Oslo, Norway. In what would soon be known as the Oslo Agreement, Israel recognized the PLO as the Palestinian people's legitimate representative. The PLO (renamed the Palestinian National Authority or PNA) renounced violence. The Oslo Agreement also set up a time frame for granting Palestinians interim sovereignty over sections of the West Bank and Gaza, culminating in the Israeli withdrawal from its settlements in Gaza in 2005. The Palestinian women who had lent their voice and their experience to the Madrid talks were shocked and dismayed by a PLO leadership that had not consulted the *intifada* leadership before participating in the Oslo negotiations.[66]

The Oslo Agreement did not bring Palestinians the state-like sovereignty for which they had struggled. Palestinian despair led to the rise of opposition groups to the PNA and to a new wave of violence against Israel. Oslo also brought an end to the leadership that women had enjoyed. Deported male party leaders returned to the West Bank and Gaza and resumed the positions they had left in the hands of women. Once told that their work was "done," activist women once again took up what they had historically been given space for in Palestinian public life: work in service societies and nongovernmental organizations (NGOs). Translating loss into opportunity, women nonetheless forged ahead. A Women's Charter, announced in 1994, named national, political, economic, and social equality as rights for women. The Women's Charter was subsequently endorsed by the GUPW and by all other Palestinian women's organizations.[67]

In the post-Oslo era, women have worked to maintain those rights. The GUPW worked to expand its membership and to get women elected to positions within the PNA. By 2003, women had made limited inroads into politics, constituting 5.7% of the Palestinian Legislative Council, 9.2% of the judiciary, and 8.3% of ministerial positions. Additionally, they sat on the central committees of Palestine's main political parties: Fatah (5%); the Popular Front (10%); the Palestinian Democratic Union or FIDA (19%); and the Democratic Front (20%).[68] In 2003, the PNA established a Ministry of Women's Affairs or MOWA, which, in addition to supporting women's increased participation in politics, has served to advance the goals and agendas established by women during the *intifada*. The post-Oslo era has witnessed the emergence of a Palestinian women's peace movement, which has formed alliances with Israeli women.[69]

When the right-wing Israeli politician and, later, prime minister Ariel Sharon (r. 2001–2006) made a provocative visit to al-Aqsa Mosque in Jerusalem on September 28, 2000, he triggered simmering Palestinian anger at both Israel and the PNA. That trigger resulted in the outbreak of a second *intifada* that would consume the Palestinian territories in an armed conflict with Israel through 2005.

Women were not the face of the Al-Aqsa *intifada*. That face belonged to the armed young men who clashed with Israeli soldiers at border crossings and checkpoints. The practice of throwing stones at the Israeli military was replaced by the firing of guns: Palestine had, as part of the Oslo Accords, martialed a 40,000-man security force. Israel responded with the use of armed helicopters and tanks. There was no safe space for old ladies and feminists on these front lines. The Israel peace organization B'Tselem reported that 6,371 Palestinians died in the Al-Aqsa *intifada*, 2,996 of whom were noncombatants and 1,317 of whom were minors. Of the 1,083 Israelis killed, 741 were civilians.[70]

Women's options for participation in such an environment were limited to providing medical care for the wounded, marching in funeral processions, and organizing demonstrations which, because of the violent nature of the conflict, were limited to the first several months of the outbreak.[71] Some women reported that they spent much of their time convincing their sons not to go out to the checkpoints or following them from a distance to make sure that they were far from harm's way. In all cases, women found that their primary role during the second *intifada* was the defense of their portrayal as mothers who willingly sent their sons to their deaths. The virtual viewing public was not kind to Palestinian women whose families were involved in the second *intifada*. Public opinion championed the homes of women whose sons displayed measured responses to Israel in 1987, but not the homes of

258 Houses in Motion: Women in War and Revolution

Figure 13.9 Graffiti marks the separation barrier in Israel. Lars Ørstavik/Alamy Stock Photo.

women who were alleged to produce martyrs only to receive government payment for their loss.[72]

In 2002, Israel began construction of a separation barrier as an effort to wall off the West Bank from Israel (despite continuing to build and expand settlements) and to wall in future uprisings (see Figure 13.9). The wall has served to further fragment and isolate Palestinians within the territories granted to them by Oslo. The wall adds to the maze of crossing terminals and checkpoints that have been the hallmarks of the occupation. (Israel withdrew its military and its settlers from Gaza in 2005, but recently completed a barrier that runs along the boundaries separating Gaza's north from Israel's south.) Movement for Palestinians now involves navigating 558 gates, roadblocks, and checkpoints in their territories.[73]

The wall has cut through social networks that are critical to Palestinian material and emotional well-being. Many say that they now experience life as if inside a gigantic prison.[74] Mothering and keeping house have since taken on increased levels of difficulty: closed crossing depots or checkpoints mean loss of revenue, unavailability of food and medicine, and separation from kin. Injured kinfolk require women's attention and care at home, as do children who cannot access their schools when checkpoints are closed. Widowhood, always a possibility when Palestinians navigate checkpoints, increases women's need to work outside the home.

In 2006, voters mandated the establishment of an Islamic state in Gaza and a de facto decoupling of Gaza's politics from the PNA. Gaza is practically surrounded by Israel (it shares a single, short border with Egypt), a country whose existence it does not recognize and against which it still continues to wage war. Upon Hamas' takeover, Israel and Egypt sealed their borders with Gaza, and Israel imposed a blockade on Gaza's coast. Gaza's roughly 2 million inhabitants therefore rely on the Rafah crossing on Egypt's border (and which Egypt opens only unreliably) as well as a network of tunnels—always in the crosshairs of Israel and Egypt—for its imports. Gaza is poor and densely crowded. Unemployment there is rampant: in late 2021, it reached 50%.[75] Cheek by jowl, Gazans work hard just to survive.

Hamas has added religious patina to an already-patriarchal society in which women are tied to the domestic realm. Women are still encouraged to devote themselves to the struggle for Palestine, in addition to their roles as wives and mothers.[76] Women's participation in Hamas is facilitated by its Women's Actions Department (WAD), whose conferences and programs provide women with avenues for demonstrating their worth both as homemakers and Hamas members. The WAD also provides women with a means of pursuing activism within Hamas. (Other means of activism in Gaza include participation in old-fashioned philanthropic organizations and NGOs.) Women also rise to positions of leadership within Hamas, both in its central and local offices and institutions. The organization's generous provision of day-care centers, in fact, facilitates mobility away from their homes for women who seek involvement in activism and politics.[77] But Hamas, like many governing powers in the Middle East, insists that the home remain the genus of women's greatest contribution to its small piece of the remaining Palestinian territories.

Hamas' charter states a role for women in the liberation struggle that is no less than that of men. But that charter also suggests that equal is also separate. As in many of the foundational national governing platforms we have encountered, guiding the next generations is women's "major role" in the Hamas regime.[78] Birthing those generations is also requisite women's work. Families in Gaza tend to be large—an average of six members per individual family in 2000.[79] Tending to those families—feeding, clothing, overseeing education—is a daily struggle for sufficient time and resources. If, in the words of one woman, "Hamas is what encourages the people to hold on," it must be acknowledged that Gazans hold on to very little.[80]

The loss of family members to Hamas' ongoing military struggle with Israel is observed within a culture that celebrates martyrdom. Even the least enthusiastic supporters of Hamas live within a culture that reifies the wife or mother of a martyr to the Palestinian cause and in which the homes of martyrs' families are elevated above all others. Hamas' military wing, the al-Kassem Brigade, praises the mothers of martyrs and honors them in a public pageantry that includes images and music celebrating the fallen (or the self-sacrificed) and their wives and mothers. That pageantry also encourages mothers to encourage martyrdom. Music and videos promoting sacrifice to the cause feature songs about the mothers who make that sacrifice, willingly or not. Conflict with Gaza's well-armed enemy next door produces heavy casualties; in the 2008 war with Israel, 1,367 Gazans were killed in a scant three weeks. Death is always close by. Gazans describe sounds made by Apache missiles and F-16 planes as if they're describing the voices of old friends. "Death motivates us to strengthen our resolve."[81]

Conclusion

Naila Ayesh (1961–), the Palestinian organizer and activist whose life is the subject of the documentary film "Naila and the Uprising," had five homes in the years leading up to and including the *intifada*. The first was her family home, located in Lifta, on the outskirts of Jerusalem. That home was demolished by the IDF in 1969. Her second home was the apartment in Gaza that she shared with her husband Jamil Zakout. That home was raided by the IDF when Naila was arrested for suspected political activity. Her third home, consequently, was the Maskubiya Prison in Jerusalem. There, a pregnant Naila was interrogated, isolated, and beaten. A return to her home in Gaza saw Naila and Jamal starting a family and taking part in the *intifada*. Consequently, her fourth home, from December 1988 through to April 1989, was Israel's Telmond Prison for female political prisoners. After her husband was deported from Gaza for association with the *intifada*, the Israeli authorities gave Naila one choice if she wanted her son Majd to know his father: a two-year exile with her husband and son in Cairo. Naila's fifth home was therefore an apartment in a foreign city.[82] It is safe to say that only rarely was Naila in a home of her choice.

While these examples do not appear to represent the experience of most women in the Middle East, they, in fact, have much to tell us about the ever-moving nature of the home throughout the region from the early twentieth century.

This book opened with a discussion of domestic life ca. 1900, in which home emerged as a place of residence, marital and family life, and work. "Close to home," as Chapter 2 describes it, meant living at a distance from the discourses that had just begun to swirl around women in the public realm. Those discourses were byproducts of changes in the global economy and of European obsession with the *harem*. In subsequent chapters, those discourses were amplified by heads of state for whom changes in the political and economic realms could not happen without women in their "proper" place. Women were therefore confined by discourses.

In subsequent chapters, we witnessed women's "liberation" from their homes as evidence of modernization and economic development. Women's "proper" place at home was not forgotten by the regimes who advanced "the modern woman" as a peer to men in education, work, or professional development. Rather, those regimes advanced the dual bread baker *and* bread earner model of that "modern woman." Women who did not request such a reconfiguration were nonetheless burdened, if not confined, by the subsequent taxing of their physical resources.

Islamism has also targeted women's homes, arguing that women have no role in public life. At home, women are reduced to wombs, nurturers of children's, morals, and symbols of the right order of political life.

In none of these cases have women had full agency over their homelife. Closed *at* home or *in* home, their experiences resemble Naila's, even as the details of their lives differ.

Notes

1. Relli Shechter, ed., *Transitions in Domestic Consumption and Family Life in the Modern Middle East: Houses in Motion* (New York: Palgrave, 2003).
2. Mary Ann Fay astutely observes that the harem becomes "mobile" and "flexible" with the veil. See her *Unveiling the Harem: Elite Women and the Paradox of Seclusion in Eighteenth-Century Cairo* (Syracuse: Syracuse University Press, 2012), 184.
3. See the introduction to Julie M. Peteet, *Gender in Crisis: Women and the Palestinian Resistance Movement* (New York: Columbia University Press, 1991).
4. Parvin Paidar, *Women and the Political Process in Twentieth-Century Iran* (Cambridge: Cambridge University Press, 1995), 125–126.
5. Paidar, *Women and the Political Process*, 106.
6. Paidar, *Women and the Political Process*, 157.
7. Mateo Muhammed Farzaneh, *Iranian Women and Gender in the Iran-Iraq War* (Syracuse, New York: Syracuse University Press, 2021), 38.
8. See Paidar, *Women and the Political Process*; Mary Elaine Hegland, "Women and the Iranian Revolution: A Village Case Study," *Dialectical Anthropology* Vol. 15, No. 2/3 (1990), 183–192.
9. Arielle Gordon, "From Guerrilla Girls to Zainabs: Reassessing the Figure of the 'Militant Woman' in the Iranian Revolution," *Journal of Middle East Women's Studies* Vol. 17, No. 1 (2021), 64–95.
10. For a more extensive discussion of the Revolution's many political possibilities, see Paidar, *Women and the Political Process*; Janet Afary and Kevin B. Anderson, *Foucault and the Iranian Revolution: Gender and the Seductions of Islamism* (Chicago: University of Chicago Press, 2005); Gordon, "From Guerrilla Girls to Zainabs," 64–95.
11. Farzaneh, *Iranian Women and Gender*, 48–49.
12. Paidar, *Women and the Political Process*, 210–212.
13. Gordon, "From Guerrilla Girls to Zainabs," 64–95.
14. Paidar, *Women and the Political Process*.
15. Shirin Ebadi, *Iran Awakening: One Woman's Journey to Reclaim Her Life and Country* (New York: Random House, 2006), Chapter 3, "The Bitter Taste of Revolution."
16. The following section is taken from Farzaneh, *Iranian Women and Gender*.
17. Faranzeh, *Iranian Women and Gender*, 198.
18. Faranzeh, *Iranian Women and Gender*, 31.
19. Faranzeh, *Iranian Women and Gender*, 323.
20. Farzaneh, *Iranian Women and Gender*, 1.
21. Haleh Esfandiari, *Reconstructed Lives: Women and Iran's Islamic Revolution* (Baltimore: Johns Hopkins University Press, 1997), 6.
22. Esfandiari, *Reconstructed Lives*, 136.
23. "Tara," cited in Mahnaz Khousha, *Voices from Iran: The Changing Lives of Iranian Women* (Syracuse, New York: Syracuse University Press, 2002), 223.
24. https://www.pbs.org/wgbh/pages/frontline/tehranbureau/2010/06/martyrs-of-the-green-movement.html.
25. Omid Khazani and Sarah Parvini, "How 'Baraye,' a song about Iran's protests, became an anthem for women, freedom and an Ordinary Life," *Los Angeles Times* (October 12, 2022); https://www.latimes.com/world-nation/story/2022-10-12/la-fg-how-baraye-a-song-about-irans-protests-became-an-anthem.
26. "Ziba," cited in Khazani and Parvini, "How 'Baraye,' a song about Iran's protests, became an anthem for women, freedom and an Ordinary Life."
27. Kousha, *Voices from Iran*, 204.
28. Human Rights Watch World Report 2021 Iran Events from 2020; https://www.hrw.org/world-report/2021/country-chapters/iran.

29 Betool Khedairi, *A Sky So Close*, Murayman Jamil, translator (New York: Anchor Books, 2002), 106.
30 Khedairi, *A Sky So Close*, 167.
31 Dina Rizq Khoury, *Iraq in Wartime: Soldiering, Martyrdom and Remembrance* (Cambridge: Cambridge University Press, 2013).
32 Khoury, *Iraq in Wartime*, 11.
33 Nadje Al-Ali, *Iraqi Women: Untold Stories from 1948 to the Present* (London: Zed Books, 2007), 155–157, 164–165.
34 Khoury, *Iraq in Wartime*, 7.
35 Khoury, *Iraq in Wartime*, 61–67.
36 Yasmin Husein Al-Jawaheri, *Women in Iraq: The Gender Impact of International Sanctions* (Boulder, CO: Lynne Reinner, 2008), 22.
37 Khedairi, *A Sky So Close*, 140–141.
38 Al-Jawaheri, *Women in Iraq*, 26.
39 Khedairi, *A Sky So Close*, 130.
40 Al-Ali, *Iraqi Women*, 177.
41 Al-Ali, *Iraqi Women*, 181.
42 Kali Rubali, "Children and the Toxic Legacy of War in Iraq," *MERIP* (September 22, 2020).
43 Al-Ali, *Iraqi Women*, 196.
44 Al-Ali, *Women in Iraq*, 240.
45 Al-Ali, *Women in Iraq*, 246.
46 www.iraqbodycount.org.
47 Al-Ali, *Women in Iraq*, 254.
48 Zahra Ali, "Iraqi Women's Activism—20 years after the US invasion," *MERIP* Vol. 306 (Spring 2023).
49 Louisa Loveluck and Mustafa Salim, "How Iraq's Children of War Found their Voice," *The Washington Post* (March 20, 2023).
50 Peteet, *Gender in Crisis*. See also Fatma Kassem, *Palestinian Women: Narrative Histories and Gendered Memory* (London: Zed Publications, 2011), particularly Chapter 6, "Home."
51 For an overview of women's activities in this era, see Lisa Taraki, "The Development of Political Consciousness among Palestinians in the Occupied Territories, 1967-1987," in *Intifada: Palestine at the Crossroads*, Jamal Nasser and Roger Heacock, eds. (New York: Birzeit University and Praeger Publishers, 1991).
52 Peteet, *Gender in Crisis*, 60.
53 Peteet, *Gender in Crisis*.
54 "Naila and the Uprising," directed by Julia Bacha, Just Vision, 2017.
55 "Naila and the Uprising."
56 Robert Hunter, *The Palestinian Uprising: A War by Other Means*, 2nd ed. (Berkeley: University of California Press, 1993), 4, cited in Cleveland and Bunton, *A History of the Modern Middle East*, 476.
57 Nahla Abdo, "Nationalism and Feminism," in *Gender and National Identity*, Valentine M. Moghadam, ed. (London: Verso Press, 1994).
58 Marriane Torres, "Women in the *Intifada*," *Palestine Papers* (August 1989); www.sonomacountyfreepress.org/palestinewomen2.
59 Ebba Augustin, "Developments in the Palestinian Women's Movement during the Intifada," in *Palestinian Women: Identity and Experience*, Ebba Augustin, ed. (London: Zed Books, 1993), 27.
60 Abdo, "Nationalism and Feminism," 148.
61 Abdo, "Nationalism and Feminism," 163.
62 Abdo, "Nationalism and Feminism," 161.

63 This is Eileen S. Kuttab's thesis; see "Palestinian Women in the *Intifada*: Fighting on Two Fronts," *Arab Studies Quarterly* Vol. 15, No. 2 (Spring 1993), 69–85.
64 Graham Usher, "Palestinian Women, the *Intifada* and the State of Independence: An Interview with Rita Giacaman," *Race and Class* Vol. 34, No. 3 (1992), 31.
65 "Naila and the Uprising."
66 "Naila and the Uprising."
67 Penny Johnson and Eileen Kuttab, "Where Have All the Women (and Men) Gone? Reflections on Gender and the Second *Intifada*," *Feminist Review* Vol. 69 (December 1, 2001), 27.
68 Sophie Richter-Devroe, "The Palestinian Women's Movement After Oslo: Peacemakers or Fighters for their Freedom?" *al-Raida* Vol. XXII, Nos. 109–110 (Spring/Summer 2005), 21.
69 Richter-Devroe, "The Palestinian Women's Movement After Oslo," 22–23.
70 https://www.btselem.org/press_releases/20100927.
71 Johnson and Kuttab, "Where Have all the Women (and Men) Gone," 34.
72 Johnson and Kuttab, "Where Have all the Women (and Men) Gone," 39.
73 https://news.cornell.edu/stories/2008/07/cornell-sociologist-studies-israels-west-bank-barrier.
74 https://news.cornell.edu/stories/2008/07/cornell-sociologist-studies-israels-west-bank-barrier.
75 https://gisha.org/en/gaza-unemployment-rate-soars-to-50-2-in-months-following-may-escalation/#:~:text=According%20to%20the%20quarterly%20unemployment%20report%20by%20the,2021%20%28July-September%29%2C%20Gaza%E2%80%99s%20unemployment%20rate%20stood%20at%2050.2%25.
76 Islah Jad, "Islamist Women of Hamas: Between Feminism and Nationalism," *Inter-Asia Cultural Studies* Vol. 12 (November 2011).
77 Jad, "Islamist Women of Hamas," 180 and 183.
78 Jad, "Islamist Women of Hamas," 188.
79 https://www.ceicdata.com/en/palestinian-territory-occupied/average-household-size/avg-household-size-gaza-strip#:~:text=State%20of%20Palestine%20%28West%20Bank%20and%20Gaza%29%20Avg,the%20previous%20number%20of%205.700%20Person%20for%202015.
80 Um Mahmod, interviewed in Sara Arraf's "Women of Hamas," Cinephil 2010.
81 Arraf, "Women of Hamas."
82 "Naila and the Uprising." Directed by Julia Bacha. 2017.

14 Arab Spring

Women's experiences during and after the Arab Spring uprisings of 2011 reflect the ambiguities of the state's relationship to its female citizens in the modern era. The women who organized and demonstrated during the uprisings are the result of state efforts to link educated, economically-productive women to modernity projects. So, too, are the women who have continued to legislate for women's rights throughout the region since Arab Spring. As in revolutions past, female participants in Arab Spring uprisings often drew on their considerable educational background and professional skills to organize and manage the uprisings' guiding hand in Tunisia, Egypt, Libya, Syria, Bahrain, and Yemen: social media. The state could take credit for the numbers of female physicians who served as medics. States could boast of professional syndicates whose membership consisted of women trained in law, education, journalism, engineering, and more. Labor unions across the region could boast of female membership and leadership. As in the past, the activities of philanthropic associations benefited the state by reaching communities outside of the reach of state welfare programs. In a pattern that has repeated itself from the early twentieth century, female participants in the Arab Spring were often the beneficiaries of the states they now challenged.

Accusations of trespass—by the state, its supporters and its detractors—accompanied these women's participation in the public realm, however. As they had historically, male revolutionaries applauded the presence of women on the streets and relied on the many services provided by them. Security and military forces, however, subjected women to arrests, detentions, physical abuse, and virginity tests to remind them that participation in the public realm had sullied their morals. As governments across the region fell and the process of rebuilding them began, women's behavior in the public and private realms was heralded by politicians (and their critics) as threatening to new regimes, as damaging to economies, as undermining moral orders. The very things that the state had "done for women" were leveraged by state institutions as evidence that women threatened the postrevolutionary order of things. As in previous revolutions, women were both symbolic of state success and of the state's uncertain future.

Nowhere were the ambiguities regarding women's role in the public realm more evident than in the case of Fayda Hamdi, the Tunisian inspector whose alleged slap across the face of Mohammed Bouazizi is said to have triggered the Arab Spring uprisings. As the story goes, Hamdi confronted Bouazizi for peddling produce without the requisite state licenses. Humiliated by the slap and exhausted by this most recent encounter with a state seemingly determined to keep him from making a living, Bouazizi ended his own life by setting himself on fire; popular expressions of sympathy for his plight and rage against the Tunisian state brought Tunisians to the street, where they protested against Zine Abidine Ben Ali (r. 1987–2011) and demanded his resignation. Ben Ali's flight from Tunisia on January 18, 2011 emboldened protestors across the Arab world to demand the removal of corrupt and suffocating regimes.

When seen as a representative of the state, Hamdi did not emerge from her encounter with Bouazizi as a sympathetic figure. The story that quickly emerged about the "slap that was heard around the world" hinged less on the veracity of the events (Hamdi claimed that she did not strike Bouazizi) than on Bouazizi's emasculation by a (female) servant of a corrupt regime. To tame anger in the streets, the regime had Hamdi arrested and briefly held her in prison. Once absolved of wrongdoing, however, Hamdi was vilified not only for her association with the state but for her behavior in private: she was a so-called *anis*, a manly spinster who hates men. Hamdi was also vilified as a stand-in for Ben Ali's wife, Leila Trabelsi, whose extended family, well known for its corruption, had dominated Tunisian politics for decades.[1] Trabelsi was said to have fled Tunisia with USD 56 billion in gold bullion stashed aboard her plane.[2]

When viewed as an emanation of the state, however, Hamdi emerges in this story differently. Through education and employment in a state agency (she was a civil servant, not a policewoman), Hamdi could be counted among the success stories of reforms initiated by Ben Ali's predecessor Habib Bourghiba (r. 1956–1987), whose legal and educational reforms for women were part of an Arab state modernization agenda. As such, Hamdi was less the villainous representative of the state as she was the model of modern Arab womanhood. In such a version of events, Hamdi's occupation as a civil servant is emblematic less of state corruption and deprivation than of the state's continued reliance upon classes of educated, employed women.

This chapter focuses on women in Arab Spring and its aftermath through this dual lens, arguing that women's participation in 2011 and beyond demonstrates not only the successes of Arab women, but also the successes of Arab state support for women's access to the public realm. We present the state's reaction to women's forceful presence in the public realm in 2011, as well as the reaction of many male citizens as examples of unfinished business regarding women's presence in that realm. Beginning with Tunisia, we account for the spoils of women's participation in Arab Spring and the obstacles that have accompanied those spoils, while at the same time illustrating the increase in sexual harassment, rape, and exclusion from the public realm that have accompanied these successes.

Arab Spring

Judging from the numbers of participants who gathered to demand their resignation over the winter and spring of 2011, Zine al-Abidine Ben Ali (Tunisia), Husni Mubarak (Egypt), Moammar Qadhafy (Libya), Bashar al-Assad (Syria), Ali

Abdullah Saleh (Yemen), and Hamad bin Isa al-Khalifa (Bahrain) were not faring well. Hundreds of thousands of demonstrators took to the streets to suggest that their heads of state had failed to govern well or wisely. Entrenched autocracies, sclerotic bureaucracies, repressive police states, and prisons full of oppositional figures, all defined the region. So too did increasing economic hardship. Neoliberal reforms had brought wealth to some and increased economic difficulty for most, especially following the 2008 global economic downturn. Food prices in the region were at an all-time high; by March 2011, they had risen for eight consecutive months. Unemployment was also high, especially for young people, 60% of the region's population, who were forced to put off marriage and family life until they found successful employment. Youth were not alone: for many of their parents' and grandparents' generations, state projects designed to offer citizens legal protection, education, employment, and social safety nets had failed to live up to their promises. Even for the wealthy, as in Bahrain, the wait for a government-provided home can be up to 25 years.[3]

The story of Mohammed Bouazizi illustrates the frustrations of both Tunisian youth (Bouazizi was 26) and their elders. Bouazizi allegedly killed himself over the job market and as the result of endless harassment from Tunisian state officials. His attempts to join the military and to gain civil employment had come to naught, and Bouazizi therefore relied on selling fruit and vegetables to provide for his widowed mother and his siblings (Bouazizi was not married). The local police routinely harassed Bouazizi because he did not have a business license. What he also lacked was the money to assure that officials would look the other way. On December 17, 2010, Bouazizi was harassed by the police for selling produce without a permit—this time by Fayda Hamdi, who confiscated his cart and scales and, allegedly, slapped Bouazizi when he did not immediately comply. When Hamdi's superiors refused to hear his case, Bouazizi allegedly set himself alight in front of a government building. Said his mother: "the government drove him to do what he did…We are poor and they thought we had no power."[4]

Khaled Said, 27, whose brutal murder at the hands of the state security forces symbolized the people's rage toward the Mubarak regime in the spring of 2011 similarly illustrates the Egyptian state's (dis)regard for its citizens. In June 2010, while blogging in an internet café in Egypt's coastal city of Alexandria, Said was apprehended by the security police, who accused him of using a blog to leak information about police corruption. Once in police custody, Said was beaten to death. While state coroners claimed that Said suffocated while trying to swallow a packet of hashish, his family maintains that police killed Said over information that would have implicated them in a drug deal.

Photographs of Said's broken and disfigured face captured the rage and frustration of the region. Similarly, the Syrian regime's arrest and brutal murder of 15 young boys from the southern Syrian city of Dara'a, accused of graffitiing the slogans that had issued from Tunisia and Egypt, illustrated both Bashar al-Assad's intolerance for dissent and his indifference toward his citizens. Fathers of the nation had seemingly turned on their children.

When viewed as a measure of those who protested such acts of aggression and indifference, the state looks less the failure. Photographs of Said, Bouazizi, and the Syrian children captured the attention of fleets of Tunisians, Egyptians, and Syrians who were educated, wired to the internet, and capable of wielding the latest martyrs against the regime. Some protestors were high profile: Mohammed El-Baradei, from Egypt, former head of the International Atomic Energy Agency, led a protest against police abuse in Alexandria in the summer of 2010. Others would see their profiles increase in due course: Egyptian Google executive Wael Ghonim memorialized Said in a Facebook page called "We Are All Khaled Said." Many members of the page were Egyptians who advocated for the struggle against police brutality. Ghonim similarly used his blog to call on Egyptians to protest in late January 2011.

Ghonim was not alone. From 2008, Egypt's April 6 Youth Movement had used Facebook to encourage support for a workers' strike, organizing demonstrations and alerting demonstrators to the presence of security police. By January 2009, 70,000 Egyptians met up on the page to vent their frustrations with nepotism, lack of free speech, and the difficult state of the Egyptian economy.

One such April 6 organizer was Asmaa Mahfouz, a then-26-year-old graduate of Cairo University. She used her training in computer science and her considerable skill at networking to galvanize support for the Egyptian textile workers, who called for better wages and working conditions in the textile center of Mahalla al-Kubra. In tandem with Ghonim, who used his blog to call Egyptians to protest on January 25, 2011—the first day of Egypt's uprisings—Mahfouz issued a vlog in which she called on Egyptians to take to the streets to protest "humiliation and hunger and poverty and degradation." "If you think yourself a man, come with me on 25 January."[5]

On February 11, 2011—the same day that Mubarak would step down—Yemeni activist Tawakkol Karman called specifically for women to take to the streets. Addressing a crowd at San'a University, gathered for what Yemenis called their "Revolution of Dignity," Karman linked women to the movement, insisting that Yemen's President Ali Abdullah Saleh must go:

> Sisters, now is the time for women to stand up and become active without asking for permission. Women are no longer victims—they have become leaders... We want to retrieve our nation, we want to become citizens in a new world.[6]

Arab Spring was not Karman's first foray into protesting the Yemeni state. Her involvement in politics extended back to her university days, after which she founded Women Journalists Without Chains (WJWC). WJWC served as Karman's springboard into social activism, which she pursued through Yemen's most prominent Islamist party, Islah. For her efforts as Yemen's "Mother of the Revolution," Karman was awarded the Nobel Peace Prize in 2011.

Yemen's then President Ali Abdullah Saleh labeled women's substantial presence in the protests against him as "un-Islamic," challenging women's claims to citizenship.[7] Karman countered that confronting the region's shared woes—dictatorship, corruption, poverty, and unemployment—without a full commitment to women's rights prevented Yemenis from fully "retrieve[ing]" their nation from despotism.[8] Said Yemeni Journalist Afrah Nasser, "It's a revolution not just against a political leader, but also against a generation that long felt it was acceptable to repress women."[9]

If Bouazizi and Said embodied states' failures, Ghonim and Mahfouz, like Tawakkol, embodied the successes of states whose educational agendas produced professionals of many ranks and skills (see Chapter 9). Both hail from middle-class Egyptian families and are graduates of Cairo University (Ghonim with a BS in computer engineering, Mahfouz in business administration). Both typified a generation of computer literate, techno-savvy youth whose worlds expanded with the rise and spread of technology, first the satellite dish and then the internet, in Egypt.[10] Both count among the ranks of well-employed graduates from state educational institutions. Both demonstrate the ideals of national education: love of nation, care for fellow Egyptians, and service on their behalf. Mahfouz was quickly dubbed the "voice of the revolution" for her care for the nation's poor and underserved citizens.

Mahfouz also embodies the successes of Arab states across the region who have linked the education and employment of women to their regimes since the 1950s. She is emblematic of the many professional women who attended the Arab Spring uprisings in their capacities as bloggers, vloggers, journalists, photographers, medics, lawyers and members of philanthropic organizations, nongovernmental organizations (NGOs), and professional syndicates. Female labor organizers, union leaders, student-committee leaders, and members of popular resistance committees all lent their talents to the effort to organize uprisings against the state.

Examples of women's activities abound. In Tunisia, women sewed revolutionary flags. As in Tunisia, Egyptian women collected food, water, and medical supplies. In Libya, female lawyers representing the families of those wrongly imprisoned by Qadhafy's regime quickly became involved in organizing demonstrations and in aiding those arrested during the uprisings.[11] In Syria, female intellectuals, including lawyers, sat on forums through which they aired their expectations for political reform. Beginning in September 2000, in what the international media hailed as the "Damascus Spring," forum participants worked tirelessly: their "Statement of the 99," published in Damascus' *al-Hayat* newspaper, called for rule by law, political pluralism, and freedom of the press. The statement addressed women specifically by calling for a reform of personal status laws based in religion (see Chapters 8 and 11).[12]

The forum's efforts bore fruit in the loosening of the state's grip on Syria's civil society and in an increase in Syrians' participation in civil-society organizations. One example was the establishment of an humanitarian aid organization, cofounded by the lawyer and activist Razan Zaitouneh, who would soon play a foundational role in Syria's uprisings. The group's establishment was in contradiction to the state's Law of Associations, which for decades had prevented such groups from forming without state permission.

While Assad's tolerance of the group was short-lived, Zaitouneh's commitment was not. Her work within the forums shaped the organizational structures undergirding Syrians' Arab Spring activism.[13] On February 17, 2011, after a young Syrian had set himself on fire in protest of the regime, over 1,000 gathered in Damascus. Protests spread across Syria by March 2011. On Friday, March 15, in what was named a "Day of Rage," Assad's troops violently dispersed protests throughout the country. The regime's spy agency made several arrests. On the following day, Syrians protested those arrests and called for the release of detainees. Present at those protests were two women who had earlier been active in Damascus Spring: Zaitouneh and Suheir al-Atassi. Al-Atassi was soon arrested and imprisoned.

The result of the March 15 protests was the founding of Syria's Local Coordination Committees or LCCs. The LCCs, which brought young men and women together in what they called an "underground parliament," brought the will and the imagination of the Damascus Spring back to life.[14] The LCCs worked to encourage unity, but they also made demands: at the top of their list was regime change. Other groups, such as the Syrian Revolution Coordinators Union and the Syrian Revolution General Commission, founded by Suhair al-Atassi, proposed boycotts of regime-sponsored businesses and liaised with armed militants calling themselves the Free Syrian Army. Students were essential to these groups and to the peaceful demonstrations sponsored by them. Women were also central. In Salamiyeh, for example, in western Syria, women established a coordination committee and organized demonstrations—in which they also participated. Photographs of the women demonstrating and being arrested were posted online and were viewed both locally and internationally.[15]

Women—veiled to avoid recognition—also provided medical and humanitarian aid at demonstrations throughout the country. In Aleppo, women established Syria's first independent radio station, Radio Naseem, which promoted gender equality along with regime change. In a number of communities, women-only LCCs focused on women-specific issues. As the regime turned weapons on its citizens in the spring of 2012, women's roles in the uprisings were diminished. Nonetheless, women continued to provide logistical support for the Free Syrian Army. Some women formed battalions, ready to engage in the fight.[16]

Bahraini women, who in addition to joining men in protest against the al-Khalifa government, also organized demonstrations of their own. While focused largely on the human rights abuses suffered by all Bahrainis, women's demonstrations added demands for greater equity in laws pertaining to divorce and child custody to calls for reform of the body politic. As in other parts of the region, the government's retaliation against female demonstrators was harsh: female doctors and nurses were arrested and imprisoned for aiding demonstrators. A similar fate awaited women caught listening to revolutionary music. Female members of the Bahrain Teachers Society were among those arrested for calling for a strike. Women in prison routinely face physical degradations, including torture and rape.[17]

The Bahraini "women of Arab Spring" did not cease their efforts as uprisings made their unsteady (and, for some, incomplete) transition to stability. Indeed, professionals, particularly lawyers, have continued to fight for women's better representation in politics, for changes to personal status laws, and for individual choice with regard to clothing.

In Tunisia, women's most enduring legacy has been their role in politics and in shaping public debates regarding women's rights. As in other parts of the region, state programs had brought very tangible improvements in women's access to education, the public realm, and increased legal rights. Women were nonetheless absent from dialogue with the state regarding their education and public and legal needs. From 1956, Tunisian women had enjoyed the most progressive personal status laws in the Arab world. Those laws ended polygamy and made women men's equals with regard to divorce. Versions of Tunisia's constitution, promulgated under Bourghiba's tenure, enshrined the "principle of equality": women could enter the army, study engineering and medicine, and have access to birth control (1963) and abortion (1965). In 1986, in celebration of 50 years of Tunisia's progressive Personal Status Codes, Ben Ali passed two new bills. One raised Tunisia's age of consent to 18 for both sexes; the other extended housing rights to divorced women with children in their custody. But, as in Nasser's Egypt and Baathist Syria and Iraq, those laws—however progressive—were promulgated without regard for women's ideas or input. Political Islam's increased popularity under Ben Ali's rule had led the president to distance himself not just from women's rights but from press and political freedoms as he worked to shore up power against his opposition. Ben Ali's regime succeeded in placing civil society, including women's movements, under state control. Women under Ben Ali's administration, however successful, were—like most men in Tunisia—not yet free to determine their own personal and political agendas.

After Ben Ali's flight from Tunisia, women lent their voices to debates surrounding Tunisia's first elections for the new National Constituent Assembly (NCA) in October 2011. When the Islamist al-Nahda Party won the majority of seats in the NCA, observers wondered if women would retain what they had gained in the overthrow of the Ben Ali regime. However, a female politician Meherzia Libidi (1963–2021) was elected to be the NCA's deputy speaker. As the region's most senior female elected official, Libidi was determined to maintain women's rights in post-Arab Spring Tunisia. Her tenure in the NCA oversaw the institution of a quota system for female representation in parliament. In the 2011 elections, the moderate Islamist al-Nahda Party took 42 of the 49 seats allocated for women.[18]

Female delegates in the NCA have been crucial in transforming debates about women into discussions *involving* them. Libidi's substantial influence shaped debates surrounding women in preparations for the new Tunisian Constitution, promulgated in August 2012, especially as drafts of that constitution failed to address women as individuals. The new constitution's Article 28, for example, had defined women's role in the family as "complementary to that of men" at the insistence of Islamists who do not see men and women as equal.[19] Women who sat in opposition to Article 28, like Libidi, suggested that it defined women only in relation to men and only in marriage. Debates and discussions among women and between women's organizations and the public resulted in the elimination of the word "complementary" in the third draft of the constitution, which was released in April 2013.[20]

The period following the ouster of Ben Ali witnessed clashes, some of them violent, between those who see Tunisia as an Islamic nation and those who insist upon protecting its secular legacy. By 2013, Tunisia was on the verge of a civil war, the result of deepening divisions over the nature of the country's future. A "quartet" of civil society associations worked with political parties to bring about a national dialogue and to usher in a new round of elections. As the result of the ensuing National Dialogue, al-Nahda's Rachid Ghanouchi, who had served as president since 2011, stepped down from office. In addition to ratifying a new constitution, the quartet succeeded in establishing an interim government and in rescheduling the elections that ultimately brought a secular party, Nidaa Tounes, and Beji Caid Essebsi to the presidency in 2014. The national dialogue reaffirmed the state's commitment to women's rights: quotas for women in the NCA remained in place; equality between men and women remained enshrined in the Tunisian Constitution; and the country's progressive Personal Status Codes were maintained. The quartet, including Madame Widad Bouchamaoui, who represented Utica (the Tunisian Union of Industry, Trade, and Handicrafts), won the Nobel Prize for Peace in 2015.

By 2017, women's steady determination to be included in the body politic had resulted in the passing of a new law which defines violence, in compliance with the UN Handbook for Legislation on Violence Against Women, as "any physical, moral, sexual or economic aggression." Under the law, which is supported by a variety of Tunisian political parties and civil society organizations, men accused of rape are no longer allowed to escape prosecution by marrying their victims. The law also raised the age of consent from 13 to 16 for both sexes. Workplace discrimination, under the new law, is subject to fines, as is sexual harassment in public. Imen Ben Mohamed, who represents the al-Nahda Party, called the law more revolutionary than Bourghiba's 1956 Personal Status Laws.[21]

Kais Saied's appointment of Najla Bouden Ramadhane as prime minister in September 2021 might appear, at first glance, to suggest that Tunisian women's goals have been accomplished. Ramadhane's appointment, however, resulted from new powers Saied has granted to himself since the summer of 2021. Saied dismissed Ramadhane's predecessor (and the cabinet that he headed), began ruling by decree, and appointed himself to head a committee to revamp the 2014 constitution. While Ramadhane's appointment is certainly a tribute to women's gains since 2011, much work nonetheless remains as women struggle to protect their constitutional rights and affirm their rights as individuals.

In the months following Mubarak's resignation on February 11, 2011, Egyptian women were critical in organizing the strikes that pressed the Supreme Council of the Armed Forces (SCAF), which ruled Egypt through 2012, to allow for elections. But the low number of seats (eight out of 508 or 2%), taken by women in the first post-Mubarak parliament, led observers both in and outside of Egypt to draw parallels between Egyptian women's experience in 2011 and that of 1919, when women were welcome in political demonstrations but left out of the body politic. When Egyptians voted—in their country's first democratic elections—they gave the presidency to Mohammed Morsi (r. 2012–2013), who had run for office on a platform showing no support for women except as mothers and family members. While scarcely represented on political councils, however, women nonetheless worked consistently to ensure that the committees responsible for drafting Egypt's new constitution protected women's rights outside of the conjugal family unit. Nonetheless, the 2012 Constitution "almost entirely erased women from public life." The constitution alluded to the idea that women's place is in the home and reminded women that their primary duties were familial.[22] Indeed, the Morsi regime failed to recognize or to address issues crucial to women, such as sexual harassment, marital rape, and human trafficking. Pakinam Sharkawi, a token female appointee in the Morsi administration, denied that Egyptian women are affected by marital rape, praising Morsi instead for his government's stance regarding women's place in Egypt.[23]

Women were pioneering in the February 17, 2011, uprising in Libya—which quickly deteriorated into a violent civil war between those loyal to Muammar Qadhafy, who had ruled Libya autocratically since 1969, and the rebels who sought an end to his rule. Qadhafy's regime was often characterized as "stateless": lacking formal state institutions and civil society organizations. Consequently, Libyans had few experienced civil servants and nongovernmental actors on whom to rely.[24] In the early days of the uprising, therefore, women rebels played revolutionary roles in building state-like institutions, often breaking gender barriers to support the revolution and to build a new state. In such capacities, women smuggled arms, provided medical aid to wounded fighters, helped identify strike zones for the North Atlantic Treaty Organization (NATO), opened NGOs to provide medical aid and education, and started newspapers.[25] In Benghazi, from which the uprising originated, women and men alike formed local committees for self-rule, participating later in forming the National Transitional Committee. This committee formed Libya's new government after the assassination of Qadhafy in August 2011. Qadhafy's sponsorship of women's education throughout the 1980s and of a reform program inaugurated in the early 2000s had created a class of Libyans—male and female—with new economic horizons and with skills that could be put to use in the building of a new national government.[26] But as one woman was quick to point out, women's education did not prepare them for the task of governing, even at the local level. They simply had no experience. Salwa Burghaigis, an attorney who participated in the Coalition of the February 17 Revolution (later to be assassinated by militias), said: "Please be patient. Please…We didn't plan it…in Egypt where they say they prepared since 1995…2005…for five years. We didn't do nothing [sic], okay? This comes [snaps fingers] like this."[27]

Patterns of resentment, violence toward, and exclusion of women who "transgress" in the public realm are not new. The state and, frequently, its male citizens have a history of asking women who have struggled to secure or defend the public realm to step out of it. The stakes have always been high: denials of suffrage, particularly, mark women's earlier spoils of victory. So, too, in Arab Spring. Female martyrs abound. In Alexandria, Egypt, 16-year-old Amira Sayyid was among the uprisings' first martyrs. In Sohag, in upper Egypt, bullets also killed Sally Zahran. A huge photo of Zahran floated around Tahrir with those of other martyrs. Next to the photo, one epitaph read: "Sally the Martyr: She taught the Egyptian people the meaning of manhood."²⁸ At the end of May 2021, the Syrian Observatory for Human Rights reported that at least 15,000 women had been killed in Syria's ongoing civil war.²⁹

If the meaning of manhood in Arab Spring was to stand up and die for the nation, the meaning of womanhood in the aftermath of Arab Spring has frequently meant struggling in public space. Throughout the region, female revolutionaries suffered (and continue to suffer) violence, harassment, imprisonment, and rape at the hands of the state security forces and the military. After Tunisia's first elections, female professors and university students experienced an increase in intimidation by Islamists. Islamist males attacked women who were not in *hijab*.³⁰ In Egypt, in the days and weeks after Mubarak's resignation, large numbers of Egyptians were arrested by the military; women detainees were sometimes subjected to virginity tests. Samira Ibrahim (1987–) later succeeded in bringing SCAF to a civilian court over the military's use of the virginity tests. She had been participating in a sit-in in Tahrir Square on March 11, 2011, International Women's Day, when she and other female protestors were arrested by the military, driven to the Egyptian Museum, and forced to strip. They were beaten and given electric shocks and virginity tests by military personnel. Only their virginity could save them from charges of prostitution. Ibrahim told this story in stark detail in court. The medical staff member who examined the women's hymens was ultimately acquitted of wrongdoing. Ibrahim's actions nonetheless led to the military's disavowal of virginity tests.³¹

Women's participation in demonstrations was particularly fraught under SCAF. Women who marched in demonstrations commemorating the 2011 International Women's Day were confronted by the military. They also found themselves surrounded by men who chanted "the people want the fall of women" in a play on one of the revolution's most popular chants "the people want the fall of the regime."³² In December 2011, an amateur videographer captured a soldier bringing his foot down on top of the face of a woman who, in the course of her confrontation with soldiers, had been stripped down to her jeans and her blue bra. The incident occurred near Tahrir Square, where the still-unidentified woman and many others were headed to protest.³³ Graffiti of a blue bra became ubiquitous in Cairo, symbolic of state violence, of women's resilience, and of women's continued demands to participate in the public realm. The woman in the blue bra was praised by Egyptians who promised not to forget what happened to this "woman among women."³⁴

Young Egyptian men interviewed after Morsi's election admitted they had voted Islamists into power because they felt emasculated and impotent under Mubarak. Similarly, Mubarak's neoliberal economic policies resulted in men feeling castrated by poverty. Some young men organized themselves and called for a reversal of women's hard-earned gains. Many young men equate feminism with the Mubarak regime, particularly because of first lady Suzanne Mubarak's high-profile role in promoting women's rights, including the right to divorce. They similarly criticize Egypt's National Council of Women because it was founded by Mrs. Mubarak. Some men therefore see support of women as granting women favor over them, of tearing down family values. "The Revolution of Egyptian Men" called for marriages only to foreign women who might not seek to overpower Egyptian men.

Religion in the aftermath of the Mubarak regime offered these men new horizons and new ways of being a man: guarantees of arranged marriage and tough physical training.[35]

It is in such a climate that sexual harassment and violence against women have escalated in the period since Mubarak's resignation. For some men, attacks against women are attacks against a system. For other men, attacks on women are attacks on opponents.[36] Some Egyptian men define their masculinity by creating a safe public space for women. These men define their rights owning the streets.[37]

The Egyptian Center for Women's Rights (ECWR; est. 2005) works to make Egypt's street safe for both sexes. The ECWR reminds men to respect and protect women: their wives, neighbors, and community members. Members fear that harassment in the streets will lead to a withdrawal of women from public life as the result of street harassment.[38]

And yet, in late June 2013, Egyptian women did once again take to the streets: with men. Those who had only recently protested against military rule now showed up in its support. Egyptians had grown weary of Morsi's ever-extending government reach. Egyptians had no hunger for a return to military rule; neither did they wish to risk the direction in which the Muslim Brotherhood was taking their country. While Morsi had once championed—even appropriated—the ideals of the revolution in order to take power, he fully abandoned those ideals once in office. The Muslim Brotherhood's political wing, the Freedom and Justice Party, had rammed through an unpopular constitution, dressed in religious ideology. By taking and holding a monopoly over Egyptian politics, the party had betrayed the revolution.[39]

The military again resumed control of Egypt, and in 2014, General Abdel-Fattah al-Sisi was given a referendum to rule as Egypt's president. Less than two weeks after his election, in the most violent state-sponsored massacre in Egypt's history, Sisi's security forces killed 800 Morsi supporters, involved in a peaceful demonstration against Morsi's deposition. Sisi's move presaged a crackdown on those who challenge his authority: under his rule, Egypt has witnessed the arrest and imprisonment of many of the leaders of the January 25 Revolution, both male and female. Sisi's regime blocks access to Tahrir and has forbidden any commemoration of the January 25 uprisings.[40]

The Sisi regime has consistently blamed foreign conspiracies for the Tahrir uprisings. Consequently, the regime has muzzled Egypt's press. Informants for the state are rampant and security regularly raids the apartments and offices of suspects. Opposition leaders have left the country. Revolutionaries' hopes that the Mubarak-era state security would be dismantled have been dashed. While State Security was renamed the National Security Agency, little about Egypt's security apparatus has changed. Egypt is arguably a harsher place than it was under Mubarak.[41]

With regard to women, his main supporters: Sisi has changed Morsi's tactics.[42] He appointed a small number of women (five) to the Committee of 50 in charge of drafting the 2014 Constitution. The president of Egypt's National Council for Women Mervat Tallaway was included among the drafters of Egypt's most progressive constitution with regard to women's rights. The new constitution enshrines men and women's equality and asserts state guarantees of that equality.

The constitution also reintroduced many advances for women from the Mubarak era.⁴³ Sisi has, accordingly, presented himself as the man who saved Egypt from the "dark ages" of Muslim Brotherhood rule (despite the fact that he had once approved of the use of virginity tests).⁴⁴

In Sisi's Egypt, those who do not participate in the family politics of the state-citizen contract are pointed to as threats to the state itself. In May 2016, for example, Egypt's National Security Council announced that the "issue of spinsters" had reached the level of a security threat. The issue? Eight million unmarried women out of the country's 100+ million citizens. Colonel Ashraf Gamal, head of the Council, signaled out these women as facilitators of the kind of social decline that leads to rape and sexual harassment. He blamed street children for further hijacking Egyptian family values by stealing on the behalf of bachelors who want to get married but lack the money. Threats to the family are seen as threats to the state itself.⁴⁵

Similarly, Sisi's state labels gays in Egypt a threat to the national order. In September 2017, photos spread through social media of Egyptians waving gay pride flags at a performance of "Mashrou' Leila," a Lebanese band whose lead singer is an openly-gay male (see Chapter 12). Claiming social outrage, the state dispatched its security apparatus to arrest anyone identified in the photos—gay or not. They shut down cafes with gay clientele and blocked websites suspected of trafficking in gay content. The scale of arrests and mistreatments was unprecedented; extra-judicial killings of gay men soared. Those imprisoned for suspected homosexuality—who join the reported 68,000 Egyptians imprisoned since Sisi took power—are subjected to beatings and to reminders to uphold Egyptian family politics: humiliating anal examinations.⁴⁶

In Syria, as peaceful demonstrations quickly gave way to an armed uprising against the Syrian government, "the vibrant popular movement gradually lost its prominence."⁴⁷ By the summer of 2013, the regime resorted to placing entire towns under siege, preventing food and aid from reaching Syrian citizens. Sarin attacks by the state against its opponents followed in August 2013, as did a scorched-earth practice of destroying the infrastructure necessary for people's survival. As millions fled the country or sought resettlement elsewhere, Syria witnessed a refugee crisis.

As the regime used increasing levels of violence against its people, the number of Syrians who took up arms increased as well. (Many Syrians did not call the conflict a civil war, referring to it instead as a one-sided assault by the regime.) Women's role in Syria's revolution has therefore been marginalized, although some women formed battalions. The most visible women combatants have been Kurds, who have taken up arms against Assad's regime. The military struggle has been fought in "a male hegemonic domain"; hosts of Syrian militias fight both the Assad regime and Islamist militias.⁴⁸

By early 2015, Syria faced a humanitarian crisis. Six percent of its population had been killed since 2011. The number of wounded sat at approximately 800,000. The regime had incarcerated 150,000. Kidnappings, extortion, and sectarian revenge-killings had become common. Eighty percent of the country lived in poverty. By the summer of 2015, four million Syrians had fled the country, taking refuge in Turkey, Lebanon, Jordan, Iraq, and Europe. Another 7.6 million were internally displaced, living in refugee camps.[49]

The flight out of Syria is perilous for all and deadly for others. Smugglers charge impossibly high prices, and migrants travel in crowded, unsafe conditions, often across the Mediterranean Sea.[50] Thousands have drowned. Those who make it out face slow-moving bureaucracies, discrimination, and xenophobia. "Media has tied the revolution to terrorism. If a Syrian asking for asylum says he was with the revolution, European authorities ask for details…It's easier not to mention the revolution, or even the regime."[51]

As in neighboring Iraq, the public domain has become increasingly dangerous for women: rape is a common practice, both by the Syrian army and by armed militias. The practice of both the state and its opponents has been to rape women in front of their male family members.[52] Checkpoints are especially dangerous for women, who have been forced by circumstances to stay home. Said one Sunni woman: "They (the regime) steal mobile phones. They kick and they punch. And what have we done to deserve this?"[53] In territories controlled by ISIS through the autumn of 2018 conditions were especially harsh for women. Like men, women suffered from the capricious and violent punishments meted out by high-ranking ISIS officials. Women had to be heavily veiled outside their homes. One unveiled woman recounted that a Jordanian member of ISIS rounded up children to throw rocks at her. None of the kids took him up on his offer. But their parents warned her that her neighborhood in Damascus had become unsafe. She and her friends thus began the process of packing and moving houses—a practice they would engage in for some time.[54]

To offer their daughters protection (and to unburden themselves of a mouth to feed), parents in refugee camps within Syria are forced to marry their daughters off at an early age, often to older men. Women in refugee camps suffer from boredom and unemployment and struggle to care for their families. Safa, a mother from Homs, was grateful to be in Lebanon. "But life is terrible here, too. This neighborhood of shacks, the lack of hygiene, the germs making the kids sick…Everyone takes advantage of Syrians. There is nothing to protect us. No state, no government, no law, no human rights. Animals have more rights than we do."[55]

In devastating circumstances, women in Syria persevere in the struggle for social change. Before her capture, Razan Zaitouneh established "Women Now" development centers across Syria. Acclaimed writer Samar Yazbek continued Zaitouneh's work in the centers, which provide safe havens for free and open discussions and offer vocational training. Some women believe that the Syrian uprising has set gender relations back, but others disagree. "This [women's movement] couldn't have happened without the revolution, and I do not see how it can be stopped."[56]

Conclusion

A final reading of Fayda Hamdi's encounter with Mohammed Bouazizi focuses on her body. That body suffered in Hamdi's encounter with the young vegetable vendor in Sidi Bouzeid, Tunisia—and afterward. In Hamdi's version of events, it was Bouazizi who struck her, pulled her hair, and cut her finger when she tried to confiscate his merchandise.[57] In some versions of the encounter, Bouazizi grabbed Hamdi's breasts, spit upon her, and showered her in vulgar insults.[58] In all versions of the encounter and of the months following it, Hamdi was twice detained for having shamed Bouazizi. She was held only briefly the first time. Subsequently, however, Hamdi was held in a women's prison for three and a half months. She struggled to find legal representation; it was a relative who finally got her acquitted.[59] While Hamdi has returned to work as a civil servant, her encounters with Bouazizi and with the state were nonetheless traumatic: she now wears a head scarf to conceal the hair loss that has plagued her since the event. She suffers from persistent tremors, particularly in her hands.[60]

Trauma unites Hamdi's body with those of the many women who tangled with the state and its representatives during and after Arab Spring. Regardless of the state's many successes regarding women, those bodies are telling indictments: injured bodies, bodies of martyrs, bodies imprisoned, bodies raped, bodies assaulted by virginity tests, bodies assassinated, bodies in refugee camps, bodies at the bottom of the Mediterranean or in unofficial gravesites along migratory paths, bodies crushed by bombs, bodies in service to those who have been injured, and the bodies of mothers who grieve for their dead children. These bodies and the bodies of the millions of women who continue to circulate in the region's fraught and dangerous public realm are indeed reminders of states' ambivalence toward their female citizens. In her interactions with Bouazizi, Hamdi was tasked with embodying the state—indeed, burdened by the weight of the state's corruption—and with managing the effects of an employment crisis that was not of her making. Her imprisoned body, alone and injured, however, served as a cautionary tale for women who take up the state's mantle. In such a regard, Hamdi is similar to that of Egypt's "woman in the blue bra," whose sole trespass was her public presence.

Unlike Hamdi, however, the "woman in the blue bra" has witnessed her image transformed by graffiti artists and cartoonists. Her encounter with the state has been transformed into every woman's conquest of public space. In one cartoon, the supine figure of the "woman among women" is given liftoff. We still see her bra, but we also see what the security officer feels: her kick to his jaw.[61]

In graffiti, the woman in the blue bra is dressed as wonder woman. Independence is her super power.[62] In meme form, the blue bra is imposed on the Egyptian flag.[63]

In Syria, where the traumas of armed conflict have led to an unprecedented flourishing of creativity among people who had not dabbled in art or literature before, women use images of female bodies to protest the Assad regime's violence against its people.[64] Art has been a form of resistance and activism for Syrians.[65] The work of painter Sulafa Hijazi uses men's bodies to critique the Assad regime's violent embrace of life and death, its simultaneous adoration of mothers and slaughter of their children.[66] One of her paintings depicts a masturbating Syrian soldier: his penis is a rifle. Another depicts a pregnant rifle, its embryo encased in metal. Another, titled "Birth," portrays a supine man giving birth to instruments of war. From his vagina emerges an automatic weapon. Women are absent from these images. Their evoked female body, however—the pregnant gun, the man giving birth—allows Hijazi to critique a state whose version of motherhood has choked the life out of Syria. "Women who give birth know the meaning of life."[67]

In what one scholar calls "shock art," Samar Yazbek used her memoir *Woman in the Crossfire* to expose the indignities committed against her body and the bodies of countless other Syrians in prison. Yazbek's descriptions of her flesh—taboo in Arab society—force readers to witness the "immensity of the violence" committed by the regime.[68] Her enterprise inscribes the imprisoned female body—in this case her own—in the collective memory of the Arab Spring in Syria.

Tunisian Aminia Sboui used her body as a tapestry with which to confront historic images of the nation—morality, motherhood, and modest dress included. In 2013, while still a member of the Ukraine-based feminist organization Femen, Sboui posted several partially-naked photographs of herself on the internet. At the time of her postings, Tunisians were undergoing intense debates about the nation's future. In those debates, women figured less as actors than as symbols of secular and Islamic political ideals. To address what she saw as an absurdity, Sboui used her body as both subject and symbol: her first posted image was of herself with the words "fuck your morals" written across her naked torso. Sboui thereby transgressed that which is implicit in the Tunisian state's contract with its female citizens: in exchange for education, enfranchisement, and a modicum of representation in politics, women maintain the symbolic role of shaping and maintaining the nation's morals. By posing topless, Sboui similarly broke "one of the most important cultural proscriptions for Arab women," placing her well outside of the images of womanhood that link Arab women's morality to the state.[69]

Sboui's images divorce her from that contract. In her second posted image, Sboui claims that her body is her own. She is absent the clothing that might mark her as "Western" or "traditional," therefore leaving her unentrapped by discourses surrounding women's proper roles.[70] Response to "My body is my own" was intense. Some reminded Sboui that her body and its associated honor, in fact, belong to her family.[71] Others simply wished that she would go away.[72]

In a third posting, and in response to a brief jail sentence, "We don't need your Di-mocracy" ("Di-mocracy," she says, "because their democracy is not a democracy"), Sboui rejects the very enterprise of debating the future of a Tunisian nation in which women's freedoms are circumscribed.[73] Here, she smokes, lighting her cigarette from the flame of a Molotov cocktail, long symbolic of the destruction of the state.[74] An anarchist symbol adorns her collarbone.[75] Outside of the nation's grasp, she is neither mother to the nation nor its daughter. She does not follow her leader. She does not use her clothing to signal allegiance to others' agendas. Stripped of the state, she is free to express herself.

Notes

1 Amal Amireh, "They Are Not Like Your Daughters or Mine: Spectacles of Bad Women from the Arab Spring," in *Bad Girls of the Arab World*, Nadia Yaqoub and Rula Quawas, eds. (Austin, TX: The University of Texas Press, 2017), 116.
2 James L. Gelvin, *The Arab Uprisings: What Everyone Needs to Know* (Oxford: Oxford University Press, 2012).

3 Elizabeth Dickenson, "Anger Mismanagement: Bahrain's Crisis Escalates," *World Affairs* Vol. 175, No. 2 (2012), 44.
4 *The Independent*, January 21, 2011.
5 Asmaa Mahfouz. https://www.youtube.com/watch?v=SgjIgMdsEuk.
6 Tom Finn, "After the Revolution: The Struggle for Women's Rights in Yemen," *Dissent* Vol. 62, No. 1 (Winter 2015), 91.
7 Human Rights Watch, "Yemen's Women: Out from the Shadows," *The Guardian* (May 7, 2011).
8 Laura Kasinof, "Women Irate at Remarks of President of Yemen," *New York Times* (April 16, 2011).
9 https://edition.cnn.com/2011/11/17/opinion/yemen-revolution-afrah-nasser/.
10 Linda Herrera, *Revolution in the Age of Social Media: The Egyptian Popular Insurrection and the Internet* (London: Verso Books, 2014), 14.
11 Ethan Chorin, *Exit the Colonel: The Hidden History of the Libyan Resistance* (New York: Public Affairs Books, 2012).
12 Robin Yassin-Kassab and Leila al-Shami, *Burning Country: Syrians in Revolution and War* (London: Pluto Press, 2018), 17.
13 Yassin-Kassab and al-Shami, *Burning Country*, 35.
14 Yassin-Kassab and al-Shami, *Burning Country*, 57–58.
15 Yassin-Kassab and al-Shami, *Burning Country*, 65.
16 Yassin-Kassab and al-Shami, *Burning Country*, 69.
17 https://www.adhrb.org/2016/07/role-women-2011-bahraini-uprising/.
18 Mehdi Hasan, *New Statesman* (April 18, 2012).
19 Khadijah Arfaoui, "Women and Leadership in the post-Arab Spring: The Case of Tunisia" https:projects.iq.harvard.edu/files/violenceagainstwomenandleadershipinthepostarabspringthecaseoftunisia.docx.pdf.
20 Mounira M. Charrad and Amina Zarrough, "The Arab Spring and Women's Rights in Tunisia." *E-International Relations*; www.e-ir.info/2013/09/04/the-arab-spring-and-womens-rights-in-tunisia/.
21 Al-Monitor.com (July 28, 2017).
22 Sawsan Bastawy, "Women's Rights in Post-Revolution Egypt." Afsar.org.uk.
23 Bastawy, "Women's Rights in Post-Revolution Egypt."
24 Elisabeth Johansson-Nogués, "Gendering the Arab Spring? Rights and (in)security of Tunisian, Egyptian and Libyan Women," *Security Dialogue* Vol. 44, Nos. 5–6 (2013), 393.
25 Ronald Bruce St. John, *Libya: From Colony to Revolution* (Oxford: One World Publications, 2012), 292.
26 Chorin, *Exit the Colonel*.
27 Anjali Kamat interviews attorneys Salwa Bughaigis and Hanaa al-Gallal, "Libyans Organize Citizen Councils to Run Cities Liberated from Pro-Qaddafi Loyalists" (February 28, 2011). www.democracynow.org/2011/2/28/libyans_organize_citizen_councils_to_run.
28 K. Laub, "Stories of Egypt's Uprisings Victims Slowly Emerge." Retrieved from http://www.salon.com/2011/02/08/egypt_protests_victims_hosni_mubarak/.
29 Reliefweb.int.
30 Mona Eltahawy, *Of Hymens and Headscarves: Why They Hate Us* (New York: Harper Collins, 2015), 18–19.
31 Adel Iskander, "Of Men and Hymen," *Egypt Independent*, December 25, 2011, cited in Adel Iskander, *Egypt in Flux: Essays on an Unfinished Revolution* (Cairo: AUC Press, 2013), 94–95.
32 Mina Kato, "Women of Egypt," *The Cairo Review of Global Affairs* (Winter 2017); www.thecairoreview.com/essays/women-of-egypt.
33 Iskander, *Egypt in Flux*, 94.
34 Cited from Dalia Labib Linssen, "Reconsidering the Image of the Blue Bra: Photography, Conflict and Cultural Memory in the 2011-2013 Egyptian Uprising," *Humanities* Vol. 7, No. 1 (2018), 27; https://doi.org/10.3390/h7010027https://www.mdpi.com/2076-0787/7/1/27.

35. Mustafa Abdulla, "Masculinity on Shifting Grounds: Emasculation and the rise of the Islamist Political Scene in post-Mubarak Egypt," in *Masculinities in Egypt and the Arab World*, Helen Rizzo, ed., *Cairo Papers in Social Science* (Cairo: AUC Press, 2014) Vol. 33, No. 1 (Spring 2014), 58–62.
36. Abdulla, "Masculinity on Shifting Grounds," 67.
37. Hellen Rizzo, "The Role of Women's Rights Organizations in Promoting Masculine Responsibility: The Anti-Sexual Harassment Campaign in Egypt," in Rizzo, ed., *Masculinities in Egypt and the Arab World*, 105.
38. Rizzo, "The Role of Women's Rights Organizations in Promoting Masculine Responsibility," 115.
39. Iskander, "Epilogue," *Egypt in Flux*, 163–164.
40. Amr Darrag, "Ten Years on from the Arab Spring, Sisi Has Made Life in Egypt Hellish," *The Guardian* (February 11, 2021); https://www.theguardian.com/commentisfree/2021/feb/11/president-sisi-mubarak-egypt-arab-spring.
41. Declan Walsh, "Why Was an Italian Graduate Student Tortured and Murdered in Egypt?" *The New York Times* (August 15, 2017).
42. Shreen Abouelnega, *Women in Revolutionary Egypt: Gender and the New Geographies of Identity* (Cairo: AUC Press, 2016), 24.
43. Mina Kato, "Women of Egypt," *The Cairo Review of Global Affairs* (Winter 2017). www.thecairoreview.com/essays/women-of-egypt.
44. Eltahawy, *Of Hymens and Headscarves*, 18.
45. Rami Galal," Egypt's Next National Security Threat: All the Single Ladies?" http://www.almonitor.com/pulse/originals/2016/05/egypt-spinsters-national-security-threat.html.
46. Sudarsan Raghavan, "Egypt Cracks Down on Gay People: Midnight Raids and Chatroom Traps Drive LGBT Community Further Underground," *The Washington Post* (October 19, 2017).
47. Yassin-Kassab and al-Shami, *Burning Country*, 76.
48. Yassin-Kassab and al-Shami, *Burning Country*, 120.
49. Yassin-Kassab and al-Shami, *Burning Country*, 147–153.
50. Maher, from Hama, cited in Wendy Pearlman, *We Crossed a Bridge and It Trembled: Voices from Syria* (New York: Custom House, 2018), 224.
51. Imad, from Selamiyeh, cited in Pearlman, *We Crossed a Bridge*, 249.
52. Yassin-Kassab and al-Shami, *Burning Country*, 79.
53. Yassin-Kassab and al-Shami, *Burning Country*, 111.
54. Marcell, cited in Pearlman, *We Crossed a Bridge*, 198–199.
55. Safa, cited in Pearlman, *We Crossed a Bridge*, 246.
56. Yassin Kassab and al-Shami, *Burning Country*, 180.
57. Al-Ahram Online, 16 December, 2014. "Interview with Fayda Hamdi."
58. Amireh, "They Are Not Like Your Daughters or Mine," 117.
59. Al-Ahram Online, December 16, 2014. "Interview with Fayda Hamdi."
60. Amireh, "They Are not like Your Daughters or Mine," 117.
61. https://search.yahoo.com/search?fr=mcafee&type=E210US714G0&p=carlos+lattuf+images+2011.
62. Cited from Dalia Labib Linssen, "Reconsidering the Image of the Blue Bra: Photography, Conflict and Cultural Memory in the 2011–2013 Egyptian Uprising," *Humanities* Vol. 7, No. 1 (2018), 27; https://doi.org/10.3390/h7010027https://www.mdpi.com/2076-0787/7/1/27.
63. Bluebra.wordpress.com.
64. "Introduction," in *Syria Speaks: Art and Culture from the Frontline*, Malu Halasa, Zaher Omareen, and Nawara Mahfoud, eds. (London: Saqi Books, 2014), viii.
65. miriam cooke, *Dancing in Damascus: Creativity, Resilience and the Syrian Revolution* (London and New York: Routledge, 2017), 1.

66 Sulafa Hijazi, "Ongoing," in Halasa, Omareen and Mahfoud, *Syria Speaks*, 11.
67 Hijazi, "Ongoing," 11, 10, 15.
68 cooke, Dancing in Damascus, 54–55.
69 Anne Marie F. Butler, "Fuck Your Morals: The Body Activism of Amina Sboui," in Yaqub and Qawwas, *Bad Girls of the Arab World*, 132.
70 Amina Sboui, "My Body Belongs to Me," cited in Butler, "Fuck Your Morals," 139.
71 Butler, "Fuck Your Morals," 139.
72 Butler, "Fuck Your Morals," 141.
73 Amina Sboui, Facebook post, cited in Butler, "Fuck Your Morals," 139.
74 Butler, "Fuck Your Morals," 139.
75 Butler, Fuck Your Morals," 141.

Further Reading

Abraham Marcus, *The Middle East on the Eve of Modernity: Aleppo in the Eighteenth Century* (New York: Columbia University Press, 1989).
Afaf Lutfi al-Sayyid Marsot, *Women and Men in Eighteenth-Century Egypt* (Austin: University of Texas Press, 1995).
Afsaneh Najmabadi, "Crafting an Educated Housewife in Iran," in *Remaking Women: Feminism and Modernity in the Middle East*, Lila Abu-Lughod, ed. (Princeton: Princeton University Press, 1998): 103–139.
Afsaneh Najmabadi, *Professing Selves: Transsexuality and Same-Sex Desire in Contemporary Iran* (Durham: Duke University Press, 2013).
Afsaneh Najmabadi, *Women with Mustaches, Men Without Beards* (Berkeley and Los Angeles: University of California Press, 2005).
Akram Khater, *Inventing Home: Emigration, Gender, and the Middle Class in Lebanon 1870-1920* (Berkeley: University of California Press, 2001).
Amrita Basu, ed., *Women's Movements in the Global Era: The Power of Local Feminisms* (Boulder, CO: Westview Press, 2016).
Arielle Gordon, "From Guerrilla Girls to Zainabs: Reassessing the Figure of the "Militant Woman" in the Iranian Revolution." *Journal of Middle East Women's Studies* 17, 1 (2021): 64–95.
Arlene Macleod, *Accommodating Protest: Working Women, The New Veiling, and Change in Cairo* (New York: Columbia University, 1991).
Asef Bayat, *Life as Politics: How Ordinary People Change the Middle East* (Stanford: Stanford University Press, 2013).
Beth Baron, *Egypt as a Woman: Nationalism, Gender, and Politics* (Berkeley: University of California Press, 2005).
Beth Baron, *The Women's Awakening in Egypt: Culture, Society and the Press* (New Haven, CT: Yale University Press, 1994).
Betool Khedairi, *A Sky So Close*, Murayman Jamil, trans. (New York: Anchor Books, 2002).
Billie Melman, *Women's Orients: English Women and the Middle East, 1718-1918: Sexuality, Religion and Work* (Ann Arbor, MI: University of Michigan Press, 2018).
Cagla Diner and Şule Toktaş, "Waves of Feminism in Turkey: Kemalist, Islamist and Kurdish Women's Movements in an Age of Globilization," *Journal of Balkan and Near East Studies* 12, 1 (March 2010).
Camron Amin, *The Making of the Modern Iranian Woman: Gender, State Policy, and Popular Culture* (Gainesville: University of Florida Press, 2002).

Cynthia Nelson, *Doria Shafik, Egyptian Feminist: A Woman Apart* (Gainesville, FL: University of Florida Press, 1996).

Darina al-Joundi with Mohamed Kacimi, *The Day Nina Simone Stopped Singing*, Marjolijn De Jager, trans. (New York: Feminist Press, 2011).

David Motadel, "Qajar Monarchs in Imperial Germany," *Past and Present* 213 (November 2011): 191–235.

Dawn Chatty and Annika Rabo, eds., *Organizing Women: Formal and Informal Women's Groups in the Middle East* (New York: Berg Publications, 2001).

Deniz Kandiyoti, ed., *Women, Islam and the State* (Philadelphia: Temple 1991).

Dina Rizq Khoury, *Iraq in Wartime: Soldiering, Martyrdom and Remembrance* (Cambridge: Cambridge University Press, 2013).

Donald Quataert, "Clothing Laws, State, and Society in the Ottoman Empire," *International Journal of Middle East Studies* 29 (1997): 403–425.

Donald Quataert, *Ottoman Manufacturing in the Age of the Industrial Revolution* (Cambridge: Cambridge University Press, 1993).

Dror Ze'evi, *Producing Desire: Changing Sexual Discourse in the Ottoman Middle East, 1500-1900* (Berkeley and Los Angeles: University of California Press, 2006).

Ebba Augustin, ed., *Palestinian Women: Identity and Experience* (London: Zed Books, 1993).

Eileen S. Kuttab, "Palestinian Women in the *Intifada*: Fighting on Two Fronts," *Arab Studies Quarterly* 15, 2 (Spring 1993).

Elif Ekin Akşit, "Fatma Aliye's Stories: Ottoman Marriages Beyond the Harem," *Journal of Family History* 25, 3 (2010): 207–218.

Elizabeth Thompson, *Colonial Citizens: Republican Rights, Paternal Privilege, and Gender in French Syria and Lebanon* (New York: Columbia University Press, 2000).

Ellen L. Fleischmann, *The Nation and its 'New' Women: The Palestinian Women's Movement 1920-1948* (Berkeley: University of California Press, 2003).

Elyse Semerdjian, *"Off the Straight Path": Illicit Sex, Law, and Community in Ottoman Aleppo* (Syracuse: Syracuse University Press, 2008).

Fadwa El Guindi, *Veil: Modesty, Privacy, and Resistance* (Bloomsbury Academic, 1999).

Faegheh Shirazi, ed., *Muslim Women in War and Crisis* (Austin: University of Texas, 2010).

Fariba Zarinebaf-Shahr, "The Role of Women in the Urban Economy of Istanbul, 1700-1850," *International Labor and Working-Class History*, 60 (2001): 141–152.

Fatma Kassem, *Palestinian Women: Narrative Histories and Gendered Memory* (London: Zed Publications, 2011).

George Gawrych, "Şamseddin Sami, Women and Social Consciousness in the Late Ottoman Empire," *Middle Eastern Studies* 46, 1 (2010): 97–115.

Haleh Esfandiari, *Reconstructed Lives: Women and Iran's Islamic Revolution* (Baltimore: Johns Hopkins University Press, 1997).

Halide Edip, *Memoirs of Halide Adivar Edib*, Hülya Adak, trans. (New York: Gorgias Press, 2004).

Helen Rizzo, ed., *Masculinities in Egypt and the Arab World*, Cairo Papers in Social Science (Cairo: AUC Press, 2014) Vol. 33, No. 1 (Spring 2014).

Irwin Schick, "Print Capitalism and Women's Agency in the Late Ottoman Empire," *Comparative Studies of South Asia, Africa, and the Middle East* 31, 1 (2011): 196–216.

Islah Jad, "Islamist Women of Hamas: between Feminism and Nationalism," *Inter-Asia Cultural Studies*, 12 (November 2011).

Jamal Nasser and Roger Heacock, eds., *Intifada: Palestine at the Crossroads* (New York: Birzeit University and Praeger Publishers, 1991).

James L Gelvin, *The Arab Uprisings: What Everyone Needs to Know* (Oxford: Oxford University Press, 2012).

Janet Afary and Kevin B. Anderson, *Foucault and the Iranian Revolution: Gender and the Seductions of Islamism* (Chicago: University of Chicago Press, 2005).

Janet Afary, *The Iranian Constitutional Revolution, 1906–1911* (New York: Columbia University Press, 2004).

Jennifer M. Scarce "The Architecture and Decoration of the Gulestan Palace: The Aims and Achievements of Fath Ali Shah (1797-1834) and Nasser al-Din Shah (1834-1896)," *Iranian Studies* 34, 1/4 (2001): 103–116.

Judith Tucker, *In the House of Law* (Berkeley: University of California Press, 1998).

Judith Tucker, *Women in Nineteenth Century Egypt* (Cambridge: Cambridge University Press, 1985).

Judy Mabro, *Veiled Half Truths: Western Travelers' Perceptions of Middle Eastern Women* (London: I.B. Tauris, 1991).

Julie M. Peteet, *Gender in Crisis: Women and the Palestinian Resistance Movement* (New York: Columbia University Press, 1991).

Khaled el-Rouayheb, *Before Homosexuality in the Arab-Islamic World, 1500-1800* (Chicago: University of Chicago Press, 2005).

Kristian Coates Ulrichsen, *The First World War in the Middle East* (London: Hurst and Company, 2014).

Lamia R. Shehadeh, ed., *Women and War in Lebanon* (Gainesville: University of Florida Press, 1999).

Laura Bier, *Revolutionary Womanhood: Feminisms, Modernity and the State in Nasser's Egypt* (Stanford: Stanford University Press, 2011).

Leila Ahmed, *A Quiet Revolution: The Veil's Resurgence from the Middle East to North America* (New Haven: Yale University Press, 2011).

Leila al-Shami, *Burning Country: Syrians in Revolution and War* (London: Pluto Press, 2018).

Leslie Peirce, *The Imperial Harem, Women and Sovereignty in the Ottoman Empire* (Oxford and New York: Oxford University Press, 1993).

Lila Abu-Lughod, *Do Muslim Women Really Need Saving?* (Cambridge, MA: Harvard University Press, 2013).

Linda Herrera, *Revolution in the Age of Social Media: The Egyptian Popular Insurrection and the Internet* (London: Verso Books, 2014).

Lisa Pollard, *Nurturing the Nation: The Family Politics of Modernizing, Colonizing, and Liberating Egypt, 1805-1923* (Berkeley: University of California Press, 2005).

Mahnaz Khousha, *Voices from Iran: The Changing Lives of Iranian Women* (Syracuse: Syracuse University Press, 2002).

Mai Ghoussoub and Emma Sinclair-Webb, eds., *Imagined Masculinities: Male Identity and Culture in the Modern Middle East* (London: Saqi Press, 2004).

Malek Abisaab, *Militant Women of a Fragile Nation* (Syracuse: Syracuse University Press, 2010).

Malu Halasa, Zaher Omareen, and Nawara Mahfoud, eds., *Syria Speaks: Art and Culture from the Frontline* (London: Saqi Books, 2014).

Margot Badran, *Feminism in Islam: Secular and Religious Convergences* (Oxford: One World Press, 2009).

Margot Badran, *Feminists, Islam and Nation: Gender and the Making of Modern Egypt* (Princeton: Princeton University Press, 1995).

Marilyn Booth, ed., *Harem Histories: Envisioning Places, Living Spaces* (Durham: Duke University Press, 2010).

Marilyn Booth, *May Her Likes Be Multiplied: Biography and Gender Politics in Egypt* (Berkeley: University of California Press, 2001).

Mary Ann Fay, *Unveiling the Harem: Elite Women and the Paradox of Seclusion in Eighteenth Century Cairo*, Middle East Studies Beyond Dominant Paradigms (Syracuse: Syracuse University Press, 2012).

Mateo Muhammed Farzaneh, *Iranian Women and Gender in the Iran-Iraq War* (Syracuse: Syracuse University Press, 2021).

Maya Mikdashi, *Sextarianism: Sovereignty, Secularism, and the State in Lebanon* (Stanford: Stanford University Press, 2022).

Melanie S. Tanielian, *The Charity of War: Famine, Humanitarian Aid and WWI in the Middle East* (Palo Alto: Stanford University Press, 2018).

Mervat Hatem, "Economic and Political Liberation in Egypt and the Demise of State Feminism," *International Journal of Middle East Studies* 24, 2 (1992): 231–251.

miriam cooke, *Dancing in Damascus: Creativity, Resilience and the Syrian Revolution* (London and New York: Routledge, 2017).

Mohja Kahf, *Western Representations of the Muslim Woman from Termagant to Odalisque* (Austin, TX: The University of Texas Press, 1999).

Mona Eltahawy, *Of Hymens and Headscarves: Why they Hate Us* (New York: Harper Collins, 2015).

Mona Russell, *Creating the New Egyptian Woman: Consumerism, Education, and National Identity, 1863-1922* (New York: Palgrave, 2004).

Monica Ringer, *Education, Religion, and the Discourse of Cultural Reform in Iran* (Costa Mesa: Mazda, 2001).

Nadia Hijab, "Women and Work in the Arab World," in *Women and Power in the Middle East*, Susan Slymovics and Suad Joseph, eds. (Philadelphia: University of Pennsylvania Press, 2001).

Nadia Yaqoub and Rula Quawas, eds., *Bad Girls of the Arab World* (Austin, TX: The University of Texas Press, 2017).

Nadje al-Ali and Nicola Pratt, *What Kind of Liberation: Women and the Occupation of Iraq* (Berkeley: University of California Press, 2009).

Nadje Al-Ali, *Iraqi Women: Untold Stories from 1948 to the Present* (London: Zed Books, 2012).

Nikki Keddie, *Women in the Middle East: Past and Present* (Princeton: Princeton University Press, 2006).

Nilüfer Göle, *The Forbidding Modern* (Ann Arbor: University of Michigan Press, 1996).

Noga Efrati, *Women in Iraq: Past Meets Present* (New York: Columbia University Press, 2012).

Nuha al-Radi, *Baghdad Diaries: A Woman's Account of War and Exile* (New York: Vintage Press, 1998).

On Barak, *On Time: Technology and Temporality in Modern Egypt* (Berkeley: University of California Press, 2013).

Orit Bashkin, "Representations of Women in the Writings of the Intelligentsia in Hashemite Iraq, 1921-1958," *Journal of Middle East Women's Studies* 4, 1 (Winter 2008).

Oz Almog, *The Sabra: The Creation of the New Jew* (Berkeley: University of California Press, 2000).

Parvin Paidar, *Women and the Political Process in Twentieth-Century Iran* (Cambridge: Cambridge University Press, 1995).

Penny Johnson and Eileen Kuttab, "Where Have All the Women (and Men) Gone? Reflections on Gender and the Second *Intifada*," *Feminist Review* 69 (December 1, 2001): 21–43.

Pernille Arenfeldt and Nawal Al-Hassan Golley, *Mapping Arab Women's Movements: A Century of Transformation from Within* (Cairo: American University in Cairo Press, 2012).

Radwa Ashour, Ferial J. Ghazoul, and Hasna Reda-Mekdashi, eds. *Arab Women Writers: A Critical Reference Guide 1873–1999* (Cairo: The American University in Cairo Press, 2008).

Rana Kabbani, *Imperial Fictions: Europe's Myths of Orient* (London: Saqi Press, 2008).

Reina Lewis, *Women, Travel and the Ottoman Harem: Rethinking Orientalism* (New Brunswick, NJ: Rutgers University Press, 2004).

Relli Shechter, ed., *Transitions in Domestic Consumption and Family Life in the Modern Middle East: Houses in Motion* (New York: Palgrave, 2003).

Rifa'at Tahtawi, *An Imam in Paris: Al-Tahtawi's Visit to Paris, 1826-1831*, Translated, Edited, and Introduced by Daniel Newman (London: Saqi Books, 2004).

Rita Stephan and Mounira M. Charrad, eds. *Women Rising in and Beyond Arab Spring* (New York: New York University Press, 2020).

Robert Hunter, *The Palestinian Uprising: A War by Other Means*, 2nd ed. (Berkeley: University of California Press, 1993).

Robin Yassin, https://www.msn.com/en-us/feedKassab.

Roksana Bahramitash and Hadi S. Esfahani, "Nimble Fingers No Longer! Women's Work in Iran," in *Contemporary Iran*, Ali Gheissari, ed. (Oxford: Oxford University Press, 2009): 77–122.

Saba Mahmoud, *Politics of Piety: The Islamic Revival and the Feminist Subject* (Princeton: Princeton University Press, 2004).

Sahar Amer, "Medieval Arab Lesbians and Lesbian-like Women," *Journal of the History of Sexuality* 18, 2 (May 2009): 215–236.

Sahar Amer, *What is Veiling* (Chapel Hill: UNC Press, 2014).

Sally K. Gallagher, *Making Do in Damascus: Navigating a Generation of Change in Family and Work* (Syracuse: Syracuse University Press, 2012).

Samar Habib, *Female Homosexuality in the Middle East* (New York: Routledge, 2007).

Sheila Katz, *Women and Gender in Early Jewish and Palestinian Nationalism* (Gainesville: University of Florida Press, 2009).

Shereen El Feki, *Sex and the Citadel: An Intimate Life in a Changing Arab World* (New York: Random House, 2013).

Sherifa Zuhur, *Revealing Reveiling: Islamist Gender Ideology in Contemporary Egypt* (Albany: SUNY Press, 1992).

Shirin Ebadi, *Iran Awakening: One Woman's Journey to Reclaim her Life and Country* (New York: Random House, 2006).

Shreen Abouelnega, *Women in Revolutionary Egypt: Gender and the New Geographies of Identity* (Cairo: AUC Press, 2016).

Susynne M. McElrone, "Nineteenth-Century Qajar Women in the Public Sphere: An Alternative Historical and Historiographical Reading of the Roots of Iranian Women's Activism," *Comparative Studies of South Asia, Africa and the Middle East* 25, 2 (2005): 297–317.

Tim Niblock, ed., *Iraq: The Contemporary State* (London: St. Martin's Press, 1992).

Valentine M. Moghadam, ed., *Gender and National Identity* (London: Verso Press, 1994).

Valentine Moghadam, "Women's Economic Participation in the Middle East: What Difference Has the Neoliberal Policy Turn Made?," *Journal of Middle East Women's Studies* 1, 1 (2005): 110–146.

Valorie K. Vojdik, "Masculinities, Feminism, and the Turkish Headscarf Ban: Revisiting Şahin v. Turkey," in *Masculinities and the Law*, Frank Rudy Cooper, ed., Vol. 13 (New York: New York University Press, 2020): 270–290.

Wendy Pearlman, *We Crossed a Bridge and It Trembled: Voices from Syria* (New York: Custom House, 2018).

Wilson Jacobs, *Working Out Egypt* (Durham: Duke University Press, 2010).

Yasmin Husein Al-Jawaheri, *Women in Iraq: The Gender Impact of International Sanctions* (Boulder, CO: Lynne Reinner, 2008).

Zehra F. Arat, ed., *Deconstructing Images of "The Turkish Woman"* (New York: Palgrave, 1999).

Zeina Abirached, *A Game for Swallows*, Edward Gauvin, trans. (Minneapolis: Graphic Universe, 2012).

Zeynep Çelik, *The Remaking of Ottoman Istanbul* (Berkeley: University of California Press, 1993).

Additional Resources

Encyclopedia of Women in Islamic Cultures, Suad Joseph and Afsaneh Najmabadi, eds. (Boston: Brill, 2003–2007). [Supplemented regularly].

Routledge Handbook on Women in the Middle East, Suad Joseph and Zeina Zaatari, eds. (London and New York: Taylor and Francis, 2022).

Index

Note: *Italic* page numbers refer to figures and page numbers followed by "n" denote endnotes.

Abduh, Muhammad 80
Abdül Hamid II 53–54, 66, 78, 80, 83–84, 100, 109, 192
Abouelnaga, Shireen 5
al-Abid Bayhum, Nazik 100, 111, 117, 121
activism 151, 169, 209; feminist activism 158; within Hamas 259; labor 184, 185; mass-based activism 251; mobilization and 210; organization and 97–98; and politics 121, 252, 259; social 112, 119, 267; and volunteerism 249; women 98, 101, 160, 168, 173, 241
Aden Women's Club 156, 157
al-Afghani, Jamal al-Din 83
Aflaq, Michel 136
African slaves 14, 72
age-specific gender segregation 181
Ahmed, Leila 5, 190
Ajami, Mary: *The Bride* 96
Akhunzadeh, Mirza Fathi Ali 77, 84
Alexandria, Why? (Chahine) 206
Al-Ali, Nadje 5
Ali, Hussein bin 113
Ali, Madiha Hasan 157
Ali, Mubarrat Muhammad 111, 116, 180
Ali, Muhammad 21–25, 47, 53, 55–56, 60, 61, 63, 103
Aliha bint Ali Chalabi 14
aliyahs 134
Aliye, Fatma 100; *The Ladies' Own Gazette* 96; *Muslim Women* 96; *Women in Islam* 92–93
Ali, Zine al-Abidine Ben 265, 270
al-Kassem, Fatma 259
All My Life 207

American invasion 148, 173, 240
American King-Crane Commission 121
American-led invasion of Iraq 186
American troops land in Lebanon 160, *161*
Amer, Sahar 5
Amin, Cameron 5
Amini, Mahsa 147
Amin, Qasim 81, 156; *The Liberation of Women* 80, 82, 94; *The New Woman* 80
Anatolian Women's Association for Patriotic Defense 112
andarun women 13, 17
Anglo-Egyptian Convention of 1877 38
Anglo-Iranian agreement 38
Anglo-Ottoman Treaty 23
anis 265
anjumans 99–100, 103
anti-Barbie campaign 233, 235
anti-foreign agenda 103
anti-protest laws 104, 184
anti-shah movement 242
anti-Westernism 227
Antun, Farah 84
April 6 Youth Movement, Egypt 267
Arab/Arabic: identity 137; literary traditions 95; modernization 141; nationalism 120, 137; nationalist movement 111, 113, 121, 137, 160, 162; socialist nationalism 169
Arab Girls' Awakening Society 117
Arabian Nights 30–33, 42
Arab Spring: accusations of trespass 264; activism 269; Bahraini "women of Arab Spring" 269; Coalition of the February 17 Revolution

272; Damascus Spring 269; Egypt's April 6 Youth Movement 267; female participants in 264; manhood in 273; National Security Agency 274; National Security Council, Egypt 275; NCA, in Tunisia 270; Qadhafy's regime 268; "quartet" of civil society associations 271; Supreme Council of the Armed Forces 271, 273; in Syria 278; Syrian Observatory for Human Rights 273; Syria's Local Coordination Committees 269; of 2011 173; UN Handbook for Legislation on Violence Against Women 271; women in 265; Women Journalists Without Chains 267
Arab Spring-like movement 250
Arab Women's Association (AWA) 122
Arab Women's Executive (AWE) 122
Arab Women's Society (AWS) 157
Arab Women's Union of Nablus 118
Arafat, Yasser 253, 255
Arfaoui, Khadijah 95
Arif, Abd al-Salam 138
Armenian community 67
Armenian women 17, 99
Armenian Women's Beneficent Society 99
Article 45 of the 1973 Constitution 142
Ashkenazi (European) Jewish women 135
Ashrawi, Hanan 255, 256, *256*
Ashtiani, Yusuf 82
al-Assad, Asma al-Akhras 148
al-Assad, Bashar 142–143, 148, 149, *150*, 265, 266
al-Assad, Hafez 136, 142, 143, *143*
Astarabadi, Bibi Khanom 94; *The Vices of Men* 93
Atatürk *see* Kemal, Mustafa
Atlantic Revolutions 72
Atlantic World 72, 86
al-Attar, Suad 138
Attiya, Rawya 137
Auto-Emancipation (Pinsker) 40
Avierino, Alexandra Khuri 95; *The Intimate Companion* 96
AWA *see* Arab Women's Association (AWA)
AWE *see* Arab Women's Executive (AWE)
AWS *see* Arab Women's Society (AWS)
Ayesh, Naila 260

Azbakiyya Gardens 56, *58*
Aziz, Abdül 51, 53
al-Azma, Yusuf 113

Ba'athists 137, 139, 170, 250
Ba'ath party 139, 142, 185, 247, 248
"bad *hijab*" 147, 220, 230
al-Badiyya, Bahithat 101
Badran, Margot 5
Baer, Gabriel 87n1
Bahai movement 83
Bahraini "women of Arab Spring" 269
al-Bakr, Ahmed Hassan 138
Balfour Declaration 115
El-Baradei, Mohammed 267
baraka 171
Baring, Evelyn 42
Baron, Beth 5
Bashkin, Orit 5
Bastard of Istanbul (Shafak) 229
Bayat, Asef 5, 174–175
Bayhum, Nazik Abid 113
Bedouin 20, 167, 193, 206
Beijing Conference 172
Beijing Declaration and Platform for Action 171–173
Beirut 3, 25, 84, 90, 95, 96, 98, 99, 111, 116, 117, 120, 121, 161–163, 164, 194, 208, 210, 231
Ben-Gurion, David 134, 135
Bey, Azmi 111
BFASS *see* British and Foreign Anti-Slavery Society (BFASS)
Bier, Laura 5
Bint al-Nil 159
"Black Friday" 243
Blunt, Anne 40
Booth, Marilyn 5
Bouazizi, Mohammed 264, 266, 276–277
Bouchamaoui, Madame Widad 271
Bourghiba, Habib 265
Bouzid, Nouri 206
boyat 208, 214, 215
Bremer, L. Paul 249
The Bride (Ajami) 96
Bridgman, Frederick Arthur 37, *38*
British and Foreign Anti-Slavery Society (BFASS) 38
British Civilizing Mission 118
British Mandate in Iraq 118, 183
British merchants 23
Burghaigis, Salwa 272
Bush, George H.W. 255

Bush, George W. *149*, 173
Butler, Anne Marie F. 5

Cairo 3, *12*, 17, 22, 25, 47, 55–61, 68, 80, 84, 90, 95, 96, 98, 100, 101, 111, 113, 171, 184, 191, 195, 226, 267, 273
capitalism 2, 82, 179, 224
capitalist forms of production 179
CCFTC *see* Central Council of Federated Trade Unions (CCFTC)
Cedar Revolution, Lebanon 163, 173, *174*
CEDAW *see* Convention on the Elimination of all forms of Discrimination Against Women (CEDAW)
Central Council of Federated Trade Unions (CCFTC) 194
Chahine, Youssef: *Alexandria, Why?* 206
Chamoun, Camille 161
Chancellor, John 122
Chardin, Jean 33
charismatic imams 228
Christian: conversion of harem 41; missionaries 30, 41, 44, 50–51, 55, 67, 118; women in Iran 99, 123, 160, 161, 203, 223
Christian Women's Solidarity Association 160
Citizens Rights Movement 166
civil initiative 4, 5, 155, 175
civil society organizations 142, 173, 268, 271, 272
civil war 8, 104, 160, 162, 163, 186, 189, 193, 204, 209, 250, 271–273, 275
clerics and women's associations 100
Coalition of the February 17 Revolution 272
Coalition Provisional Authority (CPA) 249
colonialism 2, 179, 205
Committee of Public instruction 55
Committee of Union and Progress (CUP) 109
Committee on The Political Rights of Women 159
Committee on the Status of Women 166
communities: Armenian community 67; gay/lesbian community 200; LGBTQ community, Lebanon 163; Palestine community 115, 122; pastoral communities 20
compulsory education laws 60

The Consequences and Circumstances of Words and Deeds (Taymur) 94
conservativism 169, 255
Constitutional Revolution in Iran 67, 84, 85, 91, 92, 100, 105
consumerism 16, 23, 97, 140, 185, 224, 229, 233, 241
consumption 7, 16, 19, 22, 26, 56, 60, 214, 223, 224, 228, 229, 232, 234, 241, 261
Convention on the Elimination of all forms of Discrimination Against Women (CEDAW) 172, 189–190
Conversations and Journals in Egypt and Malta (Senior) 42
cooke, miriam 5
"cosmetic tourism" company in Lebanon 231
cottage industry 7, 19, 23, 24, 180, 194–196
Council of Lebanese Woman 163
countryside women 19, 114
CPA *see* Coalition Provisional Authority (CPA)
Craven, Elizabeth 31
Cromer, Lord 43
cross-sectarianism 120
CUP *see* Committee of Union and Progress (CUP)
Curzon, George 66–67

"*dada*" 15, 79
dallalahs 17
"Damascus Spring" 268, 269
Daughter of the Nile (Shafik)) 158
Davis, James 158
Dawlatabadi, Sadiqah 99, 103; *Women's Language* 97
The Day Nina Simone Stopped Singing (Joundi) 163
decoupling 169–171, 258
Defense Service Law 135
Degher, Assia 206
"Democracy in the Family means Democracy in Society" 168
Democratic Society Party (DSP) 169
Depping, Georges-Bernard: *Historical Background on the Manners and Customs of Nations* 74
al-Din al-Bitar, Salah 136
al-Din, Huda Shams 206
al-Din, Muzzafir 67, 102, 103

292 Index

al-Din Shah, Nasir 23, 64–67, *65*, 94, 99, 101, 102
disenfranchisement 155, 159
domestic: labor 192–194; life 33, 34, 36–39; work 179, 192–194, 208
Douglas, Frederick 72
Drop of Milk Campaign 116
DSP *see* Democratic Society Party (DSP)

The Eastern Girl (Hashim) 96
Eastern Women's Conferences in Damascus 120, 121
economic reorganization 184
ECWR *see* Egyptian Center for Women's Rights (ECWR)
Edib, Halide 96, 101, 109, 111, *112*, 112–113
education: compulsory education laws 60; educational system 42–44, 50, 55, 81, 187, 189, 190; Education Council 50; and labor 140, 142; missionary educators 42; Society for Education 67; state-sponsored education for women 187; *A Trustworthy Guide to the Education of Girls and Boys* (Tahtawi) 75
Efendi, Ahmet Midhat 75
effendiyya 222
Efrati, Noga 5
EFU *see* Egyptian Feminist Union (EFU)
Egypt: agricultural production 22; Anglo-Egyptian Convention of 1877 38; April 6 Youth Movement 267; French invasion of 21; khedives 60; modernization 43; National Council for Women Mervat Tallaway 274; National Council of Women 273; National Security Council 275; security apparatus 274; textile industry 180
Egyptian Center for Women's Rights (ECWR) 274
Egyptian Constitution of 1956 137
Egyptian Correspondence Schools 192
Egyptian female labor activism 185
Egyptian Feminist Union (EFU) 119
Egyptian Nationalist Congress 101
Egyptian nationalist movement 124
Egyptian Revolution, 1919 60, 85, 96, 97, 113, 119, 123, 124, 189, 235
Egyptian woman 81, 119, 220, 228
Eight Heavens (Shaykh and Ruhi) 83
Ekram, Recaizade: *Progress* 75

elite women 13, 14, 26, 90, 91, 113, 116, 117
empire 2, 7–9, 12, 24, 30, 33, 50–54, 76, 78, 79, 82, 131, 201, 224
era of reform 223
Erdoğan, Recep Tayyip 151, 229
Essebsi, Beja Caid 271
Europe: administrators 108; Christian women 223; civilization 43; empires 30; governesses 51; ideas 116; imperialism 86, 90, 97; industrialization 7, 22, 91; influence in Iran 23; officials 118; powers 50, 91; social models and political systems 71; textile trade 16; travel literature 30–33; women 30, 44, 91, 118, 224; writers 30, 44
European and American missionaries 41
European and Russian Jewish immigrants 111
European imagination, Middle Eastern women in 29–30; domestic life 33–34, 36–39; gendered landscapes 40; harems 41–44; travel literature and women 30–33; veiled encounters 39
European-style military training 48
European-style textiles factory 182
"eve of modernity" 3
"Execution Without Trial by the Moorish King" (Régnault) 36
An Extraction of Gold in a Summary of Paris (Tahtawi) 74

factories 22, 23, 109, 247; European-style textiles factory 182; "factory girl" 3, 5, 180; Ottoman Empire 181; silk factory *181*, 181–182; women and work 180–187
Fahmy, Doriyya 220
Fainberg, Olga Pickman 118
The Family (Moyal) 96
Family Protection Law of 1967 146
Farzaneh, Mateo Mohammed 244
Fatat Shamsan 156
fatwa 102
Fawwaz, Zaynab (Zeinab) 94–95; *Fine Consequences* 95; *Scattered Pearls in the Lives of Harem Dwellers* 94–95
Fay, Mary Ann 5
Faysal, Amir 113
Federation of South Arabia 157

Federation of Women's Associations, Kuwait 171
Felatun and Rakim (Midhat) 79
female-authored biographies 95
female/feminism/feminist 5, 72, 78, 130, 132, 137, 143, 144, 148, 155–175, 273; campaigns, state building and 118–122; labor 3, 16, 26, 44, 179, 183–186, 188–190, 195; movements 155; performers (*awalim*) 17; slaves 14–15, 55, 87n1; writers 33
Female members of the Bahrain Teachers Society 269
Fine Consequences (Fawwaz) 95
The Fine Woman's Exhibition of Biographies of Famous Women (Nahhas) 95
FIRDOS *see* Fund for Integrated Rural Development (FIRDOS)
Firdos Square, Baghdad 141, *142*
First Arab Women's Congress 123
fishing and pearl diving 20–21, *21*
fjeri 20
Fleischmann, Ellen 5
FLOSY *see* Front for the Liberation of Occupied South Yemen (FLOSY)
Flying Broom Association 168
For Men Only 206
Freedom and Justice Party 274
Free Syrian Army 269
French Enlightenment thinkers 73
French invasion of Egypt 21
French Mandate rule 116
Front for the Liberation of Occupied South Yemen (FLOSY) 157
"The Fruits of Benefaction" 99
fujur 209, 214
Fulla 233–234, *234*
Fund for Integrated Rural Development (FIRDOS) 148

Gamal, Ashraf 275
Gamal, Samia 225
gay/lesbian: community 200; "gay-friendly" sites 208; identity in the Middle East 200; life 207–211
GCC *see* Gulf Cooperation Council (GCC)
GEM *see* Gender Empowerment Measure (GEM)
gender 201–203; age-specific gender segregation 181; anxieties 91–92, 109, 116, 122–124, 126; landscapes 40

gender-bending (and straight) performers 212
gendered-masculine behavior 47
Gender Empowerment Measure (GEM) 171
General Federation of Iraqi Women (GFIW) 140, 248
General Union of Palestinian Women (GUPW) 252, 257
General Union of Syrian Women 142
GFIW *see* General Federation of Iraqi Women (GFIW)
Ghonim, Wael 267
Gilani, Laila 104
A Girl Named Mahmud 206
global economies and political systems 3
Gökçen, Sabiha 188
Gölkalp, Ziya 132
Gordon, Arielle 5
Gouraud, Henri 116
Graffiti, Lebanon *164*
Great Exhibition in London 50
Green Movement 245
Gérôme, Jean-Léon 34, 36, 37, *37*
Guapa (Haddad) 212
El Guindi, Fadwa 226
Gulf Cooperation Council (GCC) 190
Gulf War 159, 190, 240, 249, 255
GUPW *see* General Union of Palestinian Women (GUPW)

Habbalin, Louisa: *Paradise* 96
Habits and Customs of the Modern Egyptians (Lane) 32
Haddad, Saleem: *Guapa* 212
hadith 13, 75, 170, 202
Hafez 136, 141, 142, *143*, 149, *150*
Hamdi, Fayda 264–266, 276, 277
Hamuda, Naima Sultan 114
Hanem, Jeshm Afet 58, 95
Hanem, Khosayr 42
Harb, Talaat: *The Woman and the Veil* 81
d' Harcourt, Charles François Marie 33–34, 81
harems 8, 12–17, 29–34, 36–38, 41–44, 48, 51, 53, 61, 64, 71, 73, 79, 84, 86, 90–93, 104, 118, 173, 260
al-Hariri, Rafik 163
Hashim, Labiba 95; *The Eastern Girl* 96; *A Man's Heart* 95
Hassanzadeh, Umleila 244
Hatem, Mervat 5
Haussman, Baron Georges-Eugène 56
al-Hayat, Ayn 100

Hayworth, Rita 225
HELEM 210
Heller, Tzila Amidror 135
Herzl, Theodor 192
High Council of Women 144
Higher Women's Committee (HWC) 254
hijab 77, 80–82, 84, 145, 157, 220, 227, 228, 235, 241, 242, 245, 255, 273; "bad hijab" 147, 220, 230; "hijab campaign" 255; laws 148
Hijazi, Sulafa 277
Historical Background on the Manners and Customs of Nations (Depping) 74
Hitchens, Robert 40
"Hoda's Clothes for Veiled Women" 228
homoeroticism 201
homosexuality 33, 77, 85, 201, 211–214
homosocial environment 211
Hosni, Soad 206
House of Cooperative Reform 119
House of the Woman 119
"houses in motion" 240, 251; Iran 241–247; Iraq 247–251; occupied Palestine 251–259
Hurrem Sultan Bathhouse 10
Hussein, Saddam 136
HWC *see* Higher Women's Committee (HWC)

Ibrahim, Samira 273
I Can't Think Straight (Kattan) 207
identity 82, 130–134, 155, 159, 162, 169, 171, 200, 201, 205–207, 211–214, 251
IDF *see* Israel Defense Forces (IDF)
imperial capitals 7–13
independent feminist organization 119
industrial revolution 21, 25, 183, 192
informal economy 192, 194–196, 213
informal labor in Iran 196
Ingres, Jean-Auguste-Dominique 34, *35*, 36
Institute for the Intellectual Development of Children and Young Adults 232
International Alliance of Women 119
International Association of Women 159
International Conference on Population and Development 146
internationalism 171–174
International Monetary Fund 184
international treaty 171, 189
International Women's conference in Rome 104, 220
International Women's Day 104, 220, 227, 273

intifada 166, 195, 221, 227, 251–257, 260
The Intimate Companion (Avierino) 96
Iran 9, 64, 67, 82, 101, 104, 142–143, 185, 189, 194, 245; Anglo-Iranian agreement 38; Christian women in 99, 123, 160, 203, 223; clerics 100; Constitutional Revolution, 1905 67, 84, 85, 91–92, 100, 105; economy 23; eight-year war with Iraq 185; European-style textiles factory 182; Europe influence in 23; "houses in motion" 241–247; informal labor in 196; lower socioeconomic classes 242; *majlis* 97, 103, 143; Medical Council of Iran (MCI) 212; morals police 232; new vision of modernity 236; oil economy 188; Organized Cybercrime Unit 230–231; parliament 147; political freedoms 144; political life 143; power dynamics 13; Qajar Iran 7, 14, 17, 25, 44, 61–68, 73, 77, 82, 187, 202, 224; reform movement 230; religious minorities 99; tobacco production 102; traditional orders 242; "White Revolution" in 143, 184, 189; women 17, 32, 101, 134, 147, 189, 230, 241–247; Women's Center 132
Iranian Revolution of 1979 105, 146, 185, 189, 194, 227, 241, 243, *243*
Iran-Iraq War 147, 185, 213, 240
Iraq 114, 138, 143, 144, 147, 148, 186, 247–251; American-led invasion of 186; British Mandate rule in 118, 183; constitution 117; General Federation of Iraqi Women (GFIW) 140, 248; "houses in motion" 247–251; humanitarian crisis 248–249; infrastructure 249; Iranian prisoner of war (POW) 244; labor force 185; minimum marriage laws 117; mobilization 247; tribes 117; women 117, 139–141, 148, 166, 186, 247, 249–250; women, in war and revolution 247–251
Iraq Body Count 249
Iraqi Constitution 117
Iraqi October Revolution *250*
Irgun 135, *136*
ISIS *see* Islamic State of Iraq and Syria (ISIS)
Islamic Republic of Iran 5, 130, 226, 229

Islamic Resistance Movement 254
Islamic Revolutionary Guards Corps 244
Islamic State of Iraq and Syria (ISIS) 186, 276
Islam/Islamic 227, 260; beliefs 226; civilizations 30; depravity 29; dress 221, 222, 226–228, 255; fashion 219, 226, 228, 232; feminists 155, 156, 170; groups 221, 226; law (*shari'a*) 8, 14, 24, 80, 147, 202, 203, 242; organizations 226, 228; reform movements 201; revivalism 228; social welfare societies 228; societies 29, 72, 80, 83, 95, 202; student groups 226
Ismail, Khedive 42–43, 56–60, 68
Israel *see* State of Israel
Israel Defense Forces (IDF) 164, 252, *253*
Israeli Declaration of Independence 134–135

al-Jazairi, Adila Bayhum 117
Jewish immigrants 111, 118
"Jewish Israeli" 135, 165
Jewish settlements in Palestine 111, 115, 118, 134, 187
Jordanian women 190
Joseph, Suad 5
al-Joundi, Darina 162, 163; *The Day Nina Simone Stopped Singing* 163
July Revolution of 1830 74
Justice and Development Party in Turkey 151, 229

al-Kabir, Amir 65–66
kafes system 8
Kaiser Wilhelm II 53, *54*
Kalam, Shams al-Muluk Javanhi 99
Kamal, Zahira 256
Karam, Afifa: *Badia and Fu'ad* 95
Kardashian, Kim 230
Karman, Tawakkol 267
Kattan, Hanan: *I Can't Think Straight* 207
Kazem, Safinaz 170
keffiyeh 221, *222*
Kemalism/Kemalist 132, 134, 149, 151, 169, 188; ideology 169; paradigm 168; single-party rule 149; Turkey 134
Kemal, Mustafa *112*, 113, 130–134, 151, 159, 188, 220, 223, 224
Kemal, Namik 75, 76–77
Kermani, Mirza 'Abd al-Hossayn Khan 77, 84

ketkhuda khatun 13
Khalid, Fayhaa 250
Khalidi, Anbara Salam 99
al-Khalifa, Hamad bin Isa 266
Khalil, Hamidah 113
Khamenei, Ayatollah 230
khanith 203
Khan, Reza 131, 133
Khan, Yephrem 104
Khanum, Tavus 13
Khassa, Hurriyat 210
Khatami, Mohammed 147
al-Khatib, Ibrahim 120
Khatun, Salun 11
Khedive Abbas I 75
Khomeini, Ayatollah Ruhallah 146, 147, 212–213, 227, 242–244; *Vilayet-e Faqih* 242
Khomeini-era laws and norms 147
Kocamaner, Hikmet 5
Kozma, Liat 5
Kurdish nationalist movement 168–169
Kurdish women 169
Kuwait 20, 159, 213–214, 232; *Baydar al-Salam* 171; Federation of Women's Associations 171; of Iraqi troops 159
Kweiri, Jocelyn 162

labor 4, 22, 24, 26, 180, 214; activism 184, 185; code 138; domestic labor 192–194; education and 140, 142; Egyptian female labor activism 185; of elite women 29; female 3, 16, 26, 44, 179, 183–186, 188–190, 195; informal labor in Iran 196; laws 144; for local manufactures 15; national federation of 135; wage 23, 24
Labor Party 134, 135, 255
The Ladies' Own Gazette (Aliye) 96
Lane, Edward: *Habits and Customs of the Modern Egyptians* 32
large-scale Jewish settlement 187
al-Lataif al-musawwara 124, 125
Law of Associations 268
laws: anti-protest laws 104, 184; compulsory education laws 60; Defense Service Law 135; Family Protection Law of 1967 146; *hijab* 148; Islam/Islamic law (*shari'a*) 8, 14, 24, 80, 147, 202, 203, 242; Khomeini-era laws 147; labor laws 144; Law of Associations

268; Lebanon repealed Law 534 209; Marriage Law of 1931 134; minimum marriage laws, Iraq 117; new trade laws 23; state's issuance of Law 39 140; sumptuary laws 219, 223–224
League of Nations 116
Lebanese Association for Human Rights 163
Lebanese Council for Women 160
Lebanese Representative Council 120
Lebanese Women's Union 160
Lebanon 1, 23, 94–96, 108, 109, 112, 116, 117, 120–122, 126, *161*, *164*, 166, *181*, 182, 183, 187, 190, 193, 209, 210, 213; American troops land in 160, *161*; Cedar Revolution 163, 173, *174*; Civil War 163, 189; "cosmetic tourism" company in 231; identity crisis 161; LGBTQ community 163; nation's Constitution 160; Palestinian refugee camps in 252; pre-civil war era 163; repealed Law 534 209; women 99, 111, 117, 119, 121, 160–162, 182, 189
Lesseps, Ferdinand de 59
Levantine harem 34
Lewis, Reina 5
The Liberation of Women (Amin) 94
Libidi, Meherzia 270
Light of Damascus Society 100
linguistic ambiguities 200–201
Local Coordination Committees (LCCs) 269
Luqman, Mohammed 156
Lutfi, Nadia 206

Madrid Conference of 1991 255
Mahd Ulya 64
Mahmud II 33, 48, *49*, 50, 222, 224
mahr 138, 158, 203
majlis 84, 85, 97, 99, 103–105, 132, 143
Malkam Khan, Mirza 83, 84
Mamluk Egypt 12–14
Mamluk grandees 9
Mamluks 9
A Man's Heart (Hashim) 95
manumission 15, 55, 73
Maronite Church leadership 181
marriage, in Islamicate societies 203–205
Marriage Law of 1931 134

masculinity 1, 2, 4, 20, 47, 61, 62, 64, 68, 102, 126, 133, 206, 208, 214, 215, 274
MAWRED *see* Modernizing and Activating Women's Role in Economic Development (MAWRED)
MCI *see* Medical Council of Iran (MCI)
media 211–214
Medical Council of Iran (MCI) 212
Meir, Golda 165
Mejid, Abdül 50, 55
Middle East 1–2, 4; gay/lesbian identity in 200; men 3; modernity in 2; reformers 48, 50; societies 179; women 1–2, 5, 200
"Middle Eastern sexuality" 201
Middle Eastern women, in European imagination 29–30; domestic life 33–34, 36–39; gendered landscapes 40; harems 41–44; travel literature and women 30–33; veiled encounters 39
Middle Eastern women's lives 7; countryside women 19; fishing and pearl diving 20–21, *21*; implications for 21–25; pastoralism 19–20; royal women 7–13; slave women 14–15; upper classes women 13–14; working classes women 15–19
Midhat, Ahmed 79; *Felatun and Rakim* 79; *Just Seventeen* 80
Midnight 205, 206
military uniforms 63, 121, 133, 140, 142, 149
Ministry of Women's Affairs (MOWA) 257
Mirror of the East 96
Mirza, Abbas 63–64
missionaries: Catholic missionaries 50; Christian missionaries 30, 41, 44, 50, 55, 67, 118; educators 42; European and American missionaries 41; schools 41–42, 50–51, 64, 67, 73
Moaveni, Azadeh 230
Modernizing and Activating Women's Role in Economic Development (MAWRED) 148
modern/modernity/modernization 2–5, 42, 43, 48, 51, 58, 61, 64, 67, 68, 87, 130, 132, 133, 137, 139, 141, 143, 211–214, 219, 222, 226, 236, 237, 241, 260, 264, 265; capitalist societies 179; Middle East 1–3,

5, 152, 201, 219; Turkish identity 132, 134
Moghaizel, Laure 163
Mohamed, Imen Ben 271
Mohammed Reza Shah Pahlavi 63–64, 67, 130, *131*, 132, 134, 143, 144, 146, 183, 184, 188–189, 194, 220, 224; "New Woman" 241–242
monikers 149, 208, 229
Montagu, Mary Wortley 31, 39
Moorish Bath, Jean-Leon Gérôme *35*
Morsi, Mohammed 235, 271
Mossadegh, Mohammed 143
Motherland Party 151
"Mother of the Revolution," Yemen 267
Mott, Lucretia 72
moustaches 102, 224
movements: anti-shah movement 242; April 6 Youth Movement, Egypt 267; Arab nationalist movement 111, 113, 121, 137, 160, 162; Arab Spring-like movement 250; Bahai movement 83; Citizens Rights Movement 166; Egyptian nationalist movement 124; feminist movements 155; Green Movement 245; Islamic Resistance Movement 254; Kurdish nationalist movement 168–169; nationalist movement 30, 105, 111, 113, 114, 118, 121, 122, 131, 137, 169, 255; reform movements 201, 230; resistance movement, Palestine 252; turban movement 227; Young Ottoman movement 77, 83, 84
MOWA *see* Ministry of Women's Affairs (MOWA)
Moyal, Ester: *The Family* 96
al-Muali, Durrat 100, 103
Mubarak, Ali 56
Mubarak, Muhammad Husni 145, 146, 228, 265, 275; neoliberal economic policies 273
Mubarak, Suzanne 273–274
Muhammad, Agha 61
mukhannathun 202–203
Murad, Leila 225
Murad V 53
Müren, Zeki 212
Musa, Nabawiyya 100–101, 119
Muslim Iranian women 30, 31, 99, 200
Muslim Women (Aliye) 96
Mustafa III 48, 223
Mustafa IV 48

Nabarawi, Ceza 119
Naguib, Mahia 156
al-Nahhas, Maryam Nasr Allah: *The Fine Woman's Exhibition of Biographies of Famous Women* 95
Najmabadi, Afsaneh 5
Nasif, Malak Hifni 101
Nasser, Afrah 268
Nasser, Gamal Abdul 137–138, *139*, 140–142, 144, 161, 184, 189, 222, 236, 270
National Charter of 1962 137
National Commission for Lebanese Women 172
National Committee for the Follow up of Women's Issues 172
National Constituent Assembly (NCA) 270
National Council of Women, Egypt 273
nationalist movement 30, 105, 111, 113, 114, 118, 121, 122, 131, 137, 169, 255
National Liberation Front (NLF) 157
National Pact 160
National Security Agency 274
National Security Council, Egypt 275
National Transitional Committee 272
National Women's Council 172
nation, as a woman 85–86
NATO *see* North Atlantic Treaty Organization (NATO)
Nawfal, Hind: *The Young Woman* 96
Nazli 95
NCA *see* National Constituent Assembly (NCA)
new philanthropic associations 98
new trade laws 23
"New Woman" 3, 4, 25, 47–48, 108, 124, 187, 242; debates 130; ethnic states and 130–152; postwar era 112–115; Redux 116–118; state building and feminist campaigns 118–122; states and gendered anxieties 122–126; WWI 109, *110*, 111
New Woman Society 116
"New Woman," through new man's gaze 71–72; early "Woman Question" authors 74–77; men writing about women 73–74; nation as a woman 85–86; Third Generation 83–85; "Woman Question" 72–73; writings after 1876 78–83
The Nightingale's Prayer 193
nineteenth-century travelers 31–32
niqab 221, 226, 228, 235

298   Index

NLF see National Liberation Front (NLF)
NLF-dominated People's Democratic Republic of Yemen 157
"No Going Back," women's slogan 255
non-elite women 91, 223
non-European Jews in Palestine 118
non-muslim women 14
North Atlantic Treaty Organization (NATO) 272

Omani society 191, 203
Omanization 190
Operation Desert Storm 147, 186, 248
Operation Protective Edge in Gaza 166
organizations: and activism 97–98; civil society organizations 142, 173, 268, 271, 272; economic reorganization 184; independent feminist organization 119; Islam/Islamic 226, 228; North Atlantic Treaty Organization 272; philanthropic organizations 97, 100, 108, 116, 134, 259, 268; and political demonstrations 101–104; and promotion of women's rights 100–101; Women's International Zionist Organization 118; Women's Organization of Iran 144
Organized Cybercrime Unit 230–231
organized feminism in Turkey 167–168
orientalist: literature 90; painters 34, 36
Orthodox Society of Compassion for Ladies 117
Oslo Accords of 1993 187, 195, 257
Oslo Agreement 256
Osman III 223
Ottoman Empire 7, 9, 16, 17, *17*, 23, 25, 31, 32, 44, 48, 50–51, 53, 67, 71–73, 75, 77, 78–80, 82, 85, 109, 112, 131, 132, 187, 193, 201, 203, 224; Aleppo 14, 96, 116, 269; Anatolia 14, 19, 23, 50, 90, 92, 96, 98, 100, 101, 108, 109, 112, 131, 180, *182*, 201; Anglo-Ottoman Treaty 23; constitutional revolt of 1876 71; Exposition in Istanbul 50; factories 181; janissary corps 33; reformers 50; rulers 8, 42, 51; sultans 4, 8, 9, 39, 56, 59, 61, 63; Syria (see Syria)

Palestine: Arab women and Jews 135; community 115, 122; Jewish settlements in 111, 115, 118, 134, 187; labor force in Israel 254; men 118, 122, 123, 187, 195, 251, 254; press 122; refugees and refugee camps in 251–252; resistance movement 252; women 111, 118, 121
Palestine Liberation Organization (PLO) 161, 252, 256
Palestine Women's Council and the Social Service Association 111
Palestinian Union of Women's Work Committees (PUWWC) 254
Palestinian Women's Association (PWA) 118
Pamuk, Orhan: *Snow* 229
Paradise (Habbalin) 96
Paris Universal Exposition 53
The Pasha Director's Daughter 206
Pasha, Farik 93
Pasha, Ibrahim *57*
Pasha, Ismail 39, 95
Pasha, Jemal 109, 111
Pasha, Mustafa Reşhid 50–51, 75
Pasha, Tawfiq 39
Pasha, Zainab 102
pastoral communities 20
pastoralism 19–20
pastoral women 20
The Paths of Egyptian Hearts in the Splendors of Contemporary Morals (Tahtawi) 74
PDRY see People's Democratic Republic of Yemen (PDRY)
Peacock Throne 62
People's Democratic Republic of Yemen (PDRY) 157
Perry, Charles 42
"Persian carpets" 24
Persian Gulf slave trade 38
Personal Status Codes 271
Phalangist militia 162
philanthropy/philanthropic organizations 97–100, 108, 112, 116, 118, 134, 155, 259, 268
Pierce, Leslie 5
A Pilgrimage to Nejd (Wilfrid and Blunt) 40
pink-collar work 180, 188, 191–192
Pinsker, Leon: *Auto-Emancipation* 40
PLO see Palestine Liberation Organization (PLO)
The Poet's Wedding (Şinasi) 75, 76
political demonstrations 101–104
political reforms 77, 83, 152, 268
post-Beijing era 172

post-Oslo era 257
postwar era 108, 109, 112–115, 120, 131
pre-Atatürk era 167
precapitalist societies 179
premodern societies 179
pre-WWI era 123
"principle of equality" 270
prisoner of war (POW) 244
Progress (Tevfik and Ekram) 75
Prophet Muhammad 14, 72, 75, 77, 95, 220
Protestantism 16
Purple Needle Campaign 167
putting-out system 16
PUWWC *see* Palestinian Union of Women's Work Committees (PUWWC)
PWA *see* Palestinian Women's Association (PWA)

al-Qadhafy, Muammar 140, 265, 268, 272
al-Qadiri, Fatima 214
Qajar Iran 7, 14, 17, 25, 44, 61–68, 73, 77, 82, 187, 202, 224
Qajar monarchs 9
Qajar women 16
Qasim, Abd al-Karim 138, 140
"quartet" of civil society associations 271
Quawas, Rula 156
al-Qubaysi, Munira 171

Rabin, Yitzhak 166, 253, 255
race-based slavery 72
Radio Naseem, Syria 269
Ramadhane, Najla Bouden 271
Ramzi, Ibrahim 81–82
Rashid, Fatima 100
RATZ party 166
al-Razzaz, Bayt 11, *12*
recoupling 156–169
Red Crescent Society 116
Red Star Association 100
Reform of Galata 51
reform programs 3, 47, 68, 71, 272
refugees and refugee camps: Iran 213; from Iraq and Syria 190; Palestine 160, 161, 190, *251*, 252; Syria 208, 276; women 111, *115*, 193, 204, 276
Régnault, Alexandre Georges-Henri: "Execution Without Trial by the Moorish King" 36
Revolutionary Guard 230
"The Revolution of Egyptian Men" 273
Rouhani, Hassan 147
royal women 7–13, 172

Ruhi, Ahmed: *Eight Heavens* 83

Al-Sabah, Emir Abdullah Al-Salim 159
sabra culture 134, 135
al-Sabuni, Nadima: *Woman* 96
Sacred Defense 244–245
Sadat, Anwar 140, 144–146, *145*, 169, 226, 228; *infitah* 184
Sadat, Jehan 144
Saddam Hussein 140–141, *141*, 147, *149*, 186, 243, 247–249
Safavids 9, 11, 61
Saied, Kais 271
al-Salam, Baydar 171
Saleh, Ali Abdullah 265–267
Salman, Umm 114
Salvation Army 207
same-sex desire 201–203, 205–207
Sami, Şamseddin 75, 76, 84; *Women* 78
Samuel, Herbert 115
sati 44
Saudization 190
Saunderson, Johnny *142*
Sboui, Aminia 278
SCAF *see* Supreme Council of the Armed Forces (SCAF)
Scattered Pearls in the Lives of Harem Dwellers (Fawwaz) 94–95
schools: Egyptian Correspondence Schools 192; missionary schools 41–42, 50–51, 64, 67, 73; traditional religious school system 225
Sciolino, Elaine 230
secluded elite women 90
secular Labor Party 134
Selim III 48–50, 224
Semerdjian, Elyse 5
Seneca Falls Convention in New York 72
Senior, William Nassau: *Conversations and Journals in Egypt and Malta* 42
sex reassignment surgery (SRS) 206, 213
sexuality 200–203, 205–207; "gay" life 207–211; gender and desire 201–203; marriage 203–205; passion on silver screen 205–207
Seyidşehri, Mahmud Emin: *A Defense of Polygamy: Addendum* 93
Shaarawi, Hoda 100, 113, 119, 220; *Daughter of the Nile* 159
shadh 200
Shafak, Elif: *Bastard of Istanbul* 229
Shafik, Doria 159
Shah, Fath Ali 13, 47, 61–64, *62*
Shamir, Yitzhak 255

sharia 134, 228, 242
Shariati, Ali 242
al-Sharif, Haram 121
Sharkawi, Pakinam 272
Sharon, Ariel 257
Shaykh, Babist: *Eight Heavens* 83
Shehadeh, Lamia R. 211
sheikhas 170–171
Shops on Jumhuri Avenue, Tehran *241*
silk factory *181*, 181–182
Şinasi, Ibrahim: *Picture of Ideas* 75; *The Poet's Wedding* 75, 76
al-Sisi, Abdel-Fattah 184, 274–275
SLA *see* Syrian Ladies Association (SLA)
"The Slave Market" 36, *37*
slave women 14–15, 59
Snow (Pamuk) 229
social activism 112, 119, 267
Society for Education 67
Society for the Advancement of Women 100
Society for the Defense of Women's Rights 100, 101
Society for the Elevation of Women 101, 111
Society for Women's Freedom 103
Sonbol, Amira 5
Sporting Clubs 222, 224, 237
SRS *see* sex reassignment surgery (SRS)
Stanton, Elizabeth Cady 72
state building 183, 211; activities 131; and feminist campaigns 118–122; platforms 130; projects 61, 71, 86
state centralization 20, 22, 183
State of Israel 108, 130, 134, 138, 140, 161, 165–167, 209–210, 251–260; invasion of 1982 162; land of 40; military 135, 251; Palestinian labor force in 254
states and gendered anxieties 122–124, 126
State Security 274
state's issuance of Law 39 140
state-sponsored education for women 187
Steppe, Mughan 61
The String 207
Sudanese emigrants 194
Suez Crisis 138
Sufism 171, 201
al-Sultanah, Taj 101
sumptuary laws 219, 223–224
Sun Throne 62
Supreme Council of the Armed Forces (SCAF) 271, 273
Swiss Legal Code 134

Syria 1, 23, 40, 95, 100, 108, 109–114, 116, 122, 126, 130, 136–138, 161–163, 170–171, 183, 186, 190, 233, 255; Arab Spring in 278; Free Syrian Army 269; General Union of Syrian Women 142; legislators 120; Local Coordination Committees 269; peaceful demonstrations 275; Radio Naseem 269; refugees 193; Syrian Observatory for Human Rights 273; uprising 117; women 121, 142, 148, 275
Syrian Congress 120
Syrian Ladies Association (SLA) 111
Syrian Observatory for Human Rights 273
Syrian Revolt of 1925 113
Syrian Revolution Coordinators Union 269
Syrian Revolution General Commission 269

al-Tahtawi, Rifaat Rafai 74; *An Extraction of Gold in a Summary of Paris* 74; *The Paths of Egyptian Hearts in the Splendors of Contemporary Morals* 74; *A Trustworthy Guide to the Education of Girls and Boys* 75
Talal, Basma Bint 172
Tanielian, Melanie 5
tanzimat reforms 24, 50, 51, 52, 73, 75, 78, 92, 224
tarboosh 222, 236
al-Tawil, Hanan 212
Taymur, Aisha 95; *The Consequences and Circumstances of Words and Deeds* 94
TCCDR *see* Tribal Criminal and Civil Disputes Regulation (TCCDR)
technology 68, 78, 184, 206, 208
techno-savvy youth 268
Tevfik, Ebüziyya 78–79; *Progress* 75
TGNA *see* Turkish Grand National Assembly (TGNA)
Third Generation 83–85
Thompson, Libby 5
Tobacco Concession crisis 83
Tobacco Rebellions of the 1890s 105
Topkapi Harem 11, *11*
Tounes, Nidaa 271
Trabelsi, Leila 265
traditional religious school system 225
transsexuality/transsexualism 208, 211–214
transvestitism 214
Treaty of Balta Liman 23
Treaty of London 56

Treaty of Turkmanchai 23
Tribal Criminal and Civil Disputes Regulation (TCCDR) 117
Troutt-Powell, Eve 5
A Trustworthy Guide to the Education of Girls and Boys (Tahtawi) 75
Tucker, Judith 5
Tunisia 160, 174, 264, 265–266, 273, 276; Constitution 270, 271; and Libya 1; National Constituent Assembly (NCA) 270; Personal Status Codes 270; political parties 271
turban movement 227
Turkey 1, 4, 31, *112*, 113, 131–134, 151, 160, 169, 188, 191, 196, 204, 210, 212, 213; greater political pluralism 169; industrialization 183–184; Justice and Development Party 151, 229; Kemalist Turkey 134; modern Turkish identity 132, 134; organized feminism in 167; rights and freedoms 167; Secularists and Islamists in 151; slavery in 80; universities 227
"The Turkish Bath" 34
Turkish Civil Code 151
Turkish Grand National Assembly (TGNA) 151
"Turkish history thesis" 132
Turkish university women 229
Turkish Workers' Party (PKK) 168

ulama 48, 101, 102, 201, 248
umm walad 8, 15
UNDP's Gender and Development Index (GDI) 171
UNGA *see* UN General Assembly (UNGA)
UN General Assembly (UNGA) 171
UN-imposed sanctions 186, 248
United National Leadership (UNL) 253
United Nations (UN) 186, 248; conferences 172; Convention about the Abolition of All Discrimination Against Women (CADAW) 168; Handbook for Legislation on Violence Against Women 271; international treaty 189; sanctions 147
upper classes women 13–14
Urabi, Ahmed 60
Urabi Revolt of 1881 60
urban women 15, 16, 18, 22, 133, 185, 189
urfi marriage 204–205
Uşakligil, Latife 133

US-led invasion of 2003 186

vaildes sultans (mother of the sultan) 9, 53
veiled encounters 39
The Vices of Men (Astarabadi) 93
Victorian era 32, 33, 179, 209

WAC *see* Women's Awakening Club (WAC)
WAD *see* Women's Actions Department (WAD)
Wafdist Women's Central Committee (WWCC) 113
waqfs 14, 26, 90
WCSS *see* Women's Cultural and Social Society (WCSS)
Western/Westernization 48, 105, 134, 219; imagination 90, 219; media 200; stereotypical misperceptions 200; students 2
"White Revolution" in Iran 143, 184, 189
Wilkie, David 56
Williams, Esther 225
Wilson, Samuel Graham 32
WJWC *see* Women Journalists Without Chains (WJWC)
WOI *see* Women's Organization of Iran (WOI)
Woman (Sabuni) 96
The Woman and the Veil (Harb) 81
Woman in the Crossfire (Yazbek) 278
"Woman Question" 30, 73–74, 76, 90–92; activism 97–98; debates 4, 44, 71–72; organization 97–98, 101–104; philanthropy 98–100; political demonstrations 101–104; press 96–97; women's rights, organization and the promotion of 100–101; writing 92–95
women: activism 98, 101, 160, 167, 173, 241; *andarun* women 13, 17; in Arab Spring 265; Arab Women's Association 122; Arab Women's Executive 122; Arab Women's Society 157; Arab Women's Union of Nablus 118; Armenian women 18, 99; Ashkenazi (European) Jewish women 135; associational life 143; blogs 210; Christian, in Iran 99, 123, 160, 161, 203, 223; Christian Women's Solidarity Association 160; civil society organizations 142; clerics and women's associations 100;

Committee on The Political Rights of Women 160; Committee on the Status of Women 166; Council of Lebanese Woman 163; countryside women 19, 114; domestic behaviors 30; Eastern Women's Conferences in Damascus 120, 121; Egyptian Center for Women's Rights 274; Egyptian woman 81, 119, 220, 226, 228; elite women 13, 14, 26, 90, 91, 113, 116, 117; European Christian women 223; European women 30, 44, 91, 118, 224; Federation of Women's Associations, Kuwait 171; First Arab Women's Congress 123; General Federation of Iraqi Women 140, 248; General Union of Palestinian Women 252, 257; General Union of Syrian Women 142; High Council of Women 144; Higher Women's Committee 254; "Hoda's Clothes for Veiled Women" 228; House of the Woman 119; industrial labor force participation 185; International Alliance of Women 119; International Association of Women 159; International Women's conference in Rome 104, 220; International Women's Day 104, 220, 227, 273; Jordanian women 190; Kurdish women 169; labor participation 183; Lebanese Council for Women 160; Lebanese women 99, 111, 117, 119, 121, 160–162, 182, 189; Lebanese Women's Union 160; in Lebanon and Syria 120; Middle Eastern women, in European imagination (*see* Middle Eastern women, in European imagination); Middle Eastern women's lives (*see* Middle Eastern women's lives); Ministry of Women's Affairs 257; Modernizing and Activating Women's Role in Economic Development 148; Muslim Iranian women 30, 31, 99, 200; *Muslim Women* (Aliye) 96; National Commission for Lebanese Women 172; National Committee for the Follow up of Women's Issues 172; National Women's Council 172, 273; nation as 85–86; non-elite women 91, 223; non-muslim women 14; opportunities for 160, 165; organizations 118; participation in demonstrations 273; pastoral women 20; periodical press 96–97; Qajar women 16; rights, organization and promotion of 100–101; royal women 7–13, 172; secluded elite women 90; slave women 14–15, 59; Society for the Advancement of Women 100; Society for the Defense of Women's Rights 100, 101; Society for the Elevation of Women 101, 111; Society for Women's Freedom 103; state-sponsored education for 187; Turkish university women 229; UN Convention about the Abolition of All Discrimination Against Women 168; UN Convention on the Elimination of all forms of Discrimination Against Women 172, 189–190; UN Handbook for Legislation on Violence Against Women 271; upper classes women 13–14; urban women 15, 16, 18, 22, 133, 185, 189; Wafdist Women's Central Committee 113; *Woman* (Sabuni) 96; *The Woman and the Veil* (Harb) 81; *Woman in the Crossfire* (Yazbek) 278; working-class women 15–19, 25, 196, 228; writing 92–95; *The Young Woman* (Nawfal) 96

Women (Sami) 78

women and work 179–180; cottage industry and informal economy 194–196; domestic service 192–194; factories 180–187; pink-collar work and service work 191–192; professions 187–191

women-focused platforms 130

Women in Black, Jerusalem *167*

Women in Islam (Aliye) 92

women, in war and revolution 240; Iran 241–247; Iraq 247–251; occupied Palestine 251–259

Women Journalists Without Chains (WJWC) 267

Women's Actions Department (WAD) 259

Women's Awakening Club (WAC) 117

Women's Charter 257

Women's Cultural and Social Society (WCSS) 159
Women's Freedom Society 99
Women's International Zionist Organization 118
Women's Language (Dawlatabadi) 97
Women's Organization of Iran (WOI) 144
Women's Revolutionary Committee 103
Women's Union in Syria and Lebanon 120
Women's Universe 97
Women Wage Peace (WWP) 166
working-class women 15–19, 25, 196, 228
World Anti-Slavery Convention 72
World Economic Forum study 192
World Exposition in Paris 56
WWCC *see* Wafdist Women's Central Committee (WWCC)
WWI 4, 30, 108, 109, *110*, 111, *115*, 116, 117, 130, 131, 155, 187, 188
WWII 149, 183, 206
WWP *see* Women Wage Peace (WWP)

yashmak 123, 220
Yazbek, Samar 276; *Woman in the Crossfire* 278
Yazdi, Safiyah 100

Yemen 156, 172, 264; Front for the Liberation of Occupied South Yemen (FLOSY) 157; "Mother of the Revolution" 267; National Liberation Front (NLF) 157; women of 157
Yom Kippur War 164
Young Ottoman movement 77, 83, 84
Young Turk Revolution 23, 85, 109, 133
The Young Woman (Nawfal) 96

Zaghloul, Saad 119, 123
Zaghloul, Saffia 124, 126
al-Zahawi, Jamil S. 85
Zaitouneh, Razan 268, 276
Zaki, Fatma 189
Zakout, Jamil 260
Zaydan, Jurji 84
Ze'evi, Dror 5
Zeina El Haj 231
zenana work 41
Zine Abidine Ben Ali 265
Zionism 111, 164, 192
Zionist immigration 111
Ziyada, Mayy 95
zuama 160

9781138800601